The. Anxiety & Phobia Workbook

SECOND EDITION

EDMUND J. BOURNE, Ph.D.

NEW HARBINGER PUBLICATIONS, INC.

The Anxiety & Phobia Workbook
Copyright © 1995 by New Harbinger Publications, Inc.
5674 Shattuck Avenue, Oakland, CA 94609

Distributed in the U.S.A. primarily by Publishers Group West; in Canada by Raincoast Books; in Great Britain by Airlift Book Company, Ltd.; in South Africa by Real Books, Ltd.; in Australia by Boobook; and in New Zealand by Tandem Press.

ISBN 1-57224-003-2 Paperback

Cover design by SHELBY DESIGNS & ILLUSTRATES.
Type and design by Gayle Zanca.

Printed in the United States of America on recycled paper.

FIRST EDITION
 1st Printing, July 1990, 11,000 copies
 2nd Printing, March 1991, 5,000 copies
 3rd Printing, August 1991, 15,000 copies
 4th Printing, May 1992, 10,000 copies
 5th Printing, December 1992, 15,000 copies
 6th Printing, July 1993, 15,000 copies
 7th Printing, January, 1994, 15,000 copies
 8th Printing, July, 1994, 15,000 copies
 9th Printing, November, 1994, 15,000 copies

SECOND EDITION
1st Printing, December, 1995, 25,000 copies
2nd Printing, July, 1996, 25,000 copies
3rd Printing, November 1996, 25,000 copies
4th Printing, April 1997, 25,000 copies
5th Printing, December 1997, 25,000 copies
6th Printing, April 1998, 30,000 copies

This book is dedicated to anyone who has
struggled with anxiety or an incomprehensible fear.

Grateful acknowledgment to

Matthew McKay for his constructive suggestions
Patrick Fanning for his patient and flexible direction, and
Barbara Quick for her skillful and sensitive editing.

Contents

But do not distress yourself with imaginings. Many fears are born of fatigue and loneliness. Beyond a wholesome discipline, be gentle with yourself.

From DESIDERATA
by Max Erhmann

Preface to the Second Edition

Five years have passed since the first edition of this book was published. At the middle of the decade, anxiety disorders are still very much with us, affecting approximately one out of ten people in the United States at any given time. What has changed most in five years is the level of consciousness and acceptance of these disorders on the part of public and professionals alike. More and more it is being recognized that anxiety disorders are very treatable problems. An increasing amount of attention by the media has enabled the public at large to gain a basic understanding of what these problems are and how they are treated. The Anxiety Disorders Association of America has expanded to give equal recognition to all of the anxiety disorders, disseminating new information on problems that were less well known in the 1980s, such as social phobia and posttraumatic stress disorder. Finally, and very fortunately, there seems to be more help available. A number of support groups and support group networks have appeared in the U.S. (see Appendix 1). There are more treating practitioners who specialize in working with anxiety disorders. And medical doctors seem better informed and more able to discriminate panic attacks and other anxiety disorders from medical conditions. While the pace and stress level of modern society continue to yield a high prevalence of problems with anxiety, at least there is an improvement in both the availability and quality of resources that can help.

Changes in the field which have occurred in the past five years called for a new edition of this book. What follows is a brief description of what has been added. Chapter 1 ("What Are the Anxiety Disorders?") has been revised to conform with the new *DSM-IV* diagnostic manual, which has changed some of the diagnostic criteria for each of the anxiety disorders, as well as adding new categories. The chapters on causes of anxiety disorders (Chapter 2) and medications (Chapter 17) have been updated to include recent research findings on the biological basis for anxiety disorders, as well as new medications that have come into use. A new cognitive approach to conceptualizing and treating panic disorder, developed by David Barlow in the U.S. and David Clark in England, has been incorporated into Chapter 6 ("Coping With Panic Attacks"). A section has been added to the chapter on relaxation (Chapter 4) entitled "Down Time and Time Management," since the ability to take time out and pace yourself is just as important to a relaxed lifestyle as engaging in a regular deep-relaxation practice. More information for support persons of agoraphobics has been added to Chapter 8 ("Help for Phobias: Real-Life Desensitization"). Much of this information is based on the writings of the late Dr. Art Hardy, who first developed exposure as a treatment for agoraphobia in the 1960s. The chapter on self-talk (Chapter 9) has a new section which helps you identify negative self-talk specific to a particular phobia or fear (the first edition had guidelines only for identifying anxiety-provoking self-talk in general). The chapter on nutrition (Chapter 16) has an added section describing reasons for adopting a more vegetarian diet. New information on the amino acid tryptophan and the uses of relaxing herbs has been included as well. There is also a discussion of three clinical syndromes which have a connection to nutrition and are often observed to aggravate anxiety disorders: adrenal exhaustion, candida, and seasonal affective disorder. Finally, the chapter on meaning, purpose, and spirituality (Chapter 19) has been expanded.

Two new chapters have been added. The first, entitled "Four Traits That Perpetuate Anxiety" (Chapter 11), describes guidelines for overcoming four personality traits which are almost universal among people struggling with anxiety: perfectionism, excessive need for approval, excessive need for control, and the tendency to ignore physical signs of stress. A second new chapter, entitled "Fears From the Past" (Chapter 18), recognizes that some phobias and fears have roots in traumatic experiences from the past. Although real-life exposure is still always the first line of treatment for phobias, a full resolution of such fears from the past may require intensive psychotherapy. Methods designed to explore and work through traumatic incidents, such as hypnosis and eye-movement desensitization and reprocessing (EMDR), have shown themselves to be especially helpful to people with trauma-based phobias.

The 1980s and early 1990s have seen the ascendancy of the cognitive-behavioral model for the treatment of anxiety disorders. Nearly all practitioners who specialize in working with anxiety disorders rely on the cognitive-behavioral approach because of its proven effectiveness. This approach is essentially *educational* in nature, teaching strategies that, with regular practice, can help you overcome panic attacks, phobias, and other problems with anxiety. Approximately 12 such strategies, all of which can be learned and practiced, are presented in this book:

- Abdominal breathing

- Relaxation training

- Regular aerobic exercise

- Identifying and eliminating catastrophic thinking that can cause panic

- Practicing coping strategies for limiting panic attacks

- Systematic (imagery) desensitization for phobias

- Incremental exposure for phobias

- Reducing worry or anticipatory anxiety by identifying and countering distorted thinking habits

- Learning to identify and express feelings

- Developing assertiveness skills

- Developing self-nurturing skills

- Modifying diet and using appropriate supplements

Although the last two strategies are technically not part of the cognitive-behavioral model, they can still be taught and learned in much the same fashion.

The cognitive-behavioral approach is likely to remain the dominant and most effective form of treatment for many years to come. Even so, a few limitations of this approach have begun to emerge recently. It's clear that no single approach can fully cover all cases, and, in some cases, a cognitive-behavioral program is not *all* that is needed. There are three additional perspectives, outlined below, which I believe can be very useful adjuncts to cognitive-behavioral therapy and self-help. The first is already well known to most practitioners who work with anxiety disorders on a day-to-day basis. The latter two are not widely used but can, in my experience, be quite useful. (These two approaches are described in more detail in the final two chapters of this book.)

1. **Biopsychiatry.** In the past ten years, the field of biopsychiatry has demonstrated that certain anxiety disorders—especially panic disorder, agoraphobia, and obsessive-compulsive disorder—have a neurobiological component. With these problems as well as others, medication can sometimes be useful. As a general rule, the more severe and chronic a particular problem with anxiety has been, the more likely a person is to benefit from a trial of medication lasting from six months up to two years.

It is preferable, if possible, not to take medication over a period of many years. It remains an assumption of this book that any neurobiological imbalance of the brain contributing to an anxiety disorder is potentially reversible by natural means. These imbalances, in my opinion, are caused either by a single, severe stressor and/or by years of cumulative stress. A committed program incorporating all of the methods in this book—and a sincere intention to increase physical wellness, relaxation, emotional expression, and a positive mental outlook—will enable the brain to self-correct to the point where medications can, in most cases, eventually become unnecessary. In fact, a belief in this "mind over matter" principle is important, in and of itself, to recovery. This holistic approach to recovery may require a few months in some instances or a few years in others.

2. **Intensive Psychotherapy.** When phobias or other fears do not fully respond to a well-administered cognitive-behavioral treatment program *or* to medication, it may be useful to explore whether the problem has roots in traumatic experiences from childhood or earlier. This is especially important in instances where childhood abuse—physical, sexual, or emotional—has occurred. Remembering, reexperiencing, and working through feelings around traumatic incidents that never were expressed is the first step. The next step is to change self-limiting decisions you made about yourself or your circumstances as a result of the trauma.

The process of remembering and reworking traumatic experiences from the past is best carried out in psychotherapy—it is not something to try on your own. Specific techniques, such as hypnosis and eye-movement desensitization and reprocessing (EMDR), can help expedite this process. (See Chapter 18 for further information.)

3. **Spirituality.** Finally, spirituality can be an important adjunct to recovery. In the past few years, spiritual perspectives on growth and healing have come to play a larger role in the self-help movement. This is evidenced by the tremendous popularity of 12-step programs, which are essentially spiritual in nature. In particular, Phobics Anonymous has come to have an increasing outreach (see Appendix 1 for the address).

There is also a growing interest in spirituality within holistic medicine. The work and writings of Bernie Siegel, Deepak Chopra, and Scott Peck, which attempt to integrate spirituality with mainstream medicine and psychiatry, have influenced many people. At present this interest in spirituality is more manifest at the grass-roots level of society than among professionals. In the future this is likely to change. Spiritually based principles and practices will eventually come to be accepted as an important adjunct to recovery from anxiety disorders as well as other behavioral problems.

Introduction

Research conducted by the National Institute of Mental Health has shown that anxiety disorders are the number-one mental health problem among American women and are second only to alcohol and drug abuse among men. Approximately ten percent of the population of the United States, or 20 to 30 million people, have suffered from panic attacks, phobias, or other anxiety disorders in the past year. Yet only a small proportion of these people receive treatment. During the 1980s panic and anxiety reached epidemic proportions (much as depression did in the 1970s). With the advent of a new decade, there appears to be no indication of any decrease in this trend.

Why are problems with panic, phobias, and anxiety so prevalent? It has been my impression that anxiety disorders are an outcome of cumulative stress acting over time. Certainly there are numerous factors which cause a person to develop panic attacks, phobias, or obsessions—but I believe that stress plays a key role. People living in western society are currently experiencing more stress than they have at any previous time in history, and it is this stress which explains the increased incidence of anxiety disorders. While it can be argued that human beings have always had to deal with stressful societal conditions (wars, famines, plagues, economic depression, and so forth), there are two reasons for suggesting that the overall stress level is higher now than before.

First, our environment and social order have changed more in the last 30 years than they have in the previous 300 years. The increased pace of modern society—and the increased rate of technological change—have deprived people of adequate time to adjust to these changes.

To compound this situation, the lack of a consistent, externally sanctioned set of standards and values (traditionally prescribed by society and religion) leaves a vacuum in which people are left to fend for themselves. Faced with a barrage of inconsistent world views and standards presented by the media, people are having to learn to cope with the responsibility of creating their own meaning and moral order.

Both of these factors make it difficult for many individuals in modern society to experience a sense of stability or consistency in their lives. Anxiety disorders are simply one outcome of a diminished ability to cope with the resulting stress, as are addictive disorders, depression, and the increased incidence of degenerative diseases.

Many good books on anxiety disorders appeared during the 1980s. A majority of these books addressed the problem of panic attacks and agoraphobia, disorders which gained during the 1980s a new prominence in the public's awareness. Most of these popular books tended to be primarily descriptive. Although several of them did talk about methods of treatment and offered practical recovery strategies, the emphasis was generally on providing readers with a basic understanding of the anxiety disorders.

In writing this workbook, my intention has been to 1) describe specific skills that you need to overcome problems with panic, anxiety, and phobias and 2) provide step-by-step procedures and exercises for mastering these skills. Although there is quite a bit of descriptive material, what makes this a *workbook* is its emphasis on coping strategies and skills along with exercises to foster your recovery.

There is probably little in this book that is altogether new. The chapters on relaxation, exercise, coping skills for panic attacks, imagery and real-life desensitization, identifying and expressing feelings, asserting yourself, self-esteem, and nutrition summarize concepts that have been dealt with in greater detail in the books listed at the end of each chapter. It has been my hope to define in a single volume the full range of strategies necessary to overcome problems with anxiety. The more of these strategies you can incorporate into your own recovery program, the more efficient and rapid your progress will be.

The approach of this workbook is strongly holistic. It presents interventions that will affect your life on many levels: body, behavior, feelings, mind, interpersonal relations, self-esteem, and spirituality. A majority of the previous popular approaches to panic and phobias have emphasized primarily behavioral and cognitive (or mental) strategies. I believe that these are very important and still constitute the core of any successful program for treating panic attacks, phobias, generalized anxiety, or obsessive-compulsive disorder. These approaches are covered in five chapters of this workbook. Chapter 6 offers concepts and coping strategies that are crucial for learning to handle panic attacks. Chapters 7 and 8 detail the processes of imagery and real-life desensitization, which are necessary to any program for recovering from agoraphobia, social phobia, or other phobias. Chapters 9 and 10 present methods for learning to counter unhelpful "self-talk" and mistaken beliefs that tend to perpetuate anxiety on a day-to-day basis.

In my own practice, I've learned that relaxation and personal wellness are also of prime importance. As previously mentioned, anxiety disorders develop as the result of cumulative, long-term stress. This stress is apparent in the well-known fact that most people with anxiety disorders tend to be in a chronic state of physiological hyperarousal. Recovery, I believe, depends on adopting lifestyle changes that promote a more relaxed, balanced, and healthy approach to life: in short, changes that upgrade your level of *physical wellness*. The strategies and skills presented in the chapters on relaxation, exercise, and nutrition constitute a necessary *foundation* on which the other skills presented throughout this workbook rest. It is much easier, for example, to implement imagery and real-life desensitization if you've first learned how to effectively enter a deep state of relaxation. You will also find it easier to identify and change counterproductive self-talk when you are feeling physically healthy and relaxed. Just as learning habits of positive self-talk will help you feel better, so improving your physical wellness through proper relaxation, exercise, and nutrition will reduce your *predisposition* to counterproductive attitudes and self-talk. In short, when you feel well you will think well.

At the other end of the spectrum, I have noticed that people who lack a sense of direction or purpose in their lives have an increased vulnerability to anxiety disorders. Panic attacks and agoraphobia—especially when they involve a fear of being closed in or unable to escape—may symbolize a sense of having "nowhere to go" or being "stuck" within your life. Given the complexity of contemporary society and the lack of any externally prescribed set of values, it is common to feel confused and uncertain about the meaning and direction of your life. By getting more in touch with a larger sense of purpose, and, where appropriate, cultivating your spirituality, you can gain a sense of meaning that will help to diminish your problems with anxiety. This is an important area to be addressed in dealing with anxiety disorders and probably most other behavior disorders as well (see Chapter 19).

In sum, I believe in the necessity of a holistic model incorporating all of the approaches presented in this workbook. Recovery from anxiety disorders depends upon intervening at all levels of the whole person.

A final important point bears mentioning. It will take a strong commitment and consistent motivation on your part to successfully utilize the skills presented in this workbook. I have assumed throughout that it is possible, if you are self-motivated and disciplined, to achieve a lasting recovery on your own. At the same time, I do not wish to give the impression that a self-motivated recovery program is the *preferred* method for dealing with anxiety disorders. It is not necessary that you go it alone. Many of you will decide to use this workbook in conjunction with your work with a therapist who has expertise in treating anxiety disorders. A therapist can provide structure and support, and can help you fine-tune the concepts and strategies found in this workbook to your own individual situation. Some of you may also find support groups or treatment groups (especially for agoraphobia and social phobia) to be very valuable. A group format can motivate and maintain your enthusiasm to learn the skills necessary for recovery. A number of people seem to benefit from the inspiration, structure, and support that a group can provide.

Ultimately you will need to choose the best way for yourself. If you decide to seek outside help for your problem, you will want to contact a specialist in the treatment of anxiety disorders to help you decide what treatment format is best for you. A list of such specialists in the United States and Canada is offered in the *National Treatment Directory for Phobias and Related Anxiety Disorders*, Sixth Edition (available from the Anxiety Disorders Association of America—see Appendix 1 for the address).

It is quite possible to overcome your problem with panic, phobias, or anxiety on your own through the use of the strategies and exercises presented in this workbook. Yet it is equally valuable and appropriate, if you feel so inclined, to use this book as an adjunct to working with a therapist or group treatment program.

1

What Are the Anxiety Disorders?

Susan awakens suddenly almost every night, a couple of hours after going to sleep, with a tightness in her throat, a racing heart, dizziness, and a fear that she's going to die. Although she's shaking all over, she hasn't a clue why. After many nights of getting up and pacing her living room floor in an attempt to get a grip on herself, she decides to go see her doctor to find out whether something is wrong with her heart.

Cindy, a medical secretary, has been having attacks like Susan's whenever she's in a confined public situation. Not only does she fear losing control over herself, but she dreads what others might think of her if this were to happen. Recently she has been avoiding going into any kind of store other than the local 7-Eleven, unless her boyfriend is with her. She has also needed to leave restaurants and movie theaters during dates with her boyfriend. Now she is beginning to wonder whether she can cope with her job. She has been forcing herself to go into work, yet after a few minutes among her office mates she starts to fear that she's losing control of herself. Suddenly she feels as though she *has to* leave.

Steve has a responsible position as a software engineer, but feels he is unable to advance because of his inability to contribute in group meetings. It's almost more than he can bear just to sit in on meetings, let alone offer his opinions. Yesterday his boss asked him whether he would be available to make a presentation on his segment of a large project. At that point Steve became extremely nervous and tongue-tied. He walked out of the room, stammering that he would let his boss know by the next day about the presentation. Privately, he thought about resigning.

Mike is so embarrassed about a peculiar fear he's had over the past few months that he can't tell anyone, not even his wife. While driving he is frequently gripped by the fear that he has run over someone or perhaps an animal. Even though there is no "thud" suggesting that anything like this has happened, he feels compelled to make a U-turn and retrace the route he's just driven to make absolutely sure. In fact, recently, his paranoia about having hit someone has grown so strong that he has to retrace his route three or four times to assure himself that nothing has happened. Mike is a bright, successful professional and feels utterly humiliated about his compulsion to check. He's beginning to wonder if he's going crazy.

Susan, Cindy, Steve, and Mike are all confronted by anxiety. Yet it is not ordinary anxiety. Their experiences differ in two fundamental respects from the "normal" anxiety people experience in response to everyday life. First, their anxiety has gone out of control. In each case, the individual feels powerless to direct what's happening. This sense of powerlessness in turn creates even more anxiety. Second, the anxiety is interfering with the normal functioning of their lives. Susan's sleep is disrupted. Cindy and Steve may lose their jobs. And Mike has lost the ability to drive in an efficient and timely manner.

The examples of Susan, Cindy, Steve, and Mike illustrate four types of anxiety disorder: panic disorder, agoraphobia, social phobia, and obsessive-compulsive disorder. Later in this chapter, you can find detailed descriptions of the characteristics of each specific anxiety disorder. But I would first like you to consider the common theme that runs through them all. What is the nature of anxiety itself?

What Is Anxiety?

You can better understand the nature of anxiety by looking both at what it is and what it is not. For example, anxiety can be distinguished from fear in several ways. When you are afraid, your fear is usually directed toward some concrete, external object or situation. The event that you fear usually is within the bounds of possibility. You might fear not meeting a deadline, failing an exam, being unable to pay your bills, or being rejected by someone you want to please. When you experience anxiety, on the other hand, you often can't specify what it is you're anxious about. The focus of anxiety is more internal than external. It seems to be a response to a vague, distant, or even unrecognized danger. You might be anxious about "losing control" of yourself or some situation. Or you might feel a vague anxiety about "something bad happening."

Anxiety affects your whole being. It is a physiological, behavioral, and psychological reaction all at once. On a physiological level, anxiety may include bodily reactions such as rapid heartbeat, muscle tension, queasiness, dry mouth, or sweating. On a behavioral level, it can sabotage your ability to act, express yourself, or deal with certain everyday situations.

Psychologically, anxiety is a subjective state of apprehension and uneasiness. In its most extreme form, it can cause you to feel detached from yourself and even fearful of dying or going crazy.

The fact that anxiety can affect you on a physiological, behavioral, and psychological level has important implications for your attempts to recover. A complete program of recovery from an anxiety disorder must intervene at all three levels to

1. Reduce physiological reactivity

2. Eliminate avoidance behavior

3. Change subjective interpretations (or "self-talk") which perpetuate a state of apprehension and worry

Anxiety can appear in different forms and at different levels of intensity. It can range in severity from a mere twinge of uneasiness to a full-blown panic attack marked by heart palpitations, disorientation, and terror. Anxiety that is not connected with any particular situation, that comes "out of the blue," is called *free-floating anxiety* or, in more severe instances, a *spontaneous panic attack*. The difference between an episode of free-floating anxiety and a spontaneous panic attack can be defined by whether you experience four or more of the following symptoms at the same time (the occurrence of four or more symptoms defines a panic attack):

- Shortness of breath
- Heart palpitations (rapid or irregular heartbeat)
- Trembling or shaking
- Sweating
- Choking
- Nausea or abdominal distress
- Numbness
- Dizziness or unsteadiness
- Feeling of detachment or being out of touch with yourself
- Hot flashes or chills
- Fear of dying
- Fear of going crazy or out of control

If your anxiety arises *only* in response to a specific situation, it is called *situational anxiety* or *phobic anxiety*. Situational anxiety is different from everyday fear in that it tends to be out of proportion or unrealistic. If you have a disproportionate apprehension about driving on freeways, going to the doctor, or confronting your spouse, this may qualify as situational anxiety. Situational anxiety becomes *phobic* when you actually start to *avoid* the situation: if you give up driving on freeways, going to doctors, or confronting your spouse altogether. In other words, phobic anxiety is situational anxiety that includes persistent avoidance of the situation.

Often anxiety can be brought on merely by thinking about a particular situation. When you feel distressed about what might happen when or if you have to face one of your phobic situations, you are experiencing what is called *anticipatory anxiety*. In its milder forms, anticipatory anxiety is indistinguishable from ordinary "worrying." But sometimes anticipatory anxiety becomes intense enough to be called *anticipatory panic*.

There is an important difference between spontaneous anxiety (or panic) and anticipatory anxiety (or panic). Spontaneous anxiety tends to come out of the blue, peaks to a high level very rapidly, and then subsides gradually. The peak is usually reached within five minutes, followed by a gradual tapering-off period of an hour or more. Anticipatory anxiety, on the other hand, tends to build up more gradually in response to encountering—or simply thinking about—a threatening situation, and then usually falls off quickly. You may "worry yourself into a frenzy" about something for an hour or more and then let go of the worry as you find something else to occupy your mind.

Anxiety Versus Anxiety Disorders

Anxiety is an inevitable part of life in contemporary society. It's important to realize that there are many situations that come up in everyday life in which it is *appropriate* and *reasonable* to react with some anxiety. If you didn't feel *any* anxiety in response to everyday challenges involving potential loss or failure, something would be wrong. This workbook can be of use to anyone experiencing normal, ordinary anxiety reactions (everyone, in other words). It is also intended for those of you who are dealing with specific anxiety disorders. Incorporating exercise, breathing skills, relaxation, and good nutritional habits into your daily life—as well as paying attention to self-talk, mistaken beliefs, feelings, assertiveness, and self-esteem—can all contribute to making your life more balanced and less anxious, regardless of the nature and extent of the anxiety you happen to be dealing with.

Anxiety disorders are distinguished from everyday, normal anxiety in that they involve anxiety that 1) is *more intense* (for example, panic attacks), 2) *lasts longer* (anxiety that may persist for months instead of going away after a stressful situation has passed), or 3) *leads to phobias* that interfere with your life.

Criteria for diagnosing specific anxiety disorders have been established by the American Psychiatric Association and are listed in a well-known diagnostic manual used by mental health professionals. This manual is called *DSM-IV* (*Diagnostic and Statistical Manual of Mental Disorders*). The following descriptions of various anxiety disorders are based on the criteria in *DSM-IV*, as is the self-diagnosis questionnaire at the end of this chapter. This workbook can help you even if your specific anxiety disorder or reaction doesn't fit any of the *DSM-IV*'s diagnostic categories. On the other hand, don't be unduly concerned if your reaction is perfectly described by one of the diagnostic categories. Approximately eight percent of the people in the United States would find themselves in your company.

Here are the various anxiety disorders defined by *DSM-IV*:

- Panic Disorder

- Agoraphobia

- Social Phobia

- Specific Phobia

- Generalized Anxiety Disorder

- Obsessive-Compulsive Disorder

- Post-Traumatic Stress Disorder

- Acute Stress Disorder

- Agoraphobia Without History of Panic Disorder

- Anxiety Disorder Due to a General Medical Condition

- Substance-Induced Anxiety Disorder

Panic Disorder

Panic disorder is characterized by sudden episodes of acute apprehension or intense fear that occur "out of the blue" without any apparent cause. Intense panic usually lasts no more than a few minutes, but, in rare instances, can return in "waves" for a period of up to two hours. During the panic itself, any of the following symptoms can occur:

- Shortness of breath or a feeling of being smothered

- Heart palpitations—pounding heart or accelerated heart rate

- Dizziness, unsteadiness, or faintness

- Trembling or shaking

- Feeling of choking

- Sweating

- Nausea or abdominal distress

- Feeling of unreality—as if you're "not all there" (*depersonalization*)

- Numbness or tingling in hands and feet

- Hot and cold flashes

- Chest pain or discomfort

- Fears of going crazy or losing control

- Fears of dying

At least four of these symptoms are present in a full-blown panic attack, while having two or three of them is referred to as a *limited-symptom attack*.

Your symptoms would be diagnosed as panic disorder if: 1) you have had two or more panic attacks and 2) at least one of these attacks has been followed by one month (or more) of persistent concern about having another panic attack, or worry about the possible implications of having another panic attack. It's important to recognize that panic disorder, by itself, does not involve any phobias. The panic doesn't occur because you are thinking about, approaching, or actually entering a phobic situation. Instead, it occurs spontaneously and unexpectedly for no apparent reason. Also, the panic attacks are not due to the physiological effects of a drug (prescription or recreational) or a medical condition.

You may have two or three panic attacks without ever having another one again or without having another one for years. Or you may have several panic attacks followed by a panic-free period, only to have the panic return a month or two later. Sometimes an initial panic attack may be followed by recurring attacks three or more times per week unremittingly until you seek treatment. In all of these cases, there is a tendency to develop *anticipatory anxiety* or apprehension between panic attacks focusing on fear of having another one.

If you are suffering from panic disorder, you may be very frightened by your symptoms and consult with doctors to find a medical cause. Heart palpitations and an irregular heartbeat may lead to EKG and other cardiac tests, which, in most cases, turn out normal. (Sometimes mitral valve prolapse, a benign arrhythmia of the heart, may coexist with panic disorder.) Fortunately, an increasing number of physicians have some knowledge of panic disorder and are able to distinguish it from purely physical complaints.

A diagnosis of panic disorder is made only after possible medical causes—including hypoglycemia, hyperthyroidism, reaction to excess caffeine, or withdrawal from alcohol, tranquilizers, or sedatives—have been ruled out. The causes of panic disorder involve a combination of heredity, chemical imbalances in the brain, and personal stress. Sudden losses or major life changes may trigger the onset of panic attacks.

People tend to develop panic disorder during late adolescence or their twenties. In a majority of cases, panic is complicated by the development of agoraphobia (as described in the following section). Between one and two percent of the population has "pure" panic disorder, while about five percent, or one in every twenty people, suffers from panic attacks complicated by agoraphobia.

Of all the anxiety disorders, panic disorder is the one for which prescription medications are most frequently given. Panic attacks can be reduced or even blocked by two different types of medications: antidepressants such as imipramine (Tofranil) or paroxetine (Paxil) or minor tranquilizers such as alprazolam (Xanax), or clonazepam (Klonopin). The problem with medications is that when they are withdrawn, even after having been taken for six months to a year, panic attacks often return. This is more often the case with tranquilizers than with antidepressant medications. Milder cases of panic disorder may be helped without medication. By reducing stress and improving your physical health, you can increase your resistance to panic attacks. A personal wellness program that includes 1) regular exercise, 2) daily practice of deep relaxation, 3) good nutrition, and 4) a shift in *attitude* to a calmer, more easy-going approach to life may enable you to reduce panic without relying on prescription medications.

Agoraphobia

Of all the anxiety disorders, agoraphobia is the most prevalent. It is estimated that one in twenty, or about five percent of the general population, suffers from varying degrees of agoraphobia. The only disorder that affects a greater number of people in the United States is alcoholism.

The word *agoraphobia* means fear of open spaces; however, the essence of agoraphobia is a fear of panic attacks. If you suffer from agoraphobia, you are afraid of being in situations from which escape might be difficult—or in which help might be unavailable—if you suddenly had a panic attack. You may avoid grocery stores or freeways, for example, not so much because of their inherent characteristics, but because these are situations from which escape might be difficult or embarrassing in the event of panic. Fear of embarrassment plays a key role. Most agoraphobics fear not only having panic attacks but *what other people will think* should they be seen having a panic attack.

It is common for the agoraphobic to avoid a variety of situations. Some of the more common ones include

- Crowded public places such as grocery stores, department stores, restaurants

- Enclosed or confined places such as tunnels, bridges, or the hairdresser's chair

- Public transportation such as trains, buses, subways, planes

- Being at home alone

Perhaps the most common feature of agoraphobia is anxiety about being far away from home or far from a "safe person" (usually your spouse, partner, a parent, or anyone to whom you have a primary attachment). You may completely avoid driving alone or may be afraid of driving alone beyond a certain short distance from home. In more severe cases, you might be able to walk alone only a few yards from home or you might be housebound altogether. I know of one agoraphobic who was unable to leave her bedroom without being accompanied.

If you have agoraphobia, you are not only phobic about a variety of situations but tend to be anxious much of the time. This anxiety arises from *anticipating* that you *might* be stuck in a situation in which you would panic. What would happen, for example, if you were asked to go somewhere you ordinarily avoid and have to explain your way out of it? Or what would happen if you suddenly were left alone? Because of the severe restrictions in your activities and life, you may also be depressed. Depression arises from feeling in the grip of a condition over which you have no control or that you are powerless to change.

Agoraphobia appears to be engendered by panic disorder. At first you simply have panic attacks that occur for no apparent reason (panic disorder). After a while, though, you become aware that your attacks occur more frequently in confined situations away from home or when you are by yourself. You begin to be afraid of these situations. At the point where you actually start to avoid these situations for fear of panicking, you've started to develop agoraphobia. From that point you might go on to develop a mild, moderate, or severe problem. In a mild case, you might feel uncomfortable in confined situations but not actually avoid them. You continue to work or shop on your own, but do not want to go far from home otherwise. In a moderate case, you might start to avoid some situations, such as public transportation, elevators, driving far from home, or being in restaurants. However, your restriction is only partial, and there are certain situations away from home or your safe person that you can handle on your own, even with some discomfort. Severe agoraphobia is marked by an all-inclusive restriction of activities to the point where you are unable to leave your house without being accompanied.

Just why some people with panic attacks develop agoraphobia and others do not is unknown at this time. Nor is it understood why some people develop much more severe cases than others. What is known is that agoraphobia is caused by a combination of heredity and environment. Agoraphobics may have a parent, sibling, or other relative who also has the problem. When one identical twin is agoraphobic, the other has a high likelihood of being agoraphobic, too. On the environmental side, there are certain types of childhood circumstances that predispose a child to agoraphobia. These include growing up with parents who are 1) perfectionist and overcritical, 2) overprotective, and/or 3) overly anxious to the point of communicating to their child that the world is a "dangerous place." The hereditary and environmental origins of agoraphobia and other anxiety disorders will be explored in greater depth in the following chapter.

Agoraphobia affects people in all walks of life and at all levels of the socioeconomic scale. Approximately 80 percent of agoraphobics are women, although this percentage has been dropping recently. It is possible to speculate that as women are increasingly expected to hold down full-time jobs (making a housebound lifestyle less socially acceptable), the percentage of women and men with agoraphobia may tend to equalize.

The good news about agoraphobia is that it is a very treatable condition. The first step in treatment is to learn to relax and to cope with panic attacks (see Chapters 4 and 6). In some cases, medication may be necessary. As a second step, situations that have been avoided are gradually confronted through a process of graded exposure. Such exposure is conducted first in imagination and then in real life (see Chapters 7 and 8). Third, constructive ways of thinking are learned and substituted in place of worrisome, fearful thinking (see Chapters 9 and 10). Finally, because agoraphobics often have difficulty standing up for themselves and their rights, assertiveness training is frequently a part of the treatment (see Chapter 13). With adequate treatment, approximately 80-90 percent of agoraphobics can achieve a lasting recovery.

Social Phobia

Social phobia is one of the more common anxiety disorders. It involves fear of embarrassment or humiliation in situations where you are exposed to the scrutiny of others or must perform. This fear is much stronger than the normal anxiety most nonphobic people experience in social or performance situations. Usually it's so strong that it causes you to avoid the situation altogether, although some people with social phobia endure social situations, albeit with considerable anxiety. Typically, your concern is that you will say or do something that will cause others to judge you as being anxious, weak, "crazy," or stupid. Your concern is generally out of proportion to the situation, and you recognize that it's excessive (children with social phobia, however, do not recognize the excessiveness of their fear).

The most common social phobia is fear of public speaking. In fact, this is the most common of all phobias and affects performers, speakers, people whose jobs require them to make presentations, and students who have to speak before their class. Public speaking phobia affects a large percentage of the population and is equally prevalent among men and women.

Other common social phobias include

- Fear of blushing in public

- Fear of choking on or spilling food while eating in public

- Fear of being watched at work

- Fear of using public toilets

- Fear of writing or signing documents in the presence of others

- Fear of crowds

- Fear of taking examinations

Sometimes social phobia is less specific and involves a generalized fear of *any* social or group situation where you feel that you might be watched or evaluated. When your fear is of a wide range of social situations (for example, initiating conversations, participating in small groups, speaking to authority figures, dating, attending parties, and so on), the condition is referred to as *generalized social phobia*.

While social anxieties are common, you would be given a formal diagnosis of social phobia only if your avoidance interferes with work, social activities, or important relationships, and/or it causes you considerable distress. As with agoraphobia, panic attacks can accompany social phobia, although your panic is related more to being embarrassed or humiliated than to being confined or trapped. Also the panic arises only in connection with a specific type of social situation.

Social phobias tend to develop earlier than agoraphobia and can begin in late childhood or adolescence. They often develop in shy children around the time they are faced with increased peer pressure at school. Typically these phobias persist (without treatment) through adolescence and young adulthood, but have a tendency to decrease in severity later in life. Recent studies suggest that social phobia affects 1.8 to 3.2 percent of the U.S. population and is three times more prevalent among men than women.

You can recover from social phobias by gradually exposing yourself to the situation you have been avoiding, first in imagination and then in real life. The processes of imagery desensitization and real-life exposure are described in Chapters 7 and 8. Working on assertiveness and self-esteem (see Chapters 14 and 15) is also critical for developing the confidence you need to be more comfortable in social and performance situations.

Treatment for social phobia is often best carried out in a group setting. The best treatment combines exposure to social settings along with restructuring of mistaken beliefs associated with embarrassment and fear of rejection.

Sometimes medications have been used to treat social phobia. Beta-blocker medications, such as Inderal and Tenormin, can reduce physiological reactions associated with social anxiety, such as rapid heart beat, blushing, and sweating. Minor tranquilizers (such as Xanax and Klonopin) or MAO-inhibitor antidepressants (such as Nardil and Parnate), although not without certain risks, have been helpful in treating particular cases of social phobia.

Specific Phobia

Specific phobia typically involves a strong fear and avoidance of *one particular* type of object or situation. There are no spontaneous panic attacks, and there is no fear of panic attacks, as in agoraphobia. There is also no fear of humiliation or embarrassment in social situations, as in social phobia. Direct exposure to the feared object or situation may elicit a panic reaction, however. The fear and avoidance are strong enough to interfere with your normal routines, work, or relationships, and to cause you significant distress. Even though you recognize its irrationalities, a specific phobia can cause you considerable anxiety.

Among the most common specific phobias are the following:

Animal Phobias. These can include fear and avoidance of snakes, bats, rats, spiders, bees, dogs, and other creatures. Often these phobias begin in childhood, where they are considered as normal fears. Only when they persist into adulthood and disrupt your life or cause significant distress do they come to be classified as specific phobias.

Acrophobia (fear of heights). With acrophobia, you tend to be afraid of high floors of buildings or of finding yourself atop mountains, hills, or high-level bridges. In such situations you may experience 1) vertigo (dizziness) or 2) an urge to jump, usually experienced as some external force drawing you to the edge.

Elevator Phobia. This phobia may involve a fear that the cables will break and the elevator will crash, *or* a fear that the elevator will get stuck and you will be trapped inside. You may have panic reactions, but you have no history of panic disorder or agoraphobia.

Airplane Phobia. This most often involves a fear that the plane will crash. Alternatively, it can involve a fear that the cabin will depressurize, causing you to asphyxiate. More recently, phobias about planes being hijacked or bombed have become common. When flying, you may have a panic attack. Otherwise you have no history of panic disorder or agoraphobia. Fear of flying is a very common phobia. Approximately 10 percent of the population will not fly at all, while an additional 20 percent experience considerable anxiety while flying.

Doctor or Dentist Phobias. This can begin as a fear of painful procedures (injections, having teeth filled) conducted in a doctor's or dentist's office. Later it can generalize to anything having to do with doctors or dentists. The danger is that you may avoid needed medical treatment.

Phobias of Thunder and/or Lightning. Almost invariably phobias of thunder and lightning begin in childhood. When they persist beyond adolescence they are classified as specific phobias.

Blood-Injury Phobia. This is a unique phobia in that you have a tendency to faint (rather than panic) if exposed to blood or your own pain through injections or inadvertent injury. People with blood-injury phobia tend to be both physically and psychologically healthy in other regards.

Illness Phobia. Usually this phobia involves a fear of contracting and/or ultimately succumbing to a specific illness, such as a heart attack or cancer. With illness phobias you tend to seek constant reassurance from doctors and will avoid any situation that reminds you of the dreaded disease. Illness phobia is different from hypochondria, where you tend to *imagine* many different types of disease rather than focusing on one.

Specific phobias are common and affect approximately 10 percent of the population. However, since they do not always result in severe impairment, only a minority of people with specific phobias actually seek treatment. These types of phobias occur in men and women about equally. Animal phobias tend to be more common in women, while illness phobias are more common in men.

As previously mentioned, specific phobias are often childhood fears that were never outgrown. In other instances they may develop after a traumatic event, such as an accident, natural disaster, illness, or visit to the dentist—in other words, as a result of conditioning. A final cause is childhood *modeling*. Repeated observation of a parent with a specific phobia can lead a child to develop it as well.

Specific phobias tend to be easier to treat than agoraphobia or social phobia since they do not involve panic attacks or multiple phobias. The treatment of choice for specific phobias is imagery desensitization and/or real-life exposure, which often succeeds in alleviating the problem.

To sum up, specific phobia is usually a benign disorder, particularly if it begins as a common childhood fear. Though it may last for years, it rarely gets worse and often diminishes over time. Typically it is not associated with other psychiatric disturbances. People with specific phobias are usually functioning at a high level in all other respects.

Generalized Anxiety Disorder

Generalized anxiety disorder is characterized by chronic anxiety that persists for at least six months *but is unaccompanied by panic attacks, phobias, or obsessions.* You simply experience persistent anxiety and worry without the complicating features of other anxiety disorders. To be given a diagnosis of generalized anxiety disorder, your anxiety and worry must focus on two or more stressful life circumstances (such as finances, relationships, health, or school performance) a majority of days during a six-month period. It's common, if you're dealing with generalized anxiety disorder, to have a large number of worries, and to spend a lot of your time worrying. Yet you find it difficult to exercise much control over your worrying. Moreover, the intensity and frequency of the worry are always out of proportion to the actual likelihood of the feared events happening.

In addition to frequent worry, generalized anxiety disorder involves having at least three of the following six symptoms (with some symptoms present more days than not over the past six months):

- Restlessness—feeling keyed up

- Being easily fatigued

- Difficulty concentrating

- Irritability

- Muscle tension

- Difficulties with sleep

Finally, you're likely to receive a diagnosis of generalized anxiety disorder if your worry and associated symptoms cause you significant distress and/or interfere with your ability to function occupationally, socially, or in other important areas.

If a doctor tells you that you suffer from generalized anxiety disorder, he or she has probably ruled out possible medical causes of chronic anxiety, such as hyperventilation, thyroid problems, or drug-induced anxiety. Generalized anxiety disorder often occurs together with depression: a competent therapist can usually determine which disorder is primary and which is secondary. In some cases, though, it is difficult to say which came first.

Generalized anxiety disorder can develop at any age. In children and adolescents, the focus of worry often tends to be on performance in school or sports events. In adults, the focus can vary. This disorder affects approximately four percent of the American population, and may be slightly more common in females than males (55-60 percent of those diagnosed with the disorder are female).

Although there are no specific phobias associated with generalized anxiety disorder, one view propounded by Aaron Beck and Gary Emery suggests that the disorder is sustained by "basic fears" of a broader nature than specific phobias, such as

- Fear of losing control

- Fear of not being able to cope

- Fear of failure

- Fear of rejection or abandonment

- Fear of death and disease

Generalized anxiety disorder can be aggravated by any stressful situation that elicits these fears, such as increased demands for performance, intensified marital conflict, physical illness, or *any situation that heightens your perception of danger or threat.*

The underlying causes of generalized anxiety disorder are unknown. It is likely to involve a combination of heredity and predisposing childhood experiences, such as excessive parental expectations or parental abandonment and rejection.

Generalized anxiety disorder may be alleviated by using the full range of strategies presented in this workbook (with the exception of imagery and real-life desensitization, which are relevant to phobias). Reducing muscle tension and improving your physical wellness through a program of regular exercise, relaxation, and good nutrition are a good beginning (see Chapters 4, 5, and 16). Modifying self-talk and the basic belief systems that perpetuate your anxiety is crucial to developing a more relaxed approach to life (see Chapters 9 and 10), as is learning to express your feelings and act assertively (see Chapters 13 and 14). Finally, working on your self-esteem will help you overcome any deep-seated feelings of insecurity or inadequacy which may underlie your anxiety, regardless of the type of anxiety disorder you happen to be facing (see Chapter 15).

Obsessive-Compulsive Disorder

Some people naturally tend to be more neat, tidy, and orderly than others. These traits can in fact be useful in many situations, both at work and at home. In obsessive-compulsive disorder, however, they are carried to an extreme and disruptive degree. Obsessive-compulsive people can spend many hours cleaning, tidying, checking, or ordering, to the point where these activities interfere with the rest of the business of their lives.

Obsessions are recurring ideas, thoughts, images, or impulses that seem senseless but nonetheless continue to intrude into your mind. Examples include images of violence, thoughts of doing violence to someone else, or fears of leaving on lights or the stove or leaving your door unlocked. You recognize that these thoughts or fears are irrational and try to suppress them, but they continue to intrude into your mind for hours, days, weeks, or longer. These thoughts or images are not merely excessive worries about real-life problems and are usually unrelated to a real-life problem.

Compulsions are behaviors or rituals that you perform to dispel the anxiety brought up by obsessions. For example, you may wash your hands numerous times to dispel a fear of being contaminated, check the stove again and again to see if it is turned off, or look continually in your rearview mirror while driving to assuage anxiety about having hit somebody. You realize that these rituals are unreasonable. Yet you feel compelled to perform them to ward off the anxiety associated with your particular obsession. The conflict between your wish to be free of the compulsive ritual and the irresistible desire to perform it is a source of anxiety, shame, and even despair. Eventually you may cease struggling with your compulsions and give over to them entirely.

Obsessions may occur by themselves, without necessarily being accompanied by compulsions. In fact, about 25 percent of the people who suffer from obsessive-compulsive disorder only have obsessions, and these often center around fears of causing harm to a loved one.

The most common compulsions include washing, checking, and counting. If you are a washer, you are constantly concerned about avoiding contamination. You avoid touching doorknobs, shaking hands, or coming into contact with any object you associate with germs, filth, or a toxic substance. You can spend literally hours washing hands or showering to reduce anxiety about being contaminated. Women more often have this compulsion than men. Men outnumber women as checkers, however. Doors have to be repeatedly checked to dispel obsessions about being robbed; stoves are repeatedly checked to dispel obsessions about starting a fire; or roads repeatedly checked to dispel obsessions about having hit someone. In the counting compulsion, you must count up to a certain number or repeat a word a certain number of times to dispel anxiety about harm befalling you or someone else.

Obsessive-compulsive disorder is often accompanied by depression. Preoccupation with obsessions, in fact, tends to wax and wane with depression. This disorder may also be accompanied by phobic avoidance—such as when a person with an obsession about dirt avoids public restrooms or touching doorknobs.

It is very important to realize that as bizarre as obsessive-compulsive behavior may sound, it has nothing to do with "being crazy." You always recognize the irrationality and senselessness of your thoughts and behavior and you are very frustrated (as well as depressed) about your inability to control them.

Obsessive-compulsive disorder used to be considered a rare behavior disturbance. However, recent studies have shown that as many as *two to three percent of the general population* may suffer, to varying degrees, from obsessive-compulsive disorder. The reason prevalence rates have been underestimated up to now is that most sufferers have been very reluctant to tell anyone about their problem. This disorder appears to affect men and women in equal numbers. Although many cases of obsessive-compulsive disorder begin in adolescence and young adulthood, about half begin in childhood. The age of onset tends to be earlier in males than females.

The causes of obsessive-compulsive disorder are unclear. There is some evidence that a deficiency of a neurotransmitter substance in the brain known as serotonin, or a disturbance in serotonin metabolism, is associated with the disorder. This is borne out by the fact that many sufferers improve when they take medications that increase brain serotonin levels, such as clomipramine (Anafranil) or specific serotonin-enhancing antidepressants such as fluoxetine (Prozac), sertraline (Zoloft), and fluvoxamine (Luvox). Further research needs to be done.

Two treatment strategies have been helpful in relieving obsessions and compulsions. The first is a behavior modification strategy called *exposure and response prevention*. This involves systematically being exposed to situations that arouse obsessive thoughts and then being prevented from engaging in any compulsive behaviors. For example, if you are obsessive about contamination and wash your hands compulsively, you would be required to expose yourself to something you considered dirty, such as a doorknob, and then to reduce the number of times you wash your hands or refrain from washing at all. Similarly, if you check the door five times whenever you leave your house, you would be required to gradually reduce the number of checks down to one. Most likely, someone would work with you in those situations in which you tend to be compulsive to enforce this "response prevention."

The other form of treatment that has been helpful involves medication. Of all the medications that have been tried, Anafranil and SSRI (selective serotonin reuptake inhibitor) antidepressants such as Prozac, Zoloft, and Paxil have been most effective, resulting in improvement or elimination of symptoms in 50-60 percent of the people treated. When medication and behavioral methods are combined, the improvement rate approaches 80 percent.

The strategies presented in this workbook will be helpful if you are affected by obsessive-compulsive disorder. Yet the primary mode of treatment I would suggest is to consult a professional who is well versed in the use of behavioral methods, such as exposure and response prevention, as well as in the use of appropriate medications. This workbook can complement behavioral and pharmacological treatment approaches.

Further discussion of obsessive-compulsive disorder can be found in Appendix 5.

Post-Traumatic Stress Disorder

The essential feature of post-traumatic stress disorder is the development of disabling psychological symptoms following a traumatic event. It was first identified during World War I, when soldiers were observed to suffer chronic anxiety, nightmares, and flashbacks for weeks, months, or even years following combat. This condition came to be known as shell shock.

Post-traumatic stress disorder can occur in anyone in the wake of a severe trauma outside the normal range of human experience. These are traumas that would produce intense fear, terror, and feelings of helplessness in anyone and include natural disasters such as earthquakes or tornadoes, car or plane crashes, rape, assault, or other violent crimes against yourself or your immediate family. It appears that the symptoms are more intense and longer lasting when the trauma is personal, as in rape or other violent crimes.

Among the variety of symptoms that can occur with post-traumatic stress disorder, the following nine are particularly common:

- Repetitive, distressing thoughts about the event

- Nightmares related to the event

- Flashbacks so intense that you feel or act as though the trauma were occurring all over again

- An attempt to avoid thoughts or feelings associated with the trauma

- An attempt to avoid activities or external situations associated with the trauma—such as a phobia about driving developing after you have been in an auto accident

- Emotional numbness—being out of touch with your feelings

- Feelings of detachment or estrangement from others

- Losing interest in activities that used to give you pleasure

- Persistent symptoms of increased anxiety, such as difficulty falling or staying asleep, difficulty concentrating, startling easily, or irritability and outbursts of anger

For you to receive a diagnosis of post-traumatic stress disorder, these symptoms need to have persisted for at least one month (with less than one month's duration, the appropriate diagnosis is "acute stress disorder"—see below). In addition, the disturbance must be causing you significant distress, interfering with social, vocational, or other important areas of your life.

If you suffer from post-traumatic stress disorder, you tend to be anxious and depressed. Sometimes you will find yourself acting impulsively, suddenly changing residence or going on a trip with hardly any plans. If you have been through a trauma where others around you died, you may suffer from guilt about having survived.

Post-traumatic stress disorder can affect people at any age. Children with the disorder tend not to relive the trauma consciously but continually reenact it in their play or in distressing dreams.

While all of the strategies in this workbook will be helpful if you're dealing with post-traumatic stress disorder, the principal treatment is psychotherapy that enables you to work through intense feelings of fear, loss, and/or guilt surrounding the original traumatic event. Insight-oriented therapy focused on expressing feelings and integrating the original experience can help reduce symptoms and increase your sense of mastery over your life. Sometimes hypnosis may be used to assist you in going back and "walking through" the original trauma.

Additional Anxiety Disorders in DSM-IV

The anxiety disorders described above were also discussed in the first edition of this workbook. Originally these seven disorders derived from an earlier classification of anxiety disorders presented in *DSM-IIIR (Diagnostic and Statistical Manual of Mental Disorders*—Third Edition, Revised). The newer *DSM-IV* classification, which appeared in May 1994, added the following four disorders.

Acute Stress Disorder

Like post-traumatic stress disorder, acute stress disorder involves developing anxiety and other disabling symptoms after exposure to a traumatic event. The principal distinction is that the symptoms subside in less than one month; if the symptoms last beyond one month, the diagnosis is changed from acute stress disorder to post-traumatic stress disorder. As with post-traumatic stress disorder, the initial trauma involves exposure to an event that carries the threat of death or serious injury (for example, military combat, violent personal assault, sexual assault, natural or manmade disasters, car accidents, or being diagnosed with a life-threatening illness). Either during or after the traumatic incident, you have symptoms such as numbness, detachment, or feelings of unreality or depersonalization. Later you tend to avoid anything that reminds you of the incident, and have persistent symptoms of anxiety (difficulty sleeping, irritability, poor concentration, exaggerated startle response, restlessness). This disturbance typically interferes with your work and your significant relationships but, as indicated, lasts no longer than four weeks following the traumatic event.

Agoraphobia Without a History of Panic Disorder

This particular anxiety disorder has all of the same features as agoraphobia—such as avoidance of a variety of situations—but there is no history of having had full-blown panic attacks. Instead, the focus of your fear is on only *one or two* symptoms among all those listed for panic disorder. For example, you might be afraid *only* of having heart palpitations if you venture too far from home or go to a crowded public place. Sometimes the fear is of an incapacitating symptom not on the list of panic attack symptoms. For example, you might be afraid to drive long distances and/or to be far from a town because of a fear of losing bladder control or having a bout of diarrhea.

Only a small percentage of people with agoraphobia do not have a history of panic disorder (estimates range from 5-15 percent). Treatment emphasizes relaxation, cognitive therapy, and *in vivo* exposure.

Anxiety Disorder Due to a General Medical Condition

This diagnostic category is reserved for situations in which significant anxiety (either in the form of panic attacks or generalized anxiety) is a direct physiological effect of a specific medical condition. Numerous types of medical conditions can cause anxiety, including endocrine conditions (hyper- and hypothyroidism, pheochromocytoma, hypoglycemia), cardiovascular conditions (congestive heart failure, pulmonary embolism), metabolic conditions (vitamin B12 deficiency, porphyria), and neurological conditions (vestibular problems, encephalitis). For a more complete listing, see the section in Chapter 2 entitled "Medical Conditions That Can Cause Panic Attacks or Anxiety."

Substance-Induced Anxiety Disorder

This category is used when panic attacks or generalized anxiety is determined to be the direct physiological effect of a substance, whether a drug of abuse, a medication, or toxin exposure. The anxiety may be a result either of exposure to the substance or withdrawal from it. For example, if you had no previous history of an anxiety disorder, then suddenly developed panic attacks as a result of withdrawing too quickly from a medication, you would receive this diagnosis.

Self-Diagnosis Questionnaire

The following questionnaire is designed to help you identify which particular anxiety disorder you may be dealing with. It is based on the official classification of anxiety disorders used by all mental health professionals and known as *DSM-IV (Diagnostic and Statistical Manual of Mental Disorders—Fourth Edition)*.

1. Do you have spontaneous anxiety attacks that come out of the blue? (Only answer "yes" if you do *not* have any phobias.)   Yes____ No____

2. Have you had at least one such attack in the last month?   Yes____ No____

3. If you had an anxiety attack in the last month, did you worry about having another one? Or did you worry about the implications of your attack for your physical or mental health?   Yes____ No____

4. In your worst experience with anxiety, did you have more than three of the following symptoms?

   ☐ shortness of breath or smothering sensation
   ☐ dizziness or unsteady feeling
   ☐ heart palpitations or rapid heartbeat
   ☐ trembling or shaking
   ☐ sweating
   ☐ choking
   ☐ nausea or abdominal distress
   ☐ feelings of being detached or out of touch with your body
   ☐ numbness or tingling sensations
   ☐ flushes or chills
   ☐ chest pain or discomfort
   ☐ fear of dying
   ☐ fear of going crazy or doing something out of control

If your answers to 1, 2, 3, and 4 were Yes, stop. You've met the conditions for **panic disorder**.

If your answer to 1 was Yes, but your anxiety reaction involved three or fewer of the symptoms listed under 4, you're experiencing what are called *limited symptom attacks*, but do not have full-blown panic disorder.

If you have panic attacks *and* phobias, go on.

5. Does fear of having panic attacks cause you to avoid going into certain situations? Yes____ No____

If your answer to 5 was Yes, stop. It is likely that you are dealing with **agoraphobia**. See question 6 to determine the extent of your agoraphobia.

6. Which of the following situations do you avoid because you are afraid of panicking?

   ☐ going far away from home
   ☐ shopping in a grocery store
   ☐ standing in a grocery store line

- ☐ going to department stores
- ☐ going to shopping malls
- ☐ driving on freeways
- ☐ driving on surface streets far from home
- ☐ driving anywhere by yourself
- ☐ using public transportation (buses, trains, etc.)
- ☐ going over bridges (whether you're the driver or passenger)
- ☐ going through tunnels (as driver or passenger)
- ☐ flying in planes
- ☐ riding in elevators
- ☐ being in high places
- ☐ going to a dentist's or doctor's office
- ☐ sitting in a barber's or beautician's chair
- ☐ eating in restaurants
- ☐ going to work
- ☐ being too far from a safe person or safe place
- ☐ being alone
- ☐ going outside your house
- ☐ other_____

The number of situations you checked above indicates the extent of your agoraphobia and the degree to which it limits your activity.

If your answer to 5 was No, but you do have phobias, go on.

7. Do you avoid certain situations *not* primarily because you are afraid of panicking but because you're afraid of being embarrassed or negatively evaluated by other people? (your embarrassment could subsequently lead you to panic)   Yes____ No____

If your answer to 7 was Yes, stop. It's likely that you are dealing with **social phobia**. See question 8 to determine the extent of your social phobia.

8. Which of the following situations do you avoid because of a fear of embarrassing or humiliating yourself?

- ☐ sitting in any kind of group (for example, at work, in school classrooms, social organizations, self-help groups)
- ☐ giving a talk or presentation before a small group of people
- ☐ giving a talk or presentation before a large group of people
- ☐ parties and social functions
- ☐ using public restrooms
- ☐ eating in front of others
- ☐ writing or signing your name in the presence of others
- ☐ dating

☐ any situation where you might say something foolish

☐ other_____

The number of situations you checked indicates the extent to which social phobia limits your activities.

If your answers to questions 5 and 7 were No, but you have other phobias, continue.

9. Do you fear and avoid any one (or more than one) of the following?

☐ insects or animals, such as spiders, bees, snakes, rats, bats, or dogs

☐ heights (high floors in buildings, tops of hills or mountains, high-level bridges)

☐ driving

☐ tunnels

☐ bridges

☐ elevators

☐ airplanes (flying)

☐ doctors or dentists

☐ thunder or lightning

☐ water

☐ blood

☐ injections or medical procedures

☐ illness such as heart attacks or cancer

☐ darkness

☐ other_____

10. Do you have high degrees of anxiety usually *only* when you have to face one of these situations? Yes_____ No_____

If you checked one or more items in 9 and answered Yes to 10, stop. It's likely that you're dealing with a **specific phobia**. If not, proceed.

11. Do you feel quite anxious much of the time but do *not* have distinct panic attacks, do *not* have phobias, and do *not* have specific obsessions or compulsions? Yes_____ No_____

12. Have you been prone to excessive worry for at least the last six months?   Yes_____ No_____

13. Have your anxiety and worry been associated with at least three of the following six symptoms?

☐ restlessness or feeling keyed up or on edge

☐ being easily fatigued

☐ difficulty concentrating or mind going blank

☐ irritability

☐ muscle tension

☐ sleep disturbance (difficulty falling or staying asleep, or restless unsatisfying sleep)

If your answers to 11, 12, and 13 were Yes, stop. It's likely that you're dealing with **generalized anxiety disorder**. If you answered Yes to 11 but No to 12 or 13, you're dealing with an anxiety condition that is not severe enough to qualify as generalized anxiety disorder.

14. Do you have recurring intrusive thoughts such as hurting or harming a close relative, being contaminated with dirt or a toxic substance, fearing you forgot to lock your door or turn off an appliance, or an unpleasant fantasy of catastrophe? (You recognize that these thoughts are irrational but you can't keep them from coming into your mind.)   Yes_____ No_____

15. Do you perform ritualistic actions such as washing your hands, checking, or counting to relieve anxiety over irrational fears that enter your mind?   Yes_____ No_____

If you answered Yes to 14 but No to 15, you are probably dealing with **obsessive-compulsive disorder**, but have obsessions only.

If you answered Yes to 14 and 15, you're probably dealing with **obsessive-compulsive disorder**, with both obsessions and compulsions.

If you answered No to 14 and 15 and most or all of the preceding questions, but still have anxiety or anxiety-related symptoms, you may be dealing with **post-traumatic stress disorder** or a nonspecific anxiety condition. Use the section in this chapter on post-traumatic stress disorder to determine whether your symptoms fit this category.

Co-Occurrence of Anxiety Disorders

In the five years that have passed since the first edition of *The Anxiety and Phobia Workbook* was published, it has become increasingly apparent that many people are dealing with more than one anxiety disorder. For example, one survey of people with panic disorder found that 15-30 percent of them also have social phobia, 10-20 percent have a specific phobia, 25 percent have generalized anxiety disorder, and 8-10 percent have obsessive-compulsive disorder. People with agoraphobia quite often have social phobias and/or obsessive-compulsive difficulties. If you find that your particular condition fits the description for more than one anxiety disorder, you are not alone.

Further Reading

American Psychiatric Association, *Diagnostic and Statistical Manual of Mental Disorders—Fourth Edition* (*DSM-IV*). Washington, D.C.: American Psychiatric Association, 1994.

Goodwin, Donald W., *Anxiety*. New York: Oxford University Press, 1986.

2

The Causes of Anxiety Disorders

If you are dealing with one of the anxiety disorders, you are likely to be concerned with the causes of your problem. You probably ask yourself "Why do I have panic attacks? Is it something hereditary or is it the way I was brought up? What causes phobias to develop? Why am I afraid of something I know isn't dangerous? What causes obsessions and compulsions?"

The symptoms of anxiety disorders often seem irrational and inexplicable: it is only natural to raise the question "Why?" But before considering in detail the various causes of anxiety disorders, there are two general points you should bear in mind. First, although learning about the causes of anxiety disorders can give you insight into how these problems develop, such knowledge is not necessary to overcome your particular difficulty. The various strategies for overcoming anxiety disorders presented in this workbook—such as relaxation, exercise, desensitization, changing self-talk and mistaken beliefs, dealing with feelings—do not depend on a knowledge of underlying causes to be effective. However interesting the information in this chapter may be, it is not necessarily what "cures." Second, be wary of the notion that there is one primary cause, or type of cause, for any of the anxiety disorders. Whether you are dealing with panic attacks, social phobia, generalized anxiety, or obsessive-compulsive disorder, recognize that there is no one cause which, if removed, would eliminate the problem. Anxiety problems are brought about by a variety of causes operating on numerous different levels. These levels include heredity, biology, family background and upbringing, conditioning, recent stressors, your self-talk and personal belief system, your ability to express feelings, and so on. The range of chapters in this book indicates the many different levels on which you can understand the causes of and the means of recovering from anxiety disorders.

Some experts in the field of anxiety disorders propose "single-cause" theories. Such theories tend to greatly over-simplify anxiety disorders and are susceptible to one of two mistaken lines of reasoning: the *biological fallacy* and the *psychological fallacy*. The biological fallacy assumes that a particular type of anxiety disorder is caused *solely* by some biological or physiological imbalance in the brain or body. For example, there has recently been a tendency to reduce the causation of panic disorder, as well as obsessive-compulsive disorder, to a strictly biological level. Panic disorder is viewed as arising from a dysfunction in a part of the brain called the *locus ceruleus*. Obsessive-compulsive disorder is thought to be caused by a deficiency in a particular neurotransmitter substance in the brain called *serotonin*. (A neurotransmitter is a chemical substance that allows nerve impulses to be transmitted from one nerve cell to another.)

It is helpful to know that there may be physiological dysfunctions involved in panic disorder and obsessive-compulsive disorder. This certainly has implications for treatment of these problems. But this does not mean that panic attacks and obsessive-compulsive disorder are physiological disturbances only. The question remains: *"What caused the physiological disturbance itself?"* Perhaps chronic stress due to psychological conflict causes the locus ceruleus to malfunction in panic disorder. Or perhaps chronically suppressed anger sets up a disturbance in brain serotonin levels that is a contributing cause of obsessive-compulsive disorder. Psychological conflicts and repressed anger, may, in turn, have been caused by a person's upbringing. Because any particular physiological disturbance may have originally been set up by stress or other psychological factors, it is a fallacy to assume that anxiety disorders are solely (or even primarily) caused by physiological imbalances.

The psychological fallacy makes the same kind of mistake in the opposite direction. It assumes that, say, social phobia or generalized anxiety disorder is caused by having grown up with parents who neglected, abandoned, or abused you, resulting in a deep-seated sense of insecurity or shame that causes your current phobic avoidance and anxiety as an adult. While it may be true that your family background *contributed* in an important way to your current problems, is it reasonable to assume that this is the *only* cause? Again, not really. To do so overlooks the possible contributions of hereditary and biological factors. After all, not all children who grow up in dysfunctional families develop anxiety disorders. It is more plausible to assume that your problem is a result of *both* 1) a hereditary predisposition toward anxiety (and possibly phobia) *and* 2) early childhood conditions that fostered a sense of shame and/or insecurity.

In sum, the idea that your particular difficulties are *just* a physiological disturbance or *just* a psychological disturbance neglects the fact that nature and nurture are interactive. Biological disturbances may be "set up" by stress or psychological factors; psychological problems, in turn, may be influenced by inborn biological disturbances. There is simply no way to say which came first or which is the so-called "ultimate" cause. By the same token, a comprehensive approach to recovery from panic, phobias, or anxiety cannot restrict itself to treating physiological or psychological causes in isolation. A variety of strategies dealing with several different levels, including biological, behavioral, emotional, mental, interpersonal, and even spiritual factors, are necessary for a full and lasting recovery. This "multidimensional" approach to recovery is discussed in the next chapter.

The causes of anxiety disorders vary not only according to the level at which they occur, but also according to the time period over which they operate. Some are *predisposing causes*, which set you up from birth or childhood to develop panic or anxiety later on. Some are *recent* or *short-term* causes—circumstances that *trigger* the onset of, say, panic attacks or agoraphobia. Others are *maintaining* causes—factors that serve to keep anxiety disorders going once they have developed.* The remainder of this chapter examines each of these types of causes in more detail. A section on biological causes is included to acquaint you with some of the better-known hypotheses about the role of the brain in causing panic attacks and anxiety.

An outline of the causes of anxiety disorders is presented below.

---

* A similar analysis of causes, applicable to agoraphobia, has been developed by Dr. Richard Raynard of The Fear Clinic, Crossroads Counseling Center, in Braintree, Massachusetts.

Causes of Anxiety Disorders

I. *Long-Term, Predisposing Causes*
  A. Heredity
  B. Childhood Circumstances
    1. Your Parents Communicate an Overly Cautious View of the World
    2. Your Parents Are Overly Critical and Set Excessively High Standards
    3. Emotional Insecurity and Dependence
    4. Your Parents Suppress Your Self-Assertiveness
  C. Cumulative Stress Over Time

II. *Biological Causes*
  A. Physiology of Panic
  B. Panic Attacks and the Noradrenergic Hypothesis
  C. Generalized Anxiety and the GABA/Benzodiazepine Hypothesis
  D. Obsessive-Compulsive Disorder and the Serotonin Hypothesis
  E. Medical Conditions That Can Cause Panic Attacks or Anxiety

III. *Short-Term, Triggering Causes*
  A. Stressors That Precipitate Panic Attacks
    1. Significant Personal Loss
    2. Significant Life Change
    3. Stimulants and Recreational Drugs
  B. Conditioning and the Origin of Phobias
  C. Trauma, Simple Phobias, and Post-Traumatic Stress Disorder

IV. *Maintaining Causes*
  A. Avoidance of Phobic Situations
  B. Anxious Self-Talk
  C. Mistaken Beliefs
  D. Withheld Feelings
  E. Lack of Assertiveness
  F. Lack of Self-Nurturing Skills
  G. Muscle Tension
  H. Stimulants and Other Dietary Factors
  I. High-Stress Lifestyle
  J. Lack of Meaning or Sense of Purpose

Long-Term, Predisposing Causes

Heredity

Are anxiety disorders inherited? The limited evidence that exists to date would argue that they are—at least in part. For example, it is estimated that 15-25 percent of children growing up with at least one agoraphobic parent become agoraphobic themselves, while the rate of agoraphobia in the general population is only 5 percent. This fact in itself doesn't prove that agoraphobia is inherited, however, because it could be argued that children *learn* from their parents to be agoraphobic.

More compelling evidence comes from studies of identical twins, who, of course, have exactly the same genetic makeup. If one identical twin has an anxiety disorder, the probability of the other identical twin having an anxiety disorder ranges from 31-88 percent, depending on the study you're looking at. By comparison, when fraternal twins (whose genes are no more similar than those of siblings born at different times) are studied, the probability is much lower. If one fraternal twin has an anxiety disorder, the odds of the other having an anxiety disorder range from about 0-38 percent—again, depending on the study. Having the same genetic makeup as someone else with phobias or anxiety makes it *more than twice as likely* that you will have a similar problem. Interestingly, the percentages for fraternal twins are generally higher than the incidence of anxiety disorders in the population (about 8-10 percent). This would argue that growing up in the same family—having the same parenting—contributes at least something to the development of anxiety disorders. Both nature and nurture seem to have an impact.

What is it that is inherited? Based on what is known at this time, it seems that you don't inherit agoraphobia, social phobia, or even panic attacks specifically from your parents. What is inherited seems to be a *general personality type* that predisposes you to be overly anxious. This is a volatile, excitable, reactive personality that is more easily set off by any slightly threatening stimulus than is the personality of individuals without anxiety disorders. Once you are born with this highly reactive personality, you might develop one or another anxiety disorder, depending on your particular environment and upbringing. For example, whether you develop agoraphobia or social phobia might depend on how much you learned to feel ashamed in situations where you were expected to perform. Whether you develop panic attacks or not might depend on the nature and degree of stress you're exposed to during adolescence and early adulthood. In short, while heredity might cause you to be born with a more reactive, excitable nervous system, childhood experiences, conditioning, and stress all serve to shape the particular type of anxiety disorder you subsequently develop.

Childhood Circumstances

What childhood experiences or family environments might predispose you to develop a particular anxiety disorder? Unfortunately, very little research on this topic has been done. Reserachers have found that panic attacks and agoraphobia in adulthood are often preceded by separation anxiety disorder in childhood. This is a condition where children experience anxiety, panic, or somatic symptoms when separated from their parents, as when going to school or even before going to sleep. Later on as adults, these same people experience anxiety when separated from a "safe" person or place. The conditions that might lead to separation anxiety disorder in the first place are matters for speculation.

What follows is a list of childhood circumstances that might predispose you to develop anxiety disorders. The list is based on my own experience with clients over several years. These factors are especially relevant if you are dealing with agoraphobia or social phobia, but may be applicable to other anxiety disorders as well.

- *Your Parents Communicate an Overly Cautious View of the World*
  Parents of people with phobias tend either to have phobias themselves or else are more fearful and anxious than average. Often they are overly concerned about potential dangers to their child. They are likely to say things like: "Don't go out

in the rain—you'll catch a cold," "Don't watch TV so much, you'll ruin your eyes," or "Be very careful" again and again. The more they communicate a fearful, overcautious attitude toward their child, the more that child comes to view the world as a "dangerous" place. When you learn that the outside world is threatening, you automatically restrict your exploration and risk-taking. You grow up with a tendency to worry excessively and be overly concerned with safety.

- *Your Parents Are Overly Critical and Set Excessively High Standards*
Children growing up with critical, perfectionist parents are never quite sure of their own acceptability. There is always some doubt about whether you are "good enough" or sufficiently worthy. As a result, you are constantly striving to please your parents and maintain their approval. As an adult, you may be overly eager to please, "look good," and "be nice" at the expense of your true feelings and capacity for assertiveness. Having grown up always feeling insecure, you may become very dependent on a safe person or safe place, and may restrict yourself from entering public or social situations where there is a risk of "losing face." You often come to internalize your parents' values, becoming exceptionally perfectionist and self-critical (as well as critical of others).

- *Emotional Insecurity and Dependency*
Up to the age of four or five, children are utterly dependent on their parents, especially their mother. Any conditions that create insecurity during this time can lead to excessive dependency and clinging later on. Excessive criticism and perfectionist standards on the part of parents seem to be a common source of insecurity for people who later develop anxiety disorders. *However, experiences of neglect, rejection, abandonment through divorce or death, and physical or sexual abuse can also produce the kind of basic insecurity (as well as emotional dependency) that form a background for anxiety disorders.*

Growing up in a family where one or both parents are alcoholic is also a common contributing factor in 20-25 percent of the clients I've seen. As described in a number of popular books over the past few years, adult children of alcoholics grow up with characteristics such as 1) obsesssion with control, 2) avoidance of feelings, 3) difficulty trusting others, 4) over-responsibility, 5) all-or-nothing thinking, and 6) excessive eagerness to please at the expense of their own needs. Although not all adult children of alcoholics develop anxiety disorders, the above characteristics are commonly seen in many people who have problems with panic and/or phobias.

A common denominator in the background of adult children of alcoholics, adult survivors of other forms of abuse, and most people who develop anxiety disorders is a deep-seated sense of insecurity. Perhaps the degree of insecurity, and the way children respond to it, will determine whether they later develop a specific type of anxiety disorder—as opposed to, say, an addictive personality or some other behavior disturbance. When children respond to insecurity with *excessive dependency*, the stage is set for over-reliance on a safe person or safe place later in life. This is a common background for agoraphobia.

- *Your Parents Suppress Your Expression of Feelings and Self-Assertiveness*
Parents may not only foster dependency but may suppress your innate capacity

to express your feelings and assert yourself. For example, as a child you may have been continually reprimanded or punished for speaking out, acting impulsively, or getting angry. Subsequently you grew up exerting a restrictive, even punitive, attitude toward your own expression of impulses and feelings. If these impulses and feelings are suppressed over a long period of time, their sudden recurrence under stress may produce anxiety or even panic. Frequently, people who learned to bottle up their feelings and self-expression as children are tenser, more prone to be anxious, and unable to express themselves as adults. Of course, this form of suppression in childhood can also lead to depression and passivity later on. In both cases, learning to express your feelings and becoming more assertive can have a very beneficial effect.

Reading about the four factors just discussed may have stimulated you to think about what happened in your own childhood. Use the *Family Background Questionnaire* on the next page to further explore what circumstances in your family may have contributed to your own problems with anxiety.

Cumulative Stress Over Time

A third contributing factor in the development of anxiety disorders is the influence of *cumulative* stress over time. When stress persists without letup over a period of time, such as several months or years, it tends to accumulate. This sort of stress is more enduring than normal, temporary stresses such as moving, the Christmas season, or a short-term financial setback. Cumulative stress can arise from unresolved psychological conflicts lasting over many years. Or it can be due to difficulties in one area of your life—such as problems with your marriage or physical health—that persist over a long period of time. Finally, it may be due to the accretion of a large number of *life events*. Life events include changes in the course of your life that require an adjustment and reordering of your priorities, such as going off to college, changing jobs, a marriage or leaving an intimate relationship, moving to a new location, having a baby, having your children leave home, and so on. While one or two life events every year is a common and manageable experience, a series of many of them stretching over one or two years' time can lead to a state of chronic stress and exhaustion.

The concept of life events arose from the work of Dr. Richard Holmes and Dr. Thomas Rahe, who developed an instrument called the *Life Events Survey* (also known as *The Social Readjustment Scale*) to assess the number and severity of life events that occur in a two-year period. They used the survey specifically to predict a person's risk of developing physical disease. However, the survey can also be used as a general measure of cumulative stress. You can get an estimate of your own level of cumulative stress by completing the *Life Events Survey* in this chapter.

For many years it has been known that stress can increase your risk of developing psychosomatic disorders such as high blood pressure, headaches, or ulcers. Only recently has it been recognized that *psychological disorders* may also be an outcome of cumulative stress. Over time, stress can affect the neuroendocrine regulatory systems of the brain, which play an important role both in mood disorders, such as depression, *and anxiety disorders*. Stress is nonspecific in its action; it simply has the greatest impact on the weak-

Family Background Questionnaire

Use the following questionnaire to reflect on your childhood. Can you identify what conditions might have contributed to your current problem with anxiety?

1. Did either of your parents suffer from panic attacks or phobias?

2. Did you have a brother, sister, grandparent, or other relative who had panic attacks or phobias?

3. Did either of your parents seem excessively prone to worry?

4. Did either of your parents seem overly concerned about potential dangers that could befall you or other family members?

5. Did your parents encourage exploration of the outside world or did they cultivate an attitude of caution, suspicion, or distrust?

6. Do you feel that your parents were overly critical or demanding of you? If so, how did you feel in response to this criticism?
   - ☐ put down or diminished
   - ☐ ashamed or guilty
   - ☐ hurt or rejected
   - ☐ angry or rebellious

7. As a child, did you feel free to express your feelings and impulses? How were feelings dealt with in your family?
   - ☐ openly expressed
   - ☐ punished
   - ☐ denied

8. Was it O.K. for you to cry? How did your parents respond when you cried?

9. Was it O.K. to express anger? How did your parents respond when you got angry?

10. What was your role in the family? How were you perceived relative to other children in the family?

11. Do you feel that you grew up feeling insecure? Which of the following might have contributed to your insecurity:
    - ☐ Excessive criticism by your parents
    - ☐ Excessive punishment
    - ☐ Your parents made you feel ashamed
    - ☐ Your parents made you feel guilty
    - ☐ Your parents neglected you
    - ☐ One or both parents abandoned you through death or divorce
    - ☐ Physical abuse
    - ☐ Sexual abuse
    - ☐ Parental alcoholism

12. If you grew up insecure, how did you respond to your feelings of insecurity?
    - ☐ By becoming very dependent on your family (Did you have difficulty leaving home?)
    - ☐ By becoming very independent of your family (Did you leave home early?)
    - ☐ By becoming angry or rebellious

est point in your system. If this happens to be your cardiovascular system, you may develop high blood pressure or migraine headaches. If it is the neuroendocrine and neurotransmitter systems of your brain, you will be more subject to developing a behavior disorder such as mood swings, generalized anxiety, or panic disorder. In short, cumulative stress might produce either headaches, fatigue, or panic attacks, depending on your particular point of greatest vulnerability. That point of vulnerability, may, in turn, be influenced by heredity. It is likely then that genes, cumulative stress, and childhood circumstances all contribute to the genesis of a particular anxiety disorder, as suggested in this diagram:

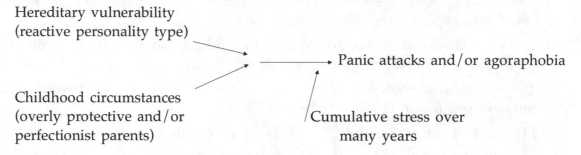

Hereditary vulnerability
(reactive personality type)

Panic attacks and/or agoraphobia

Childhood circumstances
(overly protective and/or
perfectionist parents)

Cumulative stress over
many years

When you examine long-term causes, it turns out that no *one* of them may be sufficient, by itself, to produce a particular anxiety disorder. You may live twenty years with a hereditary vulnerability to panic attacks and yet never have one. Then life events in your twenties might produce enough cumulative stress to activate what had been only a potential—and you have your first panic attack. If you grew up feeling insecure and were taught that the outside world is dangerous, you may go on to develop agoraphobia. If you grew up feeling ashamed when you performed, perhaps your particular type of phobic avoidance will be less territorial and more social (in other words, a social phobia).

Biological Causes

Biological causes refer to physiological imbalances in the body or brain that are associated with anxiety disorders. It is important to recognize that such imbalances are not necessarily the *ultimate causes* of anxiety disorders and may *themselves* be caused by

- A specific hereditary vulnerability

- Cumulative stress over time

- A hereditary vulnerability that is *brought out* by cumulative stress

Once again, it is likely that genes, life history, and stress all work together to bring about the disturbances underlying anxiety disorders.

Recent research has pointed to different types of biological explanations for different types of anxiety disorders. The type of malfunction associated with spontaneous panic attacks is probably different from the type associated with generalized anxiety disorder. And both of these, in turn, are different from physiological imbalances associated with obsessive-compulsive disorder. Each of these is discussed separately below.

Life Events Survey

Life Event	Average Stress Score
Death of spouse	100
Divorce	73
Marital separation	65
Jail term	63
Death of close family member	63
Personal injury or illness	53
Marriage	50
Being fired from work	47
Marital problems	45
Retirement	45
Change in health of family member	44
Pregnancy	40
Sexual difficulties	39
Gain of new family member	39
Business readjustment	39
Change in finances	38
Death of close friend	37
Change to different line of work	36
Change in number of arguments with spouse	35
Mortgage or loan for major purchase (such as a home)	31
Foreclosure of mortgage or loan	30
Change in responsibilities at work	29
Son or daughter leaving home	29
Trouble with in-laws	29
Outstanding personal achievement	28
Spouse begins or stops work	26
Beginning or finishing school	26
Change in living conditions	25
Revision of personal habits	24
Trouble with boss	23
Change in work hours or conditions	20
Change in residence	20
Change in school	20
Change in recreation	19
Change in church activities	19
Change in social activities	18
Mortgage or loan for lesser purchase (such as a car or TV)	17
Change in sleeping habits	16
Change in number of family get-togethers	15
Change in eating habits	15
Vacation	13
Christmas	12
Minor violations of the law	11

Determine which life events have occurred in your life over the past two years and add up your total stress score. For example, if you got married, changed to a different line of work, changed residence, and took two vacations, your total stress score would be 50+36+20+13+13= 132. If your total stress score is under 150, you are less likely to be suffering the effects of cumulative stress. If it is between 150 and 300, you *may* be suffering from chronic stress, depending on how you perceived and coped with the particular life events that occurred. If your score is over 300, it is likely you are experiencing some detrimental effects of cumulative stress. Please note that the stress scores on the above survey are averaged over many people. The degree to which any particular event is stressful to you will depend on how you perceive it.

I can't overemphasize that our state of knowledge about biological causes underlying anxiety disorders is still very tentative and incomplete. The brain mechanisms considered below, which are discussed after an initial section on the physiology of panic, should be viewed as hypothetical—not proven facts.

Finally, it is important to realize that even though there may be a physiological imbalance in the brain underlying your particular anxiety disorder, there is no reason to assume you can't correct it. *If you are willing to make lifestyle changes that reduce stress and upgrade your level of physical wellness, any physiological imbalances associated with panic, phobias, anxiety, or obsessions will tend to diminish and perhaps disappear altogether.* These lifestyle changes include making time for daily relaxation, an exercise program, good nutrition, social support, and self-nurturing activities (see the relevant chapters in this workbook). An alternative way to correct a biological imbalance is to rely on prescription medications that specifically alter the functioning of your brain. Medications work well in overcoming the physiological causes of anxiety disorders—though, in my opinion, they should be viewed as a last line of defense. It is often possible to correct physical imbalances *simply* by upgrading your level of health and wellness.

Later in this section you will read about mechanisms in the brain that are thought, based on recent research, to underlie panic attacks, generalized anxiety, and obsessive-compulsive disorder. First, however, is a description of the basic physiology of a panic attack—something which is much better understood.

Physiology of Panic

What happens to your body during a panic attack? Panic is an extreme version of an alarm reaction your body *naturally* goes through in response to any type of threat. Years ago, Walter Cannon described this as the *fight or flight response*. It is a built-in mechanism that enables all higher animals to mobilize a great deal of energy quickly in order to cope with predators or other immediate threats to their survival. This alarm reaction serves us well in situations that are realistically dangerous. Unfortunately, most of us also experience the fight or flight reaction in reponse to any situation that is viewed as *psychologically* dangerous, threatening, or overwhelming. An argument with your spouse or having to get up and go to work after a bad night's sleep can cause a pronounced stress response because *you perceive* it as threatening or overwhelming, even though it poses no direct risk to your survival.

In the case of a panic attack, there may be no perceived threat at all—the reaction may come on "out of the blue," without any noticeable provocation. Somehow, the natural flight or fight response has gotten out of control. That it occurs out of context and without apparent reason suggests that the brain mechanisms which control the response aren't functioning properly. The current hypothesis about the nature of this dysfunction is described in the next subsection. The physiology of panic itself, however, is better known.

Your nervous system has two separate actions: *voluntary* and *involuntary*. There is a voluntary nervous system that moves your muscles and obeys your direct command. Your involuntary nervous system, on the other hand, regulates automatic functions ordinarily outside voluntary control, such as your heartbeat, respiration, and digestion. This involuntary system is itself divided into two branches: the *sympathetic* and *parasym-*

pathetic nervous systems. The sympathetic nervous system is responsible for mobilizing a number of reactions throughout your body whenever you're emotional or excited. The parasympathetic nervous system has an opposite function. It *maintains* normal, smooth functioning of your various internal organs during times when you are calm and at rest.

In a panic attack, your sympathetic nervous system sets off several different bodily reactions rapidly and intensely. First, it causes your adrenal glands to release large amounts of adrenalin. What you feel is a sudden "jolt," often accompanied by a feeling of dread or terror. Within seconds, the excess adrenalin can cause 1) your heart to race, 2) your respiration to become rapid and shallow, 3) profuse sweating, 4) trembling and shaking, and 5) cold hands and feet. Your sympathetic nervous system also produces muscle contractions (the most extreme case of this is when animals "freeze" in fear), leading you to possibly experience strong contractions in your chest or throat along with a fear of not being able to breathe. Other reactions caused by the sympathetic nervous system include excess release of stomach acid, inhibition of digestion, release of red blood cells by the spleen, release of stored up sugar by the liver, an increase in metabolic rate, and dilation of the pupils.

All of these reactions occur to a lesser degree when you are emotional or excited. The problem in panic is that they peak to such an extreme level that you feel overwhelmed, terrified, and have a strong urge to run. It is important to realize that the adrenalin released during panic tends to be reabsorbed by the liver and kidneys within a few minutes. If you can "ride out" the bodily symptoms of panic without fighting them or telling yourself how horrible they are, they will tend to subside within a short time. Chapter 6 will describe strategies for learning to observe rather than react to the bodily symptoms of panic. By breathing properly and making supportive, calming statements to yourself, you can learn to manage panic instead of scaring yourself into a much more intense reaction.

While the physiology of panic is well understood, the mechanisms in the brain which initiate these physiological reactions are less well understood. The following section presents a recent hypothesis about a particular imbalance in the brain thought to be responsible for panic attacks.

Panic Attacks and the Noradrenergic Hypothesis

Your brain is by far the most complex system in your body, consisting of over 100 billion brain cells or neurons. At any given moment in time, millions of nerve impulses are being transmitted along multiple pathways which interconnect various regions of your brain. Every time a single nerve impulse moves from one nerve cell to the next, it must cross a space. Individual nerve cells are not connected but are separated by tiny spaces called *synapses*. It has been known for some time that the process by which a nerve impulse moves across a synapse is *chemical* in nature. Microscopic amounts of chemicals secreted into the synapse allow transmission of a nerve impulse from one neuron to the next. These chemicals are called *neurotransmitters;* there are over 20 different types of them in the brain.

It appears that there are different systems in the brain which are especially sensitive to particular neurotransmitters. One system, called the *noradrenergic system*, seems to be especially sensitive to a neurotransmitter substance called *norepinephrine*. Recent research implies that this system plays a significant role in the origin of panic attacks. Specifically, an important part of the noradrenergic system, the *locus ceruleus*, appears to be involved in triggering panic attacks. The locus ceruleus is at the beginning of a "chain" of neuroendocrine systems in the body which all contribute to setting off a panic attack: the locus ceruleus affects the limbic system (the brain's center for emotions), which affects the hypothalamus, which in turn affects the pituitary gland and, finally, the adrenal glands. When the locus ceruleus is stimulated in experimental animals, these animals have panic attacks which look identical to those in humans. In human trials, drugs that increase the activity of the locus ceruleus have been found to cause panic attacks, while drugs that inhibit its activity block panic attacks. It's believed that panic attacks are aggravated either by: 1) hypersensitivity of neurons in the locus ceruleus and/or 2) a defect in the inhibitory receptors of those same neurons, which causes the locus ceruleus's built-in braking mechanism not to work properly. That is, the locus ceruleus can become hyperactivated and yet be without an ability to naturally "brake" itself. When this happens, a cascade of reactions occurs down the chain of systems previously mentioned, resulting in a spontaneous, excessive adrenal gland response. Researchers believe that deficiencies or imbalances in the neurotransmitters norepinephrine and serotonin may contribute to the insufficient inhibition of the locus ceruleus. This is why antidepressant medications that increase the amounts of these neurotransmitters (by blocking their reuptake at the synapse) actually can diminish panic attacks. These medications seem to be able to *stabilize* the locus ceruleus and the noradrenergic system.

What *causes* the original dysfunction of the locus ceruleus remains unknown at this time. One hypothesis is that changes in the locus ceruleus, as well as the noradrenergic system, can take place as a result of acute stress, or as the long-term result of multiple stresses over time. Although this hypothesis remains unproven, it seems sure that cumulative stress contributes in an important way to the onset of panic attacks (as discussed in the preceding section). If the hypothesis about stress altering the locus ceruleus turns out to be true, an important implication follows: *the most effective long-term treatment for brain dysfunctions associated with panic disorder is a consistent and comprehensive program for reducing stress in your life.* Medications can certainly help restabilize the locus ceruleus and noradrenergic systems in the short run. Yet without changes in your lifestyle (such as regular relaxation and exercise, good time management, proper nutrition, personal support, and constructive attitudes)—changes that allow you to live more simply and peacefully—panic and anxiety will return soon after the medications are withdrawn.

Generalized Anxiety Disorder and the GABA/Benzodiazepine Hypothesis

Benzodiazepine tranquilizers such as Valium, Librium, Ativan, and Xanax can very effectively reduce generalized anxiety (as well as anticipatory anxiety in phobic disorders). Recently, though, it has been discovered that there is a specific system in the brain, the *benzodiazepine receptor system*, that is uniquely sensitive to benzodiazepine drugs. The implication is that the brain makes *its own* substances which are like tranquilizers. Perhaps it is a deficiency of these benzodiazepine-like substances that is responsible, at a biological level, for generalized anxiety.

To date, these substances have yet to be isolated by brain researchers (although some believe that adenosine may be one of them). What *is* known is that benzodiazepine tranquilizers increase the activity of one particular neurotransmitter substance in the brain, gamma aminobutyric acid, or GABA for short. GABA functions naturally in the brain as an inhibitory neurotransmitter—it tends to inhibit or "tone down" brain activity, particularly in the limbic system, which is the brain's center for emotions. Thus GABA is associated with the brain's own natural calming response. When you give people GABA directly, or give them drugs that increase the activity of GABA, their anxiety is reduced. Deficiencies in GABA, or having too many GABA receptors relative to the amount of GABA available, may contribute to the cause of generalized anxiety. Or a deficiency in naturally occurring benzodiazepine-like substances, which enhance the activity of GABA, may be the problem. As you can see, the situation is complicated. Any of the following mechanisms might explain the physiological basis of generalized anxiety:

- Insufficient amounts of GABA

- Insufficient amounts of natural, benzodiazepine-like substances in the brain

- Excessive sensitivity of the GABA/benzodiazepine system relative to the amounts of GABA and/or benzodiazepine-like substances available

It is not known, at present, which of the above hypotheses is correct. Nor is it known how any of the above disturbances in the benzodiazepine system might develop—in other words, whether they are inborn, develop as a result of cumulative stress, or are produced by a combination of heredity and stress. What can safely be said is that *some kind of disturbance* in the functioning of the benzodiazepine/GABA system of the brain is likely to be involved in the origin of generalized anxiety.

Obsessive-Compulsive Disorder and the Serotonin Hypothesis

The same reasoning that applied to generalized anxiety disorder also applies to obsessive-compulsive disorder (OCD). The effectiveness of specific drugs, such as clomipramine (Anafranil) and SSRI antidepressants (selective serotonin reuptake inhibitors—see Chapter 17)—fluoxetine (Prozac), sertraline (Zoloft), and fluvoxamine (Luvox)—in reducing obsessive-compulsive symptoms tells us something about the possible biological mechanisms for obsessive-compulsive disorder. These drugs are known to increase the amount of a specific neurotransmitter substance, serotonin, in the brain. They do so more effectively than most other antidepressant medications. Researchers have identified a serotonin receptor system in the brain—an elaborate network of brain cells that are specifically receptive to serotonin. Does the biological component of obsessive-compulsive disorder lie in some disturbance of this system? In many individuals with OCD involved with experimental research, a significant increase in metabolic activity has been seen in two portions of the brain, the *orbitofrontal cortex* and the *caudate nuclei*. This activity appears to be normalized when the subjects are treated with antidepressant medications that raise serotonin levels. In sum, obsessive-compulsive disorder may be associated with excessive levels of activity in certain parts of the brain. In many cases, these activity levels can be diminished by serotonin-enhancing medications.

Medical Conditions That Can Cause Panic Attacks or Anxiety

The physiology of panic described at the beginning of this section is well established. But the various proposed explanations of the biological mechanisms involving different neurotransmitter systems of the brain are, at present, still hypothetical. It is important to keep in mind that these biological hypotheses apply to a majority *but not all cases* of panic attacks and generalized anxiety. Sometimes panic reactions or anxiety can arise from medical conditions that are quite separate from recognized anxiety disorders. Hyperthyroidism and hypoglycemia, for example, can cause panic attacks that are by all appearances identical to those seen in panic disorder. A deficiency of calcium, magnesium, or an allergy to certain food additives can also produce panic or anxiety. When these conditions are corrected, the anxiety disappears.

Any of the following conditions might be a cause of panic attacks or generalized anxiety. The first six are the ones most frequently seen.

- *Hyperventilation Syndrome*
  Rapid, shallow breathing at the level of your chest can sometimes lead to excessive lowering of carbon dioxide in your bloodstream. This results in symptoms very similar to those of a panic attack, including light-headedness, dizziness, feelings of unreality, shortness of breath, trembling, and/or tingling in your hands, feet, or lips. These symptoms, in turn, may be perceived as dangerous and may stimulate a bona fide panic attack. (See the section on abdominal breathing in Chapter 4 for further discussion of hyperventilation.)

- *Hypoglycemia*
  For a large number of people, blood sugar levels can fall too low as a result of improper diet or simply stress. When this happens, such people experience a variety of symptoms similar to a panic reaction, including anxiety, shakiness, dizziness, weakness, and disorientation. Hypoglycemia can cause panic attacks, or, more often, can aggravate panic reactions which are caused by other factors. (See Chapter 16 for a detailed discusssion.)

- *Hyperthyroidism*
  Excessive secretion of thyroid hormone can lead to heart palpitations (rapid heartbeat), sweating, and generalized anxiety. Other symptoms of hyperthyroidism include weight loss, elevated body temperature, insomnia, and bulging eyes. If you have several of the above symptoms, you might want to have your doctor do a thyroid panel to see if this condition is contributing to your anxiety or panic symptoms.

- *Mitral Valve Prolapse*
  Mitral valve prolapse is a harmless condition which causes heart palpitations. It is caused by a slight defect in the valve separating the upper and lower chambers on the left side of your heart. Blood moves through the mitral valve as it passes from the upper to the lower chamber. With mitral valve prolapse, the valve doesn't close completely and some of the blood can flow back from the lower to upper chamber, causing the heart to beat out of rhythm. The resulting rhythm disturbance can be disconcerting enough to cause some people to panic—but it is *not* danger-

ous. Mitral valve prolapse is *not* a cause of heart attacks.

For reasons that are unclear, mitral valve prolapse occurs more frequently in people with panic disorder than in the population at large. In severe cases, it can be treated through the use of beta-blocking drugs such as Inderal.

- *Premenstrual Syndrone (PMS)*
  If you are a woman, it is important to observe whether your panic reactions (or generalized anxiety) worsen around the time just before your period. If so, treating your PMS may be enough to alleviate your problem with panic or anxiety. Treatment usually involves improvements in diet and exercise, taking supplements such as vitamin B_6, and in some cases taking oral progesterone. (See Chapter 16 for a more detailed discussion.)

- *Inner Ear Disturbances*
  For a small proportion of the population, panic attacks seem to be associated with a disturbance in balance caused by swelling of the inner ear (due to infection, allergy, Ménière's syndrome, or other problems). If dizziness, light-headedness, and/or unsteadiness are a *prominent* part of your problem with anxiety or panic, you may want to consult an otolaryngologist to check the labyrinth system of your inner ear.

Other medical conditions which can cause panic or anxiety include:

- Acute reaction to cocaine, amphetamines, caffeine, aspartame, or other stimulants
- Withdrawal from alcohol, sedatives, or tranquilizers
- Thyrotoxicosis
- Cushing's syndrome
- Parathyroid disease
- Complex partial seizures (temporal lobe epilepsy)
- Post-concussion syndrome
- Deficiencies of calcium, magnesium, potassium, niacin, vitamin B_{12}
- Emphysema
- Pulmonary embolism
- Cardiac arrhythmias
- Congestive heart failure
- Essential hypertension
- Environmental toxins such as mercury, carbon dioxide, hydrocarbons, food additives, pesticides

To adequately rule out any medical conditions that could be causing or aggravating your particular problem, have your doctor give you a thorough physical examination, including a blood panel, before adopting behavioral and psychological strategies for recovery. Keep in mind, though, that the above medical conditions (with the exception of hyperventilation and hypoglycemia) contribute to panic or anxiety in only a minority of cases.

For a more detailed discussion of medical conditions associated with anxiety disorders, you can refer to Chapter 6 of *The Good News About Panic, Anxiety and Phobias*, by Mark S. Gold. (See the reading list at the end of this chapter.)

Short-Term, Triggering Causes

Long-term causes such as heredity, childhood environment, and cumulative stress create a *predisposition* to anxiety disorders. Yet it takes more specific conditions, operating over a short period of time, to actually trigger panic attacks or cause a phobia to develop. In this section we will briefly consider

- Specific stressors that often precede a first panic attack

- Conditioning processes that produce phobias

- The role of trauma in certain simple phobias and post-traumatic stress disorder

Stressors That Precipitate Panic Attacks

A first panic attack is often preceded by a stressful event or situation. In my experience with people already vulnerable to panic disorder as a result of the predisposing factors previously described, I have found that the following three types of stressors often preceded their first panic attack:

- *Significant Personal Loss.* Loss of a significant person through death, divorce, or separation seems very frequently to be a trigger of a first panic attack. Other major losses, such as loss of employment, loss of health through illness, or a major financial reversal, can also precipitate a first panic attack.

- *Significant Life Change.* A major life event causing a period of adjustment lasting several months can sometimes precipitate a first panic attack. Examples of such an event might include getting married, having a baby, going off to college, changing jobs, going into the military, making a geographical move, or developing a protracted physical illness.

  It may be that *any major stressor*, whether it is a significant loss or a major life change, can trigger a first panic attack in an individual who is already vulnerable for other reasons.

- *Stimulants and Recreational Drugs.* It is not uncommon for a first panic attack to occur after excessive intake of caffeine. Often people are unaware that their use of caffeine is excessive until a full-blown panic attack brings it to their attention.

  Even more common is the incidence of panic attacks in people using cocaine. Cocaine is such a strong stimulant that it may cause panic attacks even in people who are *not* predisposed to panic disorder by the long-term factors previously described. Amphetamines ("speed"), PCP, LSD, high doses of marijuana, and withdrawal from narcotics, barbiturates, or tranquilizers can also jolt a person into a first panic attack.

Conditioning and the Origin of Phobias

A phobia is a persistent and unreasonable fear of a specific object, activity, or situation that results in a compelling desire to avoid that dreaded object, activity, or situation. There are three characteristics which distinguish a phobia from ordinary, everyday fears. First, you are *persistently* afraid of the object or situation over a long period of time. Second, you know that your fear is *unreasonable*, even though this recognition does not help to dispel it. Finally, what is most characteristic of a phobia is your avoidance of the feared situation. Being unreasonably afraid of something is not yet a phobia; the phobia begins when you actually start avoiding what you fear.

What is avoided tends to vary among the different types of phobias. If you are agoraphobic you tend to avoid situations where you're afraid you can't easily escape if you have a panic attack—examples include check-out lines in grocery stores, freeways, elevators, and bridges. If you have a social phobia you tend to avoid situations where you fear you might humiliate or embarrass yourself in front of others—examples include public speaking, parties, public bathrooms, and job interviews. Simple phobias cause you to fear potential death or injury from causes such as natural disasters or certain animals. Or you may have an enormous fear of being trapped.

How do these phobias develop? There are two types of processes which are most commonly responsible: *conditioning* and *trauma*. Trauma isn't always involved in the creation of a phobia, but conditioning processes are always present. There are two types of conditioning that contribute to the formation of a phobia: 1) *conditioning by association* and 2) *conditioning by avoidance*.

In conditioning by association, a situation that was originally neutral begins to elicit strong anxiety because on one particular day you panicked or had a strong anxiety reaction in that same situation. For example, you're driving on the freeway and spontaneously have a panic attack. The panic is made worse by fearful thoughts such as "How do I get out of here?" or "What if I get into an accident?" Your mind forms a strong association between being on the freeway and experiencing anxiety, so that later, being on, near, or even thinking about freeways elicits anxiety. In short, you have *learned* an association between freeways and anxiety. By the same token, experiencing strong anxiety the first time you try public speaking may lead to an association between the two. Subsequently, every time you attempt to speak before others, or even think about doing so, the strong anxiety is automatically triggered.

Conditioning by association may cause you to develop a fear toward a particular situation or object, but it does not by itself create a phobia. Only when you start to *avoid* that situation or object do you "learn" to be phobic. A time-honored principle in behavioral psychology is that any behavior that is rewarded tends to be repeated. Avoiding a situation you're anxious about is obviously rewarded—the reward being the reduction of anxiety. Each time you avoid the situation, the reward of being relieved of anxiety follows, and so your avoidance behavior gets strengthened and tends to be repeated. Your avoidance works very well in saving you from anxiety.

Learning to stay away from a fearful situation because it is rewarding to do so is what constitutes *conditioning by avoidance*. Avoidance conditioning is the most critical process in the formation of any phobia. It is directly reversed and overcome by the processes of imagery and real-life exposure described in Chapters 7 and 8.

Trauma, Simple Phobias, and Post-Traumatic Stress Disorder

Agoraphobia and social phobia tend to develop primarily as a result of the conditioning processes just described. Certain simple phobias, on the other hand, can develop in the wake of specific traumatic experiences. As a child, I had a phobia about bees as a result of having picked up a bee and getting stung when I was two years old. This is really an example of conditioning by association. The fear I felt at the time I got stung caused me to develop an association between bees and fear. Avoidance conditioning came into play when I later started running away from bees whenever I saw them near me. By the same token, being in an auto accident can cause a person to subsequently fear driving or even being in a car. Or nearly drowning may lead to a subsequent phobia about water. Many simple phobias can be traced back to some kind of traumatic incident in childhood. Others—especially those we have from a very early age, like the fear of darkness or fears of insects—may be part of our evolutionary heritage. Such fears may have been biologically programmed into the nervous systems of all mammals to promote survival of the species. These inborn fears people often grow up with cannot be considered phobias unless 1) they lead to persistent avoidance and 2) they persist into adulthood.

A different outcome of trauma is the occurrence of post-traumatic stress disorder, which was described in Chapter 1. No specific phobias develop; instead you tend to develop an array of symptoms that "re-create" the original trauma. Distressing recollections and dreams about what happened are the mind's attempt to gain control of the original event and to neutralize the emotional charge it carries.

Maintaining Causes

The maintaining causes of anxiety disorders are what tend to keep them going. They involve ways of thinking, feeling, and coping that serve to perpetuate anxiety, panic, or phobias. Much of this workbook is devoted to helping you deal with these maintaining causes. Of the four types of causes we are considering, only the maintaining ones operate in the here-and-now and are thus the easiest to deal with. The following list of maintaining causes isn't exhaustive and includes only those which are most obvious. Maintaining causes will be considered in greater detail throughout the rest of this workbook.

Avoidance of Phobic Situations

Phobias develop because it is very rewarding to avoid facing situations that cause you anxiety. As long as you continue to avoid dealing with a phobic situation, activity, or object, the phobia will remain securely in place. Trying to think or reason your way out of a phobia simply won't work if you continue to avoid confronting it directly. As long as you avoid a situation, you will be prone to worry about whether you can ever handle it.

Overcoming a phobia means that you unlearn certain responses while relearning others. When you finally begin to face the situation, you *unlearn* both 1) the "fear-in-advance"—the anticipatory anxiety about possibly panicking in the situation and 2) the avoidance of the situation itself. At the same time, you give yourself the opportunity to *learn* that you can enter—and remain in—a phobic situation without undue anxiety. You can learn to tolerate and eventually be comfortable in any phobic situation if you approach it in sufficiently small steps. The imagery and real-life desensitization processes discussed in later chapters are intended to foster this type of learning.

Anxious Self-Talk

Self-talk is what you say to yourself in your own mind. It is the internal monologue that you engage in much of the time, although it may be so automatic and subtle that you don't notice it unless you step back and pay attention. Much of your anxiety is created by statements you make to yourself beginning with the words "What if," for example, "What if I have another panic attack?" "What if I lose control of myself while driving?" "What will people think if I get anxious while standing in line?" This type of self-talk *anticipates* the worst before it even happens. The more common term for it is simply "worry."

Self-talk can also contribute to creating a full-blown panic attack. Such an attack may start off with bodily symptoms such as tightness in the chest and heart palpitations. If you can accept and "flow with" these symptoms without letting them scare you, they will soon peak and then subside. However, all too often you tell yourself such things as: "Oh no—I'm going to panic!" "What if I have a heart attack!" "I've got to get out of here but I can't!" "People will think I'm weird if I have to rest or lean on something for a minute because my legs feel weak." This scare-talk only aggravates the physical symptoms, which in turn produce even more extreme scare-talk, leading to a vicious cycle that produces a full-blown panic attack.

The good news is that you can learn to recognize anxiety-provoking self-talk, stop it, and replace it with more supportive and calming statements to yourself. The subject of self-talk is dealt with in detail in a later chapter.

Mistaken Beliefs

Your negative self-talk comes from underlying mistaken beliefs about yourself, others, and "the way the world is." For example, if you believe that you can't be safely alone, you will talk yourself and everyone else into assuming that there must always be someone with you. If you truly believe that life is always a struggle, then you will tell yourself that something is wrong when you start to feel better or when others offer you help. A belief that the outside world is dangerous does not promote an attitude of trust or a willingness to take risks necessary to overcome a condition like agoraphobia.

Revamping your basic beliefs about yourself and your life takes more time and work than simply reversing anxious self-talk. Yet to do so will have far-reaching effects on your self-esteem, your willingness to accept imperfections in yourself and others, and on your long-term peace of mind. The subject of mistaken beliefs is considered in detail in a later chapter.

Withheld Feelings

Denying feelings of anger, frustration, sadness, or even excitement can contribute to a state of *free-floating anxiety*. Free-floating anxiety is when you feel vaguely anxious without knowing why. You may have noticed that after you let out your angry feelings or have a good cry you feel calmer and more at ease. Expressing feelings can have a distinct physiological effect that results in a reduced level of anxiety.

As mentioned earlier, anxiety-prone people are often born with a predisposition to be more emotionally reactive or volatile. Yet they often grow up in families where obtaining parental approval takes precedence over expressing their needs and feelings. As adults they still feel it is more important to attain perfection or always be pleasing than to express strong feelings. This tendency to deny deep emotions can lead to a chronic state of tension and anxiety. It is believed by some that the external danger avoided by the phobic is actually a stand-in for a deeper-lying *internal* danger: the fear of long-repressed feelings resurfacing. Panic may occur when such feelings "threaten" to break through. For example, if you have a phobia about water, this might be viewed as a stand-in for a deeper-lying fear of denied feelings. Or a fear of ferocious animals might symbolize a deeper-lying fear of experiencing your own anger and the unmet needs from which it flows. In my view, this emotion-based theory of phobias may be at least partially right.

Fortunately, it is possible to *learn* to recognize and express your feelings more easily and frequently. Excessive ventilation of feelings, especially anger, may not always be productive, yet it is important to at least know *what* you are feeling and then allow your feelings some form of expression. Doing so will substantially lower your level of anxiety and reduce your tendency to panic. This topic is dealt with in Chapter 13.

Lack of Assertiveness

In order to express feelings to other people, it is important that you develop an assertive style of communicating that allows you to express yourself in a direct, forthright manner. Assertive communication strikes the right balance between submissiveness, where you are afraid to ask for what you want at all, and aggressiveness, where you demand what you want through coercion or threat. If you are prone to anxiety and phobias, you will tend to act submissively. You avoid asking directly for what you want and are afraid to express strong feelings, especially anger. Often you are afraid of imposing on others; you don't want to compromise your self-image as someone who is pleasing and nice. Or you are afraid that assertive communication will alienate your *safe person*—the one person you feel dependent on for your basic sense of security. The problem with a lack of assertiveness is that it breeds feelings within yourself of resentment and confinement. And resentment and a sense of confinement are notorious for aggravating anxiety and phobias.

It's possible to *learn* to be assertive and directly express your wants and feelings. An introduction to this type of communication is presented in the chapter on assertiveness.

Lack of Self-Nurturing Skills

Common to the background of many people with anxiety disorders is a pervasive sense of insecurity. This is especially apparent in agoraphobia, where the need to stay close to a safe place or safe person can be so strong. Such insecurity arises from a variety of conditions in childhood, including parental neglect, abandonment, abuse, overprotection, overcriticism, as well as alcoholism or chemical dependency in the family. Since they never received consistent or reliable nurturing as children, adult "survivors" of these various forms of deprivation often lack the capacity to properly take care of their own needs. Unaware of how to love and nurture themselves, they suffer low self-esteem and may feel anxious or overwhelmed in the face of adult demands and responsibilities. This lack of self-nurturing skills only serves to perpetuate anxiety.

The most lasting solution to parental abuse and deprivation is to become a good parent to yourself. Methods for gaining awareness of your needs, healing the "child within," and becoming more nurturing toward yourself are presented in Chapter 15.

Muscle Tension

When your muscles are tense, you feel "uptight." Muscle tension tends to restrict your breathing. And when your breathing is shallow and restricted you are more likely to experience anxiety. Tense muscles also help to keep your feelings suppressed, which, as discussed above, can increase anxiety. You may have noticed that when your body is tense, your mind has a greater tendency to race. As you relax the muscles throughout your body, your mind will begin to slow down and become calmer. The founder of systematic methods of relaxation, Edmund Jacobson, once said, "An anxious mind cannot exist in a relaxed body." Body and mind are inextricably related in anxiety.

You can reduce your level of muscle tension on a consistent basis by maintaining daily programs of deep relaxation as well as vigorous exercise. Either one of these alone can reduce muscle tension, but the combination has an even more profound effect. Detailed guidelines for incorporating relaxation and exercise into your lifestyle are presented in later chapters.

Stimulants and Other Dietary Factors

Stimulants such as caffeine and nicotine can aggravate anxiety and leave you more vulnerable to panic attacks. You may not even be aware of their impact until you reduce or eliminate them from your life. In two cases, I have seen panic attacks go away completely when clients eliminated caffeine from their diet (this was caffeine not only from coffee, but tea, cola beverages, and over-the-counter medications). For some people, other dietary factors such as sugar and food additives can aggravate or occasionally even cause panic reactions.

The nutrition-anxiety connection has hardly been explored in either popular or technical books on anxiety disorders. Chapter 16 of this book takes a detailed look at this connection.

High-Stress Lifestyle

The role of stress both as a predisposing agent and short-term cause of anxiety disorders has been described earlier. It is not surprising that a stressful lifestyle perpetuates problems with anxiety. The frequency of panic attacks and severity of phobias tends to wax and wane depending on how well you cope with the daily stresses of living. Getting a handle on all of the maintaining causes of anxiety discussed in this section—self-talk, mistaken beliefs, withheld feelings, lack of assertiveness, lack of support, muscle tension, and diet—will go a long way toward reducing stress in your life. Other factors associated with stress that are not dealt with in this workbook include time management, Type A personality, and communication. These have been discussed in many excellent popular books on stress management. I can recommend the following: *Life After Stress*, by Martin Shaffer; *Guide to Stress Reduction*, by John Mason; and *The Relaxation & Stress Reduction Workbook*, by Martha Davis, Elizabeth Eshelman, and Matthew McKay. (See the reading list at the end of this chapter.)

Lack of Meaning or Sense of Purpose

It has been my repeated experience that clients experience relief from anxiety as well as phobias when they come to feel that their life has meaning, purpose, and a sense of direction. Until you discover something larger than self-gratification—something which gives your life a sense of purpose—you may be prone to feelings of boredom and a vague sense of confinement because you are not realizing all your potential. This sense of confinement can be a potent breeding ground for anxiety, phobias, and even panic attacks.

Issues of meaninglessness and purposelessness, and their relationship to psychological well-being, have been dealt with in depth by existential psychologists such as Victor Frankl and Rollo May. Several ways of confronting and working on these issues in your own life are presented in Chapter 19.

Exercise

1. Which of the following factors do you feel might be helping to maintain your particular dificulty?

    a. Avoidance of phobic situations
    b. Anxious self-talk
    c. Mistaken beliefs
    d. Withheld feelings

e. Lack of assertiveness

f. Lack of self-nurturing skills

g. Muscle tension

h. Stimulants and other dietary factors

i. High-stress lifestyle

j. Lack of meaning or sense of purpose

2. Can you rank these maintaining causes according to how much you feel they influence your condition? Which ones do you feel are most important for you to work on?

3. Specify three maintaining causes that you would seriously be willing to work on in the next month.

a. _____

b. _____

c. _____

Further Reading

Barlow, David H. *Anxiety and Its Disorders: The Nature and Treatment of Anxiety and Panic.* New York: Guilford Press, 1988 (a textbook intended for professionals).

Davis, Martha; Eshelman, Elizabeth; and McKay, Matthew. *The Relaxation & Stresss Reduction Workbook*, Third Edition. Oakland, California: New Harbinger Publications, 1988.

Gold, Mark S. *The Good News About Panic, Anxiety and Phobias*. New York: Villard Books, 1989.

Mason, John. *Guide to Stress Reduction*. Berkeley, California: Celestial Arts, 1985.

Shaffer, Martin. *Life After Stress*. New York: Plenum Press, 1982.

3

Recovery:
A Comprehensive Approach

Chapter 2 demonstrated how many different types of factors are contributing causes of anxiety disorders. Heredity, physiological imbalances in the brain, childhood deprivation and faulty parenting, and the cumulative effect of stress over time can all work to bring about the onset of panic attacks, agoraphobia, or any of the other anxiety disorders. The maintaining causes of these disorders—what keeps them going—are many and varied as well. Such factors can operate at the level of your body (for example, shallow breathing, muscle tension, poor nutrition), emotions (such as withheld feelings), behavior (avoidance of phobic situations), mind (anxious self-talk and mistaken beliefs), and "whole self" (such as low self-esteem or a lack of self-nurturing skills).

If the causes of anxiety disorders are so varied, then an adequate approach to recovery needs to be, too. It is the basic philosophy of this workbook that the most effective approach for treating panic, phobias, or any other problem with anxiety is one which addresses the *full range* of factors contributing to these conditions. This type of approach can be called "comprehensive." It assumes that you can't just give someone the "right" medication and expect panic or generalized anxiety to go away. Nor can you just deal with childhood deprivation, having someone work through the emotional consequences of bad parenting, and expect the problem to disappear. By the same token, you can't just teach people new behaviors and new ways of talking to themselves and expect these things alone to resolve their problem. Some therapists still treat anxiety disorders solely as psychiatric conditions which can be "cured" by medication, or solely as childhood developmental problems, or solely as behavior problems; but the trend in recent years has been away from such single-gauged approaches. Many practitioners have discovered that problems with anxiety go away only temporarily when merely one or two contributing causes are dealt with. Lasting recovery is achieved when you are willing to make basic and comprehensive changes in habit, attitude, and lifestyle.

This chapter outlines and illustrates a comprehensive approach to recovery that has evolved over the several years during which I have treated anxiety problems. What makes this approach truly comprehensive is that it offers interventions addressing seven different levels of contributing causes. These levels are as follows:

- Physical

- Emotional

- Behavioral

- Mental

- Interpersonal

- Whole Self

- Existential/Spiritual

Some brief descriptions of these levels, and a preview of the rest of the chapters in this workbook, follow.

Physical Level

Physical-level causes include possible physiological imbalances in the brain and body (see the section on biological causes in the preceding chapter). Such causes also include: 1) shallow breathing, 2) muscle tension, 3) bodily effects of cumulative stress, and 4) nutritional and dietary factors (such as excess caffeine or sugar in your diet). Strategies for dealing with physical-level causes can be found in three different chapters in this workbook. Chapter 4 offers breathing techniques to help modify your breathing pattern from the shallow, chest-level breathing that contributes to anxiety. That chapter also provides two deep-relaxation techniques designed to reduce muscle tension and the effects of stress—progressive muscle relaxation and meditation. When practiced on a regular basis, either of these techniques can help you feel calmer in general, often making it unnecessary to rely on tranquilizers.

The chapter on exercise makes a strong case for getting involved in a program of regular aerobic exercise. Many of my clients have found regular exercise to be the *single most effective* strategy for reducing muscle tension, stress, and hence anxiety (both chronic and acute). Chapter 15 discusses a variety of dietary changes that can help reduce anxiety. These include elimination of stimulants and substances that stress the body, and reliance on foods and supplements that promote a calmer disposition. Chapter 17 discusses situations where it is *appropriate* for you to take medication, along with the risks and benefits of each of the major types of medications used to treat anxiety disorders.

Emotional Level

Suppressed feelings—especially withheld anger—can be a very important contributing cause to both chronic anxiety and panic attacks. Often feelings of panic are merely a "front" for buried feelings of anger, frustration, grief, or desperation. Many people with anxiety disorders grew up in families that discouraged the expression of feelings. As an adult you may have difficulty just identifying what you *are* feeling, let alone expressing those feelings. Chapter 13 provides specific guidelines and strategies for

- Recognizing symptoms of suppressed feelings

- Identifying what you are feeling

- Learning to express your feelings

- Communicating your feelings to someone else

Behavioral Level

Phobias persist because of a single behavior: avoidance. As long as you avoid driving freeways, crossing bridges, speaking in public, or being in your home alone, your fear about these situations will persist. Your phobia is maintained because your avoidance behavior is so well rewarded: you don't have to reckon with the anxiety you'd experience if you confronted what you fear. Chapters 7 and 8 describe strategies which have been found to be very effective in dealing with phobias. Desensitization through imagery allows you to first confront your fear mentally, imagining over and over that you can handle it well. Real-life desensitization involves confronting your phobia in actuality—but with the help of a support person and in small increments. Perhaps the most important feature of both types of desensitization is that they break down into small steps the process of confronting what you fear.

Certain behaviors tend to encourage panic attacks. Trying to fight or resist panic will usually only aggravate it. Most of the time it is impossible to "will" your way out of panic. Chapter 6 suggests strategies you can use to minimize panic when it first develops. Learning to observe and "go with it" instead of reacting to the bodily symptoms of panic is perhaps the most important behavioral shift you can make. Specific techniques such as talking to another person, distracting your mind, becoming physically active, expressing needs and feelings, doing abdominal breathing, and repeating affirmations can all foster an increased capacity to *actively cope* with, rather than passively react to, the bodily symptoms of panic.

Mental Level

What you say to yourself internally—what is called *self-talk*—has a major effect on your state of anxiety. People with all types of anxiety disorders tend to engage in excessive "what-if" thinking, imagining the worst possible outcome in advance of facing what they fear. Scaring yourself through what-if scenarios is what has traditionally been called worry. Self-critical thinking and perfectionist self-talk (statements to yourself that start with "I should," "I have to," "I must") also promote anxiety.

Chapter 9 presents specific strategies for recognizing and *countering* destructive thinking patterns. By reconstructing negative self-talk into more supportive, confidence-building statements, you can begin to undo the long-standing habits of worry, self-criticism, and perfectionism that perpetuate anxiety.

Beneath anxiety-provoking self-talk are *mistaken beliefs* about yourself, others, and the world that produce anxiety in very basic ways. For example, if you see yourself as inadequate compared to others—or view the outside world as a dangerous place—you'll tend to remain anxious until you revise these basic attitudes. Chapter 10 offers strategies both for identifying and countering mistaken beliefs that contribute to anxiety.

Interpersonal Level

Much of the anxiety people experience arises from difficulties in interpersonal relationships. When you have difficulty communicating your real feelings and needs to others, you may find yourself swallowing frustration to the point where you're chronically tense and anxious. The same is true when you're unable to set limits or say no to unwanted demands or requests from others. Chapter 14 offers a variety of strategies for learning to stand up for your rights and express your true wants and feelings. Assertive communication provides ways to express what you want or don't want in a manner that preserves respect for other people. Learning to be assertive is a very important part of the recovery process, especially if you're dealing with agoraphobia or social phobia.

Being able to talk about your condition with others is also an important step in the recovery process. Ways to do this are discussed at the end of Chapter 6.

"Whole Self" Level (Self-Esteem)

Of all the contributing causes to anxiety disorders, low self-esteem is among the deepest. You may have grown up in a dysfunctional family, which, through various forms of deprivation, abuse, or neglect, fostered your low sense of self-worth. As a result you may carry into adulthood deep-seated feelings of insecurity, shame, and inadequacy, which tend to show up, on a more noticeable level, as panic attacks, fear of confronting the outside world (agoraphobia), fear of humiliation (social phobia), or generalized anxiety. Frequently, low self-esteem is tied in with all of the various contributing causes described above—in particular, lack of assertiveness, self-critical or perfectionist self-talk, and difficulty expressing feelings.

There are many ways to build self-esteem. Developing a positive body image, working toward and achieving concrete goals, and countering negative self-talk with validating affirmations can all help. Many of my clients have found it particularly worthwhile to cultivate a relationship with their own *inner child*. The inner child is that part of you which is spontaneous and playful but also carries the insecurity, shame, or pain that may be left over from your childhood. It is quite possible to make up for the inadequate parenting you may have received by becoming a strong, nurturing parent to your own child within. Chapter 14 provides specific strategies and exercises for strengthening your feelings of self-worth.

Existential and Spiritual Level

Sometimes people can improve on all of the levels previously described and yet remain anxious and unsettled. They seem to have a vague sense of dissatisfaction, emptiness, or boredom about life, which can lead to panic or to chronic, generalized anxiety. Certain of my clients have found that the ultimate "solution" to their problem with anxiety was to find a broad purpose or direction that gave their life greater meaning. Frequently this involved taking up a vocation that fulfilled their true talents and interests. In one case it involved developing an artistic talent that provided a creative outlet. Anxiety symptoms (as well as depression) can be the psyche's way of pushing you to explore and actualize an unrealized potential in your life, whether this involves intellectual development, emotional development, or even getting more in touch with your body. Instead of regarding your panic or phobias *merely* as a reaction to negative physical, emotional, or mental factors, you may be surprised to discover that they represent a call to realize your full potential.

For many individuals, finally, a deep spiritual commitment and involvement provides a significant pathway to recovery from anxiety problems. Twelve-step programs have demonstrated the potency of spiritual awakening in the area of addictions—and the same is true for recovery from anxiety disorders. Developing a connection with a Higher Power (call it God, spirit, or whatever you like) can provide a profound means for achieving inner security, strength, peace of mind, and an attitude that the outer world is a benevolent place. An existential-spiritual level of recovery is considered in Chapter 19.

Four Examples of a Comprehensive Recovery Program

The preceding section may have helped to broaden your understanding of the various levels that come into play in a comprehensive approach to recovery from anxiety disorders. To make this more concrete, I want you to consider what such an approach would look like in four specific cases. These four examples are the same ones that were presented at the beginning of Chapter 1 and reflect the four most common types of anxiety disorder seen by therapists: panic attacks, agoraphobia, social phobia, and obsessive-compulsive disorder. As you read through each of the examples, you may begin to formulate what strategies you want to include in your own recovery program. The *Problem Effectiveness Chart* and *Weekly Practice Record* that follow these examples will enable you to work out your own unique program in greater detail.

Susan: Panic Disorder

You may remember from Chapter 1 that Susan was awakened every night by panic attacks marked by heart palpitations, dizziness, and a fear that she was going to die. She would get up and try to make these symptoms go away, becoming more and more anxious when they didn't, to the point where she might spend an hour or more walking about her house. Terrified and confused, she worried about whether she was going to have a heart attack. After a week of recurring panic episodes, she made an appointment with a cardiologist.

Let's suppose that her cardiologist was enlightened about anxiety disorders. After ruling out any heart problems, the cardiologist diagnosed her panic disorder and sent her to a therapist who specialized in the treatment of phobias and panic. This therapist utilized a comprehensive treatment approach with a number of components designed to diminish Susan's problem on a physical, emotional, and mental level.

First, the therapist sent her back to a medical doctor, an internist, to rule out any other possible physical bases for her problem, such as hyperthyroidism, hypoglycemia, mitral valve prolapse, or a calcium-magnesium deficiency. Once these possible medical conditions were ruled out, Susan began her recovery program by learning abdominal breathing techniques that helped her to slow down the physiological arousal response that accompanies a panic attack (see Chapter 4). She was also asked to practice progressive muscle relaxation on a daily basis (Chapter 4) to train her body to enter into a relaxed state easily. Regular practice of progressive muscle relaxation had a cumulative effect (the same would be true for regular practice of any other deep relaxation technique, such as visualization or meditation). After several weeks, Susan noticed that she was feeling more relaxed *all the time*. In addition to breathing and deep relaxation techniques, she was asked to maintain a program of regular, vigorous exercise (see Chapter 5). She had discretion in choosing the type of exercise she wanted to do, but preferably it was to be aerobic exercise lasting for half-an-hour four to five times per week. Regular exercise worked together with the breathing techniques and deep relaxation to help relieve excess muscle tension, metabolize excess adrenalin, reduce vulnerability to sudden surges of anxiety, and increase Susan's overall sense of well-being. This combination of relaxation and exercise alone went a long way to significantly reduce the intensity and frequency of her panic attacks.

Susan's therapist also discovered that she was drinking three to four cups of coffee per day. Although for some people this might be a manageable amount, most individuals dealing with panic disorder find that their condition is aggravated by even small amounts of caffeine. Susan was asked to gradually taper off her caffeine consumption and replace regular with decaffeinated coffee. Her therapist also recommended a balanced diet, consisting largely of whole, unprocessed foods with minimal sugar and salt. She was also advised to take high-potency vitamin B-complex, vitamin C, and calcium-magnesium supplements (see Chapter 16).

Susan was then taught specific techniques for interrupting the onset of panic when she first began to notice the approach of symptoms (see Chapter 6). These techniques included calling a friend, physically exerting herself by doing housework, or writing out her feelings in a journal if she was feeling angry or frustrated. Special emphasis was given to her self-talk—what she said to herself at the very onset of feeling panic symptoms (see Chapter 9). Her therapist found that Susan had a tendency to scare herself into a high state of panic by internally saying such things as, "What if I have a heart attack?" "I can't stand this!" "I've got to get out of here!" She was taught to replace this "scare-talk" with more positive, self-supportive statements such as "I can handle these sensations," "I can flow with this and wait for my anxiety to diminish," "I can let my body do its thing and this will pass." After practicing these "coping affirmations" many times, Susan found that she could simply *observe* her bodily symptoms rather than react to them. After a while she was able to avoid severe panic reactions altogether. Her therapist also helped Susan to identify some of the fundamental, mistaken beliefs underlying much of her behavior (see Chapter 10). She began to let go of such basic assumptions about herself as, "I have to be completely successful at everything I do," "Life is a struggle," "Everything must be totally predictable and in control." She was able to take life a little more easily and view its inevitable challenges with more perspective. The net result was a significant reduction in her overall level of anxiety.

A final issue associated with Susan's panic reactions was her tendency to completely suppress her anger and frustration. Early on, her therapist noticed that Susan was most vulnerable to panic on days when she had encountered numerous frustrating situations at work. She had grown up in a family where everyone was supposed to always do their best without ever complaining. Direct expression of feelings and needs was discouraged—she had learned to keep up a pleasant front both to strangers and friends, no matter how she was feeling inside. Although Susan couldn't believe it at first, she eventually concluded that her panic reactions were sometimes nothing more than intense feelings of frustration and anger in disguise. Her exercise program helped her to discharge some of these feelings. She also found it helpful to write her feelings down in a journal whenever she noticed herself beginning to feel on edge.

Susan's recovery program consisted of a variety of interventions on a physical, behavioral, emotional, and mental level, as summarized below.

Physical	Breathing exercises
	Regular practice of deep relaxation
	Regular aerobic exercise
	Elimination of caffeine
	Nutritional improvements, including vitamin supplements
Behavioral	Coping techniques to abort panic reactions at their onset—such as abdominal breathing and distraction techniques
Emotional	Identifying some panic reactions as anger in disguise
	Learning to express frustrations verbally and in writing
Mental	Changing scare-talk at the onset of panic to supportive, calming self-talk
	Practicing coping affirmations
	Reevaluating underlying mistaken beliefs and adopting a more relaxed, easy-going perspective on life

It was through a combination of all these interventions that Susan was able to find lasting relief from her panic attacks. Six months from the time she began her program she was still occasionally anxious, but only rarely experienced symptoms of panic. On those occasions when she did, she had a variety of tools that allowed her to dissipate the reaction before it gained momentum.

For Susan it was possible to achieve a lasting recovery from panic without the use of prescription medications. This is not always the case. When panic is so frequent or severe that it interferes with your work, relationships, or general ability to function (or when it does not yield to approaches like those discussed above), it may be appropriate to take medication. An antidepressant medication such as imipramine (Tofranil), taken over a period of six months to one year, can often be quite helpful in these instances (see Chapter 17).

Cindy: Agoraphobia

You may recall Cindy's case from the example in the first chapter. She not only had panic attacks but was beginning to avoid situations such as grocery stores, restaurants, and movie theaters, where she was afraid she might have an attack. She was also very concerned that she might have to stop going to work. This avoidance of situations out of fear of panic is the hallmark of agoraphobia. What would a comprehensive recovery program for Cindy look like?

Just about all the interventions described in the example of Susan were also used in Cindy's case, because she, too, was experiencing panic attacks. Breathing techniques, regular practice of progressive muscle relaxation, regular (if possible, aerobic) exercise, and nutritional improvements were all necessary to help her reduce the physiological component of panic (see the corresponding chapters in this workbook). She also learned the same coping techniques for panic, so that she was able to *act* rather than *react* when she felt the first bodily symptoms of panic coming on (see Chapter 6). Cindy also worked on changing counter-productive self-talk (see Chapter 9). In her case, this was especially important—not only for coping with panic itself, but for curbing her excessive tendency to worry about panicking when she went to work. Finally, Cindy, just like Susan, needed to reexamine some of her basic mistaken beliefs about herself such as, "I can't make mistakes," "I must always be pleasing to everybody," "Success is everything." She developed affirmations to counter these beliefs and recorded them on a tape that she listened to every night as she went to sleep (see Chapter 10).

It was important for Cindy to work not only on her panic reactions but on her avoidance behavior as well. At the outset, she was avoiding crowded public situations such as grocery stores, restaurants, and movie theaters, and had nearly reached the point where she was afraid to go to work. In only a few weeks she had severely limited where she would go. It was through the processes of imagery and real-life desensitization that she learned to reenter all these situations and be comfortable with them (see Chapters 7 and 8). There were three phases in this process. First, she broke down the goal of re-entering each specific situation into a series of steps. For example, in the case of the grocery store, she had eight steps:

1. Spending one minute near the entrance of the store

2. Spending one minute inside the door of the store

3. Going halfway to the back of the store, spending one minute, and then leaving

4. Going to the back of the store, spending one minute, and then leaving

5. Spending three minutes in the store without buying anything

6. Buying one item and going through the express checkout line

7. Buying three items and going through the express checkout line

8. Buying three items and going through a regular checkout line

The second phase involved practicing imagery desensitization—going through each of these steps in *imagination* until she could visualize the final step in detail without feeling any anxiety.

Third, Cindy practiced real-life desensitization, going through each of the eight steps in real life. She practiced each step several times at first with the help of a support person—usually her boyfriend—and then tried it out alone. For example, after she had mastered Step 3 by herself, she started practicing Step 4 with her support person. She found that the process worked best if she temporarily stopped or retreated any time she felt anxiety coming on so strongly that she felt it might get out of control. It was easier to advance from one step to the next if she didn't "overexpose" or resensitize herself by pushing herself to the point of feeling intense anxiety.

Cindy undertook this three-phase process—1) breaking the goal down into steps, 2) imagery desensitization, and 3) real-life desensitization—with each of her specific phobias. By practicing desensitization on a regular basis, she was able after three months to reenter all the situations she had previously avoided and to feel comfortable with them.

Cindy had a high degree of self-motivation. The consistent encouragement and reinforcement she got from her boyfriend, who always accompanied her on her first run of entering a phobic situation, speeded up her progress considerably.

The most direct and efficient way to overcome any fear is simply to face it. If you are agoraphobic, however, the prospect of confronting long-standing fears can seem overwhelming at first. Cindy learned that this confrontation process can be made manageable if it is broken down into sufficiently small steps which are first negotiated in imagination.

Apart from overcoming her phobias, another important part of Cindy's recovery was learning to be assertive (see Chapter 14). A major part of the stress that contributed to her first panic attack came from her inability to say no to unreasonable demands placed on her by her boss. Cindy's friends also noted that she couldn't stand up for her rights or say no to her boyfriend for fear of his leaving her. She had grown up in a family where her father had left when she was eight. In addition, her mother was very demanding and critical. Consequently Cindy was never quite sure that she was loved, and had a deep-seated insecurity about being abandoned. As a child, she feared that standing up for herself would jeopardize the tenuous and conditional love she received from her mother. Cindy carried this pattern of dependency and fear of abandonment into adulthood and "replayed" it in her relationship with her boyfriend. In subtle ways, it actually served to reinforce her agoraphobia. On an unconscious level, she felt that if she were dependent on her boyfriend to take care of her, he would never leave her.

During her recovery, Cindy realized that she wanted to rework her "life script." She was feeling increasingly frustrated about always accommodating everyone else, and began to recognize the need to develop a stronger sense of herself and her own rights. Through learning to be assertive, she discovered that she could ask for what she wanted, say no to what she didn't want, and still obtain the love and support she needed from her boyfriend and others. In fact, she was surprised to find that everyone, including her boyfriend, *respected* her more for being able to stand up for herself. The independence Cindy gained from learning to confront situations she previously avoided went hand in hand with the independence she gained from developing a more assertive interpersonal style. There was no longer any need for her agoraphobia, because there was no longer any need for the dependency that maintained it.

Because of the insecurity and fear of abandonment left over from her childhood, it was also critical for Cindy to work on self-esteem (see Chapter 15). She discovered that the only remedy for the inadequate parenting she had received was to become a good parent to herself. She did this in part by improving her body image and countering her "inner critic" (self-critical inner dialogue) with affirmations of self-acceptance and self-worth. What she found most helpful, though, was cultivating a relationship with her *inner child*. (The inner child is that part of you which is playful and creative but also carries old wounds—the pain, insecurity, or sense of inadequacy you may have felt since childhood.) Cindy learned to relabel moods in which she felt insecure or frightened as requests for nurturing from her inner child. She gained considerable inner strength and self-confidence as she learned a variety of ways to support, nurture, and care for her own child within.

In sum, Cindy's recovery program for agoraphobia contained all of the elements of Susan's program for panic attacks *plus* imagery and real-life desensitization to overcome her specific avoidances. It was also necessary for Cindy to address assertiveness and self-esteem issues. She needed to overcome feelings of insecurity and a fear of abandonment that she had carried over from childhood—an insecurity that tended to reinforce her agoraphobia. Her total program involved interventions on six different levels, including the following:

Physical	Breathing exercises
	Regular practice of deep relaxation
	Regular aerobic exercise
	Nutritional improvements, including vitamin supplements
Behavioral	Coping techniques to abort panic reactions at their onset
	Imagery and real-life desensitization to overcome specific phobias
Emotional	Learning to identify and express feelings
Mental	Countering negative self-talk that contributed to panic attacks as well as worry about panicking
	Countering underlying mistaken beliefs with self-supporting affirmations
Interpersonal	Developing a more assertive interpersonal style
Whole Self	Developing self-esteem through
	• working on her body image
	• overcoming her inner critic
	• cultivating a relationship with her inner child

It took Cindy about a year to fully implement these interventions. At the end of one year she was close to being free of her agoraphobia as well as panic attacks. She decided to go back to school part-time to train to become a registered nurse while continuing her job as a medical secretary.

Steve: Social Phobia

You may recall from Chapter 1 that Steve had difficulty attending meetings at work. He would clam up in group sessions and feared that his co-workers would look upon him critically for not contributing. His very worst fear was being asked to give a presentation before a group. When this finally happened, he was so terrified that he felt he might have to quit his job.

Steve's problem fits the picture of a social phobia very well—he feared embarrassment and humiliation as a result of being unable to perform in a group situation. His recovery program depended heavily on the processes of imagery and real-life desensitization.

Like Susan and Cindy, Steve required a comprehensive treatment approach. Because he tended generally to be anxious much of the time, the same strategies were needed that were used to reduce the physical component of anxiety for Susan and Cindy. Steve first learned abdominal breathing techniques to reduce anxiety on a short-term basis. He found these to be very helpful in reducing apprehension that came up when he was asked to attend meetings at work. He also practiced a deep relaxation technique twice a day. In Steve's case, meditation seemed to work better than progressive muscle relaxation for soothing his active mind (see Chapter 4). He also found that jogging four times a week made a substantial improvement in his level of tension and anxiety (see Chapter 5). Finally, he learned that after reducing his consumption of refined sugar, his mood swings diminished and he was less prone to bouts of depression (see Chapter 16). By upgrading his overall health and wellness, Steve became more confident about tackling his social phobia.

The phobia of being in meetings at work was dealt with first through imagery desensitization. As in Cindy's case, Steve broke down the goal of being able to handle meetings into steps:

1. Sitting in a small group (fewer than five people) for 15 minutes

2. Sitting in a small group for 45 minutes to one hour

3. Sitting in a larger group for 15 minutes

4. Sitting in a larger group for 45 minutes to one hour

5. Repeating Steps 1-4, but making at least one comment during the course of the meeting

6. Repeating Steps 1-4, but making at least two comments during the meeting

7. Giving a one-minute presentaton before a small group

8. Giving a three-minute presentation before a small group

9. Giving a five- to ten-minute presentation before a small group

10. Repeating Steps 7-9 with a larger group

The next phase was to go through each of the steps in detail in his imagination. Steve would keep working with a particular step until he no longer felt any anxiety and then would go on to the next one. If at any point his anxiety started to come on very strong—to the point where he felt it might get out of control—he would "switch off" the scene he was visualizing and retreat in his mind to a very peaceful, relaxing scene. Steve found it useful to make a tape which guided him through visualizing all ten of the steps in his program.

After he had successfully desensitized himself in his imagination, Steve undertook to conquer his fear of groups in real life (see Chapter 8). First, he sat down with his boss and discussed his problem. He explained that he wanted to be able to participate in meetings and was working through a specific, step-by-step program to overcome his phobia. He made an arrangement with his boss to attend only small, short meetings; he had permission to temporarily leave if his anxiety level became too high. After mastering small, brief meetings, he would be able to progress to larger and longer ones. Knowing he would always be free to retreat if he needed to, he felt more willing to undertake real-life desensitization. After working up to a point where he could verbally participate in large meetings, he began to work on his fear of making a presentation. Instead of starting out trying to do this at work, Steve decided to take a course in public speaking at a local junior college. The demands for performance in a classroom setting, where everyone was learning, seemed less intense than the expectations at work. After completing the public speaking class, he arranged to make a brief presentation at work before a small group of co-workers he knew well. From there he progressed to larger groups, longer presentations, and finally to speaking before groups of strangers.

Steve continued to feel anxious when he got up before a group, but he was now able to *handle* his anxiety through a combination of abdominal breathing techniques and coping affirmations such as: "I can ride through this anxiety and be fine," "As soon as I get started, I'll be fine," "What I have to say is worthwhile—everyone will be interested." With time and practice he got to the point where he no longer feared making presentations and, in fact, looked forward to them as an opportunity to contribute his own insights and ideas.

Besides practicing imagery and real-life desensitization, Steve, like Cindy, worked on assertiveness and self-esteem (see Chapters 14 and 15). He had grown up in a family where he was the youngest of three brothers. Always being bossed around by his older brothers, he learned to suppress his own feelings and ideas. Throughout his life, he had been afraid to stand up for himself. This fear played no small role in his difficulty with speaking up or making presentations before a group. Through practicing assertiveness skills, he learned how to express his feelings and wants to others directly. He was pleasantly surprised to find that others usually appreciated, and were interested in, what he had to say.

As the youngest child in his family, Steve had also been "babied" during childhood. He grew up with an underlying fear of standing up as his own person and assuming full responsibility as an adult. He had to work on self-esteem to realize that he was just as valuable, important, and able to contribute as anyone else. Overcoming his social phobia certainly helped, but, like Cindy, Steve also worked on developing a relationship with his inner child. By consistently validating and supporting the little boy within, he gradually overcame the feelings of inadequacy and shame that had fed his phobia.

Steve's program for recovery from social phobia contained many of the same components as Cindy's program for recovery from agoraphobia. The only significant difference was that Steve didn't have to deal with panic; his phobia centered around fears of embarrassment and humiliation rather than fears of losing control during a panic attack. All of the following strategies contributed to his recovery, with real-life desensitization perhaps being the most crucial:

Physical	Breathing exercises
	Regular practice of deep relaxation
	Regular aerobic exercise
	Nutritional improvements (specifically, reducing sugar intake and thus hypoglycemic mood swings)
Behavioral	Imagery desensitization
	Real-life desensitization, including a public speaking class prior to making presentations at work
Emotional	Learning to identify and express feelings
Mental	Countering negative self-talk
	Countering mistaken beliefs
Interpersonal	Developing an assertive interpersonal style
Whole Self	Developing self-esteem by cultivating a relationship with his inner child

Mike: Obsessive-Compulsive Disorder

Mike, you may recall, was a successful businessman who had a recurring, irrational fear that he had run over a person or animal while driving. So strong and insistent was this fear that he continually had to retrace the route he'd just driven to assure himself that no one was lying in the street. By the time he sought treatment, his compulsion to check was so strong that he needed to retrace his route three or four times before he could go on. Because he felt both ashamed and powerless to control his behavior, he was also significantly depressed—a common complaint of people with obsessive-compulsive disorder. Mike's problem was an example of the "checking" type of obsessive-compulsive disorder. But the comprehensive recovery program he undertook could apply equally well to other forms of obsessive-compulsive disorder including washing, counting, or other compulsions.

In many respects Mike's road to recovery was similar to that of Susan, Cindy, and Steve in the preceding examples. His therapist asked him to practice breathing exercises, progressive muscle relaxation, and aerobic exercise on a daily basis to reduce the physiological component of his anxiety. Mike also reduced the amount of caffeine and sugar in his diet and started taking high-potency B-complex and vitamin C supplements with breakfast and dinner. Mike felt so much better from these practices alone that there were certain days where he didn't need to retrace his driving route at all. However, his problem still didn't disappear altogether.

Mike worked on changing his inner dialogue or self-talk while driving. Instead of always asking himself, "What if I hit someone?" he learned to counter with the statement, "If I hit anything, I certainly would hear it or feel it. But this hasn't happened, so I'm O.K." Repeating this reassuring statement over and over helped him to reduce the number of times he needed to retrace his route from three or four to one or two, but it didn't dispel his obsession completely.

Another helpful intervention was learning to identify and express his angry feelings. Mike found that by getting angry with his compulsion to check and shouting "No!" very loudly in his car, he could sometimes dissipate his anxiety enough so that he didn't have to check. Getting in touch with and acknowledging his frustrations also helped him to reduce stress in other areas of his life apart from his specific problem with checking. Yet expressing needs and feelings was not enough, any more than the physical and mental strategies he had tried, to completely resolve his obsessive-compulsive problem.

From his reading on the subject, Mike learned that obsessive-compulsive disorder responds best to the combination of two specific interventions:

- A behavioral intervention called *exposure and response prevention*

- Medication—specifically, antidepressant medications such as clomipramine (Anafranil) and fluoxetine (Prozac)

Under the supervision of his therapist, Mike practiced exposure and response prevention in two steps. First, he was instructed to reduce to one the number of times he retraced his route. He had already brought the frequency down from four or five repetitions to two or three, and over the course of a month he was able to reduce the number further to one. At this point his therapist rode with him in the car and instructed

Mike, whenever he felt the urge to retrace, to pull the car over to the side of the road and stop. Mike then waited several minutes for the anxiety he felt about not retracing his route to subside. Then he resumed his driving. After two weeks of practicing response prevention with his therapist, Mike was finally able to do it on his own. It was very liberating to Mike not to have to spend so much time and energy on retracing his driving route.

A problem that remained, though, was that he couldn't get the obsession about having run over someone out of his mind completely—even though positive self-talk had helped somewhat. He continued to be vigilant while driving and was depressed that he had so little control over his thoughts.

Mike's therapist referred him to a psychiatrist who instructed him about the medication clomipramine, a drug that has been effective in eliminating or reducing the symptoms of obsessive-compulsive disorder in about 60 percent of the cases in which it has been used. Within three weeks of starting the medication, Mike found that his obsessions had disappeared altogether and that his depression had lifted significantly. He began to relax and enjoy driving again, free of any concern about having hit someone. His doctor told him that he would need to stay on the medication for one year, at which point Mike would gradually taper off the dose and see if he could continue to live free of obsessions without taking medication.

Although Mike's obsessive-compulsive disorder responded quite well to the combination of interventions described above, he continued to feel depressed from time to time. It became apparent to his therapist that Mike was feeling somewhat bored with his line of work and with his life in general. The final phase of his recovery program involved making two major adjustments that added meaning and direction to his life. First, he decided to make a career change. Over the course of a year, he moved from a corporate position in marketing to starting a small retail business of his own. All his life, Mike had had a strong interest in music but had never done anything to fulfill it. So, as a second step, he began taking piano lessons. After a year, he took this pursuit a step further, bought a synthesizer, and began to compose his own original piano pieces. This creative outlet added a whole new dimension to Mike's life and enabled him to express a previously unrealized potential. It was after this that his depression fully lifted.

The most critical component of Mike's recovery from obsessive-compulsive disorder was the combination of response prevention and medication. The crux of his recovery from depression was the combination of overcoming his obsessive-compulsive disorder *and* developing a creative outlet that gave his life a new dimension of meaning. His total program for recovery can be summarized as follows:

Physical	Breathing exercises
	Regular practice of deep relaxation
	Regular aerobic exercise
	Nutritional improvements plus vitamin supplements
Behavioral	Exposure and response prevention to eliminate checking
Emotional	Learning to identify and express anger and frustration
Mental	Self-talk to counter fears about having run over someone
Medication	Taking clomipramine for one year

Existential-   Pursuing a creative interest in playing the piano and musical
Spiritual   composition

Developing Your Own Recovery Program

By this point I hope that you've gained an idea about three things: 1) the wide range of strategies used in a comprehensive recovery program, 2) the specific types of strategies employed, and 3) how such strategies are actually implemented in specific cases.

You can now begin to develop your own recovery program. The following two charts are designed to assist you with this. The first is the *Problem Effectiveness Chart*. It correlates different types of anxiety disorders with specific chapters in this workbook. Chapters that are particularly relevant for *everyone* with the disorder are marked with an "X." Those chapters that are often relevant are marked with a lowercase "x." Your choice of strategies will, of course, depend on the nature and causes of your particular difficulty. After reading the first three chapters of this workbook, you should have some idea of what strategies to emphasize.

The second chart, called the *Weekly Practice Record*, enables you to outline in detail your own personal program for recovery. The chart lists all the specific strategies and skills offered in this workbook. Following each skill, in parentheses, is the recommended frequency for practice in a one-week time period. The abbreviation "var." indicates that the frequency of practice per week can vary depending on how much emphasis you want to put on that particular skill. This chart enables you to check off, for each day of the week, which exercises you have practiced.

Since this is a weekly chart, I recommend that you *make 52 copies* of it to take you through a one-year time period. (Of course, your actual recovery may turn out to take significantly less than one year.)

At the top of the chart be sure to specify the dates of the particular week as well as your goals for that week. At the bottom of the chart you can estimate, on a scale of 0 to 100 percent, how much you believe you have recovered up to the time of that particular week. (Note: Be prepared for your level of recovery to be marked by progressions and regressions from week to week.) It is obvious that you will not implement *all* of the strategies recommended in this workbook *every* week. As you go through each chapter, you'll likely emphasize the skills taught in that chapter. There are four skills, though, that I recommend trying to practice *five to seven times a week* for 52 weeks a year, regardless of the type of anxiety disorder you happen to be dealing with. These are:

1. A deep relaxation technique (such as muscle relaxation, visualization, meditation)

2. One-half hour of vigorous exercise

3. Good nutritional habits

4. Countering negative self-talk or using affirmations

If you happen to have phobias, there are two additional strategies I recommend practicing *three to five times a week* until you are phobia-free, namely

5. Imagery desensitization

6. Real-life desensitization

Beyond these guidelines, you will be working out for yourself how much time you need to spend with the various other strategies that constitute your particular recovery program.

A *consistent commitment over time* to practicing strategies that are helpful to you is what will make the difference between a partial and a complete recovery. The *Weekly Practice Record* is designed to help keep you on track with your personal program for recovery over the long haul.

Necessary Ingredients for Undertaking Your Own Recovery Program

By now you may have some idea of the strategies you want to utilize for your own recovery. The *Weekly Practice Record* will enable you to specify, on a weekly basis, the particular strategies and skills you incorporate in your personal program. You may have already guessed, though, that recovery entails much more than just a series of strategies. Your ability to *implement* the strategies recommended in this workbook depends entirely on your attitude, commitment, and motivation to really *do* something about your problem. Your recovery depends on the extent to which you can adopt and incorporate the five necessary ingredients described below.

1. Taking Responsibility—In a Context of Support

Do you feel responsible for your problem? Or do you attribute it to some quirk of heredity, abusive parents, or the stressful people in your life? Even if you feel you aren't solely responsible for having created your disorder, you are the one who is ultimately responsible either for holding onto it or doing something about it. It may be difficult initially to accept the idea that the decision is yours whether to maintain or whether to overcome your problem. Yet accepting full responsibility is the most empowering step you can take. If you are the one who keeps your condition going, you are also the one with the power to change and outgrow it.

Taking responsibility means you don't blame anyone else for your difficulties. It also means that you don't blame *yourself*. Is there truly any justification for blaming yourself that you have panic attacks, phobias, or obsessions and compulsions? Is it truly your fault that you developed these problems? Is it not more accurate to say that you've done the best you could in your life up to now with the knowledge and resources at your disposal? While it's up to you to change your condition, there is simply no basis for judging or blaming yourself for having it.

Taking responsibility for overcoming your condition does *not* mean that you have to do it all alone. In fact, the opposite is true: you are more likely to be willing to change and to take risks when you feel adequately supported. A most important prerequisite for undertaking your own program for recovery is to have an adequate support system. This can include your spouse or partner, one or two close friends, and/or a support group or class specifically set up to assist people with anxiety disorders. (Programs such as TERRAP and CHAANGE offer such groups in many cities of the United States, though the emphasis in these groups is primarily on agoraphobia—see Appendix 1 for details on how to locate these programs.)

"Ordinary" Anxiety	Post-Traumatic Stress Disorder	Obsessive-Compulsive Disorder	Generalized Anxiety Disorder	Simple Phobia	Social Phobia	Agoraphobia	Panic Attack	
×	×	×	×	×	×	×	×	Relaxation
×	×	×	×	×	×	×	×	Exercise
					×	×	×	Coping Techniques for Panic
				×	×	×		Imagery Desensitization
				×	×	×		Real-Life Desensitization
×	×	×	×	×	×	×	×	Self-Talk
×	×	×	×	×	×	×	×	Mistaken Beliefs
×	×	×	×		×	×	×	Feelings
×	×	×	×		×	×		Assertiveness
×	×	×	×	×	×	×	×	Self-Esteem
×	×	×	×	×	×	×	×	Nutrition
		×	×		×	×	×	Medication
×	×	×	×		×	×	×	Meaning/Spirituality

Problem Effectiveness Chart

Weekly Practice Record

Goals for Week
1.
2.   Date:
3.

	Mon.	Tues.	Wed.	Thurs.	Fri.	Sat.	Sun.
Used deep breathing technique (6-7)							
Used deep relaxation technique* (6-7)							
Did one-half hour vigorous exercise (4-7)							
Used coping techniques to manage panic **							
Practiced countering negative self-talk (5-7)							
Used affirmations to counter mistaken beliefs (5-7)							
Practiced imagery desensitization (3-5)							
Practiced real-life desensitization (3-5)							
Identified/expressed feelings **							
Practiced assertive communication with significant other **							
Practiced assertive communication to avoid manipulation **							
Self-esteem: worked on improving body image **							
Self-esteem: took steps toward achieving goals **							
Self-esteem: worked on countering inner critic **							
Self-esteem: worked on nurturing inner child **							
Nutrition: eliminated caffeine/sugar/stimulants (7)							
Nutrition: ate only whole, unprocessed foods (5-7)							
Nutrition: used anti-stress supplements (5-7)							
Medication: used appropriate medications as prescribed by doctor (7)							
Meaning: worked on discovering/realizing life purpose **							
Spirituality: utilized spiritual beliefs and practices to reduce anxiety **							

Estimated percent recovery (1%-100%):_____

*e.g., progressive muscle relaxation, visualization, or meditation

**Recommended frequency varies depending on focus

2. *Motivation — Overcoming Secondary Gains*

Once you've decided to acknowledge your share of the responsibility for your problem, your ability to actually do something about it will depend on your motivation. Do you feel truly motivated to change? Enough so that you'll be willing to learn and incorporate several new habits of thought and behavior into your daily routine? Enough so that you'll be willing to make some basic changes in your lifestyle?

Psychologist David Bakan once made the observation that "suffering is the great motivator of growth." If you are experiencing considerable distress from your particular problem, you're likely to be strongly motivated to do something about it. A basic belief in your self-worth can also be a strong motivation for change. If you love yourself enough to feel that you sincerely deserve to have a fulfilling and productive life, you simply won't "settle" for being impeded by panic, phobias, or other anxiety symptoms. You will demand more of life than that.

This brings up the issue of what interferes with motivation. Any person, situation, or factor that consciously or unconsciously *rewards you for holding on to your condition* will tend to undermine your motivation. For example, you may want to overcome your problem with being housebound. However, if consciously or unconsciously you don't want to deal with facing the outside world, getting a job, and earning an income, you will tend to keep yourself confined. Consciously you want to overcome agoraphobia, yet your motivation is not strong enough to overcome the unconscious "payoffs" for not recovering.

Many years ago Sigmund Freud referred to the idea of unconscious payoffs as "secondary gains." Wherever there is strong resistance to recovering from any chronic, disabling condition—whether it is an anxiety disorder, depression, addiction, or obesity—secondary gains are often operative. If you find that you have difficulty developing or *sustaining* motivation to do something about your condition, it's important to ask yourself, "What payoffs am I getting for staying this way?" The list below enumerates some of the more common secondary gains that can keep you stuck:

1. A deep-seated belief that you "don't deserve" to recover and lead a normal life—that you're unworthy of being reasonably happy. When self-punishment is a secondary gain, it is often the case that you're punishing yourself to get back at someone else. Self-punishment also can occur because you feel guilty about your condition. The way out of guilt and the tendency to hold yourself back is to work on self-esteem (see Chapter 15).

2. A deep-seated belief that "it's too much work" to truly change. After all, you may already be feeling stressed out and overwhelmed. Now you are being asked to take on considerably more responsibility and work in order to recover. Unconsciously it may just seem like too much work, leaving you discouraged about ever breaking out of your condition. The solution to this dilemma is to replace your assumption of "too much work" with more positive beliefs, such as, "I don't have to be completely well tomorrow—I can take small steps toward recovering at my own pace," or "Any goal can be achieved if broken down into sufficiently small steps." (The 12-step recovery programs have abbreviated these constructive attitudes with the slogan, "One day at a time.")

3. If you're agoraphobic and relatively housebound, you may be attached to the payoffs you get from your spouse or partner. These include attention, being taken care of, and being financially supported, or, in general, not having to deal with adult responsibilities.

4. The reverse of number 3 may also be true. Your spouse or partner may be getting payoffs from your being dependent on him or her. These can include the opportunity to take care of, control, and even take responsibility for your life (this is a case of *co-dependency*—see Chapter 15). The payoff can also be assurance that you will never leave. That is, your partner may fear that if you fully recover and become more independent, you'll leave. You need to realize that you won't be held back by your partner's secondary gains unless you are unconsciously colluding with him or her to maintain them.

The above is only a partial list of secondary gains. They may or may not apply in your case. If you feel that you're having difficulties with motivation at any point in your recovery, it's important to raise the question, "What is the payoff for avoiding change?"

3. *Making a Commitment to Yourself To Follow Through*

The initial motivation and enthusiasm you have when you first decide to do something about your problem is usually sufficient to get you started. The real test is in following through. Are you willing to make a commitment to *consistently* practice skills and strategies that work for you over the many months and sometimes years that it takes to achieve a full and lasting recovery? In my experience, it is difficult to sustain a high level of motivation over such periods of time unless you have a deep and sincere *commitment* to persist with your recovery program until you're fully satisfied with the results. On a practical level, this means going out and exercising, practicing desensitization, or working on your self-esteem even on those days when you don't feel like it. It means that you get up and keep going even after you've had a setback which makes you wonder whether you'll *ever* feel better. While your motivation may wax and wane, a personal commitment to follow through with your program is what is going to make the difference between a partial or a complete recovery.

4. *Willingness To Take Risks*

It is simply not possible to change or grow in any area of your life unless you are willing to take some risks. To recover means being willing to experiment with new ways of thinking, feeling, and acting that may be unfamiliar to you at first. It also means giving up some of the payoffs for not changing, as were described in the section on motivation. If you are dealing with phobias, the way to overcome them is simply to face those situations you've been avoiding—gradually and in your imagination at first. If you are dealing with panic attacks, it may be necessary to risk relinquishing some control and learning to flow with unpleasant bodily sensations instead of resisting and fighting them. If you're dealing with obsessions and compulsions, it may be necessary to risk experiencing anxiety when you resist engaging in compulsive behavior. Or it may be necessary to risk taking a prescription medication.

An effective program for recovery is predicated upon your willingness to risk trying out new behaviors that may cause you *more* anxiety at first, yet which in the long run can be quite helpful. As in the case of taking responsibility, having support from others who believe in you and back you up will make taking risks considerably easier.

5. Defining and Visualizing Your Goals for Recovery

It's difficult to tackle and then overcome a problem unless you have a clear, concrete idea of the goal you're aiming for. Before embarking on your own program for recovery, it is important that you answer the following questions:

- "What are the most important positive changes I want to make in my life?"

- "What would a complete recovery from my present condition look like?"

- "Specifically, how will I think, feel, and act in my work, my relationships with others, and my relationship with myself once I've fully recovered?"

- "What new opportunities will I take advantage of once I've fully recovered?"

Once you've defined what your own recovery might be like, it can be very helpful to practice *visualizing* it. During the time you allocate for practicing deep relaxation, take a few minutes to imagine what your life would look like if you were entirely free of your problems. Visualize in detail any changes in your work, recreational activities, relationships, and the body-image and appearance you would like to achieve. To assist you in developing this positive scenario, use the space below or preferably a separate sheet of paper to write out a "script" of how your life would *ideally* look when you have fully recovered. Be sure to cover as many different areas of your life as possible.

Ideal Scenario for My Life After I've Recovered

Practicing visualizing your goals for recovery on a daily basis (preferably in a relaxed state) will increase your confidence about succeeding. This practice will actually make a full recovery more likely. There is abundant philosophical evidence—both ancient and modern—that what you believe in with your whole heart and see with your whole mind has a strong tendency to come true.

Summary of Things To Do

1. Review the case histories in this chapter and examine the *Problem Effectiveness Chart* to determine which chapters of this workbook are relevant to your particular problem.

2. Decide in what order you're going to work with the various chapters that are relevant to you. I recommend using the chapters in the order they are presented.

3. Make 52 copies of the *Weekly Practice Record* to monitor your personal recovery program for one year. (Your recovery, of course, may take less than one year.)

4. Reread the final section, "Necessary Ingredients for Undertaking Your Own Recovery Program," to reinforce in your mind the five keys to a successful and complete recovery: *taking responsibility, motivation* (including overcoming secondary gains)*, commitment, a willingness to take risks,* and *defining goals.*

4

Relaxation

The capacity to relax is at the very foundation of any program undertaken to overcome anxiety, phobias, or panic attacks. Many of the other skills described in this book, such as desensitization, visualization, and changing negative self-talk, build on the capacity to achieve deep relaxation.

Relaxation is more than unwinding in front of the TV set or in the bathtub at the end of the day—though, without doubt, these practices can be relaxing. The type of relaxation that really makes a difference in dealing with anxiety is the *regular*, *daily* practice of some form of *deep relaxation*. Deep relaxation refers to a distinct physiological state that is the exact opposite of the way your body reacts under stress or during a panic attack. This state was originally described by Herbert Benson in 1975 as the *relaxation response*. It involves a series of physiological changes including

- Decrease in heart rate

- Decrease in respiration rate

- Decrease in blood pressure

- Decrease in skeletal muscle tension

- Decrease in metabolic rate and oxygen consumption

- Decrease in analytical thinking

- Increase in skin resistance

- Increase in alpha wave activity in the brain

Regular practice of deep relaxation for 20-30 minutes on a daily basis can produce, over time, a generalization of relaxation to the rest of your life. That is, after several weeks of practicing deep relaxation once per day, you will tend to feel more relaxed all the time.

Numerous other benefits of deep relaxation have been documented over the past 20 years. These include

- Reduction of generalized anxiety. Many people have found that regular practice also reduces the frequency and severity of panic attacks.

- Preventing stress from becoming cumulative. Unabated stress tends to build up over time. Entering into a state of physiological quiescence once a day gives your body the opportunity to recover from the effects of stress. Even sleep can fail to break the cumulative stress cycle unless you've given yourself permission to deeply relax while awake.

- Increased energy level and productivity. (When under stress, you may work against yourself and become less efficient.)

- Improved concentration and memory. Regular practice of deep relaxation tends to increase your ability to focus and keeps your mind from "racing."

- Reduction of insomnia and fatigue. Learning to relax leads to sleep that is deeper and sounder.

- Prevention and/or reduction of psychosomatic disorders such as hypertension, migraines, headaches, asthma, ulcers, and so on.

- Increased self-confidence and reduced self-blame. For many people, stress and excessive self-criticism or feelings of inadequacy go hand in hand. You can perform better, as well as feel better, when you are relaxed.

- Increased availability of feelings. Muscle tension is one of the chief impediments to an awareness of your feelings.

How can you achieve a state of deep relaxation? Some of the more common methods include

1. Abdominal breathing

2. Progressive muscle relaxation

3. Visualizing a peaceful scene

4. Meditation

5. Guided imagery

6. Autogenic training

7. Biofeedback

8. Sensory deprivation

For our purposes here we will focus on the first four. Guided imagery or visualization is the subject of another chapter.

Abdominal Breathing

Your breathing directly reflects the level of tension you carry in your body. Under tension, your breathing usually becomes shallow and rapid, and occurs high in the chest. When relaxed, you breathe more fully, more deeply, and from your abdomen. It's difficult to be tense and to breathe from your abdomen at the same time.

Some of the benefits of abdominal breathing include

- Increased oxygen supply to the brain and musculature.

- Stimulation of the parasympathetic nervous system. This branch of your autonomic nervous system promotes a state of calmness and quiescence. It works in a fashion exactly opposite to the sympathetic branch of your nervous system, which stimulates a state of emotional arousal and the very physiological reactions underlying a panic attack.

- Greater feelings of connectedness between mind and body. Anxiety and worry tend to keep you "up in your head." A few minutes of deep abdominal breathing will help bring you down into your whole body.

- More efficient excretion of bodily toxins. Many toxic substances in the body are excreted through the lungs.

- Improved concentration. If your mind is racing, it's difficult to focus your attention. Abdominal breathing will help to quiet your mind.

- Abdominal breathing by itself can trigger a relaxation response.

If you suffer from phobias, panic, or other anxiety disorders, you will tend to have one or both of two types of problems with breathing. Either

1. You breathe too high up in your chest and your breathing is shallow or,

2. You tend to hyperventilate, breathing out too much carbon dioxide relative to the amount of oxygen carried in your bloodstream. Shallow, chest-level breathing, when rapid, can lead to hyperventilation. Hyperventilation, in turn, can cause physical symptoms very similar to those associated with panic attacks.

These two types of breathing are discussed in greater detail below.

Shallow, Chest-Level Breathing

Studies have found differences in the breathing patterns of anxious and shy people as opposed to those who are more relaxed and outgoing. People who are fearful and shy tend to breathe in a shallow fashion from their chest, while those who are more extroverted and relaxed breathe more slowly, deeply, and from their abdomens.

Before reading on, take a minute to notice how you are breathing right now. Is your breath slow or rapid? Deep or shallow? Does it center around a point high in your chest or down in your abdomen? You might also notice changes in your breathing pattern under stress versus when you are more relaxed.

If you find that your breathing is shallow and high in your chest, don't despair. It's quite possible to retrain yourself to breathe more deeply and from your abdomen. Practicing abdominal breathing (to be described below) on a regular basis will gradually help you to shift the center of your breath downward from your chest. Regular practice of full abdominal breathing will also increase your lung capacity, helping you to breathe more deeply. A program of vigorous, aerobic exercise can also be helpful.

Hyperventilation Syndrome

If you breathe from your chest, you may tend to overbreathe, exhaling excess carbon dioxide in relation to the amount of oxygen in your bloodstream. You may also tend to breathe through your mouth. The result is a cluster of symptoms, including rapid heartbeat, dizziness, and tingly sensations that are so similar to the symptoms of panic that they can be indistinguishable. Some of the physiological changes brought on by hyperventilation include

- Increased alkalinity of nerve cells, which causes them to be more excitable. The result is that you feel *nervous* and *jittery*.

- Decreased carbon dioxide in the blood, which can cause your *heart to pump harder and faster* as well as making *lights* seem *brighter* and *sounds louder*.

- Increased constriction of blood vessels in your brain, which can cause feelings of *dizziness*, *disorientation*, and even a *sense of unreality* or *separateness from your body*.

All these symptoms may be interpreted as a developing panic attack. As soon as you start responding to these bodily changes with panic-evoking mental statements to yourself such as, "I'm losing control!" or "What's happening to me?" *you actually do panic*. Symptoms that initially only mimicked panic set off a reaction that leads to genuine panic. Hyperventilation can 1) either cause physical sensations that lead you to panic *or* 2) it can contribute to an ongoing panic attack by aggravating unpleasant physical symptoms.

If you suspect that you are subject to hyperventilation, you might notice whether you habitually breathe shallowly from your chest and through your mouth. Notice also, when you're frightened, whether you tend to hold your breath or breathe very shallowly and quickly. The experience of tingling or numb sensations, particularly in your arms or legs, is also a sign of hyperventilation. If any of these characteristics seem to apply to you, hyperventilation may play a role in either instigating or aggravating your panic reactions or anxiety.

The traditional cure for acute hyperventilation symptoms is to breathe into a paper bag. This technique causes you to breathe in carbon dioxide, restoring the normal balance of oxygen to carbon dioxide in your bloodstream. It is a method that works. Equally effective in reducing symptoms of hyperventilation are the abdominal breathing and calming breath exercises described below. Both of them help you to slow your breathing down, which effectively reduces your intake of oxygen and brings the ratio of oxygen to carbon dioxide back into balance.

If you can recognize the symptoms of hyperventilation for what they are, and then learn to curtail them by deliberately slowing your breathing, you needn't react to them with panic.

The two exercises described below can help you change your breathing pattern. By practicing them, you can achieve a state of deep relaxation in a short period of time. Just three minutes of practicing abdominal breathing or the calming breath exercise will usually induce a deep state of relaxation. Many people have successfully used one or the other technique to abort a panic attack when they felt the first signs of anxiety coming on. The techniques are also very helpful in diminishing anticipatory anxiety you may experience in advance of facing a phobic situation. While the techniques of progressive muscle relaxation and meditation described later in this chapter take up to twenty minutes to achieve their effects, the following two methods can produce a moderate to deep level of relaxation in just three to five minutes.

Abdominal Breathing Exercise

1. Note the level of tension you're feeling. Then place one hand on your abdomen right beneath your rib cage.

2. Inhale slowly and deeply through your nose into the "bottom" of your lungs—in other words, send the air as low down as you can. If you're breathing from your abdomen, your hand should actually *rise*. Your chest should move only slightly while your abdomen expands. (In abdominal breathing, the *diaphragm*—the muscle that separates the lung cavity from the abdominal cavity—moves downward. In so doing it causes the muscles surrounding the abdominal cavity to push outward.)

3. When you've taken in a full breath, pause for a moment and then exhale slowly through your nose or mouth, depending on your preference. Be sure to exhale fully. *As you exhale, allow your whole body to just let go* (you might visualize your arms and legs going loose and limp like a rag doll).

4. Do ten slow, full abdominal breaths. Try to keep your breathing *smooth* and *regular*, without gulping in a big breath or letting your breath out all at once. It will help to slow down your breathing if you slowly count to four on the inhale (1-2-3-4) and then slowly count to four on the exhale. Remember to pause briefly at the end of each inhalation. Count from ten down to one counting backwards one number with each *exhalation*. The process should go like this:
   Slow inhale … Pause … Slow exhale (count "ten")
   Slow inhale … Pause … Slow exhale (count "nine")
   Slow inhale … Pause … Slow exhale (count "eight")
   and so on down to one. If you start to feel light-headed while practicing abdominal breathing, stop for 15-20 seconds, and then start again.

5. Extend the exercise if you wish by doing two or three "sets" of abdominal breaths, remembering to count backwards from ten to one for each set (each exhalation counts as one number). *Five full minutes* of abdominal breathing will have a pronounced effect in reducing anxiety or early symptoms of panic.

   Some people prefer to count from one to ten instead. Feel free to do this if it suits you.

Calming Breath Exercise*

The *Calming Breath Exercise* was adapted from the ancient discipline of yoga. It is a very efficient technique for achieving a deep state of relaxation quickly.

1. Breathing from your abdomen, inhale through your nose slowly to a count of five (count slowly "one … two … three … four … five" as you inhale).

2. Pause and hold your breath to a count of five.

---

*The name *Calming Breath* was taken from an exercise by that name developed by Reid Wilson in *Don't Panic: Taking Control of Anxiety Attacks*. The steps presented here differ significantly from Wilson's exercise.

3. Exhale slowly, through your nose or mouth, to a count of five (or more if it takes you longer). Be sure to exhale fully.

4. When you've exhaled completely, take two breaths in your normal rhythm, then repeat steps 1 through 3 in the cycle above.

5. Keep up the exercise for at least three to five minutes. This should involve going through *at least* ten cycles of in-five, hold-five, out-five. As you continue the exercise, you may notice that you can count higher, or count higher when you exhale than when you inhale. Allow these variations in your counting to occur if they do, and just continue with the exercise for up to five minutes. Remember to take two normal breaths between each cycle. If you start to feel light-headed while practicing this exercise, stop for thirty seconds and then start again.

6. Throughout the exercise, keep your breathing *smooth* and *regular*, without gulping in breaths or breathing out suddenly.

7. Optional: Each time you exhale, you may wish to say "relax," "calm," "let go," or any other relaxing word or phrase silently to yourself. Allow your whole body to let go as you do this. If you keep this up each time you practice, eventually just saying your relaxing word by itself will bring on a mild state of relaxation.

The calming breath exercise can be a potent technique for halting the momentum of a panic reaction when the first signs of anxiety come on. It is also useful in reducing symptoms of hyperventilation.

Practice Exercise

Practice the *Abdominal Breathing* or *Calming Breath Exercise* for *five minutes every day for at least two weeks*. If possible, find a regular time each day to do this so that your breathing exercise becomes a habit. With practice you can learn in a short period of time to "damp down" the physiological reactions underlying anxiety and panic.

Once you feel you've gained some mastery in the use of either technique, apply it when you feel stressed, anxious, or when you experience the onset of panic symptoms. By extending your practice of either breathing exercise to a month or longer, you will begin to retrain yourself to breathe from your abdomen. The more you can shift the center of your breathing from your chest to your abdomen, the more consistently you will feel relaxed on an ongoing basis.

Progressive Muscle Relaxation

Progressive muscle relaxation is a systematic technique for achieving a deep state of relaxation. It was developed by Dr. Edmund Jacobson more than fifty years ago. Dr. Jacobson discovered that a muscle could be relaxed by first tensing it for a few seconds and then releasing it. Tensing and releasing various muscle groups throughout the body produces a deep state of relaxation, which Dr. Jacobson found capable of relieving a variety of conditions, from high blood pressure to ulcerative colitis.

In his original book, *Progressive Relaxation*, Dr. Jacobson developed a series of 200 different muscle relaxation exercises and a training program that took months to complete. More recently the system has been abbreviated to 15-20 basic exercises, which have been found to be just as effective, if practiced regularly, as the original more elaborate system.

Progressive muscle relaxation is especially helpful for people whose anxiety is strongly associated with muscle tension. This is what often leads you to say that you are "uptight" or "tense." You may experience chronic tightness in your shoulders and neck, which can be effectively relieved by practicing progressive muscle relaxation. Other symptoms that respond well to progressive muscle relaxation include tension headaches, backaches, tightness in the jaw, tightness around the eyes, muscle spasms, high blood pressure, and insomnia. If you are troubled by racing thoughts, you may find that systematically relaxing your muscles tends to help slow down your mind. Dr. Jacobson himself once said, "An anxious mind cannot exist in a relaxed body."

The immediate effects of progressive muscle relaxation include all the benefits of the relaxation response described at the beginning of this chapter. Long-term effects of *regular* practice of progressive muscle relaxation include

- A decrease in generalized anxiety

- A decrease in anticipatory anxiety related to phobias

- Reduction in the frequency and duration of panic attacks

- Improved ability to face phobic situations through graded exposure

- Improved concentration

- An increased sense of control over moods

- Increased self-esteem

- Increased spontaneity and creativity

These long-term benefits are sometimes called *generalization effects*: the relaxation experienced during daily sessions tends, after a month or two, to *generalize* to the rest of the day. The *regular* practice of progressive muscle relaxation can go a long way toward helping you to better manage your anxiety, face your fears, overcome panic, and feel better all around.

There are no contraindications for progressive muscle relaxation unless the muscle groups to be tensed and relaxed have been injured. If you take tranquilizers, you may find that regular practice of progressive muscle relaxation will enable you to lower your dosage.

Guidelines for Practicing Progressive Muscle Relaxation (or Any Form of Deep Relaxation)

The following guidelines will help you make the most use of progressive muscle relaxation. They are also applicable to *any* form of deep relaxation you undertake to practice regularly, including self-hypnosis, guided visualization, and meditation.

1. Practice at least *20 minutes per day*. Two 20-minute periods are preferable. Once a day is mandatory for obtaining generalization effects. (You may want to begin your practice with 30-minute periods. As you gain skill in relaxation technique, you will find that the amount of time you need to experience the relaxation response will decrease.)

2. Find a *quiet location* to practice where you won't be distracted. Don't permit the phone to ring while you're practicing. Use a fan or air conditioner to blot out background noise if necessary.

3. Practice at *regular times*. On awakening, before retiring, or before meals are generally the best times. A consistent daily relaxation routine will increase the likelihood of generalization effects.

4. Practice on an *empty stomach*. Food digestion after meals will tend to disrupt deep relaxation.

5. Assume a *comfortable position*. Your entire body, including your head, should be supported. Lying down on a sofa or bed or sitting in a reclining chair are two ways of supporting your body most completely. (When lying down, you may want to place a pillow beneath your knees for further support.) Sitting up is preferable to lying down if you are feeling tired and sleepy. It's advantageous to experience the full depth of the relaxation response consciously without going to sleep.

6. *Loosen any tight garments* and take off shoes, watch, glasses, contact lenses, jewelry, and so on.

7. Make a decision not to worry about anything. Give yourself permission to put aside the concerns of the day. Allow taking care of yourself and having peace of mind to take precedence over any of your worries. (Success with relaxation depends on giving peace of mind high priority in your overall scheme of values.)

8. Assume a *passive, detached attitude*. This is probably the most important element. You want to adopt a "let it happen" attitude and be free of any worry about how well you are performing the technique. Do not *try* to relax. Do not *try* to control your body. Do not judge your performance. The point is to let go.

Progressive Muscle Relaxation Technique

Progressive muscle relaxation involves tensing and relaxing, in succession, sixteen different muscle groups of the body. The idea is to tense each muscle group hard (not so hard that you strain, however) for about 10 seconds, and then to let go of it suddenly. You then give yourself 15-20 seconds to relax, noticing how the muscle group feels when relaxed in contrast to how it felt when tensed, before going on to the next group of muscles. You might also say to yourself "I am relaxing," "Letting go," "Let the tension flow away," or any other relaxing phrase during each relaxation period between successive muscle groups. Throughout the exercise, maintain your focus on your muscles. When your attention wanders, bring it back to the particular muscle group you're working on. The guidelines below describe progressive muscle relaxation in detail:

- Make sure you are in a setting that is quiet and comfortable. Observe the guidelines for practicing relaxation that were previously described.

- When you tense a particular muscle group, do so vigorously, without straining, for 7-10 seconds. You may want to count "one-thousand-one," "one-thousand-two," and so on, as a way of marking off seconds.

- Concentrate on what is happening. Feel the buildup of tension in each particular muscle group. It is often helpful to visualize the particular muscle group being tensed.

- When you release the muscles, do so abruptly, and then relax, enjoying the sudden feeling of limpness. Allow the relaxation to develop for at least 15-20 seconds before going on to the next group of muscles.

- Allow all the *other* muscles in your body to remain relaxed, as far as possible, while working on a particular muscle group.

- Tense and relax each muscle group once. But if a particular area feels especially tight, you can tense and relax it two or three times, waiting about 20 seconds between each cycle.

Once you are comfortably supported in a quiet place, follow the detailed instructions below:

1. To begin, take three deep abdominal breaths, exhaling slowly each time. As you exhale, imagine that tension throughout your body begins to flow away.

2. Clench your fists. Hold for 7-10 seconds and then release for 15-20 seconds. *Use these same time intervals for all other muscle groups.*

3. Tighten your biceps by drawing your forearms up toward your shoulders and "making a muscle" with both arms. Hold ... and then relax.

4. Tighten your *triceps*—the muscles on the undersides of your upper arms—by extending your arms out straight and locking your elbows. Hold ... and then relax.

5. Tense the muscles in your forehead by raising your eyebrows as far as you can. Hold ... and then relax. Imagine your forehead muscles becoming smooth and limp as they relax.

6. Tense the muscles around your eyes by clenching your eyelids tightly shut. Hold ... and then relax. Imagine sensations of deep relaxation spreading all around the area of your eyes.

7. Tighten your jaws by opening your mouth so widely that you stretch the muscles around the hinges of your jaw. Hold ... and then relax. Let your lips part and allow your jaw to hang loose.

8. Tighten the muscles in the back of your neck by pulling your head way back, as if you were going to touch your head to your back (be gentle with this muscle group to avoid injury). Focus only on tensing the muscles in your neck. Hold ... and then relax. Since this area is often especially tight, it's good to do the tense-relax cycle twice.

9. Take a few deep breaths and tune in to the weight of your head sinking into whatever surface it is resting on.

10. Tighten your shoulders by raising them up as if you were going to touch your ears. Hold ... and then relax.

11. Tighten the muscles around your shoulder blades by pushing your shoulder blades back as if you were going to touch them together. Hold the tension in your shoulder blades ... and then relax. Since this area is often especially tense, you might repeat the tense-relax sequence twice.

12. Tighten the muscles of your chest by taking in a deep breath. Hold for up to 10 seconds ... and then release slowly. Imagine any excess tension in your chest flowing away with the exhalation.

13. Tighten your stomach muscles by sucking your stomach in. Hold ... and then release. Imagine a wave of relaxation spreading through your abdomen.

14. Tighten your lower back by arching it up. (You can omit this exercise if you have lower back pain.) Hold ... and then relax.

15. Tighten your buttocks by pulling them together. Hold ... and then relax. Imagine the muscles in your hips going loose and limp.

16. Squeeze the muscles in your thighs all the way down to your knees. You will probably have to tighten your hips along with your thighs, since the thigh muscles attach at the pelvis. Hold ... and then relax. Feel your thigh muscles smoothing out and relaxing completely.

17. Tighten your calf muscles by pulling your toes toward you (flex carefully to avoid cramps). Hold ... and then relax.

18. Tighten your feet by curling your toes downward. Hold ... and then relax.

19. Mentally scan your body for any residual tension. If a particular area remains tense, repeat one or two tense-relax cycles for that group of muscles.

20. Now imagine a wave of relaxation slowly spreading throughout your body, starting at your head and gradually penetrating every muscle group all the way down to your toes.

The entire progressive muscle relaxation sequence should take you 20-30 minutes the first time. With practice you may decrease the time needed to 15-20 minutes. You might want to record the above exercises on an audio cassette to expedite your early practice sessions. Or you may wish to obtain a professionally made tape of the progressive muscle relaxation exercise. (See Appendix 4.) Some people always prefer to use a tape, while others have the exercises so well learned after a few weeks of practice that they prefer doing them from memory.

Remember—regular practice of progressive muscle relaxation once a day will produce a significant reduction in your overall level of anxiety. It will also reduce the frequency and intensity of panic attacks. Finally, regular practice will reduce anticipatory anxiety that may arise in the course of systematically exposing yourself to phobic situations (see Chapters 7 and 8).

The Peaceful Scene

After completing progressive muscle relaxation, it's helpful to visualize yourself in the midst of a peaceful scene. Progressive muscle relaxation addresses particular groups of muscles; imagining yourself in a very peaceful setting can give you a global sense of relaxation that frees you from anxious thoughts. The peaceful scene can be a quiet beach, a stream in the mountains, or a calm lake. Or it can be your bedroom or a cozy fireside on a cold winter night. Don't restrict yourself to reality: you can imagine, if you want to, floating on a cloud or flying on a magic carpet. The important thing is to visualize the scene in sufficient detail so that it completely absorbs your attention. Allowing yourself to be absorbed in a peaceful scene will deepen your state of relaxation, giving you actual physiological results. Your muscular tension lessens, your heart rate slows down, your breathing deepens, your capillaries open up and warm your hands and feet, and so on. A relaxing visualization constitutes a light form of self-hypnosis.

Here are two examples of peaceful scenes. (See also the "Beach" and "Forest" Visualizations in Chapter 12).

> *You're walking along a beautiful, deserted beach. You are barefoot and can feel the firm white sand beneath your feet as you walk along the margin of the sea. You can hear the sound of the surf as the waves ebb and flow. The sound is hypnotic, relaxing you more and more. The water is a beautiful turquoise blue flecked with whitecaps far out where the waves are cresting. Near the horizon you can see a small sailboat gliding smoothly along. The sound of the waves breaking on the shore lulls you deeper and deeper into relaxation. You draw in the fresh, salty smell of the air with each breath. Your skin glows with the warmth of the sun. You can feel a gentle breeze against your cheek and ruffling your hair. Taking in the whole scene, you feel very calm and at ease.*

> *You're snuggled in your sleeping bag. Daylight is breaking in the forest. You can feel the rays of the sun beginning to warm your face. The dawn sky stretches above you in pastel shades of pink and orange. You can smell the fresh, piney fragrance of the surrounding woods. Nearby you can hear the rushing waters of a mountain stream. The crisp, cool morning air is refreshing and invigorating. You're feeling very cozy, comfortable, and secure.*

Note that these scenes are described in language that appeals to the senses of sight, hearing, touch, and smell. Using multisensory words increases the power of the scene to compel you, enabling you to experience it as if you were actually there. The whole point of imagining a peaceful scene is to transport yourself from your normal state of restless thinking into an altered state of deep relaxation.

Use a separate sheet of paper to design your own peaceful scene. Be sure to describe it in vivid detail, appealing to as many senses as possible. It may help to answer the following questions: What does the scene look like? What colors are prominent? What sounds are present? What time of day is it? What is the temperature? What are you touching or in physical contact with in the scene? What does the air smell like? Are you alone or with somebody else?

Just as with progressive muscle relaxation, you may wish to record your peaceful scene on tape so that you can conjure it up without effort. You might want to record your scene on the same tape following the instructions for progressive muscle relaxation.

Use the script below to introduce your peaceful scene when you make your own recording:

… Just think of relaxing every muscle in your body, from the top of your head to the tips of your toes.

… As you exhale, imagine releasing any remaining tension from your body, mind, or thoughts … just let that stress go.

… And with every breath you inhale, feel your body drifting down deeper … down deeper into total relaxation.

… And now imagine going to your peaceful scene…. Imagine your special place as vividly as possible, as if you were really there. (Insert your peaceful scene.)

… You are very comfortable in your beautiful place, and there is no one to disturb you…. This is the most peaceful place in the world for you…. Just imagine yourself there, feeling a sense of peace flow through you and a sense of well-being. Enjoy these positive feelings … Allow them to grow stronger and stronger.

… And remember, anytime you wish, you can return to this special place by just taking time to relax.

… These peaceful and positive feelings of relaxation can grow stronger and stronger each time you choose to relax.

Once you have imagined your own ideal peaceful scene, practice returning to it every time you do progressive muscle relaxation, deep breathing, or any other relaxation technique. This will help to reinforce the scene in your mind. After a while it will be so solidly established that you will be able to return to it on the spur of the moment—whenever you wish to calm yourself and turn off anxious thinking. This technique is one of the quickest and most effective tools you can use to counter ongoing anxiety or stress during the day. Fantasizing a peaceful scene is also an important part of imagery desensitization, a process for overcoming phobias described in a later chapter.

Meditation

From the time we awaken until we go to bed, most of us are engaged almost continually in external activities. We tend to be only minimally in touch with our inner feelings and awareness. Even when we withdraw our senses and are falling asleep at night, we usually experience a melange of memories, fantasies, thoughts, and feelings related to the preceding or coming day. Rarely do we get behind all of this and experience ourselves "just being" in the present moment. For many people in Western society, in fact, the idea of doing nothing or "just being" is difficult to comprehend.

Meditation can bring you to this place of "just being." It is the one process that allows you to completely stop, let go of thoughts about the immediate past or future, and simply focus on being in the here and now. It can be a helpful discipline to practice when you find that your mind is racing or excessively busy.

Meditation practices have been around for at least 5,000 years. Traditionally, the purposes and benefits of meditation have been spiritual in nature: becoming one with

God, attaining enlightenment, achieving selflessness. While many people still practice meditation today for spiritual purposes, just as many practice meditation apart from any religious framework for personal growth or for the simple purpose of relaxing.

Meditation was popularized in the United States in the mid-sixties as Transcendental Meditation or TM. In Transcendental Meditation, an instructor selects a Sanskrit *mantra* (a word or sound) for you, such as "Om Shanti" or "So-Hum." You are then instructed to repeat the sound mentally while sitting in a quiet place. You must concentrate completely—but unforcefully—on the mantra while letting any distractions just pass through your mind.

In the 1970s Herbert Benson did research on Transcendental Meditation, which he published in his well-known book, *The Relaxation Response*. Benson developed his own version of meditation, which involved mentally repeating the word *one* with each exhalation of breath. He documented a number of physiological effects of meditation, including

- A decrease in heart rate

- A decrease in blood pressure

- A decrease in oxygen consumption

- A decrease in metabolic rate

- A decrease in the concentration of lactic acid in the blood (associated with anxiety reduction)

- An increase in forearm blood flow and hand temperature

- An increase in electrical resistance of the skin (associated with deep relaxation)

- An increase in alpha brain wave activity

Benson also established that the positive benefits of meditation are not exclusive to TM, and that an individually selected mantra is unnecessary. His own "respiratory-one" method achieved the same physiological effects as Transcendental Meditation.

Since the time of Benson's work, considerable research on the long-term benefits of meditation has established that it *can alter personality traits, behaviors*, and *attitudes*. If you suffer from anxiety disorders, meditation can break up obsessional mental patterns and help you restructure your thoughts more productively. (Regular meditation has an even greater impact on repetitive mental patterns than the practice of progressive muscle relaxation, which is directed more to relieving muscle tension.)

Meditation has repeatedly been found to reduce chronic anxiety. Often the dosage of tranquilizers can be reduced if you are meditating every day. Other long-range benefits include

- Sharpened alertness

- Increased energy level and productivity

- Decreased self-criticism

- Increased *objectivity* (the capacity to view situations nonjudgmentally)

- Decreased dependence on alcohol or recreational drugs

- Increased accessibility of emotions
- Heightened self-esteem and sense of identity

Some Precautions

Meditating can release emotional material that may be difficult to handle for someone who has a history of mental illness, especially psychosis. Meditation may also enhance the action of certain drugs in some individuals. Have your doctor carefully monitor your dosage of antianxiety or antihypertensive medications if you are regularly practicing meditation.

Guidelines for Practicing Meditation

1. Find a quiet environment. Do what you can to reduce external noise. If this is not completely possible, play a record or tape of soft, instrumental sounds, or sounds from nature. The sound of ocean waves makes a good background.

2. Reduce muscle tension. If you're feeling tense, spend some time, no more than 10 minutes, relaxing your muscles. Progressive muscle relaxation of the upper portion of the body—your head, neck, shoulders—is often helpful. The following sequence of head and neck exercises may also be helpful (some progressive muscle relaxation in addition to this sequence is probably optimal).

   - Slowly touch your chin to your chest three times
   - Bend your head back to gently stretch the back of your neck three times
   - Bend your head over to your right shoulder three times
   - Bend your head over to your left shoulder three times
   - Slowly rotate your head clockwise for three complete rotations
   - Slowly rotate your head counterclockwise for three complete rotations

3. Sit properly.
   Eastern Style: Sit cross-legged on the floor with a cushion or pillow supporting your buttocks. Rest your hands on your thighs. Lean slightly forward so that some of your weight is supported by your thighs as well as your buttocks.
   Western Style (preferred by most Americans): Sit in a comfortable, straight-backed chair, with your feet on the floor and legs uncrossed, hands on your thighs.
   In either position keep your back and neck *straight* without straining to do so. Do not assume a tight, inflexible posture. If you need to scratch or move, do so. In general, do not lie down or support your head, this will tend to promote sleep.

4. Set aside 20-30 minutes for meditation (beginners might wish to start out with 5-10 minutes). You may wish to set a timer (within reach) or run a background tape that is 20-30 minutes long so that you'll know when you're done. If having a clock or watch available to look at makes you more comfortable, it's O.K. After you have practiced 20-30 minutes per day for several weeks, you may wish to try longer periods of meditation up to an hour.

5. Make it a regular practice to meditate every day. Even if you meditate for only five minutes, it's important to do it every day. It's ideal if you can find a set time to practice meditating.

6. Meditating is easier if you don't do it on a full stomach or when you are tired.

7. Select a focus for your attention. The most common devices are your own breathing cycle or a mantra (see below). Alternatives include a physical object—such as a picture or candle flame.

8. Assume a nonjudgmental, passive attitude.

   • Concentrate on whatever you've chosen as an object of meditation but don't force or strain yourself to do so. If it is an internal image, you may want to close your eyes. When thoughts or daydreams come to your mind, attempt neither to hold on to them or to reject them too vigorously. Just allow them to come and go. This process might be compared to watching leaves float by on the surface of a stream.

   • Every time your attention wanders from your object of focus, gently bring it back again. Distractions are *normal*—don't judge yourself when they come up.

   • *Don't dwell on the outcome of your meditation.* Don't trouble yourself with such doubts as whether you will be able to go deep enough in the remaining time. Refrain from judging your experience. There's no need to wonder how well you're doing during the meditation. Some meditations will feel good, some mediocre, and sometimes it may be difficult to meditate at all.

   • The more you let go and refrain from trying to do anything (other than gently guiding your attention back to your object of focus), the deeper your experience of the meditation will be.

Two Common Forms of Meditation

Using a Mantra

1. Select a word to focus on.

   • A neutral word such as "one."

   • A Sanskrit mantra such as "Om Shanti," "Sri Ram," "So-Hum."

   • A word or phrase that has some special significance within your personal belief system. In his recent book, *Beyond the Relaxation Response*, Benson describes how a word or phrase of special personal significance (such as, "I am at peace," "Let go, let God") deepens the effects of meditation.

2. Repeat this word or phrase, ideally on each exhalation.

3. As any thoughts come to mind, just let them pass over and through you and gently bring your attention back to the repetitive word or phrase.

Counting Breaths

1. As you sit quietly, focus on the inflow and outflow of your breath. Each time you breathe out, count the breath. You can count up to 10 and start over again, or

keep counting as high as you like, or you can use Benson's method of repeating "one" on each exhalation.

2. Each time your focus wanders, bring it back to your breathing and counting. If you get caught in an internal monologue or fantasy, don't worry about it or judge yourself. Just relax and return to the count again.

3. If you lose track of the count, start over at 1 or at a round number like 50 or 100.

4. After practicing breath-counting meditation for a while, you may want to let go of the counting and just focus on the inflow and outflow of your breathing.

Whichever form of meditation you try, you might want to start out with short periods of 5-10 minutes and gradually lengthen them to 20-30 minutes over a period of two to three weeks. Most people find that it takes persistent and disciplined effort over a period of several months to become proficient at meditating. Even though meditation is the most demanding of relaxation techniques to learn, it is for many people the most rewarding. Research has found that among all relaxation techniques, meditation is the one people are most likely to persist in doing regularly.

If you are truly interested in establishing a meditation practice, I recommend that you find a class, group, or teacher to study with. This will make it easier for you to stick with your practice.

Some Common Obstacles to a Daily Program of Deep Relaxation

There are many difficulties you may encounter in trying to practice any form of deep relaxation on a regular basis. You may start out enthusiastically, setting aside time to practice every day. Yet after a week or so, you may find yourself "forgetting" to practice. In a fast-paced society that rewards us for speed, efficiency, and productivity, it's difficult to stop everything and simply relax for 20-30 minutes. We are so used to "doing" that it may seem like a chore just to "be."

If you find that you've broken your personal commitment to practice deep relaxation on a daily basis, take time to examine very carefully what you are *saying to yourself*—what excuses you make—on those days when you don't relax. If you just don't "feel" like relaxing, there is usually some more specific reason for feeling that way that can be found by examining what you're telling yourself.

Some common excuses for not practicing include

- "I don't have time to relax."
  What this usually means is that you haven't given relaxation sufficient priority among all the other activities you've crowded into your schedule.

- "I don't have any place to relax."
  Try creating one. You might let the kids watch their favorite TV show or play with their favorite toys while you go into another room, with instructions not to interrupt you. If you and the kids have only one room, or if they are too young to respect your privacy, then you need to practice at a time when they are out of the house or asleep. The same goes for a demanding spouse.

- "Relaxation exercises seem too slow or boring."
  If you're telling yourself this, it's a good indication that you are too speeded up, too frantically pushing yourself through life. Slow down—it's good for you.

- "I feel more anxious when I relax."
  In some individuals, deep relaxation may bring up suppressed feelings, which are often accompanied by sensations of anxiety. If this happens to you, be sure to start off with relatively short periods of relaxation, working up gradually to longer periods. The moment you start feeling any anxiety, simply open your eyes and stop whatever procedure you're practicing until you feel better. With time and patience this particular problem should diminish. If it doesn't, it would be helpful to consult a professional therapist skilled in treating anxiety disorders to assist you in desensitizing yourself to relaxation.

- "I just don't have the discipline."
  Often this means that you haven't persisted with practicing relaxation long enough to internalize it as a habit. You may have made similar statements to yourself in the past when you were attempting to acquire a new behavior. Brushing your teeth didn't come naturally when you first started. It took some time and diligence to reach the point where it became an honored habit. If you expend the effort to practice deep relaxation five to seven days per week for at least one month, it will likely become so ingrained that you won't need to think about doing it anymore— you'll just do it automatically.

Practicing deep relaxation is more than learning a technique: it involves making a basic shift in your attitude and lifestyle. It requires a willingness to give priority to your health and internal peace of mind over the other pressing claims of productivity, accomplishment, money, or status.

Down Time and Time Management

This chapter on relaxation would not be complete without discussion of the concepts of down time and time management. In fact, fully appreciating and implementing these ideas in your life is *the most important thing you can do if you would like to achieve a more relaxed lifestyle.*

You can practice deep muscle relaxation or meditation every day and feel a pleasant respite for 20-30 minutes. These practices can definitely enhance your overall feeling of relaxation if you practice them regularly. Yet if you're on a treadmill the rest of the time, with too much to get done and no breaks in your schedule, you're likely to remain under stress, prone to chronic anxiety or panic attacks, and ultimately headed toward burnout.

Down Time

Down time is exactly what it sounds like—*time out f*rom work or other responsibilities to give yourself an opportunity to rest and replenish your energy. Without periods of down time, any stress you experience while dealing with work or other responsibilities tends to become *cumulative*. It keeps building without any remission. You may tend to keep pushing yourself until finally you drop from exhaustion or experience an aggravation of your anxiety or phobias. Sleep at night doesn't really count as down time. If you go to bed feeling stressed, you may sleep for eight hours and still wake up feeling tense, tired, and stressed. Down time needs to be scheduled apart from sleep during the day. Its primary purpose is simply to allow a break in the stress cycle—to prevent stress you're experiencing from becoming cumulative. I recommend to my clients that they give themselves the following periods of down time:

> 1 hour per day
> 1 day per week
> 1 week out of every 12-16 weeks

If you don't have four weeks of paid vacation per year, then be willing to take time off without pay. During these periods of down time, you disengage from any task you consider work, put aside all responsibilities, and don't answer the phone unless it's someone you would enjoy hearing from.

There are three kinds of down time, each of which has an important place in developing a more relaxed lifestyle: 1) rest time, 2) recreation time, and 3) relationship time. It's important that you provide yourself enough down time so that you have time for all three. Often recreation and relationship time can be combined. However, it's important to use rest time for just that—and nothing else.

Rest time is time when you set aside all activities and just allow yourself to *be*. You stop action and let yourself fully rest. Rest time might involve lying on the couch and doing nothing, quietly meditating, sitting in your recliner and listening to peaceful music, soaking in a jacuzzi, or taking a catnap in the middle of the workday. The key to rest time is that it is fundamentally passive—you allow yourself to stop doing and accomplishing and just *be*. Contemporary society encourages each of us to be productive and always accomplish more and more every moment of the waking day. Rest time is a needed counterpoint. When you're under stress, one hour of rest time per day, separate from the time you sleep, is optimal.

Recreation time involves engaging in activities that help to "re-create" you, that is, serve to replenish your energy. Recreation time brightens and uplifts your spirits. In essence, it is doing anything that you experience as fun or play. Examples of such activities might include puttering in the garden, reading a novel, seeing a special movie, going on a hike, playing volleyball, taking a short trip, baking a loaf of bread, or fishing. Recreation time can be done during the work week and is most important to have on your days off from work. Such time can be spent either alone or with someone else in which case it overlaps with the third type of down time.

Relationship time is time when you put aside your private goals and responsibilities in order to enjoy being with another person—or, in some cases, with several people. The focus of relationship time is to honor your relationship with your partner, children, extended family members, friends, pets, and so on, and forget about your individual pursuits for a while. If you have a family, relationship time needs to be allocated equitably between time alone with your spouse, time alone with your children, and time when the entire family gets together. If you're single with a partner, time needs to be judiciously allocated between time with your partner and time with friends.

When you slow down and make time to be with others, you're less likely to neglect your basic needs for intimacy, touching, affection, validation, support, and so on (see the section called "Your Basic Needs" in Chapter 15). Meeting these basic needs is absolutely vital to your well-being. Without sufficient time devoted to important relationships, you will surely suffer—and the people you most care about are bound to as well.

How can you allow for more down time (all three kinds) in your life? An important prerequisite is to get past workaholism. Workaholism is an addictive disorder in which work is the *only* thing that gives you a sense of inner fulfillment and self-worth. You devote all your time and energy to work, neglecting both your physical and your emotional needs. Workaholism describes an unbalanced way of life which often leads first to chronic stress, then to burnout, and ultimately to serious illness.

If you're a workaholic, it's possible to *learn* to enjoy nonwork aspects of your life, as discussed above and achieve a more balanced approach in general. Deliberately making time for rest, recreation, and relationships may be difficult at first, but tends to get easier, and to become self-rewarding, as time goes on.

Another important step is simply *to be willing to do less.* That is, you literally reduce the number of tasks and responsibilities you handle in any given day. In some cases this may involve changing jobs; in others, merely restructuring how you allocate time for work versus rest and relaxation. For some individuals, this translates to a fundamental decision to make earning money less important and a simpler, more balanced lifestyle more important. Before you think about leaving your present job, however, consider how you can shift your values in the direction of placing more emphasis on the *process* of life ("how" you live) as opposed to accomplishments and productivity ("what" you actually do) within your current life situation.

Exercise

Take some time to reflect on how you might allocate more time for each of the three types of down time discussed. Write your answers in the space provided below.

Rest time:

Recreation time:

Relationship time:

Time Management

A very important skill to have if you want more time away from work and responsibilities is good time management. Time management describes the way in which you organize or structure your daily activities over time. Ineffective time management can lead to stress, anxiety, burnout, and, eventually, illness. Effective time management, on the other hand, will allow you more time for the three Rs described above: (rest, recreation, and relationships).

Developing good time management skills may necessitate giving up some cherished habits. Are any of the following tendencies true for you? Check off any of the statements below that apply:

☐ I tend to underestimate the amount of time it takes to complete an activity or task. By the time I finish, I've taken up time I needed for something else.

☐ I tend to squeeze too many things into too little time. As a result, I end up rushing.

☐ I find it difficult to let go of something I'm involved in. So I end up not leaving myself enough time to get to (or complete) the next activity I need to do.

☐ I have difficulty prioritizing activities—getting the most essential ones done before I attend to the less important ones.

☐ I have difficulty delegating nonessential tasks to others, even when it is possible to do so.

If you checked off any of the above statements as true, you might benefit from learning and cultivating effective time management skills.

The skills described below—prioritization, delegation, allowing extra time, letting go of perfectionism, overcoming procrastination, and learning to say no—can help you work with—rather than against—time.

Prioritization

Prioritization means learning to discriminate between tasks or activities that are essential and those that are nonessential. You attend to what's most important and put everything else on hold (or delegate tasks to other people—see below).

You may find it useful to divide your daily tasks and responsibilities into three categories: *essential*, *important*, and *less important* or trivial. *Essential* tasks or activities include those that require immediate attention: they are absolutely necessary—such as getting the kids off to school. Alternatively, they can be activities that are very important to you— such as physical exercise, if you're working on reducing your anxiety. *Important* tasks and activities are those that have significant value but can be delayed for a limited time, such as spending quality one-on-one time with your spouse or partner. Important tasks cannot be delayed for a long time, however. Less important or trivial tasks can be postponed a long time without serious risk, or can be delegated to others (tasks such as taking the stack of newspapers in the garage to the recycling center, or putting photos in your new album).

You may find it helpful, perhaps when you first get up in the morning, to categorize the tasks facing you as *essential*, *important*, or *less important*. Actually divide a piece of paper into three columns and write everything down. Then start with tasks in the *essential* and *important* columns. Only move on to the tasks in the *less important* category when you're done with all the tasks in the first two columns. In general, I would advise postponing all the tasks in the *less important* column in favor of giving yourself more down time.

If you're serious about achieving a more relaxed lifestyle, then you'll need to place down time—time for rest, recreation, and relationships—into the *essential* category. When down time becomes a regular and high-priority item in your schedule—something you refuse to postpone—you begin to take life more slowly and easily. As a result, you'll feel less stressed, better able to sleep, and more capable of enjoying yourself in general. Making down time essential requires giving up addictions to work, outer achievement, and success, as well as letting go of perfectionism.

You may also want to include under the essential column those activities that contribute to the achievement of your long-term ideals or life goals. Long-term ideals and life goals tend to remain just that for most people—postponed until the distant future—*unless* you take time to do something toward achieving them on a step-by-step basis in the present.

Delegation

Skill in delegation means being willing to let someone else take care of a task or activity that has lower priority for you, or is an important task that *you* don't have to do personally. By delegating, you free up more time for those tasks that are essential and require your personal attention. Often delegation means paying someone else to do what you might do yourself if you had unlimited time: housecleaning, car washing, cooking, childcare, basic repairs, and so on. At other times delegation simply means distributing tasks equitably among family members: your spouse and the kids do their fair share of household chores. A key to delegation is a willingness to trust and rely on others' capabilities. You give up the idea that only you can do an adequate job, and are willing to entrust responsiblity for a task to someone else.

Allowing Extra Time

A common problem in time management is underestimating the amount of time required to complete a task. The result is that you end up rushing to try to get something done, or else run into overtime and encroach on time that was needed for the next activity in your schedule. As a general rule, it helps to allow a little more time than you would expect for each activity during the day. It's better to err in favor of overestimating the time required for a task, leaving yourself plenty of time to proceed in a leisurely manner to the next activity.

An important prerequisite for allowing extra time is to be *willing to do fewer things*—not to cram as many tasks or activities into a given time frame. This may be very difficult for people addicted to their own adrenalin, who seem to get a certain exhilaration and fulfillment from rushing around or feeling busy. However, allowing extra time has termendous rewards in terms of letting you proceed throughout your day at a more relaxed and easy pace. To do so will save you a lot of stress.

Letting Go of Perfectionism

Perfectionism essentially means setting your standards and expectations too high. There is no allowance for the inevitable mistakes, frustration, delays, and limitations that come up in the process of working toward any goal. Perfectionism can keep you on a treadmill of overwork or overdedication to the point where you don't allow time out for your own needs. Letting go of perfectionism requires a fundamental attitude shift. It becomes all right simply to do your best, to make some mistakes along the way, and to accept the results you get, even if your best efforts fall short. It also involves learning to laugh on occasion rather than despair at the limitations inherent to human existence.

For a more in-depth discussion about letting go of perfectionism, see Chapter 11.

Overcoming Procrastination

Procrastination is always self-defeating when you leave yourself too little time. Whether preparing for an exam or preparing to go to work, putting off the inevitable leaves you harried and stressed in the end.

One reason for procrastinating can be that you really don't want to do whatever it is that needs doing in the first place. If this is your reason for stalling, the solution lies either in delegating or prioritizing. If you can delegate an undesirable task to someone else, then by all means do so. If you can't, then get the undesirable task done *first*—in other words, give it essential priority before the other things you need to do. Promising yourself to do something fun or interesting afterward as a reward for getting the undesirable task done often works well. In overcoming procrastination, the carrot usually works much better than the stick.

Another reason for procrastinating is perfectionism. If you feel that something has to be done perfectly, you may keep postponing getting started because you fear that you can't do it "just right." The solution here is to jump in and get started whether or not you feel you're ready to do it right. An important principle to remember is that *motivation often follows behavior.* Just getting started with a task will often generate the motivation to follow through and complete it. Then you may have enough time left over to go back and rework or refine what you did during the first round to a higher standard. If you keep stalling, however, you can use up all the time needed to do the kind of job you'd like to do. The worst outcome is when you don't attempt the task at all because of your impossibly high standards.

Saying No

There are many reasons why people have difficulty saying no. You may always want to be pleasing and responsive to family and friends, no matter what they ask of you. So you have difficulty setting limits, even when their demands or needs become more than you can handle. Or you may be so bound up with your work that it's your primary source of identity and meaning. No matter how demanding and time-consuming work responsibilities become, you keep taking them on, because not to do so would leave you feeling empty.

In short, difficulty saying no is usually tied up with your self-image. If your image of yourself requires you to be nice all the time and always available to everyone, then there is probably no limit to what others will ask of you. If your work is who you are, then it will be hard for you to say no to work demands in order to make time for your personal needs.

Learning to say no requires a willingness to relinquish cherished beliefs about yourself—which can be one of the hardest things for anyone to do. This may involve expanding your identity beyond taking care of others, or taking care of business, and learning to take the time to nurture and attend to your own needs. It means accepting the reality that taking care of yourself—even at the expense of what you do for others—isn't selfish. Can you really offer your best to others or your work if you yourself are tired, stressed, or burnt out?

In my own case, it was necessary to go to the edge of serious illness before the importance of saying no fully sank in. In many cases illness—whether in the form of panic attacks, depression, or some other persistent problem—may force you to re-evaluate the way you live your life. Illness can be the catalyst that makes you slow down, pay attention, and learn how to live in a simpler, more balanced fashion.

Summary of Things To Do

1. Reread the section on abdominal breathing and decide which breathing exercise you want to work with. Practice the exercise you prefer for five minutes per day for at least two weeks. Practice for one month or longer if you wish to change your breathing pattern from your chest downward toward your abdomen.

    Use the abdominal breathing or calming breath exercise whenever you spontaneously feel symptoms of anxiety beginning to come on.

2. Practice progressive muscle relaxation for 20-30 minutes per day (two practice periods per day is even better) for at least two weeks. For the first few times, have someone read you the instructions or record them on tape—that way you can follow them effortlessly. Eventually, you'll learn the sequence so well that you may choose to dispense with a tape.

3. Visualize going to a peaceful scene following progressive muscle relaxation. It may help to record a detailed description of such a scene following your recorded instructions for progressive muscle relaxation. Try going to your peaceful scene (along with doing abdominal breathing) at those times during the day when anxiety comes up.

4. After practicing progressive muscle relaxation for at least two weeks, you may enjoy its benefits so much that you decide to adopt it as your preferred deep relaxation technique. Alternatively, you may want to use one of the guided visualizations in the chapter on visualization or learn to meditate. *The type of relaxation technique you use is less important than your willingness and commitment to practice some method of deep relaxation on a daily basis.*

5. If you encounter difficulties in maintaining your commitment to practicing deep relaxation over the long term, reread the section called "Some Common Obstacles to a Daily Program of Deep Relaxation."

6. Spend some time considering the section "Down Time and Time Management." Do you need to allocate more time in your life for rest, relaxation, and personal relationships? What changes would you need to make in your daily schedule to achieve this? Think about at least one change you could make, starting this week. Are you willing to commit to it?

Further Reading

Benson, Herbert. *The Relaxation Response.* New York: Morrow, 1975.

Benson, Herbert. *Beyond the Relaxation Response.* New York: Berkley Books, 1985.

Carrington, Patricia. *Freedom in Meditation.* New York: Anchor Press/Doubleday, 1977.

Davis, Martha; Eshelman, Elizabeth Robbins; and McKay, Matthew. *The Relaxation & Stress Reduction Workbook.* Third Edition. Oakland, California: New Harbinger Publications, 1988.

Harp, David. *The Three Minute Meditator.* Third Edition. Oakland, California: New Harbinger Publications, 1996.

Jacobson, Edmund. *Progressive Relaxation.* Midway Reprint. Chicago: The University of Chicago Press, 1974.

Lakein, Alan. *How to Get Control of Your Time and Your Life.* New York: Signet, 1973.

LeShan, Lawrence. *How to Meditate.* New York: Bantam Books, 1974.

Mason, John. *Guide to Stress Reduction.* Berkeley, California: Celestial Arts, 1985. (This book is particularly recommended as a good resource for relaxation scripts you can record for yourself.)

Naranjo, Claudio, and Ornstein, Robert. *The Psychology of Meditation.* New York: The Viking Press, 1971.

5

Physical Exercise

One of the most powerful and effective methods for reducing generalized anxiety and overcoming a predisposition to panic attacks is a program of regular, vigorous exercise. You have panic attacks when your body's natural "fight-or-flight" reaction—the sudden surge of adrenalin you experience in response to a realistic threat—becomes excessive or occurs out of context. Exercise is a natural outlet for your body when it is in the fight-or-flight mode of arousal. A majority of my clients who have undertaken a regular exercise program are less vulnerable to panic attacks and, if they do have them, find them to be less severe. Regular exercise also diminishes the tendency to experience anticipatory anxiety toward phobic situations, expediting recovery from all kinds of phobias ranging from fear of public speaking to fear of being alone.

Regular exercise has a direct impact on several physiological factors that underlie anxiety. It brings about

- *Reduced skeletal muscle tension*, which is largely responsible for your feelings of being tense or "uptight"

- *More rapid metabolism of excess adrenalin and thyroxin* in the bloodstream, the presence of which tends to keep you in a state of arousal and vigilance

- *A discharge of pent-up frustration*, which can aggravate phobic or panic reactions

Some of the general physiological benefits of exercise include

- Enhanced oxygenation of the blood and brain, which increases alertness and concentration

- Stimulation of the production of *endorphins*, natural substances which resemble morphine both chemically and in their effects: endorphins increase your sense of well-being

- Lowered pH (increased acidity) of the blood, which increases your energy level

- Improved circulation

- Improved digestion and utilization of food

- Improved elimination (from skin, lungs, and bowels)

- Decreased cholesterol levels
- Decreased blood pressure
- Weight loss as well as appetite suppression in many cases
- Improved blood sugar regulation (in the case of hypoglycemia)

Several *psychological* benefits accompany these physical improvements, including

- Increased subjective feelings of well-being
- Reduced dependence on alcohol and drugs
- Reduced insomnia
- Improved concentration and memory
- Reduced depression
- Increased self-esteem
- Greater sense of control over anxiety

Symptoms of Being Out of Shape

How do you know that you are out of shape and in need of exercise? Here are some common symptoms:

- Being out-of-breath after walking up a flight of stairs
- Long recovery time after walking up a flight of stairs
- Feeling exhausted after short periods of exertion
- Chronic muscle tension
- Poor muscle tone
- Obesity
- Muscles cramped and aching for days after participating in a sport
- General tiredness, lethargy, boredom

Your Fitness Level

The worksheet below can help you assess the extent of your fitness. Think about the most strenuous physical activity you practice in an *average week*. When you have completed the questions below, determine your fitness score and evaluate your fitness level.

INTENSITY	FREQUENCY	DURATION
How strenuous is your exercise?	How many times do you exercise per week?	How long do you exercise each time?
Heavy = 5 points (fast cycling, running, aerobic dancing)	3 or more times = 5 points	21 minutes to 1 hour = 5 points
Moderate = 3 points (jogging, cycling, very fast walking)	1-2 times = 2 points	11-20 minutes = 3 points
Light = 1 point (golf, strolling, most housework)	not at all = 0 points	10 minutes or less = 1 point

Add your score:_____ + _____ + _____ = _____
                                                      Total

TOTAL SCORE	FITNESS LEVEL	RECOMMENDED ACTION
13 to 15	Very good	Congratulations! Maintain your present level of activity
8 to 12	Average	You are moderately sedentary and should increase your level of activity
7 or less	Poor	Begin planning an exercise program now!

An alternative way to assess your level of fitness is to measure your *resting pulse rate*, the average number of heartbeats per minute when you're at rest. As a rule of thumb, a resting pulse of 80 or above suggests that you could definitely improve your fitness. A resting pulse of 70-80 suggests that you *may* need to obtain more exercise. If you are in a fitness program and have an average resting pulse below 70, you are likely to be in good shape. To measure your pulse, allow yourself to get relaxed, then take the number of pulse beats in 20 seconds and multiply by 3.

Are You Ready for a Fitness Program?

If you've decided you would like to get more exercise, you need to ask yourself whether you are fully ready to do so. There are certain physical conditions that limit the amount and intensity of exercise you should undertake. If your answer to any of the questions below is yes, be sure to consult with your physician before beginning any exercise program. He or she may recommend a program of restricted or supervised exercise appropriate to your needs.

YES   NO

____   ____   Has your physician ever said you have heart trouble?

____   ____   Do you frequently have pains in your heart or chest?

____   ____   Do you often feel faint or have spells of dizziness?

____   ____   Has your physician ever told you that you have a bone or joint problem (such as arthritis) that has been or might be aggravated by exercise?

____   ____   Has a physician ever said that your blood pressure was too high?

____   ____   Do you have diabetes?

____   ____   Are you over 40 years old and unaccustomed to vigorous exercise?

____   ____   Is there a physical reason, not mentioned here, why you should not undertake an exercise program?

If you answered no to all of the above questions, you can be reasonably assured that you are ready to start an exercise program. Begin slowly and increase your activity gradually over a period of weeks. If you are over 40 and unaccustomed to exercise, plan to see your doctor for a physical before undertaking an exercise program.

Some individuals are reluctant to take up exercise because the state of physiological arousal accompanying vigorous exercise reminds them too much of the symptoms of panic. If this applies to you, you might want to start out doing 45 minutes of walking on a daily basis.

Or you can *very gradually* build up to a more vigorous level of exercise. You might try just two to three minutes of jogging or cycling and then gradually increase the duration of your daily exercise a minute at a time, remembering to stop every time you feel even the slightest association with panic (see the descriptions of step-by-step desensitization in Chapters 3, 7, and 8). It might also be helpful to have a support person exercise with you intially. If you feel phobic about exercise, a program of gradual exposure will help you to desensitize to it in the same way you would to any other phobia.

Choosing an Exercise Program

There are many types of exercise to choose from. Check off below which type you feel you might be interested in. If you are already exercising, consider whether there are any other forms you would like to try.

___ running/jogging	___ downhill skiing	___ baseball
___ vigorous cycling	___ weight lifting	___ basketball
___ brisk walking	___ tennis	___ bowling
___ jumping rope	___ racquetball	___ golf
___ rowing	___ square-dancing	___ housework
___ stationary cycling	___ isometrics	___ gardening
___ cross-country skiing	___ handball	___ football
___ swimming	___ calisthenics	___ ballroom dancing
___ running in place	___ ping pong	___ yoga
___ aerobic dancing	___ mini-trampoline	___ roller skating
___ ice skating		

Deciding what form of exercise to do depends upon your objectives. For reducing generalized anxiety and/or a proneness to panic, aerobic exercise is the most effective for many individuals. The activities listed in the first column on the preceding page are aerobic. Aerobic exercise requires sustained activity of your larger muscles. It reduces skeletal muscle tension, and increases *cardiovascular conditioning*—the capacity of your circulatory system to deliver oxygen to your tissues and cells with greater efficiency. Regular aerobic exercise will reduce stress and increase your stamina.

Beyond aerobic fitness, you may have other objectives in taking up exercise. If increased muscle *strength* is important, you may want to include weight lifting or isometric exercise in your program (if you have a heart condition or angina, you should probably *not* engage in weight lifting or bodybuilding). If *socializing* is important, then tennis, racquetball, golf, or team sports such as baseball or football might be what you're looking for. Exercise which involves stretching, such as dancing or yoga, is ideal for developing muscular *flexibility*. If you want to *lose weight*, jogging or cycling are probably most effective. If *discharging aggression and frustration* are important, you might try competitive sports. Finally, if you just want to get outdoors, then hiking or gardening would be appropriate. Rigorous hiking (as done by the Sierra Club, for example) can increase both strength and endurance. For further information on the various benefits of different types of exercise, see Covert Bailey's classic book on the subject, *Fit or Fat?*

Many people find it helpful to *vary* the type of exercise they do. Popular combinations involve doing an aerobic type of exercise such as jogging or cycling three to four times a week and a socializing exercise (such as tennis), or a bodybuilding exercise, twice a week. Maintaining a program with two distinct types of exercise prevents either from becoming too boring.

Finally, if you have not exercised in many years—or are over 40 and out of shape—walking 30-45 minutes daily is probably the best way to start.

Getting Started

If you haven't been exercising, it is important not to start off too fast or hard. Doing so often results in prematurely "burning out" on the idea of maintaining a regular exercise program. The following guidelines for getting started are recommended:

- Approach exercise gradually. Set limited goals at the outset, such as exerting only 10 minutes (or to the point of being winded) every other day for the first week. Add 5 minutes to your workout time each successive week until you reach 30 minutes.

- Give yourself a one-month trial period. Make a commitment to stay with your program for one month despite aches and pains, inertia, or other resistance to exercise. By the end of the first month you may be starting to experience sufficient benefits to make the exercise self-motivating. Be aware that achieving a high level of fitness after being out of shape takes three to four months.

- Keep a record of your daily exercise practice. Use the *Daily Record of Exercise* below to keep track of the date, time, duration, and type of exercise you engage in on a daily basis for one month. (You may want to make copies of the Daily Record to track your exercise program beyond the first month.) If you're doing aerobic exercise, record your pulse immediately after completing your workout and enter it under "Pulse Rate." Also be sure to rate your level of satisfaction, using a 1-10 scale, where 1 equals no satisfaction at all and 10 equals total satisfaction with your exercise experience. As you begin to get into shape, the ratings should increase. Finally, if you fail to exercise when you intended to, indicate your reason for not doing so. Later on it may be useful to reevaluate these reasons to see if they are truly valid or "mere excuses." (See the final section of this chapter for dealing with resistance to exercise.)

- *Expect* some initial discomfort. Aches and pains when starting out are normal if you've been out of shape. You can expect the discomfort to pass as you grow in strength and endurance.

- Try to focus on the *process* of exercise rather than the product. See if you can get into the inherently enjoyable aspects of the exercise itself. If jogging or cycling is what you like, it helps to have a scenic environment. Focusing on competition with others or yourself will tend to increase rather than reduce anxiety and stress.

- Reward yourself for maintaining a commitment to your exercise program. Give yourself dinner out, a weekend trip, or new athletic clothes or equipment in exchange for sticking to your program during the first weeks and months.

- *Warm up*. Just as your car needs to warm up before you begin driving, your body needs a gradual warm-up before engaging in vigorous exercise. This is especially important if you are over 40. Five minutes of calisthenics or stretching exercises will usually be sufficient.

- After vigorous exercise, it is important to give yourself a few minutes to cool down. Walking around for two or three minutes will help bring blood back from peripheral muscles to the rest of your body.

- Avoid exercising within 90 minutes of a meal and don't eat until one hour after exercising.

- Avoid exercising when you feel ill or overstressed (try a deep relaxation technique instead).

- Stop exercising if you experience any sudden, unexplainable bodily symptoms.

- If you find yourself feeling bored with exercising solo, find a partner to go with you or a form of exercise that requires a partner.

Optimizing the Anxiety-Reducing Effects of Exercise

Exercise needs to be of sufficient regularity, intensity, and duration to have a significant impact on anxiety. The following standards can be viewed as goals to aim for:

Daily Record of Exercise* for _____

(month)

Date	Time	Type of Exercise	Duration	Pulse Rate	Satisfaction Level	Reason for Not Exercising

*Based on a maximum frequency of six days of exercise per week

- Ideally exercise should be *aerobic*

- Optimal frequency is *4-5 times* per week

- Optimal duration is *20-30 minutes* or more per session

- Optimal intensity for aerobic exercise is a heart rate of *(220 - your age) x .75* for at least 10 minutes.

The table below indicates aerobic pulse ranges for various ages:

Age	Pulse (Heart) Rate
20-29	145-164
30-39	138-156
40-49	130-148
50-59	122-140
60-69	116-132

- *Avoid exercising only once per week.* Engaging in infrequent spurts of exercise is stressful to your body and generally does more harm than good (walking is an exception).

Obstacles To Implementing an Exercise Program

If you have difficulty starting or maintaining an exercise program, ask yourself what excuses or rationalizations you are giving yourself. What are you saying to yourself that tends to make you procrastinate? Try making a record of your opportunities and excuses like the one below.

A Couch Potato's Logbook

Janine is fifty pounds overweight. She wants to lose weight, but she also uses her weight as an excuse not to exercise. Here is a logbook of Janine's battle with her sedentary lifestyle.

Opportunity To Exercise Not Taken	Reason I Didn't Exercise	How I'll Talk Myself Into It Next Time
Friend invited me to go to her aerobics class.	I kept thinking how grotesque I'll look in leotards. What if my competitiveness makes me work too hard and I have a heart attack?	I'll find some loose, comfortable clothes that won't show every bulge quite so much. I'll focus on pacing myself—if I start to feel too stressed, I won't feel self-conscious about slowing down or just standing and stretching for a while.

Walk to the grocery store.	I'd have too much to carry home—and, anyway, it looked like rain.	I'll spread out my shopping over more trips so that I have only one bag to carry each time. I can wear a daypack to free up my hands while I'm walking home. Now that I think of it, my fold-up umbrella fits inside my pack—and, anyway, it's easy enough to carry.
Local chapter of the Sierra Club was advertising a bird walk.	I don't know the names of any of the birds. I don't have binoculars. I might get panicky if we have to climb up anywhere high.	I guess people go on these things because they *don't* know the names of the birds: I'll be in good company. Even if I don't have binoculars, it will be good for me to get out in the air—and maybe we'll see some birds close up. I'll look into borrowing some binoculars. I'll ask my friend George along—he knows about my panic attacks and he'll be able to help me if I start feeling stressed out.

Common Excuses for Not Exercising

Below is an annotated list of common excuses people make for avoiding exercise.

- "I don't have enough time."
  What you are really saying is that you're not willing to make time. You aren't assigning enough importance to the increased fitness, well-being, and improved control over anxiety you could gain from exercise. The problem is not a matter of time but one of priorities.

- "I feel too tired to exercise."
  One solution is to exercise before going to work—or on your lunch break—rather than at the end of the day. If this is simply impossible, don't give up. What many nonexercisers fail to realize is that moderate exercise can actually *overcome* fatigue. Many people exercise *in spite* of feeling tired and find that they feel rejuvenated and reenergized afterwards. Things will grow easier once you get past the initial inertia of starting to exercise.

- "Exercise is boring—it's no fun."
  Is it really true that *all* the activities listed earlier are boring to you? Have you tried out all of them? It may be that you need to find *someone* to exercise with in order to have more fun. Or perhaps you need to go back and forth between two different types of exercise to stimulate your interest. Exercise can begin to feel wonderful after a few months when it becomes inherently rewarding, even if it initially bored you. If you've considered jogging but think of it as too boring, I suggest that you read *Beyond Jogging—The Inner Space of Running,* by Mike Spino.

- "It's too inconvenient to go out somewhere to exercise."
  This is really no problem, as there are several ways to obtain vigorous exercise in the comfort of your home. Stationary bicycles have become very popular, and 20 minutes per day on one will give you a good workout. If this seems boring, try listening to a portable tape recorder with headphones or place your stationary bike in front of the TV set. Aerobic exercise at home is convenient and fun if you have a VCR. Jane Fonda's low-impact aerobics video is a good one to start out with. Other indoor activities include jumping on a rebounder, calisthenics, using a rowing machine, and/or using a universal gym with adjustable weights. There are also early morning exercise programs on TV. If you can't afford exercise equipment or a VCR, just put on some wild music and dance for 20 minutes. In short, it is quite possible to maintain an adequate exercise program without leaving your home.

- "I'm afraid I'll have a panic attack."
  Brisk walking every day for 45 minutes is an excellent form of exercise that is very unlikely to produce symptoms you might associate with panic. If you would prefer doing something more vigorous, start off with a very short period of two or three minutes and gradually add a minute at a time. Anytime you start to feel uneasy, simply stop, wait until you fully recover, and then try completing your designated period of exercise for that day. The principles of graded exposure described in the chapters on desensitization can be applied effectively to a phobia about exercise.

- "Exercise causes a buildup of lactic acid—doesn't that cause panic attacks?"
  It is true that exercise increases the production of lactic acid, and that lactic acid can promote panic attacks in some people who are already prone to them. However, regular exercise also increases *oxygen turnover* in your body: that is, the capacity of your body to oxidize substances it doesn't need, including lactic acid. Any increase in lactic acid produced by exercise will be offset by your body's increased capacity to remove it. The net effect of regular exercise is an overall *reduction* in your body's tendency to accumulate lactic acid.

- "I'm over 40—and that's too old to start exercising."
  When clients over 40 tell me "it's too late" to take up exercise, I remind them that many of the people chosen to be astronauts are in their forties. I also tell them about marathon runners who *began* running in their fifties and sixties after having not exercised at all. Unless your doctor gives you a clear medical reason for not exercising, age is never a valid excuse. With patience and persistence, it is possible to get into excellent physical shape at almost any age.

- "I'm too overweight and out of shape," or "I'm afraid I'll have a heart attack if I stress my body by exercising vigorously."

  If you have physical reasons to worry about stressing your heart, be sure to design your exercise program with the help of your physician. Vigorous walking is a safe exercise for virtually everyone, and is considered by some physicians to be the ideal exercise, as it rarely causes muscle or bone injuries. Swimming is also a safe bet if you're out of shape or overweight. Be sensible and realistic in the exercise program you choose. The important thing is to be consistent and committed, whether your program involves walking for one hour every day or training for a marathon.

- "I've tried exercise once and it didn't work."

  The question to ask here is *why* didn't it work. Did you start off too hard and fast? Did you get bored? Did you balk at the initial aches and pains? Did you feel lonely exercising by yourself? Perhaps it is time for you to give yourself another chance to discover all the physical and psychological benefits of a regular exercise program.

Regular exercise is an essential component of the total program for overcoming anxiety, panic, and phobias presented in this workbook. If you combine exercise with a program of regular deep relaxation, you are undoubtedly going to experience a substantial reduction in generalized anxiety and will very likely increase your resistance to panic attacks as well. Exercise and deep relaxation are the two methods *most* effective for altering a hereditary-biochemical predisposition to anxiety. The techniques described in the remaining chapters of this workbook depend for their effectiveness on your commitment to, and mastery of, deep relaxation and a program of regular exercise.

Summary of Things To Do

1. Evaluate your level of fitness, using the worksheet in the section "Your Fitness Level."

2. Determine whether you are ready to begin a fitness program by answering the questions in the section "Are You Ready for a Fitness Program?"

3. Choose one or more types of exercise you would prefer to do. If you're out of shape, begin with walking for periods of at least 30 minutes, or with a more vigorous form of exercise for 10-15 minutes. Increase the duration and intensity of your exercise gradually. Exercise at least four times per week.

4. Monitor your exercise program, using the *Daily Record of Exercise*, for at least one month.

5. Observe all the guidelines for maintaining a regular exercise program listed in the section "Getting Started." It's particularly important to give yourself time to warm up and cool down before and after engaging in vigorous exercise.

6. If you encounter resistance to exercise—or lose your motivation to keep exercising after the first week or so—reread the section "Obstacles to Implementing an Exer-

cise Program." Try to identify what you're telling yourself about exercise that creates your resistance or lack of motivation. Work on countering your negative self-talk by giving yourself positive reasons to exercise the next time you have an opportunity.

Further Reading

Bailey, Covert. *Fit or Fat?* Boston: Houghton Mifflin, 1977.

Brems, M. *Swim for Fitness*. San Francisco: Chronicle Books, 1979.

Cooper, K.H. *The Aerobic Way*. New York: M. Evans and Company, 1977.

Fixx, J.F. *Jim Fixx's Second Book of Running*. New York: Random House, 1980.

Gale, B. *The Wonderful World of Walking*. New York: William Morrow, 1979.

Gould, D. *Tennis Everyone*. Third Edition. Palo Alto, California: Mayfield, 1978.

Hittleman, R. *Richard Hittleman's Yoga 28-Day Exercise Plan*. New York: Workman Publishing Co., 1969.

Kostrubala, T. *The Joy of Running*. New York: Pocket Books, 1976.

Smith, D.L. and Gaston, E.A. *Get Fit with Bicycling*. Emmaus, Pennsylvania: Rodale Press, 1979.

Sorenson, J. *Aerobic Dancing*. New York: Rawson Way, 1979.

Spino, M. *Beyond Jogging: The Inner Space of Running*. New York: Pocket Books, 1979.

Thomas, G.S. *Exercise and Health: Evidence and Implications*. New York: Oelger, Shlager, Gunn & Hain, 1981.

Wiener, H.S. *Total Swimming*. New York: Simon and Schuster, 1980.

Wood, P.D. *Run to Health*. New York: Charter, 1980.

Yamada, Y. *Akido Complete*. New York: Castle Books, 1969.

6

Coping With Panic Attacks

A panic attack is a sudden surge of mounting physiological arousal that can occur "out of the blue" or in response to encountering (or merely thinking about) a phobic situation. *Bodily symptoms* that occur with the onset of panic can include heart palpitations, tightening in the chest or shortness of breath, choking sensations, dizziness, faintness, sweating, trembling, shaking, and/or tingling in the hands and feet. *Psychological reactions* that often accompany these bodily changes include feelings of unreality, an intense desire to run away, and fears of going crazy, dying, or doing something uncontrollable.

Anyone who has had a full-fledged panic attack knows that it is one of the most intensely uncomfortable states human beings are capable of experiencing. Your very first panic attack can have a traumatic impact, leaving you feeling terrified and helpless, with strong anticipatory anxiety about the possible recurrence of your panic symptoms. Unfortunately, in some cases, panic does come back and occurs repeatedly. Why some people have a panic attack only once—or perhaps once every few years—while others develop a chronic condition with several attacks a week, is still not understood by researchers in the field.

The *good* news is that you can learn to cope with panic attacks so well that they will no longer have the power to frighten you. Over time you can actually diminish the intensity and frequency of panic attacks *if* you are willing to make some changes in your lifestyle. Lifestyle changes which are most conducive to reducing the severity of panic reactions are described in other chapters of this workbook. They include

- Regular practice of deep relaxation (see Chapter 4)

- A regular program of exercise (see Chapter 5)

- Elimination of stimulants (especially caffeine, sugar, and nicotine) from your diet (see Chapter 16)

- Learning to acknowledge and express your feelings, especially anger and sadness (see Chapter 13)

- Adopting self-talk and "core beliefs" which promote a calmer and more accepting attitude toward life (see Chapters 9 and 10)

These five lifestyle changes vary in importance for different people. To the extent that you can cultivate all five of them, you will find that, over time, your problem with panic reactions will diminish.

The approach in this workbook is not oriented toward medication. Yet there *are* some people who suffer from panic attacks for whom it's appropriate to take medication. If you're having panic attacks with sufficient intensity and frequency that they interfere with your ability to work, your close personal relationships, or your sleep, or if such attacks persistently give you the feeling that you are "losing your grip" on yourself, then medication may be an appropriate intervention.

The two types of medications most frequently prescribed for panic attacks are minor tranquilizers (for instance, Xanax or Ativan) and antidepressants (such as Tofranil, Elavil, or Prozac). For more information on the use of prescription medications in treating panic attacks, see Chapter 17.

The remainder of this chapter will present some specific guidelines for dealing with panic attacks on a *short-term*, immediate basis. These are practical strategies for coping with panic attacks *at the very moment they occur.*

Deflate the Danger*

A panic attack can be a very frightening and uncomfortable experience, but it is absolutely not dangerous. You may be surprised to learn that panic is an *entirely natural bodily reaction that simply occurs out of context*. Earlier chapters discussed the fight-or-flight reaction—an instinctual response in all mammals (not just humans) to physiologically prepare to fight or flee when their survival is threatened. This instantaneous reaction is necessary to ensure the survival of the species in life-threatening situations. It serves to protect the lives of animals in the wild when they are faced by their predators. And it serves to protect your life by informing and mobilizing your impulse to flee from danger.

Suppose, for example, that your car stalled on the railroad tracks while a train approached you from about 200 yards away. You would experience a sudden surge of adrenalin, accompanied by feelings of panic, and a very strong and sensible urge to flee your predicament. In fact, your body would undergo a whole range of reactions, including

- An increase in your heart rate

- An increase in your respiratory rate

- A tensing of your muscles

- Constriction of your arteries and reduced blood flow to your hands and feet

- Increased blood flow to your muscles

- Release of stored sugar from your liver into your bloodstream

- Increased production of sweat

The very intensity of this reaction and the strong urge to flee are precisely what would ensure your survival. The surge of adrenalin and flow of blood to your muscles increases your alertness and physical strength. Your energy is mobilized and directed toward escape. If these reactions were less intense or less rapid, you might never get

*Some of the ideas presented in this section are adapted from David Barlow, Ph.D., and Michelle Craske, Ph.D., *Mastery of Your Anxiety and Panic.* Albany, New York: Graywind Publications, 1989.

out of the way in time. Perhaps you can recall times in your life when the flight response worked properly and served you well.

In a spontaneous panic attack, your body goes through *exactly the same* physiological flight reaction that it does in a truly life-threatening situation. The panic attack that wakes you up at night or occurs out of the blue is *physiologically indistinguishable* from your response to such experiences as your car stalling on the railroad tracks or waking to hear a robber going through your house.

What makes a panic attack unique and difficult to cope with is that these intense bodily reactions occur *in the absence of any immediate or apparent danger*. Or, in the case of agoraphobia, they occur in response to situations that have no apparent life-threatening potential (such as standing in line at the grocery store or being at home alone). In either case, you don't know why the reaction is happening. And not knowing why—not being able to make any sense out of the fact that your body is going through such an intense response—only serves to make the entire experience even more frightening. Your tendency is to react to sensations that are intense and *inexplicable* with even more fear and a heightened sense of danger.

No one fully knows at this time why spontaneous panic attacks occur—why the body's natural flight mechanism can come into play for no obvious reason or out of context. Some people believe that there is always *some* stimulus for a panic attack, even if this is not apparent. Others believe that sudden attacks arise from a temporary physiological imbalance. It *is* known that there is a greater tendency for panic attacks to occur when a person has been undergoing prolonged stress or has recently suffered a significant loss. However, only some people who have undergone stress or loss develop panic attacks, while others might develop headaches, ulcers, or reactive depression. It is also known that a disturbance in the part of the brain called the *locus ceruleus* is implicated in panic attacks; but it seems that this disturbance is only one event in a long chain of causes without being the primary cause. A full understanding of what causes panic attacks awaits future research. (For a more detailed account of what is known, see Chapter 2.)

Because there is no immediate or apparent external danger in a panic attack, you may tend to *invent* or *attribute danger* to the intense bodily sensations you're going through. In the absence of any real life-threatening situation, your mind may misinterpret what's going on *inside* as being life-threatening. Your mind can very quickly go through the following process: "If I feel this bad, I must be in some danger. If there is no apparent external danger, the danger must be inside of me." And so it's very common when undergoing panic to invent any (or all) of the following "dangers":

In response to heart palpitations: "I'm going to have a heart attack" or "I'm going to die."

In response to choking sensations: "I'm going to stop breathing and suffocate."

In response to dizzy sensations: "I'm going to pass out."

In response to sensations of disorientation or feeling "not all there": "I'm going crazy."

In response to "rubbery legs": "I won't be able to walk" or "I'm going to fall."

In response to the overall intensity of your body's reactions: "I'm going to lose complete control over myself."

As soon as you tell yourself that you're feeling any of the above dangers, you multiply the intensity of your fear. This intense fear makes your bodily reactions even worse, which in turn creates still more fear, and you get caught in an upward spiral of mounting panic.

This upward spiral can be avoided if you understand that what your body is going through is *not dangerous*. All of the above dangers are illusory, a product of your imagination when you're undergoing the intense reactions which constitute panic. *There is simply no basis for any of them in reality*. Let's examine them one by one.

- *A panic attack cannot cause heart failure or cardiac arrest.*
  Rapid heartbeat and palpitations during a panic attack can be frightening sensations, but they are not dangerous. Your heart is made up of very strong and dense muscle fibers and can withstand a lot more than you might think. According to Claire Weekes, a healthy heart can beat 200 beats per minute for days—even weeks—without sustaining any damage. So, if your heart begins to race, just allow it to do so, trusting that no harm can come of it and that your heart will eventually calm down.

  There's a substantial difference between what goes on with your heart during a panic attack and what happens in a heart attack. During a panic attack, your heart may race, pound, and at times miss or have extra beats. Some people even report chest pains, which pass fairly quickly, in the left-upper portion of their chest. None of these symptoms is aggravated by movement or increased physical activity. During a true heart attack, the most common symptom is continuous pain and a pressured, even crushing sensation in the center of your chest. Racing or pounding of the heart may occur but this is secondary to the pain. Moreover, the pain and pressure get worse upon exertion and may tend to diminish with rest. This is quite different from a panic attack, where racing and pounding may get worse if you stand still and lessen if you move around.

  In the case of heart disease, distinct abnormalities in heart rhythm show up on an electrocardiogram (EKG) reading. It has been demonstrated that during a panic attack there are no EKG abnormalities—only rapid heartbeat. (If you want to gain additional reassurance, you may want to have your doctor perform an EKG.)

  In sum, there is simply no basis for the connection between heart attacks and panic. Panic attacks are not hazardous to your heart.

- *A panic attack will not cause you to stop breathing or suffocate.*
  It is common during panic to feel your chest close down and your breathing become restricted. This might lead you to suddenly fear that you're going to suffocate. Under stress your neck and chest muscles are tightening and reducing your respiratory capacity. Be assured that there is nothing wrong with your breathing passage or lungs, and that the tightening sensations will pass. Your brain has a built-in reflex mechanism that will eventually *force* you to breathe if you're not getting enough oxygen. If you don't believe this, try holding your breath for up to a minute and observe what happens. At a certain point you'll feel a strong reflex to take in more air. The same thing will happen in a panic attack if you're not getting enough oxygen. You'll automatically gasp and take a deep breath long before reaching the point where you could pass out from a lack of oxygen. (And even if you did pass out, you would immediately start breathing!) In sum, choking

and sensations of constriction during panic, however unpleasant, are not dangerous.

- *A panic attack cannot cause you to faint.*
The sensation of light-headedness you may feel with the onset of panic can evoke a fear of fainting. What is happening is that the blood circulation to your brain is slightly reduced, most likely because you are breathing more rapidly (see the section on hyperventilation in Chapter 4). This is *not* dangerous and can be relieved by breathing slowly and regularly from your abdomen, preferably through your nose. It can also be helped by taking the first opportunity you have to walk around a bit. Let the feelings of light-headedness rise and subside without fighting them. Because your heart is pumping harder and actually increasing your circulation, you are very unlikely to faint (except in rare instances if you have a blood phobia and happen to be exposed to the sight of blood).

- *A panic attack cannot cause you to lose your balance.*
Sometimes you may feel quite dizzy when panic comes on. It may be that tension is affecting the semicircular canal system in your inner ear, which regulates your balance. For a few moments you may feel dizzy or it may even seem that things around you are spinning. Invariably this sensation will pass. It is not dangerous and very unlikely to be so strong that you will actually lose your balance. If sensations of pronounced dizziness persist for more than a few seconds, you may want to consult a doctor (preferably an otolaryngologist) to check if infection, allergies, or other disturbances might be affecting your inner ear.

- *You won't fall over or cease to walk when you feel "weak in the knees" during a panic attack.*
The adrenalin released during a panic attack can dilate the blood vessels in your legs, causing blood to accumulate in your leg muscles and not fully circulate. This can produce a sensation of weakness or "jelly legs," to which you may respond with the fear that you won't be able to walk. Be assured that this sensation is just that—a sensation—and that your legs are as strong and able to carry you as ever. They won't give way! Just allow these trembling, weak sensations to pass and give your legs the chance to carry you where you need to go.

- *You can't "go crazy" during a panic attack.*
Reduced blood flow to your brain during a panic attack is due to arterial constriction, a *normal* consequence of rapid breathing. This can result in sensations of disorientation and a feeling of unreality that can be frightening. If this sensation comes on, remind yourself that it's simply due to a slight and temporary reduction of arterial circulation in your brain and does not have anything to do with "going crazy," no matter how eerie or strange it may feel. No one has ever gone crazy from a panic attack, even though the fear of doing so is common. As bad as they feel, sensations of unreality will eventually pass and are completely harmless.

It may be helpful to know that people do not "go crazy" in a sudden or spontaneous way. Mental disorders involving behaviors that are labeled "crazy" (such as schizophrenia or manic-depressive psychosis) develop very gradually over a period of years and do not arise from panic attacks. No one has ever started to hallucinate or hear voices during a panic attack (except in rare instances where panic was induced by an overdose of a recreational drug such as LSD or cocaine). In short, a panic attack cannot result in your "going crazy," no matter how disturbing or unpleasant your symptoms feel.

- *A panic attack cannot cause you to "lose control of yourself."*
  Because of the intense reactions your body goes through during panic, it is easy to imagine that you could "completely lose it." But what does completely losing it mean? Becoming completely paralyzed? Acting out uncontrollably or running amok? I am aware of no reported instances of this happening. If anything, during panic your senses and awareness are heightened with respect to a single goal: escape. Running away or trying to run away are the only ways in which you would be likely to "act out" while panicking. Complete loss of control during panic attacks is simply a myth.

The first step in learning to cope with panic reactions is to recognize that they are not dangerous. Because the bodily reactions accompanying panic feel so intense, it's easy to imagine them being dangerous. Yet in reality no danger exists. The physiological reactions underlying panic are *natural* and *protective*. In fact, *your body is designed to panic* so that you can quickly mobilize to flee situations that genuinely threaten your survival. The problem occurs when this natural, life-preserving response occurs outside the context of any immediate or apparent danger. When this happens, you can make headway in mastering panic by learning not to imagine danger where it doesn't exist.

Breaking the Connection Between Body Symptoms and Catastrophic Thoughts

There is an important difference between people who have panic attacks and those who do not. *Individuals who are prone to panic have a chronic tendency to interpret slightly unusual or uncomfortable body sensations in a catastrophic way.* For example, heart palpitations are seen as signals of an impending heart attack, chest constriction and shortness of breath are seen as signs of imminent suffocation, or dizziness is seen as a precursor to fainting or collapse. People who do not have panic attacks may notice (and not particularly like) having such body symptoms, *but they do not interpret them as catastrophic or dangerous.*

If you have a tendency to interpret unpleasant body sensations as portending something dangerous or catastrophic, you will also tend to constantly monitor your body to see if you're having those sensations. You're probably very tuned in to your internal bodily states and overreact easily if something begins to feel slightly "off" or unusual. This increased *internalization* compounds the problem, because you're more likely to notice and magnify any sudden change in your body's internal state that is slightly unusual or unpleasant.

The variety of circumstances that might cause a sudden aberration in your body's internal physiological state are legion. Sometimes the cause lies outside of your body. For example, an argument with your spouse, seeing something unpleasant on TV, hearing your alarm clock go off, or being in a hurry to get somewhere could trigger an increase in heart rate, chest constriction, stomach queasiness, or any of a wide range of body symptoms associated with anxiety. At other times, the cause resides in some subtle physiological shift within your body—for example, oxygen deprivation due to under-breathing, a spontaneous shift in the neuroendocrine systems of your brain, an increase in muscle tension in your neck and shoulders, or a fall in your blood sugar level. Whether the initial cause lies primarily outside or within your body, you are usually unaware of these physiological shifts until you actually feel the resultant symptoms. The above examples illustrate only a few among many possibilities, any of which might constitute the triggering event for an increase in anxiety. Whether or not you actually develop a full-blown panic attack depends on *how you perceive and respond* to the particular increase in body symptoms that occurs.

To sum up, people who panic are likely to experience: 1) increased internalization or preoccupation with subtle shifts in body symptoms or mood and 2) an increased tendency to interpret slight aberrations or incremental changes in body symptoms as dangerous or catastrophic. The diagram below illustrates this tendency:

Development of Panic Attack

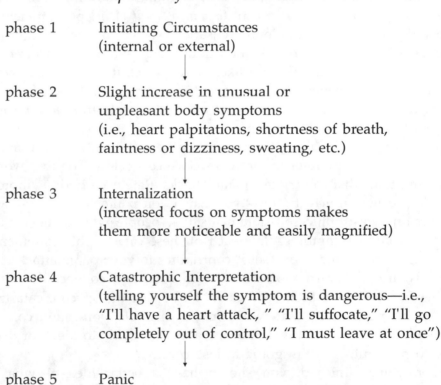

phase 1	Initiating Circumstances (internal or external)
phase 2	Slight increase in unusual or unpleasant body symptoms (i.e., heart palpitations, shortness of breath, faintness or dizziness, sweating, etc.)
phase 3	Internalization (increased focus on symptoms makes them more noticeable and easily magnified)
phase 4	Catastrophic Interpretation (telling yourself the symptom is dangerous—i.e., "I'll have a heart attack, " "I'll suffocate," "I'll go completely out of control," "I must leave at once")
phase 5	Panic

The good news is that it's possible to intervene at any point in this sequence. At phase 1 it may be *generalized stress* that leads to the initial unpleasant body sensations—heart palpitations, chest constriction, dizziness, and so on. Incorporating regular relaxation, exercise, low-stress nutritional habits, and other stress management techniques into your lifestyle (see Chapters 4, 5, 11, and 16) on a daily basis can go a long way toward reducing the propensity for sudden increases in your body's state of sympathetic nervous system arousal associated with stress. Beyond generalized stress, you may be able to identify the particular initiating circumstances that cause your panic attacks by noting carefully what was going on just before—or in the several hours before—a panic attack occurs. You can use the *Panic Attack Record* described in this chapter to help you determine what initial circumstances may have led to a particular panic attack. You can then try to avoid or eliminate these circumstances so they don't cause you trouble in the future. Interventions that reduce the propensity for having unpleasant body sensations in the first place (phases 1 and 2 in the chart) all require making changes in your lifestyle and attitudes.

Phase 3 of the panic cycle is comprised of internalization—being too focused on your internal body state. When you actually feel panic coming on, you can reduce internalization by using any of the active coping techniques described later in this chapter in the section, "Coping Techniques To Counteract Panic at an Early Stage." These techniques serve to distract your attention away from internal body symptoms, and also have a directly relaxing effect.

Perhaps the most important change you can make to defuse panic attacks, however, is to intervene at phase 4. That is, you can learn to stop interpreting unpleasant body sensations as being dangerous or potentially catastrophic. In fact, recent research both in the United States and England has determined that eliminating catastrophic interpretations of body symptoms can, *in and of itself alone,* be sufficient to relieve panic attacks. If you can learn to tolerate sensations such as dizziness, tightness in your chest, rapid heartbeat, and so on as innocuous body symptoms—rather than as signs of imminent danger—you will very likely have fewer, if any, panic attacks. That is not to say that stress management techniques and coping strategies for panic are not still important; it does imply, though, that eliminating catastrophic interpretations by itself can go a long way to relieve panic.

To assist you in breaking the connection between body symptoms and catastrophic interpretations, please refer to the two worksheets below. The first worksheet is a list of body symptoms that can trigger panic attacks. Rate each body symptom on a 0-5 scale according to how much it affects you when you panic. The second worksheet is a list of common catastrophic self-statements that people who panic make in response to unpleasant body symptoms. Rate each of these catastrophic statements on a 1-4 scale according to how much you feel it contributes to your panic attacks.

Finally, use the third worksheet to go back and connect the two lists. For each troublesome body symptom you rated 4 or 5, list the specific catastrophic statements likely to be triggered by that symptom. For example, you might connect heart palpitations with "I'm having a heart attack, " and "I'm going to die, " or dizziness with "I'm going to pass out," or "I'm going to lose control."

When you're finished, you should have a better idea of what particular body symptoms and associated catastrophic interpretations trigger your panic attacks. This knowledge will likely help you break the false connection you've made between your body symptoms and mistaken interpretations. Keep in mind throughout this exercise that *none of the body symptoms you've listed is actually dangerous. However unpleasant such symptoms might feel, they are completely harmless.* Equally important, keep in mind that *none of the catastrophic thoughts you have checked off is true or valid, even though you might have convinced yourself that it is. Every one of the catastrophic thoughts is simply false—a mistaken belief that you can learn to let go of.*

How do you break the automatic connection between unpleasant body symptoms and false, catastrophic thoughts? Three ways have been found to be helpful:

1. Recognition

2. Writing down alternative explanations of symptoms

3. Symptom inductions

Recognition

Just recognizing your tendency to believe that harmless body symptoms are signs of imminent danger is the first step. Awareness of specific connections between particular symptoms and particular catastrophic thoughts, which you may have gained from the previous exercise, will help you begin diffusing the danger when those symptoms come up in day-to-day life.

Writing Down Alternative Explanations of Body Symptoms

The catastrophic self-statements you make in an attempt to make sense of unpleasant body symptoms during a panic attack are simply false. It's just not true, for example, that rapid heartbeat or palpitations occur because you are having a heart attack. Nor is constriction in your chest or shortness of breath happening because you're about to suffocate. Nor is dizziness and light-headedness occurring because you're about to faint or "go crazy." In each of these cases, there is an alternative explanation that is non-catastrophic and based in fact. Alternative logical explanations might go something like this:

1. An increase in heartbeat and/or heart palpitations is very likely caused by increased output of adrenalin and sympathetic nervous system activity that accompany the early stage of an anxiety reaction. Such reactions are part of the body's normal means of handling any *perceived* threat—they are part of the flight-or-fight response. They are in no way dangerous, even if they continue for some time. For example, a healthy heart can beat rapidly for hours without putting you at any risk.

2. An increase in chest constriction and shortness of breath can be explained in terms of contraction of the muscles surrounding the chest cavity, also due to increased sympathetic nervous system activity. Such symptoms have nothing to do with the process of suffocating. Your chest muscles cannot contract to the point where you would be at risk of suffocating, no matter how unpleasant the tightness in your chest happens to feel.

3. Becoming dizzy or light-headed, common symptoms that can occur when you become anxious, are not caused by the fact that you are about to faint. They are caused by minor constrictions in the arteries of your brain, which lead to a slight reduction in blood circulation. It's extremely unlikely that you would faint, even if you feel quite light-headed. Fainting typically occurs during a drop in blood pressure; when you start to feel anxious, you usually experience an *increase* in blood pressure due to increased adrenalin and sympathetic nervous system tone.

Panic Attack Worksheet 1

Body Symptoms

Any of the following body symptoms can occur during a panic attack. Please evaluate each of them according to their effect when you are having an attack, and indicate your answers on the 0-5 scale in the righthand column.

0 = No Effect	3 = Strong Effect
1 = Mild Effect	4 = Severe Effect
2 = Medium Effect	5 = *Very* Severe Effect

	0	1	2	3	4	5
1. Sinking feeling in stomach	0	1	2	3	4	5
2. Sweaty palms	0	1	2	3	4	5
3. Warm all over	0	1	2	3	4	5
4. Rapid or heavy heartbeat	0	1	2	3	4	5
5. Tremor of the hands	0	1	2	3	4	5
6. Weak or rubbery knees or legs	0	1	2	3	4	5
7. Shaky inside and/or outside	0	1	2	3	4	5
8. Dry mouth	0	1	2	3	4	5
9. Lump in throat	0	1	2	3	4	5
10. Tightness in chest	0	1	2	3	4	5
11. Hyperventilation	0	1	2	3	4	5
12. Nausea or diarrhea	0	1	2	3	4	5
13. Dizzy or lightheaded	0	1	2	3	4	5
14. A feeling of unreality—as "in a dream"	0	1	2	3	4	5
15. Unable to think clearly	0	1	2	3	4	5
16. Blurred vision	0	1	2	3	4	5
17. A feeling of being partially paralyzed	0	1	2	3	4	5
18. A feeling of detachment or floating away	0	1	2	3	4	5
19. Palpitations or irregular heartbeats	0	1	2	3	4	5
20. Chest pain	0	1	2	3	4	5
21. Tingling in hands, feet, or face	0	1	2	3	4	5
22. Feeling faint	0	1	2	3	4	5
23. Fluttery stomach	0	1	2	3	4	5
24. Cold, clammy hands	0	1	2	3	4	5

Panic Attack Worksheet 2

Catastrophic Thoughts*

Catastrophic thoughts play a major role in aggravating panic attacks. Using the scale below, rate each of the following thoughts according to the degree to which you believe that thought contributes to your panic attacks.

1 = Not at all   3 = Quite a lot
2 = Somewhat   4 = *Very* much

1. I'm going to die.	1	2	3	4
2. I'm going insane.	1	2	3	4
3. I'm losing control.	1	2	3	4
4. This will never end.	1	2	3	4
5. I'm really scared.	1	2	3	4
6. I'm having a heart attack.	1	2	3	4
7. I'm going to pass out.	1	2	3	4
8. I don't know what people will think.	1	2	3	4
9. I won't be able to get out of here.	1	2	3	4
10. I don't understand what's happening to me.	1	2	3	4
11. People will think I'm crazy.	1	2	3	4
12. I'll always be this way.	1	2	3	4
13. I'm going to throw up.	1	2	3	4
14. I must have a brain tumor.	1	2	3	4
15. I'll choke to death.	1	2	3	4
16. I'm going to act foolish.	1	2	3	4
17. I'm going blind.	1	2	3	4
18. I'll hurt someone.	1	3	2	4
19. I'm going to have a stroke.	1	2	3	4
20. I'm going to scream.	1	2	3	4
21. I'm going to babble or talk funny.	1	2	3	4
22. I'll be paralyzed by fear.	1	2	3	4
23. Something is really physically wrong with me.	1	2	3	4
24. I won't be able to breathe.	1	2	3	4
25. Something terrible will happen.	1	2	3	4
26. I'm going to make a scene.	1	2	3	4

Connecting Body Symptoms and
Catastrophic Thoughts

In the left-hand column below list body symptoms you rated 5 or 4 on the first Panic Attack Worksheet. Describe your most troublesome body symptoms, one at a time. Then list catastrophic self-statements from the second worksheet "Catastrophic Thoughts" which you rated 4 or 3. *List those catastrophic statements you would be most likely to make in response to each particular body symptom.* For example, "Rapid heartbeat" is a body symptom that might elicit such catastrophic self-statements as, "I'm having a heart attack," and "I'm going to die."

Body Symptom:	Catastrophic Thoughts:
Body Symptom:	Catastrophic Thoughts:
Body Symptom:	Catastrophic Thoughts:
Body Symptom:	Catastrophic Thoughts:

Even less plausible is the idea that dizziness and light-headedness are caused by the fact that you're about to go crazy. The process of "going crazy" has nothing to do with panic attacks, and takes place over a much longer period of time than the duration of any panic attack.

These examples can serve as guidelines for developing your own alternative, non-catastrophic explanations for troublesome body symptoms. You'll likely find it helpful to refer to the first section of this chapter, "Deflate the Danger," in coming up with your own alternative explanations. The process of writing down such explanations will help you strengthen your conviction that uncomfortable body symptoms are truly harmless rather than signs of imminent danger.

You might want to put your alternative explanations of body symptoms on 3x5 index cards—one explanation of a particular symptom per card. Keep the cards with you in your purse or wallet and take them out and read them if you feel body symptoms coming on.

Symptom Inductions

A recent, very effective treatment for panic attacks involves voluntarily inducing body symptoms that can trigger panic. This is typically done in a therapy session. For example, if dizziness and shortness of breath are troublesome symptoms, the therapist has the client hyperventilate for two minutes and then stand up suddenly to actually bring on these symptoms. This might sound like an unusual and extreme therapeutic procedure, but, in fact, it is harmless and often quite helpful. Unless the client has a respiratory disorder, hyperventilation for two minutes is harmless. Deliberately hyperventilating gives her or him an opportunity to *actually experience uncomfortable body symptoms without anything negative or dangerous happening.* The key here is that the client learns on a "gut" or experiential level that nothing terrible follows body sensations that he or she used to interpret as dangerous. Repeated inductions of dizziness in this way help a panic-prone person to develop a strong conviction that dizziness is not dangerous.

A more detailed discussion of symptom inductions can be found at the end of this chapter.

Don't Fight Panic

Resisting or fighting initial panic symptoms is likely to make them worse. It's important to avoid tensing up in reaction to panic symptoms or trying to "make" them go away by suppressing them or gritting your teeth. Although it's important to act rather than be passive (as discussed below), you still shouldn't fight your panic. Claire Weekes, in her popular books *Hope and Help for Your Nerves* and *Peace from Nervous Suffering*, describes a four-step approach for coping with panic:

Face the symptoms—don't run from them.
Attempting to suppress or run away from the early symptoms of panic is a way of telling yourself that you can't handle a particular situation. In most cases, this will only create more panic. A more constructive attitude to cultivate is one that says,

"O.K., here it is again. I can allow my body to go through its reactions and handle this. I've done it before."

Accept what your body is doing—don't fight against it.
When you try to fight panic, you simply tense up against it, which only makes you more anxious. Adopting just the opposite attitude, one of *letting go* and *allowing* your body to have its reactions (such as heart palpitations, chest constriction, sweaty palms, dizziness, and so on) will enable you to move through panic much more quickly and easily. The key is to be able to *watch* or *observe* your body's state of physiological arousal—no matter how unusual or uncomfortable it feels—without reacting to it with further fear or anxiety.

Float with the "wave" of a panic attack rather than forcing your way through it.
Claire Weekes makes a distinction between *first fear* and *second fear*. First fear consists of the physiological reactions underlying panic; second fear is making yourself afraid of these reactions by saying scary things to yourself like, "I can't handle this!" "I've got to get out of here right now!" "What if other people see this happening to me!" While you can't do much about first fear, you can eliminate second fear by learning to "flow with" the rising and falling of your body's state of arousal rather than fighting or reacting fearfully to it. Instead of scaring yourself about your body's reactions, you can move with them and make reassuring statements to yourself like: "This too will pass," "I'll let my body do its thing and move through this," "I've handled this before and I can handle it now." A list of positive, coping statements you can use to help you float through a panic attack follows after the fourth point below.

Allow time to pass.
Panic is caused by a sudden surge of adrenalin. If you can allow, and float with, the bodily reactions caused by this surge, much of this adrenalin will metabolize and be reabsorbed in three to five minutes. As soon as this happens, you'll start to feel better. *Panic attacks are time limited.* In most cases, panic will peak and begin to subside within only a few minutes. It is most likely to pass quickly if you don't aggravate it by fighting against it or reacting to it with even more fear (causing "second fear") by saying scary things to yourself.

Coping Statements

Use any or all of the following positive statements to help you cultivate attitudes of accepting, "floating," and allowing time to pass during a panic attack. You may find it helpful to repeat a single statement over and over the first minute or two when you feel panic symptoms coming on. You may also want to do deep abdominal breathing in conjunction with repeating a coping statement. If one statement gets tiresome or seems to stop working, try another.

"This feeling isn't comfortable or pleasant, but I can accept it."

"I can be anxious and still deal with this situation."

"I can handle these symptoms or sensations."

"This isn't an emergency. It's O.K. to think slowly about what I need to do."

"This isn't the worst thing that could happen."

"I'm going to go with this and wait for my anxiety to decrease."

"This is an opportunity for me to learn to cope with my fears."

"I'll just let my body do its thing. This will pass."

"I'll ride this through—I don't need to let this get to me."

"I deserve to feel O.K. right now."

"I can take all the time I need in order to let go and relax."

"There's no need to push myself. I can take as small a step forward as I choose."

"I've survived this before and I'll survive this time, too."

"I can do my coping strategies and allow this to pass."

"This anxiety won't hurt me—even if it doesn't feel good."

"This is just anxiety—I'm not going to let it get to me."

"Nothing serious is going to happen to me."

"Fighting and resisting this isn't going to help—so I'll just let it pass."

"These are just thoughts—not reality."

"I don't need these thoughts—I can choose to think differently."

"This isn't dangerous."

"So what."

"Don't worry—be happy." (Use this to inject an element of lightness or humor.)

If you have frequent panic attacks, I suggest writing your favorite coping statements on a 3x5 card and carrying it in your purse or wallet. Bring the card out and read it when you feel panic symptoms coming on.

Explore the Antecedents of Your Panic Attacks

You can increase your mastery over panic attacks by investigating the types of circumstances which tend to precede them. If you are agoraphobic, you are very familiar with these circumstances. You know that you are more likely to panic, for example, if you are far from home, driving over a bridge, or sitting in a restaurant, and so you systematically avoid these particular situations. If you have spontaneous panic attacks that come "out of the blue," you might find it helpful to monitor their occurrence for two weeks and take careful note of what was going on immediately—as well as for several hours—before each one occurs. You might observe whether any of the following conditions makes a difference in the likelihood of your having a panic reaction:

- Were you under stress?

- Were you by yourself or with someone?

- If with someone, was it family, friends, or a stranger?

- What kind of mood were you in for several hours before panic came on? Anxious? Depressed? Excited? Sad? Angry? Other?

- Were you engaging in negative or fearful thoughts just before you panicked?

- Did you feel tired or rested?

- Were you experiencing some kind of loss?

- Were you feeling hot or cold?

- Were you feeling restless or calm?

- Had you consumed caffeine or sugar just before panic came on?

- Are there any other circumstances that correlate with your panic reactions?

You can use the *Panic Attack Record* to monitor every panic attack you experience over a two-week period.* Make copies of the form and fill one out for each separate panic attack. Answer all the questions for the entire day from the time you awoke until the time you panicked. If the attack happened at night, answer for the day preceding that night.

By making the effort to record your panic attacks and carefully observing any circumstances that consistently precede them, you are taking an important step. You are learning that you need not be a passive victim of an event that seems totally outside your control. Instead, you can begin to alter the circumstances of your daily life in a direction that significantly reduces the odds of having panic attacks.

Learn To Discriminate Early Symptoms of Panic

With practice you can learn to identify the preliminary signs that a panic attack may be imminent. For some individuals this might be a sudden quickening of the heartbeat. For others it might be a tightening in the chest, sweaty hands, or queasiness. Still others might experience a slight dizziness or disorientation. Most people experience some preliminary warning symptoms before reaching the "point of no return" when a full-blown panic attack is inevitable.

It's possible to distinguish among different levels or degrees of anxiety leading up to panic by imagining a ten-point scale.

---

*The *Panic Attack Record* is adapted from a similar form developed by David Barlow and Michelle Craske in their previously cited book.

Panic Attack Record

(Fill out one form for each separate panic attack during a two-week period.)

Date: _____

Time: _____

Duration (minutes): _____

Intensity of panic on anxiety scale (see next section, rate 5-10): _____

Antecedents

1. Stress level during preceding day (rate on 1-10 scale): _____

2. Alone or with someone? _____

3. If with someone, was it family, friend(s), stranger? _____

4. Your mood for three hours preceding panic attack. Anxious _____ Depressed _____ Excited _____ Angry _____ Sad _____ Other (specify) _____

5. Were you facing a challenge _____ or taking it easy _____?

6. Were you engaging in negative or fearful thoughts before you panicked? Yes _____ No _____ If so, what thoughts? _____

7. Were you tired _____ or rested _____?

8. Were you experiencing some kind of emotional upset or loss? Yes _____ No _____

9. Were you feeling hot _____ cold _____ neither _____?

10. Were you feeling restless and impatient? Yes _____ No _____

11. Were you asleep before you panicked? Yes _____ No _____

12. Did you consume caffeine or sugar within eight hours before you panicked? Yes _____ No _____ If yes, how much? _____

13. Have you noticed any other circumstances which correlate with your panic reactions? (specify)

_____

_____

Anxiety Scale*

7-10 *Major Panic Attack*	All of the symptoms in Level 6 exaggerated; terror; fear of going crazy or dying; compulsion to escape
6 *Moderate Panic Attack*	Palpitations; difficulty breathing; feeling disoriented or detached (feeling of unreality); panic in response to perceived loss of control
5 *Early Panic*	Heart pounding or beating irregularly; constricted breathing; spaciness or dizziness; definite fear of losing control; compulsion to escape
4 *Marked Anxiety*	Feeling uncomfortable or "spacey"; heart beating fast; muscles tight; beginning to wonder about maintaining control
3 *Moderate Anxiety*	Feeling uncomfortable but still in control; heart starting to beat faster; more rapid breathing; sweaty palms
2 *Mild Anxiety*	Butterflies in stomach; muscle tension; definitely nervous
1 *Slight Anxiety*	Passing twinge of anxiety, feeling slightly nervous
0 *Relaxation*	Calm, a feeling of being undistracted and at peace

The symptoms at various levels of this scale are typical, although they may not correspond exactly to your specific symptoms. The important thing is to identify what constitutes a Level 4 for *you*. This is the point at which—whatever symptoms you're experiencing—*you feel your control over your reaction beginning to diminish.* Up to and through Level 3, you may be feeling very anxious and uncomfortable, but you still feel that you're coping. Starting at Level 4, you begin to wonder whether you can manage what's happening, which can lead you to further panic. With practice you can learn to "catch yourself"—abort a panic reaction *before* it reaches this point of no return. The more adept you become at recognizing the early warning signs of panic up through Level 4 on the scale, the more control you will gain over your panic reactions. Mark this page with a paper clip or in some other fashion, as we will frequently refer to the Anxiety Scale here and in subsequent chapters.

Coping Strategies To Counteract Panic at an Early Stage

You must first learn to identify your own preliminary warning signs of a potential panic attack. What are your own Level 4 symptoms? Then it is time to *do something* about them. Fighting panic is not a good idea, but doing nothing and just remaining passive

---

*This anxiety scale was adapted from a similar one developed by Dr. Arthur Hardy in the *TERRAP Program Manual*, Menlo Park, California: TSC Publications, 1981.

can be even less helpful. The best solution is to utilize a number of tried-and-true coping strategies.

If you've been able to detect the early symptoms of panic before they get out of control (before they reach or exceed Level 5), any of the following coping strategies can be used to prevent a full-fledged panic reaction.

1. Retreat

If you are near or already in a situation in which you feel phobic, simply exit the situation until your anxiety subsides. In most cases, you can find a "trap door" that allows you to get yourself out of a situation. If you feel the onset of panic on the freeway, get over into the far right lane, slow down, and pull off onto the shoulder, or leave at the next exit. If you're standing in line at the grocery store, you can simply put your groceries aside and walk out without explaining. Very few situations have absolutely "no exit." Even on a bridge you can, in an emergency, put your flashers on and slow down to stop.

It's very important to distinguish *retreat* from *escape* in withdrawing from a phobic situation. Retreat means that you leave a situation *temporarily* with the intention of *returning* when you feel better. Escape, on the other hand, only serves to reinforce your phobia. When you don't go back into a situation, you begin to think of it as intolerable: you've learned only how to escape, nothing more. If you exit a difficult situation to head off a panic attack, be sure to attempt returning after you feel better. It is like the old saying about getting back up onto the horse after it has thrown you: getting back on proves that you are the one who is in control.

The following strategies are helpful for panic attacks that occur spontaneously and are not necessarily associated with a specific phobic situation. They may also be used in a phobic situation when you want to cope with anxiety up to and including Level 4 on the Anxiety Scale. Anxiety above Level 4 should always be dealt with, if possible, by retreating.

2. Talk to Another Person

Talking to someone nearby will help you get your mind off your panic symptoms and anxious thoughts. Whether you are driving with a passenger in the car, standing in line at the grocery store, standing in an elevator, or flying on a plane, this can work very well. In a public speaking situation, confiding to your audience about your nervousness can help to reduce it.

3. Move Around or Engage in Physical Activity

Moving and doing something physical lets you dissipate the extra energy or adrenalin created by the fight-or-flight reaction. Instead of resisting the normal physiological reaction that accompanies panic, you can move with it.

At work you can walk to the bathroom and back or walk outdoors for ten minutes. At home you can do household chores requiring physical activity or work out on your stationary bicycle or rebounder. Alternatively, you can engage in your usual physical exercise—jogging, swimming, or whatever. Gardening is also an excellent way to harness the physical energy of a panic reaction.

4. Stay in the Present

Focus on concrete objects around you in your immediate environment. In a grocery store, for example, you might look at the people standing around or the various magazines next to the cash register. While driving, you might focus on the cars in front of you or on other details of the surrounding environment (so long as you don't look away from the highway, of course). Staying in the present and focusing on external objects will help minimize the attention you might give to troublesome physical symptoms or catastrophic thoughts. If possible, you might try actually touching objects nearby to reinforce staying in the immediate present.

5. Engage in a Simple Repetitive Activity

There are many simple, repetitive acts that can distract your attention from your panic symptoms or anxiety-provoking thoughts. You can

- Unwrap and chew a piece of gum

- Count backward from 100 by 3s

- Count the number of people in line at the grocery store; time how long it takes each person to get to the head of the line; count the money in your wallet; or take out and read a 3x5 card on which you've listed coping statements for panic

- While driving, count the bumps on the steering wheel; count the number of red cars you see; time the length of the stoplight; add up numbers on license plates

- Feel the sharp edge of a key or the tines of a comb

- Snap a rubber band against your wrist

- Place a wet towel on your face or take a cold shower

- Sing

This list can be extended indefinitely. The point is to find some simple form of distraction that redirects your attention away from your bodily sensations or anxiety-provoking thoughts. See the book by Fredrick Newman, *Fighting Fear*, for a more extensive list.

6. Do Something That Requires Focused Concentration

These activities are harder to initiate when you're feeling anxious or panicky. They work very well as distractors from worry, however. Once you're involved in them, they have a greater and more lasting capacity to distract your attention.

- Read a good novel or magazine

- Solve puzzles (crosswords, jigsaw, puzzle books)

- Knit or sew
- Write a running account of your changing level of anxiety
- Engage in card or board games
- Calculate or compute
- Play a musical instrument
- Plan your day's activities
- Paint or play with clay

7. Express Anger

Anger and anxiety are incompatible reactions. It's impossible to experience both at the same time. Many of my clients have found that symptoms of anxiety and panic are a stand-in for deeper-lying feelings of anger, frustration, or rage. If you can express anger *physically onto an object*—not just talk about it—at the moment you feel sensations of panic coming on, you often can abort the occurrence of a panic attack. Below are some effective ways to do this:

- Pound on a pillow or your bed with both fists
- Put a large, durable pillow or cushion on your bed and hammer it with a tennis racket or plastic baseball bat
- Scream into a pillow or in your car alone with the windows rolled up
- Throw a dozen eggs into the bathtub (the remains wash away easily)
- Hit a punching bag or life-sized inflatable mannequin
- Chop wood

"Getting mad at" the early symptoms of a panic attack often works well. This does *not* mean struggling against panic (which is never a good idea); it is rather a matter of transmuting the energy behind fear into another emotion—in this case, anger.

Getting angry at panic means that you might say such things to your symptoms as, "The hell with this—I don't care what other people think!" "This reaction is ridiculous! I'm going into this situation anyway!" This approach of "doing it to the panic before it does it to you" can be effective for some individuals.

I suggest that you try this particular strategy after having worked with some of the other ones first. Getting angry at panic reactions may not always be the best strategy to start out with when you haven't explored any other coping strategies first.

8. Experience Something Immediately Pleasurable

Just as anger and anxiety are incompatible, so is a feeling of pleasure incompatible with an anxiety reaction. Any of the following may work to abort a panic attack:

- Have your spouse or significant other hold you

- Have a pleasurable snack or meal (this snack should consist of complex carbohydrates and protein—such as cheese and crackers or nuts—*not* sugar or junk food)

- Engage in sexual activity

- Take a hot shower or sit and relax in a hot bath

9. *Visualize a Comforting Person or Scene*

If you are visually inclined and you catch your anxiety while it's still at a relatively low level, try imagining a safe person or a peaceful scene. When you visualize a safe person, see him or her standing right there with you, offering you support and reassurance. For the peaceful scene, try using the one you developed for your daily relaxation practice (see Chapter 4).

10. *Practice Thought Stopping*

This is a time-honored behavior modification technique for disrupting a pattern of negative or anxious thoughts. Many people have found thought stopping (either alone or in combination with deep breathing) to be a highly effective technique for diverting panic attacks as well as obsessive "what-if" thinking in anticipation of entering a phobic situation. Follow these steps:

1. Take a deep breath and then shout "Stop!" "Stop It!" or "Get out!" (if there are other people around, you might want to do this silently or just visualize a huge stop sign).

2. Repeat several times, if necessary.

3. Replace anxious thoughts with calming and supportive statements to yourself, such as "This too will pass," "I am calm and strong," or any of the coping statements listed earlier.

    If shouting "Stop!" doesn't serve to interrupt your thoughts, you may want to try snapping a rubber band against your wrist. A number of my clients have found this more physical alternative to be very helpful. Dousing your face with cold water or applying a cold washrag may also serve to disrupt a train of negative thoughts.

    After you have disrupted your negative thinking, you may find it helpful to shift your focus to deep abdominal breathing, as described below. Paying attention to deep breathing will help you to "get out of your head" and divert your attention away from further negative thinking. *In fact, any technique you can find which moves you from being "stuck" in your head into your whole body (breathing, vigorous exercise, being held, and so on) can be effective in helping you to slow down your mind when it seems to be racing out of control.*

All the coping strategies described up to this point can be helpful in aborting or diminishing a panic attack before it gains momentum. These strategies involve various forms of distraction. They are very practical and work well for many people. You will need to experiment with them all to find out which ones work best for you.

The four strategies to be described below involve distraction, but at the same time go beyond it. They are often more powerful than the first eight strategies because they go to the *core* of a panic attack. That is, they directly address the two principal factors that produce panic:

1. Physiological arousal (the fight-or-flight reaction) and

2. Fear-provoking self-talk

A panic attack occurs when you react fearfully to the initial bodily sensations of panic (such as increased heartbeat, respiration, sweating, and other symptoms) and scare yourself into a much more intense reaction with negative self-talk (such as, "Am I going to have heart attack?" "I'm losing control of myself!" "What if someone sees this happening to me!").

Strategies 11 and 12, abdominal breathing and muscle relaxation, directly counteract the physiological arousal reaction that initiates panic. Strategy 13, repeating positive coping statements, counteracts the tendency to create a spiral of fear through negative self-talk.

11. *Practice Abdominal Breathing*

Breathing slowly from your abdomen can help reduce the bodily symptoms of panic in either of two ways:

- By slowing down your respiration and breathing from your abdomen, you can reverse two of the reactions associated with the fight-or-flight response—increased respiratory rate and increased constriction of your chest wall muscles. After three or four minutes of slow, regular, abdominal breathing, you are likely to feel that you have slowed down a "runaway reaction" that was threatening to get out of control.

- Slow abdominal breathing, especially when done through your nose, can reduce symptoms of hyperventilation that may cause or aggravate a panic attack. The dizziness, disorientation, and tingly sensations associated with hyperventilation are produced by rapid, shallow, chest-level breathing. Three or four minutes of slow, abdominal breathing reverses this process and will eliminate hyperventilation symptoms.

Review the section on abdominal breathing in Chapter 4 along with the Abdominal Breathing and Calming Breath exercises. Pick the exercise you prefer and practice it for five minutes every day until you feel that you've mastered it. (Practicing abdominal breathing every day will also help you to retrain yourself to breathe from a deeper level in your lungs.) Once you feel comfortable and confident with a particular technique, try using it anytime you feel the initial symptoms of panic coming on. Remember to keep up slow, abdominal breathing for three to five minutes until you can feel your panic symptoms beginning to subside. If the breathing exercise itself causes you to feel light-headed, stop for 30 seconds, and then start again.

An alternative practice that helps some people to offset panic is simply to take a deep breath and hold it as long as you can at the moment you feel panic symptoms coming on. If you still feel anxious after this, repeat the procedure two or three times.

12. Practice Muscle Relaxation

Much of the discomfort you feel during a panic attack is due to your voluntary muscles tensing up. By practicing deep muscle relaxation at the first onset of panic, you can reverse this particular component of the fight-or-flight reaction. For some people muscle relaxation will work even better than abdominal breathing for reducing the physiological intensity of panic. For others, a combination of abdominal breathing and deep-muscle relaxation will work best.

How do you practice muscle relaxation when you feel panic coming on? Go back and review the section on progressive muscle relaxation in Chapter 4. Practice the following *abbreviated* version when you feel your anxiety starting to increase:

- Clench your fists. Hold for 10 seconds and then release for about 15-20 seconds.

- Tighten your biceps muscles by drawing your forearms up toward your shoulders and "making a muscle" with both arms. Hold about 10 seconds ... and then relax for 15-20 seconds.

- Tighten your forehead muscles by raising your eyebrows as high as you can. Hold about 10 seconds ... and then relax for 15-20 seconds.

- Tighten up the muscles around your eyes by clenching them tightly shut. Hold about 10 seconds ... and then relax for 15-20 seconds.

- Tighten the muscles in the back of your neck by gently pulling your head way back, as if you were going to touch your head to your back. Focus only on tensing the muscles in your neck. Hold about 10 seconds ... and then relax for 15-20 seconds. Repeat this step if your neck feels especially tight.

- Tighten your shoulders by raising them up as if you were going to touch your ears. Hold about 10 seconds ... and then relax for 15-20 seconds.

- Tighten the muscles around your shoulder blades by pushing your shoulder blades back as if you were going to touch them together. Hold the tension in your shoulder blades about 10 seconds ... and then relax for 15-20 seconds. Repeat this step if your upper back feels especially tight.

Taking a few minutes to run through these seven steps will not only divert your attention away from the bodily symptoms of a panic reaction, but will actually slow down the reaction itself. Use muscle relaxation alone or combine it with abdominal breathing by inhaling when you tense a muscle group and exhaling when you release it.

As in the case of abdominal breathing, it is a good idea to gain skill with progressive muscle relaxation in its entirety before using the abbreviated version above to reduce panic symptoms. Practice progressive muscle relaxation for half an hour every day for two weeks so that you can initiate the above steps automatically and effortlessly to counter a panic reaction.

13. Repeat Positive Coping Statements

One of the central points of this chapter has been to emphasize the role of negative self-talk in aggravating a panic attack. While the physical bodily reactions associated with panic (first fear) may come out of the blue, your emotional reaction to these bodily symptoms (second fear) does not. It is based on *what you tell yourself* about these symptoms. If you tell yourself that your physiological symptoms are horrible and very threatening, that you can't stand them, you're going to lose control, or that you might die, you will scare yourself into a very high state of anxiety. On the other hand, if you accept what's happening and make calming, reassuring statements to yourself, such as, "It's only anxiety—I'm not going to let it get to me," "I've been through this before and it's not dangerous," or "I can handle this until it passes," you can minimize or eliminate the escalation of your symptoms.

Use any of the positive coping statements listed earlier in this chapter when you feel the first symptoms of panic coming on. This will help divert your mind away *both* from the bodily symptoms of panic *and* from fear-inducing self-talk that can only make things worse. Many people find it helpful to write several coping statements down on a 3x5 card which they carry with them at all times. Should symptoms start to come on, you simply pull the card out and repeat a particular statement over and over. Keep this up for several minutes if necessary, until you feel the physiological intensity of your panic beginning to subside.

Learning to use coping statements effectively to overcome panic will take practice and perseverance. If you make the effort, you will be surprised how well coping statements can work to prevent your anxiety symptoms from going above Level 4 on the Anxiety Scale. Positive self-talk also can help to limit a panic attack that has already gone above Level 4.

In sum, the way you respond to early physical symptoms of panic will be determined largely by *what you say to yourself,* as illustrated below.

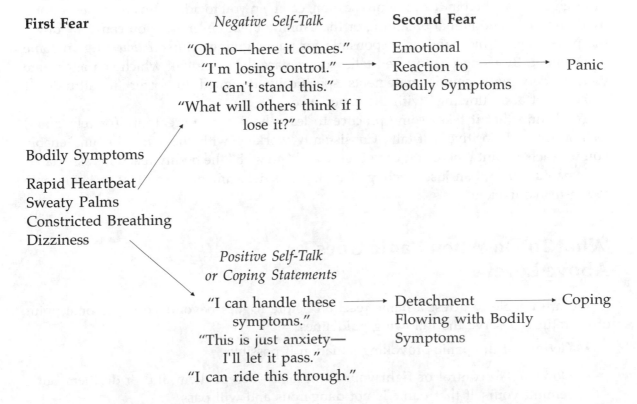

First Fear   *Negative Self-Talk*   **Second Fear**

                                  "Oh no—here it comes."   Emotional
                                  "I'm losing control." ——→   Reaction to ——————→ Panic
                                  "I can't stand this."   Bodily Symptoms
                                  "What will others think if I
                                      lose it?"

Bodily Symptoms

Rapid Heartbeat
Sweaty Palms
Constricted Breathing
Dizziness

                                  Positive Self-Talk
                                  or Coping Statements

                                  "I can handle these ——————→ Detachment ——————→ Coping
                                      symptoms."   Flowing with Bodily
                                  "This is just anxiety—   Symptoms
                                      I'll let it pass."
                                  "I can ride this through."

The choice is up to you.

14. *Use Breathing (or Relaxation) in Combination With Coping Statements*

You might find that a *combination* of abdominal breathing (or progressive muscle relaxation) and repeating a positive coping statement will work best in limiting your panic. Generally it's best to address the physical sensations of panic first with an abdominal breathing exercise (or muscle relaxation), and to follow up shortly thereafter with methodical repetition of a coping statement. You may prefer to completely overlap the two types of techniques or, alternatively, you may want to work exclusively on reducing your physiological arousal for a minute or two and then start working with a positive statement. Experiment to see what works best for you. I suggest that you gain some skill and familiarity with each type of strategy by itself, first, before attempting to put them together. With practice, you may develop a combination of breathing (or muscle relaxation) and self-talk that is very effective against all types and degrees of panic.

Learn To Observe Rather Than React to Bodily Sensations of Anxiety

You can take a major step forward by learning to detach emotionally from the first physical symptoms of panic: simply *observe* them. To the extent that you are able to *watch* the intense reactions your body goes through when aroused without interpreting them as a threat, you will be able to save yourself considerable distress. Strategies 11 through 14, described in the previous section, can help you to adopt this detached stance. By doing deep abdominal breathing or the calming breath exercise, you can slow down the physiological mechanisms responsible for panic, giving yourself *time* to gain some detachment. By using positive self-talk, you replace the scare talk which can aggravate your anxiety with coping statements specifically designed to foster an attitude of detachment and "flowing" with the experience.

You'll find that it takes some practice to learn how to use breathing (or relaxation) techniques and positive self-talk. Consistently working with them *will* in time enable you to reach a point where you can observe and "go with" the bodily reactions associated with panic rather than just reacting. This kind of detachment is the key to being able to master your panic.

What To Do When Panic Goes Above Level 4

If you are unable to arrest a panic reaction before it goes beyond your personal point of no return, observe the following guidelines:

- Get out of the panic-provoking situation if possible

- Don't try to control or fight your symptoms—accept them and "ride them out"; remind yourself that panic is not dangerous and will pass

- Call someone—express your feelings to them

- Move around or engage in physical activity

- Focus on simple objects around you

- Touch the floor, the physical objects around you, or "ground" yourself in some other way

- If you are in a place where you can do so, discharge tension by pounding your fists, crying, or screaming

- Breathe slowly and regularly through your nose to reduce possible symptoms of hyperventilation

- Use positive self-talk (coping statements) in conjunction with slow breathing

- As a last resort, take an extra dose of a minor tranquilizer (with the general approval of your doctor)

During an intense panic attack, you may feel very confused and disoriented. Try asking yourself the following questions to increase your objectivity (you may want to write these out on a 3x5 card which you carry with you at all times).

1. *Are these symptoms I'm feeling truly dangerous?* (Answer: No)

2. *What is the absolute worst thing that could happen?* (Usual answer: I might have to leave this situation quickly or I might have to ask for assistance.)

3. *Am I telling myself anything that is making this worse?*

4. *What is the most supportive thing I could do for myself right now?*

Putting It All Together

To sum up, there are three approaches you can use to deal with the oncoming symptoms of panic:

1. *Retreat*

2. *Distraction*

3. *Breathing* (or muscle relaxation) *and positive self-talk*

The first technique is useful for dealing with panic that arises in the process of confronting a phobic situation; the latter two can be used for phobic panic or for spontaneous panic attacks.

Retreat

If panic symptoms begin to come on when you're approaching or dealing with a phobic situation (such as driving on the freeway, entering the grocery store, or staying at home alone), then retreat if your symptoms exceed Level 4 on the Anxiety Scale.

Bodily symptoms of panic arise while entering a phobic situation

↓

Retreat from the situation

↓

Recover from the symptoms (allow anxiety to fall to a Level 1 or 2)

↓

Reenter the situation

The last step is very important. Not attempting to return to the situation after symptoms of panic have subsided will only reinforce your fear.

Distraction

If panic symptoms come on spontaneously, apart from any phobic situation, you may find it helpful to try distraction first. Distraction can also be helpful in managing your anxiety, up to Level 4, while you are confronting a phobic situation.

Bodily symptoms of panic

↓

Divert your attention from bodily symptoms
(use any of the strategies described in this chapter)

1. Talk to someone

2. Focus on objects in your surroundings

3. Do simple, repetitive tasks (count change, time a stoplight, read your list of affirmations, and so on)

4. Engage in physical activity

5. Express anger physically or at the panic itself

6. Do something pleasurable (get a backrub, eat a delicious snack)

7. Practice thought stopping

↓

Stay involved with the distraction until symptoms
of panic subside (down to Level 1)

Deep Breathing (or Relaxation) and Positive Self-Talk

While distraction techniques can be very practical and effective, you may prefer to get at the "root" of a panic attack by practicing an arousal-reduction technique (abdominal breathing or muscle relaxation) and/or repeating positive coping statements. For many people, these are the most powerful strategies for counteracting panic. They can be used separately or in combination and are useful for spontaneous panic attacks as well as for panic encountered while attempting to confront a phobia.

Bodily symptoms of panic

Do deep breathing (see Chapter 4), either:

(1) Slow, abdominal breathing, preferably through your nose, for up to 3-5 minutes

or

(2) Calming breath (inhale to 5, hold to 5, exhale to 5) up to 10 times

or

Do abbreviated version of progressive muscle relaxation (see above)

and/or

Repeat a positive coping statement over and over (during or following deep breathing or muscle relaxation), for example:

"I can handle this,"

"This will pass and I'll relax,"

"This is just anxiety—it's not dangerous."

Continue deep breathing and/or positive self-talk until symptoms of panic subside (down to Level 1)

Optional: The Use of Symptom Induction Techniques

As discussed earlier in this chapter, symptom inductions are a highly effective technique used by therapists to treat panic disorder. They enable people to learn on an *experiential* level that unpleasant body symptoms are harmless and devoid of negative or catastrophic consequences.

You may want to try symptom induction techniques with a professional therapist who has had experience using them. This is fine, and likely to be a little more comfortable for you. Nevertheless, some people have tried these techniques on their own and found them to be quite helpful. If you decide that you want to include these techniques in your self-help program, please observe the following guidelines:

1. *Check with your doctor if you are over 40 or suspect that you might have any physical condition that would preclude using symptom induction procedures.* For example, you wouldn't try hyperventilation if you have a chronic respiratory problem like asthma or emphysema. You also wouldn't run up and down stairs if you have

any kind of heart condition that restricts physical exercise. Nor would you do induction procedures if you were pregnant or had epilepsy.

2. Although the techniques are harmless, it's a good idea to have a friend or family member present when you first do them to provide support and encouragement. If you can get your support person to do the procedure with you, so much the better.

3. You need to persist in doing the induction procedure long enough so that the sensations produced are unpleasant and/or cause an increase in anxiety. You want to simulate, if possible, the actual sensations you experience during a panic attack. As a general rule, keep doing the procedure about 30 seconds after you first notice it producing unpleasant sensations and/or anxiety.

4. Practice each induction technique once per day, every day, until it loses its ability to make you anxious. With repeated practice, the symptoms you experience from induction procedures should lose their capacity to cause anxiety. This is precisely what you want.

Induction Techniques

After obtaining clearance from your physician, try practicing the following six symptom induction techniques.

1. Hyperventilate continuously for two minutes. This involves breathing deeply and rapidly with your mouth open. At the end of two minutes, stand up.

2. Breathe through a straw while holding your nose for one minute (don't allow any air through your nose).

3. Walk up and down stairs rapidly about 90 seconds or until your heart rate increases noticeably. Stop if you experience dizziness or your heart rate exceeds 140 beats per minute. (Alternatively, you can use a stationary bike or stairmaster to increase your heart rate.)

4. Spin—preferably in a desk chair or else standing up for one minute. It's not necessary to go a full minute if you find yourself getting significantly dizzy. Be near a chair or couch where you can sit back down easily.

5. Tense every part of your body and hold yourself tight for one minute before releasing.

6. Repeat out loud the list of paired associations.

breathless	suffocate
palpitations	dying
numbness	stroke
unreality	insane

After doing this long enough to create anxiety (about one or two minutes), then repeat the same associations inserting "does not mean" in the middle.

Remember to persist with each of these procedures long enough to produce unpleasant sensations. It's ideal if you allow yourself to feel the unpleasant sensations up to 30 seconds, although you may want to start out with a shorter period when you first try the induction. You'll learn the most from this exercise if the procedure actually makes you somewhat uncomfortable or anxious. The idea is to teach yourself that you can have unpleasant body symptoms without anything terrible or dangerous happening. To the extent that this learning carries over to real life panic symptoms, you will likely stop having full-blown panic attacks—that is, you'll be able to withstand the unpleasant body sensations during the early stage of panic without reacting to them as dangerous. Keep in mind that you may need to practice the symptom induction procedures many times before you get to the point where the symptoms don't cause you any anxiety.

After doing a symptom induction procedure, always practice the coping skills you've learned to reduce anxiety, such as abdominal breathing, repeating coping statements, moving around, or talking to your support person. Symptom inductions provide an excellent opportunity to gain confidence in your mastery of coping skills.

What if the inductions don't produce any anxiety, even from the beginning? This might happen for at least two reasons. It could happen because you feel safe doing the procedure in the comfort of your own home or with your support person. Or the process of inducing body symptoms *voluntarily* may give you a sense of control over what's happening that isn't present when a real-life panic situation occurs. In order to give the symptom induction procedures a little more "charge," you can modify the conditions in which you do them as follows:

1. Do the procedures alone.

2. Do the procedures away from your home or safe place.

3. Do them while *visualizing* yourself in your phobic situation.

4. Do them (e.g., hyperventilation or spinning) while actually confronting a phobic situation in real life.

The last procedural modification may actually have a paradoxical effect. If you can *deliberately* bring on panic-like symptoms without negative consequences in your phobic situation, you may come to believe that you have more control over such symptoms when they arise spontaneously.

For a more in-depth discussion of how to use and benefit from symptom inductions, please see the books by David Barlow or Denise Beckfield listed under "Further Reading" at the end of this chapter.

Sharing About Your Condition

A very important way to minimize the likelihood of panic in a large number of situations is simply to inform someone in charge that you have a problem with panic attacks and/or agoraphobia.

This is especially critical if you are afraid of panic attacks interfering with your capacity to perform your job. If you try to work without letting anyone know about your problem, you may come to feel increasingly trapped in the situation—trapped by your fear of what other people might think of you if you "lost it." This is likely to increase rather than decrease the probability of actually panicking.

If you say a little bit about your problem to your boss or a co-worker, you will make your workplace into more of a "safe place." You'll worry less about what others might think if you panic, because someone important already knows. More importantly, you will have given yourself permission to temporarily leave work in the event that you do lose it. With this permission, you are much less likely to feel trapped, and any fears you might have developed about going to work are likely to dissipate.

The same applies to any other situations in which you're afraid of panicking and yet where there is someone in charge you might talk to—such as in classrooms, doctors' and dentists' offices, at parties (talk to the host or hostess), or at group meetings (talk to the facilitator).

To assist you in sharing about your condition, use the *Dear Person Letter*, which is used by permission from the *TERRAP Program Manual* by Dr. Art Hardy. (TERRAP offers group treatment programs for agoraphobia throughout the United States—see Appendix 1.) You can either use the letter verbatim or use it as the basis for developing your own script of what you want to share about your condition. The letter is most applicable to agoraphobia, but can be adapted for social phobia and panic disorder as well. Either hand the letter to someone you wish to tell about your problem or else read it to them.

Remember that *everyone* has experienced anxiety, and *everyone* feels uncomfortable in some situations. If you take the risk of sharing something about your condition, you'll be surprised at the support and acceptance you'll receive.

Dear Person Letter

Dear_____:

I want to tell you something about myself. I have a problem with a type of anxiety called agoraphobia. This is *not* a mental illness, but a kind of anxiety which causes panic attacks.

Although 5 in 100 people suffer from agoraphobia, few people have heard of the condition. It is difficult for me to talk about it, but sharing this information with you is important to me.

Agoraphobia is similar to claustrophobia, except that panic attacks can be triggered by many things, such as crowds, distance from home, freeways, bridges, and/or many other situations. I can neither anticipate nor control these anxiety attacks. Because these attacks are extremely uncomfortable, sometimes terrifying and always embarrassing, I have been avoiding situations which might arouse them.

I have found help for this problem and am making progress. At this point I am doing some things and want to do even more, but I still need a way out of situations that are frightening to me. I have found that when other people understand that I may need to leave an uncomfortable situation, I can do better and it helps in my recovery.

It is extremely important to me to feel free to leave any given situation at any time, no matter how innocuous the situation may appear. I don't ask that you understand my condition, but I would appreciate your help.

In telling you this I am not soliciting your sympathy, but I would like your moral support as I work toward recovery. I realize that the way I confront the problem may seem confusing and even inappropriate to you. Be assured that I have been treated by other methods, but have found that the system I am using now is helping me to recover. By your acceptance, you will be working with me in licking this problem.

Summary of Things To Do

1. Reread the section "Deflate the Danger" several times to reinforce the idea that the various symptoms of a panic attack are not dangerous.

2. Complete the two *Panic Attack Worksheets*. Then make connections between physical sensations or symptoms that accompany your panic reactions, and any catastrophic interpretations you tend to make of those sensations. Remember that it's your catastrophic self-statements that are mainly responsible for triggering panic attacks.

3. Reread the section on Claire Weekes' four-step approach for coping with panic attacks to help you cultivate attitudes of acceptance and nonresistance toward panic symptoms. Learn to flow with panic rather than fight it.

4. Monitor your panic attacks for two weeks, using the *Panic Attack Record* to look for conditions and stimuli that precede your panic reactions.

5. Work on learning to recognize your own early symptoms of panic. Identify what symptoms constitute a Level 4 for you on the *Anxiety Scale* (the point at which you feel like you're beginning to lose control).

6. Experiment with different coping strategies when you feel panic symptoms progressing up through Level 4. Which strategies work best for you?

7. Give special attention to the last four coping strategies.

   a. Practice abdominal breathing (using either the Abdominal Breathing or Calming Breath exercise from the chapter on relaxation) for five minutes per day until you've mastered the technique. Then use it to reduce arousal when you feel the initial physical symptoms of panic coming on.

   b. Practice the abbreviated muscle relaxation exercise for five minutes per day until you've mastered the technique. Then use it to counter the early physical symptoms of panic.

   c. Choose one or more coping statements and practice using them at the moment when you notice that you're starting to scare yourself into more anxiety or panic with negative self-talk. Repeat your coping statements until you are able to overcome any negative self-talk going on in your head.

   d. After you've gained mastery in the use of a, b, and c, try combining them. Start with abdominal breathing or muscle relaxation and follow this up with the repetition of a coping statement. The right combination of these techniques can be even more effective than any one of them alone.

8. Experiment with coping strategies for panic reactions *above* Level 4 on the *Anxiety Scale* to find out which ones work best for you.

9. If you feel so inclined, try the symptom induction procedures in the section designated as "optional." These procedures will desensitize you to physical sensations that you associate with panic. If you're working with a therapist, you may wish to ask him or her to assist you in carrying out symptom inductions.

10. Talk about your condition with a relative, friend, or your supervisor at work, using the *Dear Person Letter* as a framework for what you say.

Further Reading

Barlow, David and Craske, Michelle. *Mastery of Your Anxiety and Panic.* Albany, New York: Graywind Publications, 1989.

Beckfield, Denise F. *Master Your Panic and Take Back Your Life.* San Luis Obispo, California: Impact Publishers, 1994. (A very thorough and useful self-help guide for overcoming panic attacks.)

Clum, George A. *Coping With Panic.* Pacific Grove, California: Brooks/Cole, 1990.

Sheehan, David. *The Anxiety Disease.* New York: Bantam Books, 1986. (Especially recommended as an introductory book for people suffering panic attacks.)

Weekes, Claire. *Hope and Help for Your Nerves.* New York: Bantam Books, 1978.

Weekes, Claire. *Peace from Nervous Suffering.* New York: Bantam Books, 1978. (An excellent resource for learning to deal with panic and other forms of anxiety.)

Wilson, Reid. *Don't Panic: Taking Control of Anxiety Attacks.* New York: Harper and Row, 1986.

7

Help for Phobias:
Imagery Desensitization

The most effective way to overcome a phobia is simply to face it. Continuing to avoid a situation that frightens you is, more than anything else, what keeps the phobia alive.

Having to face a particular situation you have been avoiding for years may at the outset seem an impossible task. Yet this task can be made manageable by breaking it down into sufficiently small steps. Instead of entering a situation all at once, you can do it very gradually in small or even minute increments. And instead of confronting the situation directly in real life, you can face it first in your imagination. This is where imagery desensitization comes in.

Sensitization is a process of becoming sensitized to a particular stimulus. In the case of phobias, it involves learning to associate anxiety with a particular situation. Perhaps you once panicked while sitting in a restaurant or by yourself at home. If your anxiety level was high, it's likely that you acquired a strong association between being in that particular situation and being anxious. Thereafter, being in, near, or perhaps just thinking about the situation automatically triggered your anxiety: a connection between the situation and a strong anxiety response was established. Because this connection was automatic and seemingly beyond your control, you probably did all you could to avoid putting yourself in the situation again. Your avoidance was rewarded because it saved you from reexperiencing your anxiety. At the point where you began to *always* avoid the situation, you developed a full-fledged phobia.

Desensitization is the process of *unlearning* the connection between anxiety and a particular situation. For desensitization to occur, you need to enter a phobic situation while you're in a relaxed or relatively relaxed state. With *imagery* desensitization, you *visualize* being in a phobic situation while you're relaxed. If you begin to feel anxious, you retreat from your imagined phobic situation and imagine yourself instead in a very peaceful scene. With *real-life* desensitization, you confront a phobic situation directly, but physically retreat to a safe place if your anxiety reaches a certain level. In both cases the point is to 1) *unlearn* a connection between a phobic situation (such as driving on the freeway) and an anxiety response and 2) *reassociate* feelings of relaxation and calmness with that particular situation. Repeatedly visualizing a phobic situation while relaxed—or actually entering it while relaxed—will eventually allow you to overcome your tendency to respond with anxiety. If you can train yourself to relax in response to something, you will no longer feel anxious about it. Relaxation and anxiety are incompatible responses, so the goal of desensitization is to learn to remain in the phobic situation and be relaxed at the same time.

You may be asking why it's necessary to go through the desensitization process initially in your imagination. Why not just face the dreaded object or situation in real life? More than 30 years ago, the behavioral psychologist Joseph Wolpe discovered the efficacy of desensitization through imagery. In some cases it is so effective that it supplants the need for real-life desensitization. In other cases, imagery desensitization reduces anxiety sufficiently to make the task of real-life desensitization possible.

Much of the anxiety you have, say, about flying, driving, or being in an elevator is connected with your thoughts and fantasies about these situations. Becoming desensitized first to anxious thoughts and scenes experienced in fantasy can pave the way toward handling the phobic situation in real life. Even if the real-life situation continues to evoke some anxiety, this anxiety may be considerably reduced after having practiced imagery desensitization. This *transfer effect* from imagery to real life was discovered in the early sixties and has been confirmed by research and practice in desensitization techniques over the past 30 years. I strongly recommend that you use the guidelines in this chapter and practice desensitizing yourself to your phobia through imagery *before* attempting real-life desensitization.

Practicing imagery desensitization before confronting a phobia in real life also helps to overcome *anticipatory anxiety*. As the term implies, this is the anxiety you experience in anticipation of having to deal with a phobic situation. Hours or days before making a speech or your first flight, for example, you may experience numerous anxious thoughts and images about the upcoming situation. Dwelling on these anxious thoughts and images only creates more and more anxiety, long before you ever deal with the actual situation. By systematically training youself to relax as you imagine scenes of a future phobic situation, you can reduce your anticipatory anxiety substantially.

A final important reason for practicing desensitization through imagery is that there are many situations in which it is inconvenient if not impossible to expose yourself to your phobic situation in real life. This is particularly a problem if your phobia has to do with natural disasters such as earthquakes or hurricanes. It will also certainly be inconvenient and expensive to undergo a series of real-life exposures if you're phobic about the Bar Exam or transcontinental flights. Much of the fear and anticipatory anxiety around these phobias can be removed through a systematic program that never strays from the realm of your imagination.

Success with imagery desensitization depends on *four* things:

1. Your capacity to attain a deep state of relaxation

2. Constructing an appropriate *hierarchy*: a series of scenes or situations relating to your phobia which are ranked from mildly anxiety-provoking to very anxiety-provoking

3. The vividness and detail with which you can visualize each scene in the hierarchy, as well as your peaceful scene

4. Your patience and perseverance in practicing desensitization on a regular basis

The topic of relaxation was covered in an earlier chapter. Below you will find instructions on how to construct a hierarchy and how to practice desensitization through imagery.

Constructing an Appropriate Hierarchy

A well-constructed hierarchy allows you to approach a phobic situation gradually through a sequence of steps. You can use the following guidelines and sample hierarchies to develop your own:

1. Choose a particular phobic situation you want to work on, whether this involves going to the grocery store, driving on the freeway, or giving a talk before a group.

2. Imagine having to deal with this situation in a very limited way—one that hardly bothers you at all. You can create this scenario by imagining yourself somewhat removed in space or time from full exposure to the situation—such as parking in front of the grocery store without going in, or imagining your feelings one month before you have to give a presentation. Or you can diminish the difficulty of the situation by visualizing yourself with a supportive person at your side. Try in these ways to create a very mild instance of your phobia and designate it as the first step in your hierarchy.

3. Now imagine what would be the strongest or most challenging scene relating to your phobia, and place it at the opposite extreme as the highest step in your hierarchy. For example, if you're phobic about grocery stores, your highest step might be waiting in a long line at the checkout counter by yourself. For flying, such a step might involve taking off on a transcontinental flight, or encountering severe air turbulence midflight. For public speaking, you might imagine either presenting to a large crowd, giving a long presentation, or speaking on a very demanding topic. See if you can identify what specific parameters of your phobia make you more or less anxious and use them to develop scenes of varying intensity. The scenes in the first example below become progressively more challenging in terms of three distinct parameters: 1) distance driven, 2) degree of traffic congestion, and 3) driving alone.

4. Now take some time to imagine six or more scenes of graduated intensity related to your phobia and rank them according to their anxiety-provoking potential. It is desirable to have these scenes correspond to things you will actually do later in real-life exposure (see the next chapter). Place your scenes in ascending order between the two extremes you've already defined. Use the sample hierarchies below to assist you. Then write down your list of scenes on the *Hierarchy Worksheet* on page 143.

Phobia About Driving on Freeways

Visualize:

1. Watching from a distance as cars drive past on the freeway

2. Riding in a car on the freeway with someone else driving (this could be broken down into several steps, varying the distance traveled or time spent on the freeway)

3. Driving on the freeway the distance of one exit with a friend sitting next to you at a time when there is little traffic

4. Driving the distance of one exit with a friend when the freeway is busier (but not at rush hour)

5. Repeat Step 3 alone

6. Repeat Step 4 alone

7. Driving the distance of two exits with a friend sitting next to you at a time when there is little traffic

8. Driving the distance of two exits with a friend sitting next to you at a time when there is moderate traffic

9. Repeat Step 7 alone

10. Repeat Step 8 alone

In steps above this level you would increase the distance you drive and also include driving during rush-hour conditions.

Phobia About Giving Presentations at Work

Visualize:

1. Preparing a talk which you don't give

2. Preparing a talk and delivering it in front of one friend

3. Preparing a talk and delivering it in front of three friends

4. Giving a brief presentation to three or four people at work who you know well

5. Same as Step 4 but a longer presentation

6. Giving a brief presentation to 10-15 acquaintances at work

7. Same as Step 6 but a longer presentation

8. Giving a brief presentation to three or four strangers

9. Same as Step 8 but a longer presentation

10. Giving a brief presentation to 10-15 strangers

11. Giving a brief presentation to 50 strangers

Phobia About Getting Injections

Visualize:

1. Watching a movie in which a minor character gets a shot

2. A friend talking about her flu shot

3. Making a routine doctor's appointment

4. Driving to a medical center

5. Parking your car in the medical center parking lot

6. Thinking about shots in the doctor's waiting room

7. A woman coming out of the treatment room rubbing her arm

8. A nurse with a tray of syringes walking past

9. Entering an examination room

10. A doctor entering the room and asking you about your symptoms

11. The doctor saying you need an injection

12. A nurse entering the room with injection materials

13. The nurse filling a syringe

14. The smell of alcohol being applied to a cotton ball

15. A hypodermic needle poised in the doctor's hand

16. Receiving a penicillin shot in the buttocks

17. Receiving a flu shot in the arm

18. Having a large blood sample taken

Note that in all three examples, increments from one step to the next are very small. One of the keys to success with imagery desensitization is creating a hierarchy with sufficiently small steps so that it is relatively easy to progress from one level to the next.

5. Generally, 8-12 steps in a hierarchy are sufficient, although in some cases you may want to include as many as 20. Fewer than 8 steps is usually an insufficient number to make the hierarchy meaningful.

6. Sometimes you may find it difficult to go from one step to the next in your hierarchy. You may be able to relax in the context of the scene you've created in Step 9, but become very anxious when you visualize Step 10. In this instance you need to construct an *intermediate* scene (at "9-1/2") that can serve as a bridge between the two original scenes.

7. If you have difficulty feeling comfortable with the initial scene in your hierarchy, you need to create a still-less-threatening scene to start out with.

How To Practice Imagery Desensitization

Desensitization through imagery is a two-step process. First, you need to take the time to get very relaxed. Second, you go through the desensitization process itself, which involves alternating back and forth between visualizing a particular step in your hierarchy and recapturing your feelings of deep relaxation. Be sure to follow all of the steps outlined below.

1. **Relax.** Spend 10-15 minutes getting relaxed. Use progressive muscle relaxation or any other relaxation technique that works well for you (see Chapters 4 and 11).

2. **Visualize yourself in a peaceful scene.** This is a relaxing place you can vividly picture in your mind (see Chapter 4). It can be a scene outdoors (such as a beach, a meadow, or the mountains), indoors (curling up by a fireplace), or can come completely from your imagination. Above all it is a place where you feel *safe*. Spend about one minute there.

3. **Visualize yourself in the first scene of your phobia hierarchy.** Stay there for 30 seconds to 1 minute, trying to picture everything with as much vividness and detail as possible, as if you were "right there." Do *not* picture yourself as being anxious. If you see yourself in the scene at all, imagine yourself acting and feeling calm and confident—dealing with the situation in the way you would most like to. If you feel *little or no anxiety* (below Level 2 on the Anxiety Scale), proceed to the next scene up in your hierarchy.

4. **If you experience *mild to moderate anxiety* (Level 2 or 3 on the Anxiety Scale), spend 30 seconds to 1 minute in the scene, allowing yourself to relax to it.** You can do this by breathing away any anxious sensations in your body or by repeating a calming affirmation such as, "I am calm and at ease." *Picture yourself handling the situation in a calm and confident manner.*

5. **After up to a minute of exposure, retreat from the phobic scene to your peaceful scene.** Spend about 1 minute in your peaceful scene or long enough to get *fully* relaxed. Then *repeat* your visualization of the same phobic scene as in Step 4 for 30 seconds to 1 minute. Keep alternating between a given phobic scene and your peaceful scene (about 1 minute each) until the phobic scene loses its capacity to elicit any (or more than very mild) anxiety. *Then* you are ready to proceed to the next step up in your hierarchy.

6. **If visualizing a particular scene causes you *strong anxiety* (Level 4 or above on the Anxiety Scale), do *not* spend more than 10 seconds there.** Retreat immediately to your peaceful scene and stay there until you're fully relaxed. Expose yourself gradually to the more difficult scenes, alternating short intervals of exposure with retreat to your peaceful scenes. If a particular scene in your hierarchy continues to cause difficulty, you probably need to add another step—one that is intermediate in difficulty between the last step you completed successfully and the one that is troublesome.

7. **Continue progressing up your hierarchy step by step in imagination.** Generally it will take a minimum of two exposures to a scene to reduce your anxiety to it. Keep in mind that it's important not to proceed to a more advanced step until you're fully comfortable with the preceding step. Practice imagery desensitization for 15-20 minutes each day and begin your practice *not* with a new step but with the last step you successfully negotiated. (Then proceed to a new step.)

Hierarchy for _____
                        (specify phobia)

Instructions: Start with a relatively easy or mild instance of facing your phobia. Develop at least eight steps which involve progressively more challenging exposures. The final step should be your goal or even a step beyond what you've designated as your goal.

Step   *Scene*

 1. _____

 2. _____

 3. _____

 4. _____

 5. _____

 6. _____

 7. _____

 8. _____

 9. _____

10. _____

11. _____

12. _____

13. _____

14. _____

15. _____

16. _____

17. _____

18. _____

19. _____

20. _____

Note: Make copies of this sheet and use one copy for each of your phobias.

To sum up, imagery desensitization involves four steps that you apply to *each* scene in your hierarchy:

1. *Visualize* the phobic scene as vividly as possible.

2. *React to the scene* allowing yourself to relax with it for 30 seconds to 1 minute if your anxiety stays below Level 4. Picture yourself handling the scene in a calm and confident manner. If your anxiety to the scene reaches Level 4 or above, retreat to your peaceful scene after 5-10 seconds of exposure.

3. *Relax* in your peaceful scene for up to a minute, until you're fully calm.

4. *Repeat* the process of alternating between a phobic scene and your peaceful scene until the phobic scene loses its power to elicit anxiety. At this point proceed to the next scene up in your hierarchy.

How To Get the Most Out of Imagery Desensitization

The process of desensitization will work best if you adhere to the following guidelines:

1. Spend about 15-20 minutes the first time you practice imagery desensitization. As you gain skill in relaxation and visualization, you can lengthen your sessions to 30 minutes. In this time period (on a good day), you can expect to master two or three scenes in your hierarchy.

2. You need to be very relaxed for this sort of desensitization to be effective. If you feel that you aren't deeply relaxed, then you might spend more time—20-30 minutes—relaxing at the outset, and spend more time relaxing in your peaceful scene after each exposure to a particular phobic scene. Make sure that you *fully* recover from any anxiety after each exposure.

3. If you have difficulty developing a peaceful scene of your own, refer to the examples given in Chapter 4.

4. You need to be able to visualize each phobic scene as well as your peaceful scene in detail, as if you were really there. If you are having difficulty with visualizing effectively, you might ask yourself the following questions about each scene to heighten its vividness and detail:

   - What objects or people are in the scene?
   - What colors do you see in the scene?
   - Is the light bright or dim?
   - What sounds can you hear in the scene?
   - Can you hear the wind or a breeze?
   - What is the temperature of the air?
   - What are you wearing?
   - Can you smell or taste anything?
   - What other physical sensations are you aware of?
   - What are your emotions within the scene?

5. Stop a particular session if you feel tired, bored, or overly upset.

6. Try to practice every day if possible. Desensitization through imagery will be most effective following your regular period of relaxation.

7. Even if the first few scenes in your hierarchy don't elicit any anxiety at all, it's important to expose yourself to each of them at least once. (You can proceed from one to the next without retreating to your peaceful scene if your anxiety stays below Level 2.) Imagery desensitization is at work even when you're not feeling any anxiety in response to a given scene because you are still associating relaxation with your phobia.

Putting Imagery Desensitization on Tape

You might find it helpful to put instructions for desensitization on tape to reduce any distractions while going through the process. Use the guidelines below for making your own tape.

- Begin your tape with 10-15 minutes of instructions for deep relaxation. Use the instructions for progressive muscle relaxation given in Chapter 4 or any visualization that can induce a state of deep relaxation (see Chapter 11).

- Following the relaxation phase, visualize yourself in your peaceful scene. Use the instructions given in Chapter 4 to introduce your scene. Spend at least one minute there.

- After going to your peaceful scene, record your own instructions for desensitization, according to the guidelines below.

   Picture yourself in the first scene of your phobia hierarchy ... Imagine what it would be like if you were actually there.

   (Pause 15-20 seconds.)

   Now allow yourself to relax in this scene ... do whatever you need to do to relax.

   (Pause 15-20 seconds.)

   Picture yourself handling the situation in just the way you would like to... Imagine that you are feeling relaxed, calm, and confident. You might also wish to take in a deep breath ... and as you exhale, let out any tense or uncomfortable feelings.

   (Pause 15-20 seconds.)

   Now let go of this scene and go back to your peaceful scene. Remain there until you feel fully relaxed. Put your recorder on pause if you need to until all your anxiety is gone.

   (Let one minute elapse on the tape, then continue recording.)

   If you felt any anxiety imagining the previous scene in your hierarchy, go back and imagine yourself there again ... Take a minute to let go and relax in the context of that scene, and then return to your peaceful scene until you are fully relaxed ... You can place your cassette player on pause to do this ... If you felt little or no anxiety within the previous scene, you're ready to go on.

(Leave a 10-second pause on the tape, then continue recording.)

Now, if you were fully relaxed in the previous scene, go on to the next scene in your hierarchy ... Imagine what it would be like if you were actually there.

(Pause 15-20 seconds.)

(Repeat the above instructions a second time, starting from the phrase: "Now allow yourself to relax in this scene ... ")

Your tape should consist of 1) 10-15 minutes of instructions for deep relaxation, 2) instructions for going to your peaceful scene, with a minute of silence for being there, and 3) the above instructions for systematic desensitization repeated twice.

In general, it is best not to work on more than two new scenes in your hierarchy at a given time if they are triggering any anxiety. You can work through more than two scenes in your hierarchy only if they are not causing you any discomfort. Please note that *it is important not to move up to a new scene in your hierarchy until you've completely desensitized to the preceding scene*. This means that you can visualize it in detail and feel little or no anxiety. When you begin your practice session, it's a good idea to go back and practice on the scene you most recently desensitized to before proceeding to a new scene. You can then allow yourself to progress to new scenes further up in your hierarchy.

Practicing Desensitization With Your Support Person

It's possible to have a friend or support person give you instructions for imagery desensitization. Such instructions can be found in Appendix 2.

Summary of Things To Do

1. Construct a hierarchy consisting of at least eight scenes for each phobia you want to work on. Use the examples in this chapter as well as in Appendix 3 to assist you with this.

2. Review the section "How To Practice Imagery Desensitization" so that you're thoroughly familiar with the procedure.

3. Practice imagery desensitization for your phobia three to five times per week. You may wish to put instructions for desensitization on tape, as suggested above. Or you can have a support person give you instructions, following the format presented in Appendix 2.

4. When you've progressed about halfway up your hierarchy in fantasy, you're ready to undertake real-life desensitization with your phobia (see the following chapter).

5. If you're having difficulty reducing your anxiety with imagery desensitization, the problem may lie in one of four areas. You may need to

- Be more completely relaxed before you begin—desensitization works best when you're very relaxed

- Work on visualizing your phobic scenes, or your peaceful scene, in more detail

- Become completely desensitized to a particular step in your hierarchy before proceeding to the next step, or

- Add additional steps in your hierarchy, especially if the "gap" betweeen one scene and the next one up is too wide

Further Reading

McKay, Matthew; Davis, Martha; and Fanning, Patrick. *Thoughts and Feelings: The Art of Cognitive Stress Intervention*. Oakland, California: New Harbinger Publications, 1981. (See Chapter 6)

Wolpe, Joseph. *The Practice of Behavior Therapy*, Second edition. New York: Permagon Press, 1973.

Wolpe, Joseph, and Wolpe, David. *Life Without Fear*. Oakland, California: New Harbinger Publications, 1988.

8

Help for Phobias:
Real-Life Desensitization

Real-life desensitization is the single most effective available treatment for phobias. While imagery desensitization is often an important prerequisite, actually facing the situations you've been avoiding in real life is essential for recovery.

Other terms for real-life desensitization are *in vivo desensitization*, *exposure therapy*, or simply *exposure*. In many controlled studies, direct exposure to phobic situations has consistently been found to be more effective than other, nonbehavioral treatments such as insight therapy, cognitive therapy by itself, or medication. Nothing works better towards overcoming a fear than facing it—especially when this is done systematically and in small increments. Furthermore, improvement resulting from real-life exposure does not disappear weeks or months later. Once you've fully desensitized yourself to a phobic situation in real life, you can remain free of fear.

Real-life desensitization is the treatment of choice for agoraphobia, social phobias, and many simple phobias. It's useful in overcoming the *territorial* phobias that are common in agoraphobia—for example, grocery stores, shopping malls, driving on bridges or freeways, riding on buses, trains, or planes, scaling heights, and being alone. *Social* phobias that respond to direct exposure include fears of public speaking, making presentations, being in groups, attending social functions, dating, using public restrooms, and taking examinations. And simple phobias ranging from fears of insects to a fear of water can all be overcome by direct exposure.

For all types of phobias it's desirable to practice desensitization through imagery before undertaking real-life exposure. When you're at least halfway up your desensitization hierarchy of phobic scenes, you can begin to confront your phobia in real life. Again, you must start at the lowest step in your hierarchy and progress upwards. As with imagery desensitization, you advance to each new step in your real-life hierarchy only after you can easily handle the preceding step.

If real-life exposure is such an effective treatment, why are there still so many phobic people around? Why hasn't everybody availed themselves of a treatment that is so powerful? The answer is simple. For all its effectiveness, exposure isn't a particularly easy or comfortable process to go through. Not everyone is willing to tolerate the unpleasantness of facing phobic situations or to persist with practicing real-life desensitization on a regular basis. *Exposure therapy demands a strong commitment on your part.* If you're genuinely committed to your recovery, then you'll be willing to

- Take the risk to start facing situations you may have been avoiding for many years

- *Tolerate the initial discomfort* that entering phobic situations—even in small increments—often involves

- *Persist in practicing* exposure on a consistent basis, despite probable setbacks, over a long enough period of time to allow your complete recovery (generally this takes from six months to two years)

If you're ready to make a genuine commitment to real-life desensitization over a period of up to a year or two, you *will* recover from your phobias.

How To Practice Real-Life Desensitization

The basic procedure for real-life desensitization is essentially the same as for imagery desensitization, with some modifications. You can use the same basic hierarchy of phobic scenes you constructed for your desensitization through imagery, progressing from a low-anxiety to a high-anxiety situation. The difference is that you will be carrying out the steps of the hierarchy in real life rather than in your imagination. You may find that you need to add some additional steps to your real-life hierarchy. You may also want to have a support person accompany you as you confront your phobic situations, although it's possible to do this work alone. Finally, you need to retreat when your anxiety reaches Level 4 on the Anxiety Scale (see Chapter 6), or when you reach the point where you feel like you're beginning to lose control. Use the guidelines below to design your exposure therapy.

Set Goals

Start out by clearly defining your goals. What would constitute being fully recovered from your phobias? Do you want to be able to drive on the freeway alone? Buy the week's groceries by yourself? Give a presentation at work? Fly on a jet?

Be sure to make your goals specific. Instead of aiming for something as broad as being comfortable shopping, define a specific goal such as "buying three items in the grocery store by myself" or "making a one-hour flight." Eventually you will want to remove all restrictions—in other words, be comfortable in any store or on any flight. For the purpose of setting up a hierarchy, keep your goals concrete. Once you've defined goals, set up timelines. By what date would you like to be able to give a speech, drive the freeway, or make a flight? Six months from now? One year from now? Give yourself a timeframe within which to work and then make a commitment to stick with it. It's often useful to differentiate between short- and long-term goals. Use the worksheet on the next page to define where you would like to be with your recovery process at various points in the future. Make a copy of this statement of your goals and post it in a conspicuous place to remind yourself of your plan for overcoming your fears.

GOALS

A. In Three Months

B. In Six Months

C. In One Year

D. After Two Years

Create a Hierarchy for Each Goal

You're ready now to break each goal down into small steps. Use the hierarchy you constructed in the last chapter, keeping in mind that you will be enacting each step in real life. Make sure that you start off with a very easy, only mildly anxiety-arousing step and work up to a final step that you would be able to do if you were fully recovered from your phobia. Your hierarchy should have from 8 to 20 progressively more difficult steps.

In some instances, it will be necessary to construct a different hierarchy for real-life exposure than what you used for imagery desensitization. You may need more and smaller steps when you face a situation in real life than when you're visualizing it in your mind. A scene that was part of your visualization may be impractical to enact in real life, as in the case of a public speaking phobia.

Remember to add an additional step in the middle if you are having difficulty moving from one step to the next. For example, suppose you're exposing yourself to grocery shopping. You've reached the point where you can stay in the store for several minutes but you can't bring yourself to buy an item and go through the express checkout line. One intermediate step you could add would be taking an item in your basket up to the checkout line, waiting in line as long as your anxiety level remained mild (below Level 4 on the Anxiety Scale), and then returning the item to where you found it. You would repeat this step without buying anything until the action became monotonous. Another example of an intermediate step would be to go through the checkout line with your support person carrying and paying for the item you picked out. After several repetitions of this, you might be ready to go through the line and buy an item on your own.

If you have a problem getting beyond a particular step, try going back to the preceding step in your hierarchy for your next practice session and work your way back up. For example, if you've mastered driving over a small bridge but have difficulty advancing to the next largest one, go back and repeat driving over the smaller bridge several times. The object is to get yourself so bored with the smaller bridge that you feel a strong incentive to attempt the next step up in your hierarchy. When you do, have your support person go with you.

If you have difficulty getting started with exposure therapy, try beginning with an even less challenging step than your original first step. For example, you might have a phobia about flying and you don't feel ready even to drive to the airport. As a preliminary step, watch a video that shows jets taking off and in flight, or get used to looking at photos of planes in a magazine. If you still can't make it to the airport, drive *by* it repeatedly until you feel able to drive to the airport parking lot, turn around, and return home.

As mentioned earlier, it's helpful to master desensitization through imagery before undertaking real-life exposure. As a general rule, you should start real-life exposure after you've been practicing imagery desensitization for about two weeks—or after you've worked through about half of your hierarchy.

Three examples follow of hierarchies developed for real-life exposure. More examples may be found in Appendix 3. Please note that these are only sample hierarchies; your own hierarchy of phobic scenes involving elevators or grocery stores may differ depending on what aspects of the situations elicit your greatest anxiety.

Elevators

1. Look at elevators, watching them come and go.

2. Stand in a stationary elevator with your support person.

3. Stand in a stationary elevator alone.

4. Travel up or down one floor with your support person.

5. Travel up or down one floor alone, with your support person waiting outside the elevator on the floor where you will arrive.

6. Travel two to three floors with your support person.

7. Travel two to three floors alone, with your support person waiting outside the elevator on the floor where you will arrive.

8. Extend the number of floors you travel, first with your support person and then alone with your partner waiting outside the elevator.

9. Travel on an elevator alone without your support person.

Grocery Stores

1. Drive to the grocery store with your support person and spend one minute in the parking lot.

2. Drive to the grocery store with your support person and spend five minutes in the parking lot.

3. Walk up to the entrance of the grocery store and walk around outside for two minutes with your support person.

4. Repeat Steps 1, 2, and 3 alone.

5. Enter the grocery store for 15 seconds with your support person and then walk out.

6. Enter the grocery store for one minute with your support person and then walk out.

7. Walk to the back of the store with your support person and spend two minutes in the store.

8. Enter the store with your support person and go along while he or she buys one item.

9. Enter the store with your support person and go along as he or she buys two items from different aisles.

10. Repeat Steps 5, 6, and 7 with your support person waiting outside.

11. Enter the store with your support person and buy one item.

12. Enter the store with your support person and buy two items from different aisles.

13. Buy one item alone with your support person waiting outside.

14. Buy two items alone with your support person waiting outside.

15. Go shopping by yourself, buying only one item the first time and gradually increasing the number of items bought and your time spent inside the grocery store.

Flying

1. Approach the airport with your support person and drive around it.

2. Park at the airport with your support person for five minutes.

3. Enter the terminal with your support person and walk around for five minutes.

4. Go to a departure gate with your support person and watch planes take off and land.

5. Repeat Steps 1-4 alone.

6. Arrange to visit a grounded plane and spend one minute on board with your support person.

7. Same as 6 but stay on board for five minutes. You might try buckling into a seat.

8. Repeat Steps 6 and 7 alone.

9. Schedule a short flight (15-30 minutes) and go with your support person.

10. Schedule a longer flight and go with your support person.

11. Repeat Steps 9 and 10 alone.

On the following page is a form on which you can design your own hierarchy of steps for a particular phobia. Make several copies of this page and write down hierarchies for the specific phobias you wish to work on. You may not need all 20 steps, but try to create a minimum of 8 different steps, proceeding from the least to the most challenging steps.

Hierarchy for _____
(specify phobia)

Instructions: Start with a relatively easy or mild instance of facing your phobia. Develop at least eight steps which involve progressively more challenging exposures. The final step should be your goal or even a step beyond what you've designated as your goal.

Write down the date on which you complete each step as you work your way up in the hierarchy.

Step   *Date Completed*

1. _____

2. _____

3. _____

4. _____

5. _____

6. _____

7. _____

8. _____

9. _____

10. _____

11. _____

12. _____

13. _____

14. _____

15. _____

16. _____

17. _____

18. _____

19. _____

20. _____

Note: Make a copy of this sheet for each of your phobias.

Procedure for Direct Exposure

1. ***Proceed*** *into your phobic situation* (whatever step in your hierarchy you're on) *up to the point where your anxiety reaches Level 4 on the Anxiety Scale.* In other words, keep going into or stay in the situation up to the point where your anxiety *first begins to feel a little unmanageable.* Even if you are *uncomfortable* in the situation, *stay with it* as long as your anxiety level does not go beyond Level 3.

2. ***Retreat*** from the situation at the point where your anxiety reaches Level 4 or the point where it begins to feel less than fully manageable—the point where it feels like it might get out of control. Retreat means *temporarily* leaving the situation until you feel better and then *returning.* In most situations this is literally possible (when aboard an airplane, you can retreat to your peaceful scene in your mind). *Retreat is not the same as escaping or avoiding the situation.* It is designed to prevent you from "flooding" and risking the possibility of resensitizing yourself to the situation and reinforcing the strength of your phobia.

   Flooding means to let your anxiety rise above Level 4 without retreating. Some poeple find that staying in a phobic situation without retreating, and enduring a high level of anxiety, may be a useful strategy. This flooding approach does seem to work for a minority of people who suffer from phobias. However I do not recommend it for most people, as it often tends to lead to increased sensitization and a reinforcement of fear. If you do decide to try the flooding approach, it is best to just *stay* at your current step in your hierarchy without going any further. For example, you would not go any further back into a grocery store—nor would you retreat—at the point where your anxiety begins to rise above Level 4. You allow your anxiety to rise and run its course without fighting or resisting it until it subsides. If you're one of the minority of people for whom flooding works, by all means use it as a tool in your recovery.

3. ***Recover.*** After you temporarily pull back from your phobic situation, wait until your anxiety level recedes to no more than Level 1 or 2 on the Anxiety Scale. Be sure to give yourself sufficient time for your anxiety to subside. You may find that abdominal breathing or walking around at this point helps you recover your equanimity.

4. ***Repeat.*** After recovering, reenter your phobic situation and continue to progress into it up to the point where your anxiety, once again, reaches Level 4 on the Anxiety Scale. If you are able to go further or stay longer in the situation than you did before, fine. If not—or if you can't go even as far as you did the first time—that's fine, too. Do not chastise yourself if your performance after retreating turns out to be less spectacular than it was initially. This is a common experience. In a day or two you'll find that you'll be able to continue in your progression up your hierarchy.

5. ***Continue going through the above cycle—Expose-Retreat-Recover-Repeat—***until you begin to feel tired or bored, then stop for the day. This constitutes one practice session, and it will typically take you from thirty minutes to two hours. For most people one practice session per day is enough. In a single session you may be unable to master the first step in your hierarchy or you may progress through the

first four or five steps. *The limit for how far you go in any practice session should be determined by the point when your anxiety reaches Level 4 on the Anxiety Scale.*

On some days you'll enjoy excellent progress, on others you'll hardly progress at all, and on still others you will not go as far as you did on preceding days. On a given Monday you might spend five minutes alone in the grocery store for the first time in years. On Tuesday you can endure five minutes again but no more. Then on Wednesday you are unable to go into the store at all. Thursday or Friday, however, you discover that you can last ten minutes in the store. This up-and-down, "two steps forward, one step back" phenomenon is typical of exposure therapy. Don't let it discourage you!

Rely on a Support Person — Especially at the Beginning

It's often very helpful to rely on a person you trust (such as your spouse, partner, friend, or a helping professional) to accompany you on your forays into your phobia hierarchy when you first begin the process of real-life desensitization. The support person can provide reassurance and safety, distraction (by talking with you), encouragement to persist, and praise for your incremental successes.

However, your support person shouldn't push you. Your partner *should* encourage you to enter a phobic situation without running away. But it's up to you to decide on the intensity of your exposure and to determine when you reach Level 4 and need to retreat. Your support person should not criticize your attempts or tell you to try harder. Yet it is good if she or he can identify any resistance on your part and help you to recognize whether such resistance is present. Your partner's main job is to provide encouragement and support without judging your performance. Guidelines for support people can be found at the end of this chapter.

Become Aware of Your Particular Sensitivities

As you undertake exposure, look for which particular characteristics of your phobic situation make you anxious. In the grocery store, for example, is it the number of people, the size of the store, the brightness of the lights, or simply the multiplicity of stimuli that causes you anxiety? While participating in a group, is it the number of people, the proximity of an exit, a fear of being judged or of making a bad impression that bothers you the most? Becoming aware of the specific elements of any phobic situation that makes you anxious will increase your sense of control over that situation and accelerate desensitization. You may want to list your specific sensitivities for each phobia on the back of your hierarchy worksheet for that phobia.

Making the Most of Exposure

These instructions are intended to help you get the most out of real-life desensitization:

1. **Be Willing To Take Risks**
   Entering a phobic situation that you've been avoiding for a long time is going to

involve taking a mild to moderate risk. There's simply no risk-free way to face your fears and recover. Risk-taking is easier, however, when you start with small, limited goals and proceed incrementally. Establishing a hierarchy of phobic situations allows you to take this incremental approach toward mastering your phobias.

2. *Deal With Resistance*

Undertaking exposure to a situation that you've been avoiding may bring up resistance. Notice if you delay getting started with your exposure sessions or find reasons to procrastinate. The mere thought of actually entering a phobic situation may elicit strong anxiety, a fear of being trapped, or self-defeating statements to yourself such as, "I'll never be able to do it" or "This is hopeless." Instead of getting stuck in resistance, try to regard the process of desensitization as a major therapeutic opportunity. By plunging in you will learn about yourself and work through long-standing avoidance patterns that have held up your life. Give yourself pep talks about how much your life and relationships will improve when you are no longer plagued by your phobias.

You might also want to review the section on motivation under "Necessary Ingredients for Undertaking Your Own Recovery Program" in Chapter 3. Consider whether there are any secondary gains that might be contributing to your resistance.

Once you get through any initial resistance to real-life exposure, the going gets easier. If you feel you're having problems with resistance at any point, you may want to consult a therapist who is familiar with exposure therapy.

3. *Be Willing To Tolerate Some Discomfort*

Facing situations that you've been avoiding for a long time is not particularly comfortable or pleasant. It's inevitable that you will experience some anxiety in the course of becoming desensitized. In fact, it is common to feel *worse initially* at the outset of exposure therapy before you feel better. Recognize that feeling worse is *not* an indication of regression but rather that exposure is really *working*. Feeling worse means that you're laying the foundation to feel better. As you gain more skill in handling symptoms of anxiety when they come up during exposure, your practice sessions will become easier and you'll gain more confidence about following through to completion.

4. *Avoid Flooding—Be Willing To Retreat*

Your exposure sessions are entirely different from the phobic situations you are forced into by circumstance. In the process of desensitization, you are in control of the intensity and length of your exposure to the situations that frighten you: circumstance does not offer this luxury. Always be willing to retreat from a practice situation if your anxiety reaches Level 4 on the Anxiety Scale. Then wait until you recover before confronting the phobic situation again. *Retreat is not cowardly*—it is the most efficient and expedient way to master a phobia. Overexposure or *flooding* may resensitize you to a situation and ultimately prolong the time it takes to overcome your phobia.

5. *Plan for Contingencies*

Suppose you're practicing on an elevator and the worst happens— it stops between floors. Or suppose you are just beginning to drive on the freeway and you start to panic when you're far away from an exit. It's good to plan ahead for those worst-case scenarios whenever possible. In the first example, give yourself some insurance by practicing on an elevator that has a functioning emergency phone. Or in the case of the freeway, tell yourself in advance that it will be all right to retreat to the shoulder or at least drive slowly with your emergency flashers on until you reach an exit. If you'll be entering a situation that doesn't have a "trap door," keep your list of coping statements (see Chapter 6) near at hand, or bring along your relaxation cassette and a tape player with headphones.

6. *Trust Your Own Pace*
   It's important not to regard real-life exposure as some kind of race. The goal is not to see how fast you can overcome the problem: pressuring yourself to make great strides quickly is generally not a good idea. In fact to do so carries a risk of resensitizing yourself to your phobia if you attempt advanced steps in your hierarchy before becoming fully comfortable with earlier steps. Decide on the pace you wish to adopt in exposing yourself to a difficult situation, realizing that very small gains count for a lot in this type of work.

7. *Reward Yourself for Small Successes*
   It's common for people going through real-life desensitization to castigate them- selves for not making sufficiently rapid progress. Bear in mind that it's important to consistently reward yourself for small successes. For example, being able to go into a phobic situation slightly further than the day before is worthy of giving yourself a reward, such as a new piece of clothing or dinner out. So is being able to stay in the situation a few moments longer—or being able to tolerate anxious feelings a few moments longer. Rewarding yourself for small successes will help sustain your motivation to keep practicing.

8. *Learn To Cope With the Early Stages of Panic*
   Use your array of coping techniques (see Chapter 6) if you are unable to easily retreat from a situation when your anxiety reaches Level 4:

   • Deep abdominal breathing
   • Affirmative self-talk
   • Conversation with your support person
   • Distractions (such as counting the number of blue cars on the freeway)
   • Anger (get angry with the anxiety)
   • Thought stopping

   Remember to maintain an overall attitude of "floating" or "going with" your bodily sensations rather than balking or resisting them. Using abdominal breath- ing and positive self-talk in combination often helps. As soon as retreat becomes possible, use this option!

9. *Use Positive Coping Statements When Entering a Phobic Situation*
   Repeating positive statements over and over before or during exposure sessions can be quite helpful. Repetition of coping statements serves to direct your attention away from physical symptoms of anxiety and prevents you from talking yourself into a higher level of panic. Such statements encourage a confident and composed attitude that can help you through the most difficult moments in your exposure practice. Use the list of positive coping statements provided later in this chapter.

You may want to write some of them on a 3x5 card which you carry with you during your practice sessions.

10. *Practice Regularly*

Methodical and regular practice—rather than hurrying or pressuring yourself—will do the most to expedite your recovery. Ideally it is good to practice real-life desensitization *three to five times per week*. Longer practice sessions, with several trials of exposure to your phobic situation, tend to produce more rapid results than shorter sessions. As long as you retreat when appropriate, it's impossible to undergo too much exposure in a given practice session (the worst that can happen is that you might end up somewhat tired or drained).

The *regularity* of your practice will determine the rate of your recovery. If you're not practicing regularly, notice what excuses you're making to yourself and sit down with someone else to evaluate them. Then find arguments for refuting those excuses the next time they come up. Regular practice of exposure is *the key* to a full and lasting recovery.

11. *Expect and Know How To Handle Setbacks*

Not being able to tolerate as much exposure to a situation as you did previously is a normal part of recovery. Recovery simply doesn't proceed in a linear fashion—there will be plateaus and regressions as well as times of moving forward. Setbacks are an integral part of the recovery process.

For example, suppose you are working on overcoming a phobia about driving on freeways. Your practice sessions over a four-week period might go like this:

Week 1: During three out of five practice sessions you can drive the distance of one exit on the freeway.

Week 2: For five out of five practice sessions you can't get on the freeway at all. (This degree of regression is not at all uncommon.)

Week 3: For two out of five practice sessions you are able to drive the distance of one exit. During two other sessions you're able to drive the distance of two exits. One day you can't get on the freeway at all.

Week 4: Due to illness you only get in two practice sessions. On one of those days you're able to manage three exits.

It's very important not to let a setback discourage you from further practice. Simply chalk it up to a bad day or bad week and learn from it. Nothing can take away the progress you've made up to now. You can use each setback as a learning experience to tell you more about how to best proceed in mastering a particular phobic situation.

12. *Be Prepared To Experience Stronger Emotions*

Facing phobic situations you've been avoiding for a long time often stirs up suppressed feelings—not only of anxiety but anger and sorrow as well. Recognize that this is a normal and expected part of the recovery process. *Allow* these feelings to surface and let yourself express them. Let yourself know "It's O.K. to have these feelings" even though you may be uncomfortable with them. An important part of recovery from a phobic condition is learning to accept, express, and communicate your feelings (see Chapter 13).

13. *Follow Through To Completion*
Finishing exposure therapy means that you reach a point where you are no longer afraid of panic attacks in *any* situation that was formerly a problem (obviously this does not include extreme situations that anyone would be afraid of). The recovery process generally takes from six months to two years to complete. Getting comfortable with most situations but still having one or two you are afraid of is generally insufficient. To attain lasting freedom from your phobias, it's important to keep working until you get to the point where 1) you can go into any situation that nonphobic people would regard as safe, and 2) you regard panic reactions themselves as manageable and not at all dangerous.

Factors That Can Promote or Impede Your Success

Numerous studies have examined the conditions affecting the success of exposure therapy. This section summarizes the findings of this research. For a more detailed discussion, see the 1988 volume by David Barlow, *Anxiety and Its Disorders: The Nature and Treatment of Anxiety and Panic* (see especially Chapter 11).

What Promotes Success

1. *Cooperation of Your Partner or Spouse*
When your partner or spouse supports your recovery and is willing to assist you in the exposure process itself, results are often excellent. Conversely, if your partner is indifferent, uncooperative, or consciously or unconsciously opposes your recovery, success with exposure may be difficult to attain. If you feel that your partner is interfering with your progress in overcoming your phobias, you both may want to consult a competent couples' therapist who is knowledgeable about the treatment of phobias.

2. *Willingness To Tolerate Some Discomfort*
As discussed in the previous section, it is inevitable that you will feel more anxiety when you begin to confront phobic situations in real life. Practicing exposure therapy is hard work and requires a willingness to tolerate some discomfort. It may be tempting not to begin or not to follow through with exposure because you dread the unpleasantness involved. That is why it is so important to reward yourself for your efforts. In some cases, *low* doses of a minor tranquilizer, such as Xanax, may be a useful adjunct in the early stages of exposure therapy. Low doses of a minor tranquilizer can reduce your anxiety just enough to make the process feasible while still allowing desensitization to occur. (See Chapter 17 for a more detailed discusssion of the pros and cons of using tranquilizers.)

3. *Ability To Handle the Initial Symptoms of Panic*

   Fear of having a panic attack is perhaps the greatest deterrent to undertaking a course of real-life desensitization. If you've developed a broad repertory of skills for handling the early symptoms of panic (as detailed in Chapter 6), you can approach exposure with considerable confidence. Many phobia treatment programs these days train clients to cope with physical reactions associated with panic *before* beginning a program of gradual exposure.

4. *Willingness To Retreat When Retreat Is Appropriate*

   Moving too fast or pushing yourself too hard to confront phobic situations is likely to backfire. If you don't retreat when your anxiety reaches Level 4 on the Anxiety Scale, you're likely to resensitize rather than desensitize yourself to whatever situation you're confronting. In recent years, most phobia treatment programs have given up the old approach of flooding and have allowed clients to *pace themselves*, emphasizing the importance of retreating when anxiety begins to rise. This newer approach has resulted in higher success rates and a greater number of people following through with exposure to complete recovery. In short, it is wise to avoid taking a "Rambo" approach to your exposure sessions.

5. *Ability To Handle Setbacks*

   Some people stop their program of exposure after experiencing one or two setbacks, failing to recognize that setbacks are a normal and predictable part of the process. Your ability to tolerate setbacks and still persist in your daily practice sessions will be a crucial determinant of your success.

6. *Willingness To Practice Regularly*

   Regular, consistent practice—in other words, three to five times per week—is unquestionably the *strongest* predictor of success with exposure. There is simply no substitute for regular practice. It has been my experience over the years that the clients who practice regularly are the ones who recover. There is no phobia that cannot be overcome by a steady and persistent commitment to practice exposure. This is definitely an area of human experience where "persistence wins the race."

What Interferes With Success

The opposite of any of the above-mentioned conditions will tend to impede your success with exposure: lack of cooperation from your partner, your own inability to tolerate some discomfort, a lack of skills for coping with panic, an unwillingness to retreat when retreat is appropriate, an inability to handle setbacks, and/or an unwillingness to practice consistently. In addition, clinical research has shown that the following two conditions can impede success with exposure therapy:

1. *Depression*

   People who suffer from clinical depression associated with agoraphobia or social phobia are generally less motivated to practice exposure. They also have a tendency to discount successes and progress when they do practice. Common symptoms of clinical depression include

- Fatigue and lack of energy
- Self-reproach and feelings of worthlessness
- Loss of interest or pleasure in usual activities
- Difficulty concentrating
- Reduced appetite
- Difficulty sleeping
- Suicidal thoughts

If you feel you're experiencing three or more of the above symptoms, it would be advisable to have a clinical consultation before undertaking a self-paced program of exposure. Cognitive behavior therapy is an extremely effective treatment for depression. In more serious cases, antidepressant medication, taken under a doctor's supervision, can help lift your mood enough to allow you to practice real-life desensitization.

2. *Alcohol and Tranquilizers*
Alcohol or high doses of minor tranquilizers such as Xanax tend to interfere with exposure. It's necessary to experience *some* anxiety during exposure to a phobic situation if you are to learn new and more adaptive responses to it. People who undergo exposure therapy while on high doses of minor tranquilizers often relapse when they go off the medication. This is less likely when you've been taking a low dosage (for example, 1 mg or less of Xanax per day). In fact, *low* doses of tranquilizers may in some cases be helpful toward undertaking and maintaining a program of exposure.

Using Coping Statements During Exposure

It's often helpful when doing real-life exposure to work with coping statements. These are positive statements you can say to yourself just before you begin to face your phobic situation—or during the exposure process itself. If you have a problem with public speaking, for example, you would use them before you do your presentation. With most other phobias, you can use coping statements before or during exposure.

The purpose of using coping statements is to help distract your mind from any negative, anxiety-provoking self-talk you might be prone to engage in when you face what you fear. These positive statements also help put your mind in a positive frame. They can help you relax and maintain your confidence just before or during the time you confront your phobia. Any anxiety you experience during exposure tends to make you more suggestible. By repeating positive coping statements at the time of exposure, you will induce a positive state of mind which can help keep your anxiety at a lower level.

There are two ways in which you might want to work with coping statements. First, you might want to record your favorite statements on an audio cassette and listen to them right before you directly confront your phobic situation. If you have a portable cassette recorder, you might even want to listen to them during the exposure process itself.

An alternative, more active way to work with coping statements is to write them down on 3x5 cards—one or two statements per card. Keep the cards in your purse or wallet and then take them out and rehearse the coping statements before or during your real-life exposure sessions. Some people find repeating a single coping statement over and over to be more effective, while others like to read down a list of several coping statements at once.

Keep in mind that to get the most benefit from coping statements, you will need to practice working with them many times. They may not be as effective in offsetting anxiety the first few times you use them as they will be after repeated practice. It took many repetitions to reinforce your negative, anxiety-provoking self-statements that trigger your anxiety. By the same token, it will take repeated use of positive coping statements—before or during real-life exposure—to reach a point where you fully internalize them.

The following 30 coping statements are divided into three categories: statements to use when you are *preparing* to face your phobic situation; statements you can use when you *first confront* the situation and *during* the exposure process; and, finally, statements you can use to help you handle any symptoms or feelings that come up during exposure.

Preparing To Face Your Phobia

Today I'm willing to go just a little outside my comfort zone.

This is an opportunity for me to learn to become comfortable with this situation.

Facing my fear of _____ is the best way to overcome my anxiety about it.

Each time I choose to face _____, I take another step toward becoming free of fear.

By taking this step now, I'll eventually be able to do what I want.

There's no right way to do this. Whatever happens is fine.

I know I'll feel better once I'm actually in the situation.

Whatever I do, I'll do the best I can.

I praise myself for being willing to confront my fear of _____.

There's always a way to retreat from this situation if I need to.

First Confronting (and During Exposure to) Your Phobia

I've handled this before and I can handle it now.

Relax and go slowly. There's no need to push right now.

I can take some abdominal breaths and take my time.

Nothing serious is going to happen to me.

It's okay to take my time with this and do only as much as I'm ready to do today.

I'm going to be all right. I've succeeded with this before.

I don't have to do this perfectly. I can let myself be human.

I can think about being in my peaceful place as I undertake this.

I can monitor my anxiety level and retreat from this situation if I need to.

This is not as bad as I thought.

As I continue to practice exposure, it will get easier.

Coping With Body Sensations and Feelings That Come Up During Exposure

I can handle these symptoms or sensations.

These sensations (feelings) are just a reminder to use my coping skills.

I can take some abdominal breaths and allow these feelings to pass.

These feelings will pass and I'll be okay.

This is just adrenalin—it will pass in a few minutes.

This will pass soon.

These are just thoughts—not reality.

This is just anxiety—I'm not going to let it get to me.

Nothing about these sensations or feelings is dangerous.

I don't need to let these feelings and sensations stop me. I can continue to function.

It's always okay to retreat for a while if I need to.

Guidelines for the Support Person

Support people come in many guises, including spouses, lovers, relatives, friends, other people with phobias, recovered phobics, and therapists. The most important characteristics of an effective support person include: a caring and supportive attitude, the ability to be nonjudgmental, and a willingness to encourage you to face your fears with patience and persistence.

The following guidelines are intended for support people who may work with you during your exposure therapy.*

---

*I am indebted to Barbara Bringuel for much of the content of these guidelines.

1. Be familiar with the material presented in this workbook, especially the concepts of desensitization, retreat, and the Anxiety Scale.

2. Before beginning a practice session, communicate clearly with your phobic partner about what is expected of you during practice. Do they want you to talk a lot to them? Stay right with them? Follow behind them? Wait outside? Hold their hand?

3. If your partner is easily overwhelmed, help them to break each problem down into small, incremental steps.

4. It's up to the phobic—not the partner—to define the goals of a given practice session. Partners should be cooperative rather than assuming the initiative.

5. Partners should be familiar with the phobic's early warning signs of anxiety. Encourage them to verbalize when they're beginning to feel anxious (reaching Level 4 on the Anxiety Scale). Don't be afraid to ask them from time to time how they're doing.

6. Create with your phobic partner a list of coping statements and relaxation procedures that you can remind them of during exposure sessions.

7. Don't allow your partner's distress to rattle you, but don't fail to take it seriously. Remember that anxiety isn't necessarily rational. In case of a panic attack, quietly lead your partner away from the threatening situation, end the practice session for the day, and take your partner home. Above all, stay close by until the panic completely subsides.

8. A hug can go much further than a lot of words. If you see that your partner is frightened in a particular situation, your hug or the offer of your hand will help relieve anxiety better than any lecture about how there is no reason to be afraid.

9. Be reliable. Be where you say you're going to be during a practice session. Don't move to another location because you want to test your partner. It can be very frightening for the phobic to return to a prearranged meeting place and find you gone.

10. Don't push a person with phobias! Phobics know what's going on in their body and may panic if pushed further than they're ready to go at a particular point in their recovery.

11. On the other hand, encourage your partner to make the most out of practice. It's better to attempt to enter a frightening situation and have to retreat than not to try at all. Your partner's resistance may be making practice impossible or may be impeding progress. If your partner seems stalled or unmotivated to practice, ask what is getting in the way of proceeding. Assist, if you can, in exploring and identifying psychological resistance.

12. In spite of all your desire to help, phobics must have responsibility for their own recovery. Be supportive and encouraging but avoid trying to step in and do it all for them. This will only undermine their confidence.

13. Try to see things from the phobic's point of view. Things which seem insignificant to others—such as walking down a street or eating in a restaurant—may involve

a great deal of work and courage for the phobic to achieve, even for a short period of time. These accomplishments and the efforts leading to them should be recognized.

14. Phobics generally are very sensitive and need a great deal of praise for every step they take. Be sure to give your partner recognition for small achievements. Praise them for whatever they accomplish and be understanding and accepting when they regress.

15. Encourage practice with rewards. For example, you might say, "When you can handle restaurants, let's have lunch together somewhere special."

16. Accept the phobic's "bad" days and reinforce the idea that they can't have a perfect day every time. Backsliding is part of the normal course of exposure therapy.

17. It may be necessary to readjust your own schedule to facilitate your partner's practice. Be sure you're willing to make a commitment to work with your partner regularly over a sustained period of time before offering to be a support person. If you're unable to see them through the full period of recovery (which can take typically six months to two years), let them know specifically how long a commitment you can make.

18. Know your own limits. Be forgiving when you are a less-than-perfect partner. If your capacity to be supportive has been stretched to the limit, take a break.

What Type of Support Person (or Partner) Are You?

The kind of support you can offer your phobic partner or friend depends to a great degree on what type of person you are. Dr. Art Hardy, founder of the TERRAP Program (the first program to offer effective treatment for agoraphobia) outlined six types of personalities that can interfere with being an effective, helpful support person:

1. The overly capable type

2. The overly dictatorial, domineering type

3. The overly protective type

4. The overly critical type

5. The overly quiet, inhibited type

6. The overly objective type

If you're trying to be of assistance to a phobic person, consider whether any of these categories fits you. It's especially important to be aware of these issues if you happen to be the spouse or partner of an agoraphobic.

1. Overly Capable Type
The overly capable type wants to take charge and do more and more for the phobic person. In essence, they believe that through their skill and capability, they can take responsibility and "fix" the phobic's problems. The result is that phobics, often insecure and lacking in confidence in the first place, give up their independence, self-sufficiency,

and self-esteem until a point is reached where they no longer know what they want or how to go about finding it. They look to the support person to take charge. Thus the overly capable support person needs to learn how to consciously restrict his or her own efforts to do too much for the phobic. Only in that way can phobics grow in their sense of self-sufficiency and independence.

2. Overly Dictatorial, Domineering Type

In some ways similar to the overly capable type, the overly domineering support person or partner tries to control and regiment the phobic's attempts at recovery much as an overcontrolling parent would attempt to supervise a child. The dictatorial type enjoys power and believes that the agoraphobic's recovery is dependent on an enforced program and consistent discipline. The usual result of this approach is to undermine the phobic's spontaneity and increase his or her overall level of fear and inhibition. As phobic people in such a partnership increasingly withhold their spontaneous feelings and impulses, anxiety rises and the relationship becomes more strained. Finally, such relationships may need to come to an end if the phobic person is to learn to express her or himself and become self-sufficient.

In this case, both the partner and the phobic might do well to seek counseling. The former needs to take the risk of relinquishing control; the latter needs to risk becoming an assertive, independent individual.

3. Overly Protective Type

Overly protective support people or partners tend to infantalize the phobic by being too inclined to take care of them, trying to respond to their every need. What phobics learn from this is that they can get a lot of attention and comfort by keeping this type of dysfunctional relationship going. They can also lose their sense of self-sufficiency and self-esteem by becoming overly dependent on the ministrations of their oversolicitous partner. The result is that they become too comfortable to risk the difficulties and anxiety involved in overcoming their phobias.

Again, it is useful for both the overly protective partner and the phobic to seek counseling. Overly protective partners need to give up the habit of obtaining their sense of self-worth by playing parent to the phobic. Phobics need to be willing to give up some of the comfort of being overly protected in order to individuate and become their own person.

The three preceding patterns, on the part of the support person or partner, constitute variations on the common theme of co-dependency, which is discussed elsewhere in this book (see Chapters 11 and 15). The following three personality types, though less likely to create co-dependent relationships with the phobic, still tend to interfere with the latter's recovery.

4. Overly Critical Type

Overly critical types often learned their characteristic way of behaving from overly critical parents. Frequently their tendency to put down and ridicule the phobic is fueled by frustration and anger over having their life limited by their partner's restrictions. Sometimes they rationalize their behavior with the erroneous belief that pointing out the phobic's faults and weaknesses will somehow correct the situation.

Phobic people are insecure and inclined to be highly self-critical. Being overly critical toward them only increases their low self-esteem and anxiety, further impeding any chance at progress. It's important that overly critical partners learn to relax their standards and accept the phobic's limitations and weaknesses. This can go a long way toward helping phobics get past their own perfectionism and tendencies toward self-criticism. In order to deal with the inevitable frustration that living with a phobic person can evoke, it's important for both partners to cultivate some of their own interests and pursuits that provide a sense of satisfaction outside the immediate context of the relationship.

5. Overly Quiet, Inhibited Type

The quiet, overly inhibited support person (or partner) may not provide sufficient stimulation for the phobic. The example such a person provides may lead the phobic to hold back and suppress his or her feelings and self-expression. After a sustained period of time, withheld feelings lead to chronic stress and tension. The body keeps score and may eventually develop anxiety or panic reactions (see the chapter on feelings).

It's important that quiet, introverted partners learn how to get in touch with and express their own feelings. This can happen through individual or group therapy, attending and participating in support groups, or even going to classes or workshops on communication. In this way partners can help phobics learn to express rather than repress their feelings.

6. Overly Objective Type

The overly objective approach to working with a phobic is an attempt to base everything on reason and logic. The problem with this approach is that fear is neither reasonable nor logical. It's important to realize that phobic thinking, especially during times of anxiety or panic, is likely to be entirely subjective. At these times phobics are simply unable to respond to logic. Their response is likely to be, "Yes, I know that being in the supermarket is not actually dangerous, but the way my body is reacting sure makes it *feel* dangerous. I feel like I *have* to leave." If you attempt to reason with phobic people under these circumstances, they will likely clam up, withdraw, or even become considerably more anxious because they feel misunderstood. A better approach is to allow phobics to talk about exactly how they are feeling. Listen to them carefully at these times so that they can gain reassurance and confidence by feeling understood. This is the most effective way to offer support. In general, don't criticize phobics because their reactions don't seem to be logical. Even if you've never experienced what they're going through, make an effort to understand that the ability to think rationally drops out when anxiety runs high.

Living with a person restricted by phobias can be frustrating. Yet it is vital that your frustration and resentment are not directed toward the phobic, either overtly (through outbursts and verbal bashing) or covertly (through overcontrolling or passive-aggressive behavior). Support people or partners need support, too, and a chance to deal with their feelings. They also need to have opportunities to pursue their own interests, on occasion, apart from the relationship. Here are some recommendations for accomplishing both of these aims:

1. Give yourself the opportunity to express your frustrations regarding your phobic partner either in counseling or with a supportive friend.

2. Set clear limits on what you can do for the phobic—but don't withdraw your support and encouragement.

3. Listen to the phobic's needs, making your best effort to respond, but don't take responsibility for his or her recovery.

4. Take "time out" from your relationship with the phobic to pursue creative hobbies, interests, and goals that give you a sense of forward movement and meaning in your life.

5. Remember that recovery from agoraphobia is time-limited. If the phobic person gets appropriate treatment—and engages in that treatment—he or she should make substantial gains in one or two years. Thus the present restrictions on your life are not long term.

When Are Medications Useful?

The emphasis of this chapter up to this point has been to offer practical strategies you can use to help you face and overcome your phobias in real life. If practiced regularly and conscientiously, these strategies are very effective. Direct exposure has repeatedly proven itself to be the most helpful method for overcoming phobias.

Sometimes, however, it is difficult for some people to get started with exposure. When your anxiety level is very high, or you've been avoiding particular situations for a long time, your initial resistance to beginning the first few sessions of exposure may be strong. You may, quite literally, have difficulty "getting out the door." It is in this situation that medication can sometimes be useful. While not providing a long-term solution, medication can sometimes help you get over initial blocks and barriers to getting started. Once you've gained more confidence about being able to handle previously avoided situations, the medication can gradually be phased out.

Two types of medication may be useful in facilitating early exposure. Both types can reduce the frequency and intensity of panic attacks sufficiently to help you get past your initial resistance. In so doing, they will also tend to reduce anticipatory anxiety.

1. The newer SSRI antidepressant medications, Paxil and Zoloft (see the chapter on medications), often help by reducing both anxiety and depression. This can certainly help increase motivation to undertake exposure. It's usually necessary to take these medications three to four weeks before therapeutic benefits occur. Also, if you're sensitive to these medications, it's best to start out with a *low dose, for example, 1/2 or even 1/4 of a tablet per day*, and gradually to work up to 1 tablet per day, usually taken in the morning.

2. A low dose of a benzodiazepine tranquilizer, such as .25 mg Klonopin or .25 mg Xanax, can be taken about one-half hour prior to your practice session. With benzodiazepines, two conditions need to be observed. First, it's important that the dose be low, since if you take a dose high enough to mask your anxiety, you will not experience desensitization. It's always necessary to experience some anxiety for desensitization to be effective. Second, if possible, use the medication *only*

before you go out to practice. Taking the medication several times per day, although sometimes necessary and often prescribed this way, is more likely to lead to dependence and eventual addiction. If you are not taking any medication, I suggest you try the antidepressant approach before trying a low dose of a benzodiazepine tranquilizer, since the former carries no risk of addiction. In either case, it will eventually be necessary to undertake exposure without the assistance of the medication if you wish to gain a sense of complete mastery over your fear.

See the chapter on medications for further guidelines on how to use either antidepressant medications or tranquilizers.

Summary of Things To Do

1. Decide on those phobias for which you're ready to undertake real-life desensitization. It's best to have practiced imagery desensitization with these phobias first, as described in Chapter 7.

2. Establish a hierarchy with at least eight steps for each phobia you wish to work on. Use the hierarchies you created for imagery desensitization. You may find it helpful to add some additional steps to your real-life hierarchies. If you haven't yet constructed any hierarchies for your phobias, use the examples in this chapter and in Appendix 3 as models.

3. Review the section "Procedure for Direct Exposure" so that you're thoroughly familiar with the correct procedure for real-life desensitization. Learning to retreat and recover when your anxiety reaches Level 4 on the Anxiety Scale is especially important.

4. Practice real-life desensitization three to five days per week. Monitor your progress by indicating the date you complete each step in your hierarchy on the hierarchy worksheets. Regular practice is the best way to ensure your success.

5. Rely on a support person (your spouse, partner, a close friend, a recovered phobic, or a therapist) when you begin to work on your hierarchy and also the first time you confront each new step. Having a support person with you should help make exposure easier unless you have a strong preference for doing it on your own.

6. Review the section "Making the Most of Exposure" so that you fully understand all of the ingredients that contribute to success with real-life desensitization. Your willingness to a) deal with initial resistance, b) tolerate some discomfort, c) learn to retreat, d) practice regularly, and e) handle setbacks is particularly important.

7. Practice using coping statements when you're preparing to undertake an exposure session, or during the exposure process itself.

8. Have your support person read the section "Guidelines for the Support Person" before she or he accompanies you on your practice sessions.

9. If you've utilized everything in this book up to and including this chapter, and you're still having a difficult time getting started with exposure, consult with your doctor about the possibility of using medication to help you move forward.

Resources

Audio tapes by the author are available to help you prepare for real-life desensitization. Each tape contains two guided visualizations: one for imagery desensitization and the other to help build confidence and optimism about overcoming a particular phobia. These tapes can assist you in mastering the following eight phobias:

- Shopping in a Supermarket
- Driving Further From Home
- Driving Freeways
- Flying
- Heights
- Giving a Talk
- Speaking Up in Public
- Fear of Illness

For further information on these tapes, see the notice at the end of this book.

Further Reading

Barlow, David. *Anxiety and Its Disorders*. New York: Guilford Press, 1988. (For professional readers.)

Chambless, Dianne, and Goldstein, Alan. *Agoraphobia: Multiple Perspectives on Theory and Treatment*. New York: Wiley, 1982.

Hardy, Arthur. *Agoraphobia: Symptoms, Causes and Treatment*. Menlo Park, California: TSC Corporation, 1976. (Available from TERRAP Programs—see Appendix 1)

Newman, Fredrick. *Fighting Fear: The Eight-Week Program for Treating Your Own Phobia*. New York: Bantam Books, 1986.

Ross, Jerilyn. *Triumph Over Fear*. New York: Bantam Books, 1994. (An inspiring and valuable guide for both clients and professionals.)

Zane, Manuel, and Milt, Harry. *Your Phobia: Understanding Your Fears Through Contextual Therapy*. New York: Warner Books, 1986.

9
Self-Talk

Imagine two individuals sitting in stop-and-go traffic at rush hour. One perceives himself as trapped, and says such things to himself as "I can't stand this," "I've got to get out of here," "Why did I ever get myself into this commute?" What he feels is anxiety, anger, and frustration. The other perceives the situation as an opportunity to lay back, relax, and put on a new tape. He says such things to himself as "I might as well just relax and adjust to the pace of the traffic," or "I can unwind by doing some deep breathing." What he feels is a sense of calm and acceptance. In both cases, the situation is exactly the same, but the feelings in response to that situation are vastly different because of each individual's internal monologue, or *self-talk*.

The truth is that it's *what we say to ourselves* in response to any particular situation that mainly determines our mood and feelings. Often we say it so quickly and automatically that we don't even notice, and so we get the impression that the external situation "makes" us feel the way we do. But it's really our interpretations and thoughts about what is happening that form the basis of our feelings. This sequence can be represented as a time-line:

External Events	→	Interpretation of Events and Self-Talk	→	Feelings and Reactions

In short, you are largely responsible for how you feel (barring physiological determinants, such as illness). This is a profound and very important truth—one that sometimes takes a long time to fully grasp. It's often much easier to blame the way you feel on something or someone outside yourself than to take responsibility for your reactions. Yet it is through your willingness to accept that responsibility that you begin to take charge and have mastery over your life. The realization that you are mostly responsible for how you feel is empowering once you fully accept it. It's one of the most important keys to living a happier, more effective, and anxiety-free life.

Anxiety and Self-Talk

People who suffer from phobias, panic attacks, and general anxiety are especially prone to engage in negative self-talk. Anxiety can be generated on the spur of the moment by repeatedly making statements to yourself that begin with the two words "what if." Any anxiety you experience in anticipation of confronting a difficult situation is manufactured out of your own what-if statements to yourself. When you decide to avoid a situation altogether, it is probably because of the scary questions you've asked yourself: "What if I panic?" "What if I can't handle it?" "What will other people think if they see me anxious?" Just noticing when you fall into what-if thinking is the first step toward gaining control over negative self-talk. The real change occurs when you begin to *counter* and *replace* negative what-if statements with positive, self-supportive statements that reinforce your ability to cope. For example, you might say, "So what," "These are just thoughts," "This is just scare-talk," "I can handle this," or "I can breathe, let go, and relax."

I want you to consider some basic facts about self-talk. Following these facts is a discussion of the different types of self-defeating inner monologues.

Some Basic Points About Self-Talk

- Self-talk is usually so automatic and subtle that you don't notice it or the effect it has on your moods and feelings. You react without noticing what you told yourself right before you reacted. Often it's only when you relax, take a step back, and really examine what you've been telling yourself that you can see the connection between self-talk and your feelings. What is important is that *you can learn to slow down and take note of your negative internal monologue.*

- Self-talk often *appears in telegraphic form.* One short word or image contains a whole series of thoughts, memories, or associations. For example, you feel your heart starting to beat faster and say to yourself, "Oh no!" Implicit within that momentary "Oh no!" is a whole series of associations concerning fears about panic, memories of previous panic attacks, and thoughts about how to escape the current situation. Identifying self-talk may require unravelling several distinct thoughts from a single word or image.

- Anxious self-talk is typically *irrational but almost always sounds like the truth.* What-if thinking may lead you to expect the worst possible outcome in a given situation, one that is highly unlikely to occur. Yet because the association takes place so quickly, it goes unchallenged and unquestioned. It's hard to evaluate the validity of a belief you're scarcely aware of—you just accept it as is.

- Negative self-talk *perpetuates avoidance.* You tell yourself that a situation such as the freeway is dangerous and so you avoid it. By continuing to avoid it, you reinforce the thought that it's dangerous. You may even project images of catastrophe around the prospect of confronting the situation. In short, anxious self-talk leads to avoidance, avoidance begets further anxious self-talk, and around and around the cycle goes.

  Avoidance $\longleftrightarrow$ Anxious Self-Talk

- Self-talk can *initiate or aggravate a panic attack.* A panic attack often starts out with symptoms of increasing physiological arousal, such as a more rapid heartbeat, tightness in the chest, or sweaty palms. Biologically, this is the body's *natural* response to stress—the fight-or-flight response that all mammals, including humans, normally experience when subjected to a perceived threat. There is nothing inherently abnormal or dangerous about it. Yet these symptoms can remind you of previous panic attacks. Instead of simply allowing your body's physiological reaction to rise, peak, and subside in its own good time, you scare yourself into a considerably more intense panic attack with scary self-talk: "Oh no, it's happening again," "What if I lose control?" "I *have* to get out of here now," or "I'm going to fight this and make it go away." This scare-talk aggravates the initial physical symptoms, which in turn elicits further scare-talk. A severe panic attack might have been aborted or rendered much less intense had you made reassuring statements to yourself at the onset of your first symptoms: "I can accept what's happening even though it's uncomfortable," "I'll let my body do its thing," "This will pass," "I've gotten through this before and I will this time," or "This is just a burst of adrenalin that can metabolize and pass in a few minutes."

- Negative self-talk is a *series of bad habits*. You aren't born with a predisposition to fearful self-talk: you *learn* to think that way. Just as you can replace unhealthy *behavioral* habits, such as smoking or drinking excess coffee, with more positive, health-promoting behavior, so can you replace unhealthy thinking with more positive, supportive *mental* habits. Bear in mind that the acquisition of positive mental habits takes the same persistence and practice required for learning new behaviors.

Types of Negative Self-Talk

Not all negative self-talk is the same. Human beings are not only diverse but complex, with multifaceted personalities. These facets are sometimes referred to as "subpersonalities." Our different subpersonalities each play their own distinct role and possess their own voice in the complex workings of consciousness, memory, and dreams. Below I've outlined four of the more common subpersonality types that tend to be prominent in people who are prone to anxiety: the Worrier, the Critic, the Victim, and the Perfectionist.* Since the strength of these inner voices varies for different people, you might find it useful to rank them from strongest to weakest in yourself.

1. The Worrier (promotes anxiety)

Characteristics: Usually this is the strongest subpersonality in people who are prone to anxiety. The Worrier creates anxiety by imagining the worst-case scenario. It scares you with fantasies of disaster or catastrophe when you imagine confronting something you fear. It also aggravates panic by reacting to the first physical symptoms of a panic attack. The Worrier promotes your fears that what is happening is dangerous or embarrassing ("What if I have a heart attack?!" "What will they think if they see me?!").

In short, the Worrier's dominant tendencies include 1) anticipating the worst, 2) overestimating the odds of something bad or embarrassing happening, and 3) creating grandiose images of potential failure or catastrophe. The Worrier is always vigilant, watching with uneasy apprehension for any small symptoms or signs of trouble.

---

* These subpersonalities are based on Reid Wilson's descriptions of the Worried, Critical, and Hopeless Observers in his book *Don't Panic: Taking Control of Anxiety Attacks.*

Favorite Expression: By far the favorite expression of the Worrier is "What if..."

Examples: Some typical dialogue from the Worrier might include: "Oh no, my heart's starting to beat faster! What if I panic and lose complete control of myself?" "What if I start stammering in the middle of my speech?" "What if they see me shaking?" "What if I'm alone and there's nobody to call?" "What if I just can't get over this phobia?" or "What if I'm restricted from going to work for the rest of my life?"

2. The Critic (promotes low self-esteem)

Characteristics: The Critic is that part of you which is constantly judging and evaluating your behavior (and in this sense may seem more "apart" from you than the other subpersonalities). It tends to point out your flaws and limitations whenever possible. It jumps on any mistake you make to remind you that you're a failure. The Critic generates anxiety by putting you down for not being able to handle your panic symptoms, for not being able to go places you used to go, for being unable to perform at your best, or for having to be dependent on someone else. It also likes to compare you with others, and usually sees them coming out favorably. It tends to ignore your positive qualities and emphasizes your weaknesses and inadequacies. The Critic may be personified in your own dialogue as the voice of your mother or father, a dreaded teacher, or anyone who wounded you in the past with their criticism.

Favorite Expression: "What a disappointment you are!" "That was stupid!"

Examples: Typical of the Critic's self-talk are statements such as the following: "You stupid... (the Critic relishes negative labels). "Can't you ever get it right?" "Why are you always this way?" "Look at how capable _____ is," or "You could have done better."

3. The Victim (promotes depression)

Characteristics: The Victim is that part of you which feels helpless or hopeless. It generates anxiety by telling you that you're not making any progress, that your condition is incurable, or that the road is too long and steep for you to have a real chance at recovering. The Victim also plays a major role in creating depression. The Victim believes that there is something inherently wrong with you: you are in some ways deprived, defective, or unworthy. The Victim always perceives insurmountable obstacles between you and your goals. Characteristically, it bemoans, complains, and regrets things as they are at present. It believes that nothing will ever change.

Favorite Expressions: "I can't." "I'll never be able to."

Examples: The Victim will say such things as: "I'll never be able to do that, so what's the point in even trying?" "I feel physically drained today—why bother doing anything?" "Maybe I could have done it if I'd had more initiative ten years ago—but it's too late now."

4. The Perfectionist (promotes chronic stress and burnout)

Characteristics: The Perfectionist is a close cousin of the Critic, but its concern is less to put you down than to push and goad you to do better. It generates anxiety by constantly telling you that your efforts aren't good enough, that you *should* be working harder, that you *should* always have everything under control, *should* always be competent, *should* always be pleasing, *should* always be _____ (fill in whatever you keep telling yourself that you "should" do or be). The Perfectionist is the hard-driving part of you that wants to be best and is intolerant of mistakes or setbacks. It has a tendency to try to convince you that your self-worth is dependent on *externals* such as vocational achievement, money and status, acceptance by others, being loved, or your consistent ability to be pleasing and nice to others regardless of what they do. The Perfectionist isn't convinced by any notions of your inherent self-worth, but instead pushes you into stress, exhaustion, and burnout in pursuit of its goals. It likes to ignore warning signals from your body.

Favorite Expressions: "I should." "I have to." "I must."

Examples: The Perfectionist may provide such instructions as "I should always be on top of things," "I should always be considerate and unselfish," "I should always be pleasant and nice," "I *have to* (get this job, make this amount of money, receive _____'s approval, etc.) or I'm not worth much." (See the discussion of "should statements" at the end of the next section.)

Exercise: What Are Your Subpersonalities Telling You?

Take some time to think about how each of the above subpersonalities plays a role in your thinking, feelings, and behavior. First, estimate how much each one affects you by rating its degree of influence from "not at all" to "very much" on a six-point scale (see the worksheets below). Which subpersonality is strongest and which is weakest for you? Then think about what each subpersonality is saying to you to create or aggravate anxiety in each of four different situations.

1. *Work* (in other words, on your job, at school, or in other performance situations)

2. *Personal Relationships* (with your spouse or partner, parents, children, and/or friends)

3. *Anxiety Symptoms* (on occasions where you experience panic, anxiety, or obsessive-compulsive symptoms)

4. *Phobic Situations* (either *in advance* of facing a phobia or while actually *confronting* the phobic situation)

Here are some examples for each subpersonality:

The Worrier

Work:	"What if my boss finds out that I have agoraphobia? Will I get fired?"
Relationships:	"My husband is getting tired of having to take me places. What if he refuses? What if he leaves me?"
Anxiety Symptoms:	"What if they see me panic? What if they think I'm weird?"
Phobic Situation:	"What if I get into an accident the first time I try to drive on the freeway?"

Many of you will find that the Worrier's self-talk in the latter two situations is by far the most common source of your anxiety. If you have panic attacks, the Worrier is prone to create anxiety about when and where your next one might occur. Should the bodily symptoms of panic actually start to come on, the Worrier will magnify them into something dangerous, which only creates more panic. Many of the coping strategies described in Chapter 6 (in particular, the use of positive coping statements) are designed to help you deal with the Worrier during a panic attack.

If you have phobias, the Worrier is typically busy telling you about all kinds of things which might happen if you were to actually face your fear. As a result, you often experience "anticipatory anxiety" (anxiety in advance of facing a phobia) and try to avoid dealing with whatever your phobia may be. You'll find it helpful to do a separate analysis of what your Worrier is telling you (in other words, your what-ifs) for *each* of your specific phobias. Ask yourself what you're afraid could happen if you faced each phobia.

The Critic

Work: "I'm incompetent because of my condition."

Relationships: "I'm a burden to my husband."

Anxiety Symptoms: "I'm such a weakling—I go to pieces when I panic."

Phobic Situation: "Everybody else can drive—I feel like a loser."

The Victim

Work: "My situation at work is hopeless—sooner or later I'll be fired."

Relationships: "My parents really messed me up" or "I can't make it without my boyfriend."

Anxiety Symptoms: "I'll *never* get over these panic attacks—there must be something very wrong with me."

Phobic Situation: "It's useless going on any more job interviews. No one's going to hire me when they see that I'm so anxious."

The Perfectionist

Work: "I should be able to make sales like I used to no matter how anxious I feel."

Relationships: "I shouldn't need to depend on my husband or anyone else to take me places."

Anxiety Symptoms: "I *have to* be able to stop these thoughts from going through my mind."

Phobic Situation: "I *have to* learn to drive like anyone else."

Use the worksheets that follow to write down anxiety-provoking statements your subpersonalities are using in each of the above situations. You don't need to do this for all four subpersonalities or for all four types of situations in each case. Only include those subpersonalities and situations which you suspect are a problem for you. (You'll be filling in the right-hand columns of the worksheets later. Just complete the left-hand columns for now. Use additional sheets of paper if you need more room.)

Monitor what your subpersonalities are telling you for at least one week. Pay attention especially to occasions where you are feeling anxious (panicky), depressed, self-critical and ashamed, or otherwise upset. Look for the thoughts that were going through your mind that led you to feel the way you did. "I felt scared" is not a good example of self-talk because it doesn't indicate what you were thinking (telling yourself) that caused you to feel scared. On the other hand, the self-statement, "What if I panic on the job today?" is an example of a thought that could have led you to feel scared. (See Step 4 in the section later in this chapter called "General Guidelines for Identifying and Countering Self-Talk" for further suggestions about separating thoughts from feelings.) When you've identified what you were telling yourself that provoked anxiety or caused you to feel upset, write it down in the "Negative Self-Talk" column of the appropriate subpersonality and situation on the forms that follow.

Countering Negative Self-Talk

The most effective way to deal with the negative self-talk of your Worrier and other subpersonalities is to *counter* it with positive, supportive statements. Countering involves *writing down* and *rehearsing* positive statements which directly refute or invalidate your negative self-talk. If you're creating anxiety and other upsetting emotional states through negative mental programming, you can begin to change the way you feel by substituting positive programming. Doing this will take some *practice*. You've had years to practice your negative self-talk and naturally have developed some very strong habits. Your Worrier and other subpersonalities are likely to be very well entrenched. By starting to notice when you're engaging in negativity, and then countering it with positive, supportive statements to yourself, you'll begin to turn your thinking around. With practice and consistent effort, you'll change both the way you think *and feel* on an ongoing basis.

Sometimes countering comes naturally and easily. You are ready and willing to substitute positive, reasonable self-statements for ones that have been causing you anxiety and distress. You're more than ready to relinquish negative mental habits that aren't serving you. On the other hand, you may object to the idea of countering and say, "But what if what my Worrier (Critic, Victim, or Perfectionist) says is true? It's hard for me to believe otherwise." Or you may say, "How can I substitute positive self-statements for negative ones if I don't really believe them?"

Perhaps you're strongly attached to some of your negative self-talk. You've been telling yourself these things for years and it's difficult to give up both the habit and the belief. You're not someone who's easily persuaded. If that's the case, and you want to do something about your negative self-talk, it's important that you subject it to rational scrutiny. You can weaken the hold of your negative self-statements by exposing them to any of the following Socratic questions. (These questions are *Socratic* because, like Socrates, they expose a negative argument to rational investigation.)

1. What is the evidence for this?

2. Is this *always* true?

3. Has this been true in the past?

4. What are the odds of this really happening (or being true)?

5. What is the very worst that could happen? What is so bad about that? What would I do if the worst happened?

6. Am I looking at the whole picture?

7. Am I being fully objective?

The validity of your negative self-statements has nothing to do with how attached you are to them or how ingrained they might be. Rather, it has to do with whether they stand up under careful, objective scrutiny. Consider the following examples:

Worrier: "What if I have a heart attack the next time I panic?"

Questioning: "What is the evidence that panic attacks cause heart attacks?" (Answer: None—see Chapter 6.)

Counterstatement: "A panic attack, however uncomfortable, is not dangerous to my heart. I can let panic rise, fall, and pass, and my heart will be fine."

Critic: "You're weak and neurotic because of your stupid phobias."

Questioning: "What is the evidence for this?" (Answer: Phobias are caused by a conditioning process that occurs in a high anxiety state—see Chapter 2. "Weak" and "neurotic" are pejorative labels which explain nothing.)

Counterstatement: "My phobias developed because of a conditioning process that caused me to be sensitized to certain situations. I'm learning to overcome my phobias through a process of gradual exposure."

Victim: "I'll never get over this problem. I'll be limited in my mobility for the rest of my life."

Questioning: "What is the evidence that agoraphobia is a life-long condition? What other outcomes are possible?" (Answer: Ninety percent of agoraphobics recover with effective treatment.)

Counterstatement: "My condition isn't hopeless. I can overcome it by establishing and committing myself to a program for recovery."

Perfectionist: "I have to receive my parents' acceptance and approval or I'll be devastated."

Questioning: "Am I being fully objective? Is it actually true that my parents' approval is absolutely necessary for my well-being? What is the worst that could happen?" (Answer: "I could still survive and have people who care for and support me even without my parents' approval.")

Counterstatement: "I'm willing to go forward with my life and try to better myself regardless of what my parents think."

Subpersonality: The Worrier

Affects me: not at all .   .   .   .   . very much

                    1   2   3   4   5   6

Negative Self-Talk	*Positive Counterstatements*
Situation: *Work/School*	
Relationships	
Anxiety Symptoms (give this special attention if you have panic attacks)	
Phobias (determine the Worrier's self-talk for each of your phobias— use a separate sheet if necessary)	

Subpersonality: The Critic

Affects me: not at all ._____._____._____._____._ very much

   1   2   3   4   5   6

Negative Self-Talk	Positive Counterstatements
Situation:	
Work/School	
Relationships	
Anxiety Symptoms	
Phobias	

Subpersonality: The Victim

Affects me: not at all _____ very much

                     1   2   3   4   5   6

Negative Self-Talk	*Positive Counterstatements*
Situation: *Work/School*	
Relationships	
Anxiety Symptoms	
Phobias	

Subpersonality: The Perfectionist

Affects me: not at all .___.____.____.____._ very much
              1   2   3   4   5   6

Negative Self-Talk	Positive Counterstatements
Situation:	
Work/School	
Relationships	
Anxiety Symptoms	
Phobias	

If you feel attached to your negative self-talk, use any of the above Socratic questions to evaluate the validity of what you're telling yourself. In most cases, you'll find that the negative statements of your Worrier, Critic, Victim, and Perfectionist have little basis in reality. At worst, they will be only partially or occasionally true. Once you've discredited a particular subpersonality's views, you will be ready to counter with positive, supportive statements.

Rules for Writing Positive Counterstatements

1. *Avoid negatives* in writing your counterstatements. Instead of saying, "I'm not going to panic when I board the plane," try, "I am confident and calm about boarding the plane." Telling yourself something will *not* happen is more likely to create anxiety than giving yourself a direct affirmation.

2. Keep counterstatements in the *present tense* ("I can breathe and let these feelings pass" is preferable to "I will feel better in a few minutes"). Since much of your negative self-talk is in the here-and-now, it needs to be countered by statements that are also in the present tense. If you're not ready to *directly* affirm something, try beginning your positive statement with: "I am willing to…," "I am learning to …," "I am coming…," "I can…."

3. Wherever possible, keep your statements in the *first person*. Begin them with "I" or refer to "I" somewhere in the statement. It's O.K. to write a sentence or two explaining the basis for your counterstatement (see the previous examples of counterstatements for the Worrier and Critic), but try to end with an I-statement.

4. It's important that you have some *belief* in your positive self-talk. Don't write something down just because it's positive if you don't actually believe it. If appropriate, use the Socratic questions to challenge your negative self-talk first, and then follow this up with a positive counterstatement that holds some personal credibility for you.

To get you started, here are some more examples of positive counterstatements you can use with each of the above subpersonalities:

The Worrier
Instead of "What if…" you can say, "So what," "I can handle this," "I can be anxious and still do this," "This may be scary, but I can tolerate a little anxiety, knowing that it will pass," "I'll get used to this with practice," or "I can retreat if necessary."

The Critic
Instead of putting yourself down, you can say, "I'm O.K. the way I am," "I'm lovable and capable," "I'm a unique and creative person," "I deserve the good things in life as much as anyone else," "I accept and believe in myself," or "I am worthy of the respect of others."

The Victim
Instead of feeling hopeless, you can say, "I don't have to be all better tomorrow," "I can continue to make progress one step at a time," "I acknowledge the progress I've

made and will continue to improve," "It's never too late to change," or "I'm willing to see the glass as half-full rather than half-empty."

The Perfectionist
Instead of demanding perfection, you can say, "It's O.K. to make mistakes," "Life is too short to be taken too seriously," "Setbacks are part of the process and an important learning experience," "I don't have to always be _____," "My needs and feelings are as important as anyone else's."

Working With Counterstatements

Now you are ready to go back and counter all of the negative statements you recorded on the worksheets for your various subpersonalities. Write down counterstatements corresponding to each negative statement in the right-hand column. Use extra sheets of paper if you need to.

Once you've completed writing out positive self-talk for each subpersonality in each situation, there are several ways you can work with your positive counterstatements.

1. Read through your list of positive counterstatements slowly and carefully for a few minutes each day for at least two weeks. See if you can feel some conviction about their truth as you read them. This will help you to integrate them more deeply into your consciousness.

2. Make copies of your worksheets and post them in a conspicuous place. Take time once a day to carefully read through your positive counterstatements.

3. Put your counterstatements on tape, leaving about five seconds between each consecutive positive statement so that it has time to sink in. You can significantly enhance the effect of such a tape by giving yourself 10-15 minutes to become very relaxed before listening to your counterstatements. You will be more receptive to them in a relaxed state. You may want to record the instructions for progressive muscle relaxation (see Chapter 4) or one of the relaxing visualizations described in Chapter 12 on the first 10-15 minutes of the tape.

4. If you're having a problem with a particular phobia, you might want to work with positive counterstatements that are *specific just to that phobia*. For example, if you're afraid of speaking before groups, make a list of all your fears (*what-ifs*) about what could happen, and develop positive statements to counter each fear. Then read through your list of counterstatements carefully each day for two weeks or make a short tape as described in 3, above.

Changing Self-Talk That Perpetuates Specific Fears and Phobias

Three factors tend to perpetuate fears and phobias: 1) sensitization, 2) avoidance, and 3) negative, distorted self-talk. Chapters 7 and 8 focused on the first two conditions. A phobia develops when you become sensitized to a particular situation, object, or event—in other words, when anxiety becomes conditioned or associated with that situation, object, or event. If panic suddenly arises while you happen to be driving on the freeway or while you're home alone, you may start feeling anxious every time you're in either of these situations. Becoming *sensitized* means that the mere presence of—or even thinking about—a situation may be enough to trigger anxiety automatically.

After sensitization occurs, you may start to *avoid* the situation. Repeated avoidance is very rewarding, because it saves you from having to feel any anxiety. Avoidance is the most powerful way to hold on to a phobia, because it prevents you from ever learning that you can handle the situation.

The third factor that perpetuates fears and phobias is distorted self-talk. The more *worry* and *anticipatory anxiety* you experience about something you fear, the more likely you are to be involved in unconstructive self-talk connected with that fear. You may also have negative *images* about what could happen if you had to face what you fear, or about your worst fears coming true. Both the negative self-talk and negative images serve to perpetuate your fears, guaranteeing that you remain afraid. They also undermine your confidence that you can ever get over your fear. Without negative self-talk and negative images, you would be much more likely to overcome your avoidance and confront your fear.

Fears come in many forms, but the nature of fearful self-talk is always the same. Whether you are afraid of crossing bridges, speaking up in a social situation, the sensation of rapid heartbeat, the possibility of serious illness, or about your children getting into trouble, the types of distorted thinking which perpetuate these fears are the same. *There are three basic distortions:*

1. Overestimating a Negative Outcome

Overestimating the odds of something bad happening. Most of the time your worries consist of "what-if" statements which overestimate a particular negative outcome. For example, "What if I panic and lose complete control of myself?" "What if they see me panic and think I'm weird?" "What if I flunk the exam and have to drop out of school?"

2. Catastrophizing

Thinking that if a negative outcome did occur, it would be catastrophic, overwhelming, and unmanageable. Catastrophic thoughts contain such statements as "I couldn't handle it," "I'd be overwhelmed," "I'd never live it down," "They'll never forgive me."

3. Underestimating Your Ability To Cope

Not recognizing or acknowledging your ability to cope if a negative outcome did, in fact, occur. This underestimation of your ability to cope is usually implicit in your catastrophic thoughts.

If you take any fear and examine the negative thinking that contributes to maintaining that fear, you'll probably find these three distortions. To the extent that you can overcome these distortions with more reality-based thinking, the fear will tend to drop away. In essence, you can define fear as *the unreasonable overestimation of some threat, coupled with an underestimation of your ability to cope.*

Here are some examples of how the three types of distortions operate with various fears. In each example, all three types of distorted thoughts are identified. Then, the distortions are challenged in each case and modified with more appropriate, reality-based counterstatements.

Example 1: Fear of Having a Panic Attack While Driving on a Freeway

Overestimating Thoughts

"What if I can't handle the car? What if my attention wanders and I lose control of the car? What if I cause an accident and kill someone?"

Catastrophic Thoughts

"I couldn't handle it if I lost control of the car. It would be a totally unmanageable situation—the end of the world—if I caused an accident." (Note: An image of a horrendous accident can accompany and amplify the force of a catastrophic thought.)

Underestimating Your Ability To Cope

"I couldn't cope if I lost control of the car, especially if I got into an accident. I'll die of embarrassment if other drivers notice how frightened I am. What would I say to a policeman—that I'm phobic? I wouldn't be able to start driving again if I got stopped for a ticket. I couldn't live with myself if I caused physical injury to another person—and I know I couldn't face life in a wheelchair."

Refuting Distorted Thinking

It's possible to refute each of these types of distorted thinking with questions and counterstatements. Examples follow below:

Overestimating

With overestimating thoughts, the appropriate question is: *"Viewing the situation objectively, what are the odds of the negative outcome actually happening?"*

In the case of the previous example, the question is, "If I did panic while driving, what are the true odds that I would lose control of the car?"

You could use this counterstatement: "It's unlikely that having a panic attack would cause me to lose complete control. The moment I felt my anxiety coming on, I could pull over to the shoulder on the side of the road and stop. If there weren't any shoulders, I could slow way down in the right lane, perhaps to 45 mph, put my flashers on, and keep a grip on myself until I reached the nearest exit. Once I got off the highway, my panic would begin to subside."

Catastrophizing

With catastrophizing, the relevant question to ask is: *"If the worst did happen, is it actually true that I couldn't handle it?"* The idea is to go ahead and imagine the worst that could happen and then ask yourself whether *in reality* you could handle the consequences or not.

In the above example, you would raise the question, "If the worst did happen—if I did get into an accident, one that even caused injury—would I be totally unable to handle it?"

You could then use a counterstatement such as: "As bad as having an accident would be, in most cases I would be able to handle it if I weren't injured. It's common for people to function in an emergency situation and then handle their anxiety later. So in all likelihood, I would keep functioning in the event of an accident as long as I wasn't injured."

"Even if I were injured, and unable to handle the situation, the police and paramedics would soon arrive on the scene and take charge. There is simply no way in which the situation could become completely unmanageable."

Underestimating Your Ability To Cope

Countering the idea that you couldn't cope often takes place in the process of answering catastrophic thinking with a more objective appraisal. However, the process isn't complete until you actually *identify and list specific ways in which you could cope*. In the above example, some possible coping strategies could include:

- "If I did have a panic attack, I could cope by getting off the highway immediately or driving slowly to the nearest exit and getting off."

- "In the very unlikely case that I actually caused an accident, I would still cope. I would exchange names and addresses with other parties involved. If my car were undriveable, the police would likely drive me to a place where I could call to have the car towed. It would be a very unpleasant experience, to say the least; but, realistically, I would continue to function. I've functioned in emergencies in the past, and I could function in this case, if I weren't injured."

- "Even given the remote possibility that I were injured, I wouldn't 'go crazy' or 'totally lose it.' I would simply wait until the paramedics came and took charge of the situation."

Example 2: Fear of Panicking While Speaking Up in a Class or Meeting

Overestimating Thoughts:

"What if I panicked while speaking? Wouldn't others think I was really weird or crazy?"

Questioning: "Realistically, how likely is it that I would panic while speaking? What are the odds, if I *did* panic, that people would be aware of what I was thinking, or make any judgments about me at all?"

Counterstatements: "It is possible that I could start to panic while speaking. If I did, I could simply abbreviate what I wanted to say and sit back down. As people tend to be caught up in their own thoughts and fears, no one would likely notice my difficulty or judge that I'd cut my comments short."

"Even if people did see me panic—if they saw my face turn red or heard my voice trembling—the odds are very slim that they'd think I was weird or crazy. It's much more likely that they'd express concern."

Catastrophic Thoughts:

"If I panicked while speaking and people thought I was weird, that would be *terrible*. I'd never live it down."

Questioning: "Suppose the unlikely happened and people really thought I was strange or weird because I panicked. How terrible would that be?"

Counterstatements: "It's not going to be the end of the world if some people think I'm strange or that something's wrong with me. They have no way of knowing what it's like to have panic attacks, so they couldn't really understand. Even if people don't understand, or if they misperceive me, that doesn't decrease one bit my value or worth as a human being. If I believe in myself, then it really doesn't matter what others think. Certainly if others knew what it was like to have a panic attack, they would likely be sympathetic."

Underestimating Your Ability to Cope
"I couldn't cope if people thought I was strange."

Questioning: "Is it realistic to assume that I couldn't cope? Is it realistic to suppose I'd never live it down?"

Counterstatements: "Even if people thought I was strange or different because I panicked, I could explain to them that I sometimes have panic attacks in social situations. With all the publicity about anxiety disorders that's around these days, they would likely understand. Being totally honest is one way I could handle the situation. And no matter what happened, I would forget about it after a while. It's just not true that I would never live it down."

Example 3: Fear of Serious Illness

Overestimating Thoughts:
"I have no energy and feel tired all the time. Maybe I have cancer and don't know it!"

Questioning: "What are the odds that symptoms of low energy and fatigue mean that I have cancer?"

Counterstatements: "Symptoms of fatigue and low energy can be indicative of all kinds of physical and psychological conditions, including a low-grade virus, anemia, adrenal exhaustion or hypothyroidism, depression, and food allergies, to name a few. There are many possible explanations of my condition, and I don't have any specific symptoms that would indicate cancer. So the odds of my fatigue and low energy indicating cancer are very low."

Catastrophic Thoughts:
"If I were diagnosed with cancer, that would be the end. I couldn't take it. I'd be better off ending things quickly and killing myself."

Questioning: If the unlikely happened and I really were diagnosed with cancer, how terrible could that be? Would I actually go to pieces and just want to die?"

Counterstatements: "As bad as a cancer diagnosis would be, it's unlikely that I would totally go to pieces. After an initial difficult adjustment to the fact—which might take days to weeks—I would most likely begin to think about what I needed to do to deal with the situation. It would certainly be difficult, yet it wouldn't be a situation that I was less equipped to handle than anyone else."

Underestimating Your Ability To Cope

"If I were given a diagnosis of cancer, I simply couldn't cope."

Questioning: "Realistically, is it actually true that I would have no way of coping with the situation?"

Counterstatements: "Of course I would cope. After an initial period of adjusting to the situation, my doctor and I would plan the most effective possible treatment strategies. I would join a local cancer support group, and get lots of support from my friends and immediate family. I would try alternative methods, such as visualization and dietary changes, that could help. In short, I would try everything possible to attempt to heal the condition."

The above three examples illustrate how overestimating and catastrophic thoughts can be challenged and then countered by more realistic, less anxiety-provoking thinking. Now it's your turn. During the next two weeks, monitor the times when you feel anxious or panicky. Each time you do, use the following five steps to work with negative self-talk.

Step 1: If you're feeling anxious or upset, do something to relax, such as abdominal breathing, progressive muscle relaxation, or meditation. It's easier to notice your internal dialogue when you take time to slow down and relax.

Step 2: After you get somewhat relaxed, ask yourself, "What was I telling myself that made me anxious?" or "What was going through my mind?" Remember to separate thoughts from feelings. For example, "I felt terrified" describes a feeling, while "This panic will never end" is an overestimating thought which might have led you to feel terrified.

Step 3: Identify the three basic types of distortions among your anxious self-talk. Sort out *overestimating thoughts*, *catastrophic thoughts*, and *thoughts that underestimate your ability to cope*.

Step 4: When you've identified your anxious, distorted thoughts, *challenge* them with appropriate questions.

- *For overestimating thoughts:* "What are the realistic odds that this feared outcome would actually happen?"

- *For catastrophic thoughts:* "If the feared outcome actually did occur, how terrible would it be? Is it really true that I would go to pieces and lose all my ability to cope?"

- *For thoughts underestimating your ability to cope:* "If the feared outcome did occur, what could I actually *do* to cope?"

Step 5: Write counterstatements to each of your anxious self-statements. These counterstatements should contain language and logic that reflect more balanced, realistic thinking.

Use "The Worry Worksheet" on page 193 to write down your anxious thoughts and corresponding counterstatements for any specific fear or phobia you choose to work with. In the section at the bottom, list ways in which you could cope if the negative (but unlikely) outcome you fear actually occurred.

It would be a good idea to make 10-20 photocopies of the worksheet before you begin, so that you can fill out a separate sheet for each specific fear or phobia you have.

Other Types of Distorted Thinking (Cognitive Distortions)

Overestimating and catastrophizing, along with underestimating your ability to cope, are the most common types of distortions in thinking which contribute to most phobias and fears. There are other types of distortions, however, which can skew the ways in which you perceive and evaluate both yourself and innumerable situations in everyday life. These distortions can contribute not only to anxiety, but to much of the depression, guilt, self-criticism, and/or cynicism you might feel. Learning to identify and counter these unhelpful modes of thinking with more realistic and constructive self-talk can go a long way towards helping you handle everyday stresses in a more balanced, objective fashion. This, in turn, will significantly reduce the amount of anxiety, depression, and other unpleasant emotional states you experience. Remember that your immediate experience of the outside world is largely shaped and colored by your own personal thoughts about it. Change your thoughts and you'll change the way your world appears.

Four additional cognitive distortions that are especially relevant to people dealing with anxiety disorders are described below. Use the examples given under each one to help you identify these distortions when they occur in your own self-talk. Then write out both your distorted thoughts and appropriate counterstatements, using the worksheet on page 194. You'll want to make 10-20 copies of this worksheet, reserving several separate sheets for each of the four types of cognitive distortions.

1. Overgeneralizing

To overgeneralize is to assume (usually falsely) that because you've had one bad experience, in a particular situation, your bad experience will always repeat itself in similar situations. This happens automatically in the process of developing a phobia— you have a panic attack in one store and after a while you start to avoid all stores. (The generalizing of a phobia from one to all instances of a situation is also influenced by a conditioning phenomenon that behavioral psychologists call "stimulus generalization.")

For example, you conclude that because you've had one bad experience with public speaking, you'll *never* be able to speak in public successfully. Or because you had one panic attack where you felt terrified and out of control, you assume that the next one and every one thereafter will be equally bad. Or because one person made an unflattering remark about your performance at work or school, you conclude that *everyone* must see it that way (which then leads you to believe that your work is "objectively" substandard).

The essence of overgeneralizing consists of jumping from one instance in the present to *all* instances in the future. You can tell that you're overgeneralizing when your self-talk includes words such as *never, always, all, every, none, no one, nobody, everyone, everybody,* or *absolute statements* incorporating these words ("I'll never be able to drive again," or "No one would remain my friend if they really knew me").

The Worry Worksheet

Specific Fear or Phobia _____

Anxious Self-Talk	Counterstatements
Overestimating thoughts (or images):	
"What if ..."	
Catastrophic Thoughts (or images):	
"If the worst happened, then ..."	

Coping Strategies: List ways in which you would cope if a negative (but unlikely) outcome did occur. Use the other side of the sheet if needed. Change "What if" to *"What I would do if* (one of the negative predictions actually did come about) ..."

1.

2.

3.

Make 10-20 copies of this worksheet before you start, and use a separate sheet for each of your phobias or fears.

Cognitive Distortion Worksheet

Type of Distorted Thinking: _____	Rational Counterstatements

Three types of Socratic questions are effective for rationally challenging and refuting overgeneralizations:

1. What is the evidence for this?

2. What are the odds of this really happening (or being true)?

3. Has this been true in the past?

Most cases of overgeneralizing won't stand up in the face of these questions. The example below illustrates how to question and counter overgeneralizing thoughts.

Overgeneralization: "That panic attack I had on the freeway yesterday was so bad that I'll *never* be able to drive on freeways again."

Questioning: "What are the odds of this really being true? Has this been true in the past?"

Counterstatement: "I may need to lay off driving freeways for a while. After some time has passed, I'll feel good enough to try it again. I believe I can succeed if I break the task down into small enough steps. After all, I was able to drive freeways in the past, so I know I can do so again."

Note that one of the keys to countering overgeneralizations is to look for *balancing evidence*, that is, balancing your negative outlook with other evidence that is more positive and compelling.

Exercise

Monitor your self-talk for one week and notice occasions when you use words such as *always, never, everyone, no one,* and so on. Write down your overgeneralizations in the left-hand column of one of your copies of the Cognitive Distortion Worksheet, and then write rational counterstatements in the right-hand column. Use balancing evidence and be as specific as possible in your counterstatements.

2. Filtering

Filtering involves selecting out and focusing on one negative aspect of a situation so that you ignore any positive aspects. It is a favorite tactic of the Critic. Applied to yourself, you focus on a single fault and ignore any of your assets and strengths. Or at times you may filter out anything positive in your view of a personal relationship.

Filtering commonly occurs in the course of exposure to a phobic situation, when you focus on one setback and ignore all the progress you've made. Just because you were able to drive to work alone last week, but can't do it this week, you begin to question the entire process of real-life desensitization. Or because you have one bad panic attack, you ignore the fact that you've had fewer panic attacks in the last two months than you did before. Other examples might include getting a job performance evaluation that is mostly positive, yet focusing exclusively on the one or two criticisms it contains. Or your partner compliments you on your cooking, praising the meat, potatoes, vegetables, and dessert, while adding that next time you might try using less salt in the salad dressing. You then feel let down and regard the entire dinner as a failure. It is as if you were wearing a special pair of eyeglasses that filters out anything positive. It's like the old joke about the mother who gives her grown son two ties. When he shows up at her house wearing one of them, she asks him, "So what's wrong with the other tie?"

Be wary of filtering when the following words crop up in your self-talk: *worthless, pointless, hopeless, stupid, failure, dangerous, unfair*. In fact, any word that is globally negative in scope may indicate that you're filtering. If you describe someone or something in such terms, reexamine your thinking to see whether you're viewing things in a *balanced* way—one which takes both positive and negative aspects into full account.

Two Socratic questions are often helpful in challenging cognitive distortions due to filtering.

1. Am I looking at the whole picture (or am I taking both sides of this into account)?

2. Are there positive aspects of this situation (person, object) that I'm ignoring?

Both questions remind you to look for other, more positive evidence and to consider both sides of an issue. The following example illustrates this:

Filtering:	"I just flunked my midterm in calculus. I'm going down the tubes! I'll never make it through the semester!" (Note the use of catastrophizing as well as filtering.)
Questioning:	"Am I looking at the whole picture?"
Counterstatement:	"I'm doing satisfactory to good work in my other courses. In calculus, I'm doing well enough on the homework to offset bad grades on the exams, so that I can at least pass. There's no basis for the idea that I can't make it through the semester."

The counterstatement in this example of filtering relied on balancing evidence, much like the counterstatements to overgeneralizing in the previous section. These two types of cognitive distortion are similar in that they both *ignore* refuting evidence.

Exercise

Monitor your self-talk for one week and notice any examples of filtering, especially when you find yourself viewing something exclusively in a negative light or using globally negative labels such as *failure, worthless, hopeless*. Write self-talk based on filtering in the left-hand column of one of your worksheets and then refute each negative statement with rational counterstatements that take the whole picture into account.

3. Emotional Reasoning

Emotional reasoning refers to the tendency to judge or evaluate something illogically, totally on the basis of your feelings. There may, of course, be some instances where relying on feelings alone can be useful and appropriate. For example, if you simply don't feel good about someone you're just meeting, interviewing, or dating, that may be sufficient reason for you to decide not to proceed with the relationship. In many other cases, though, going solely on feelings and suspending your reason can lead to very erroneous conclusions.

One common example of this is to conclude that because you *feel* a certain way, then you necessarily *are* that way as well ("I feel useless, therefore I must *be* useless," "I feel incompetent, therefore I *am* incompetent," or "I feel ugly, therefore I *am* ugly."). To infer from one negative feeling or a mood that you inherently and for all time possess that negative quality is like inferring from one rainy day that the sun never shines. "I feel, therefore I am" simply isn't accurate or true.

An indication of emotional reasoning is when you make decisions totally on impulse, without the mediation of reasoning. While spontaneity argues in favor of doing this on certain occasions, there are many situations where impulsive decisions made without time to think things through can create problems. Be wary about making such "snap judgments."

Questions you can use to challenge emotional reasoning include:

1. Am I going solely by my feelings?

2. Am I looking at this objectively?

3. What is the evidence that my judgment (based on feelings) is completely accurate?

Note the use of such questions in the following examples:

Emotional Reasoning:	"It feels impossible to go in and participate in that meeting. I just can't do it."
Questioning:	"Am I going solely by my feelings? Am I looking at this objectively?"
Counterstatement:	"Just because it *feels* impossible doesn't mean facing this situation *is* impossible. If necessary, I can leave the meeting (saying I have to go to the bathroom) if I need to. Knowing that, I'll go in and give it a try."
Emotional Reasoning:	"I feel terrible today—there's got to be something seriously wrong with me."
Questioning:	"Am I being completely objective? What is the evidence for this?"
Counterstatement:	"Just because I feel bad doesn't mean that I'm inherently flawed. Even though I'm depressed, there's no evidence for the idea that I'm irrevocably defective. So what if I'm feeling bad? I know that there are things I can do (exercise, call a friend, work in the garden) to get myself out of this mood."

Exercise

During the next week, see if you can track down instances where you make judgments or draw conclusions solely on the basis of your feelings. Notice especially those occasions where you make snap judgments without reasoning things out. Use the suggested questions above to dispute emotional reasoning and write down your counterstatements in the right-hand column of one of your worksheets.

4. "Should Statements"

Should statements are the hallmark of the Perfectionist subpersonality described earlier. You are using them whenever you tell yourself "I should do this," "I must do that," or "I have to" in an attempt to motivate yourself to do something. In cases of ethical responsibility or common courtesy, shoulds *can* be appropriate. There's nothing wrong with such should statements as "I should let him know that I appreciate the favor he did," "I should be honest on my income tax," "I should teach Johnny to look both ways when he crosses the street." The difficulty arises when you use "I should" or "I must" to pressure yourself to meet self-imposed expectations that are unreasonably high. For example:

"I should always be pleasing and cheerful to others, despite my feelings."

"I should be totally competent."

"I should be a `perfect' spouse, parent, lover, friend, worker, student, etc."

"I should be totally self-reliant."

"I should never get tired or sick."

"I should never feel negative emotions like anger or jealousy."

"I should have achievements that bring me status and/or wealth."

"I should not be susceptible to panic attacks."

"I should never be afraid."

Imposing should statements on yourself such as the ones above is guaranteed to keep you anxious and tense. Such statements also lower your confidence and self-esteem. After the Perfectionist tells you what you should do, the Critic comes in to inform you about how far you fall short.

How can you tell when your should statements are appropriate and when they are reflections of a stress-inducing bad habit? In Chapter 7 of their book *Self-Esteem*, Matthew McKay and Patrick Fanning outline four criteria for determining when a should reflects "healthy" versus "unhealthy" standards.

1. Is the standard flexible—in other words, does it allow for exceptions, or is it rigid and global with no exceptions?

2. Is the standard based on your own experience or is it "inherited"—without your ever having questioned it—from your parents?

3. Is the standard realistic (does it take into account all the consequences its application may lead to), or is it based on an arbitrary sense of rightness, regardless of consequences?

4. Is the standard life-enhancing (does it acknowledge your needs and feelings)—or is it life-restricting (ignore your needs and feelings)?

When you find that you're telling yourself "I should" or "I must," you can evaluate the appropriateness of your self-talk according to these criteria. Failing even one of the criteria is enough to cast serious doubt on the reasonableness of a particular should statement. Consider the following example:

Should Statement: "I should always be pleasing and positive toward others."

Questioning: "Is this something I've tested out for myself, or did I accept it unquestioningly from my parents? Does this acknowledge my needs and feelings or does it ignore them?"

Counterstatement: "My mother gave me the message that I should always be pleasing, no matter what the situation. In my own experience, I've learned that there are times when it's hypocritical to act this way. This should also ignores my needs and feelings, as there are times when I don't really feel like being cheerful and pleasing. Conclusion: It's O.K. not to always be pleasing and cheerful."

Exercise

Notice during the course of a week how often you tell yourself "I should do this," "I must do that," or "I have to." Write these down in the left-hand column of one of your worksheets. Use the four criteria above to challenge shoulds involving excessively high and rigid standards imposed on *yourself*. Use the suggested Socratic questions to refute shoulds involving unrealistic expectations about *life*. Write your counterstatements in the right-hand column of your worksheet.

General Guidelines for Identifying and Countering Self-Talk

Negative self-talk is nothing more than an accumulation of self-limiting mental habits. You can begin to break these habits by noticing occasions when you engage in unconstructive dialogues with yourself and then countering them, preferably in writing, with more positive, rational statements. It took repetition over many years to internalize your habits of negative self-talk; it will likewise take repetition and practice to learn more constructive and helpful ways of thinking.

Follow the steps below:

1. *Notice*—"Catch yourself in the act" of engaging in negative self-talk. Be aware of situations that are likely to be precipitated or aggravated by negative self-talk. For example:

   - Any occasion when you're feeling anxious, including the onset of a panic attack (watch for the Worrier and the cognitive distortions of overestimating and catastrophizing)

   - Anticipation of having to face a difficult task or a phobic situation (again the Worrier, overestimating, and catastrophizing play a large role)

- Occasions when you've made some kind of mistake and feel critical of yourself (watch for the Critic and overgeneralizing, filtering, and should statements)

- Occasions when you're feeling depressed or discouraged (watch for the Victim, overestimating, catastrophizing, filtering, and overgeneralizing)

- Situations where you're angry at yourself or others (watch for the Critic, the Perfectionist, and any of the above-described cognitive distortions)

- Situations where you feel guilty, ashamed, or embarrassed (watch especially for the Perfectionist and should statements)

2. *Stop*—Ask yourself any or all of the following questions:

"What am I telling myself that is making me feel this way?"

"Do I really want to do this to myself?"

"Do I really want to stay upset?"

If the answer to the last two questions is no, proceed.

Realize that sometimes your answers may be yes. You may actually wish to continue to be upset rather than change the underlying self-talk. Often this is because you're having strong feelings that you haven't allowed yourself to fully express. It's common to *stay* anxious, angry, or depressed for a period of time when there are strong feelings that you haven't fully acknowledged—let alone expressed.

If you're feeling too upset to easily undertake the task of identifying and countering self-talk, give yourself the opportunity to acknowledge and express your feelings. If there's no one available to share them with, try writing them down in a journal. When you've calmed down and are ready to relax, proceed with the steps below. (See Chapter 13 for more guidelines and strategies.)

Another reason you may maintain your anxiety is because you perceive a strong need to "keep everything under control." Often you're overestimating some danger or preparing for an imagined catastrophe—and so staying tense and vigilant is the way in which you give yourself a sense of control. Your vigilance is validated by the feeling of control it gives you. Unfortunately, in the process you can make yourself more and more tense until you reach a point where your mind seems to race out of control, and you dwell on danger and catastrophe almost to the exclusion of anything else. This, in turn, leads to more anxiety and tension. The only way out of this vicious cycle is to let go and relax. The next step, relaxation, is crucial for you to be able to slow down your mind and sort out patterns of negative self-talk.

3. *Relax*—*Disrupt* your train of negative thoughts by taking some deep abdominal breaths or using some methods of distraction. The point is to *let go, slow yourself down*, and *relax*. Negative self-talk is so rapid, automatic, and subtle that it can escape detection if you're feeling tense, speeded up, and unable to slow down. You'll find it difficult to recognize and undo such self-talk by merely thinking about it: it's necessary to physically relax first. In extreme cases, it may take 15-20 minutes of deep relaxation, using breathing, progressive muscle relaxation, or

meditation, to slow yourself down enough so that you can identify what you've been telling yourself. If you're not excessively wound up, you can probably do this step in a minute or two.

4. *Write down* the negative self-talk or inner dialogue that led you to feel anxious, upset, or depressed. It's often difficult to decipher what you're telling yourself by merely reflecting on it. It can be confusing to try to think about what you've just been thinking. The act of writing things down will help to clarify what specific statements you actually made to yourself. Use the *Daily Record of Dysfunctional Thoughts* in the exercise following this section to write down your self-talk.

This step may take some practice to learn. *It's important in identifying self-talk to be able to disentangle thoughts from feelings.* One way to do this is to write down just the feelings first and then uncover the thoughts which led to them. As a general rule, feeling statements contain words expressing emotions, such as "scared," "hurt," and "sad," while self-talk statements do not contain such words. For example, the statement "I feel stupid and irresponsible" is one in which thoughts and feelings are still entangled. It can be broken down into a particular feeling ("I feel upset," or "I feel disappointed") and the thoughts (or self-talk) which logically produce such feelings ("I'm stupid," or "I'm irresponsible").

To give another example, the statement "I'm too scared to undertake this" mixes a feeling of fear with one or more thoughts. It can be broken down into the feeling ("I'm scared") which arises from the negative self-statement ("This is unmanageable," or "I can't undertake this"). You can ask yourself first, "What was I feeling?" Then ask, "What thoughts were going through my mind to cause me to feel the way I did?"

Always keep in mind that *self-talk consists of thoughts, not feelings.* Most of the time these thoughts are judgments or appraisals of a situation or yourself. The feelings are emotional reactions that *result* from these judgments and appraisals.

5. *Identify the type* of negative self-talk you engaged in (is it from the Worrier, the Critic, the Victim, or the Perfectionist?). Also, look for any *cognitive distortions* that were present (such as overestimating, catastrophizing, overgeneralizing, and filtering). After doing this for a while, you'll become aware of the particular types of negative inner dialogue and particular types of cognitive distortions you're especially prone to use. With practice, you'll identify them more quickly when they come up.

6. *Answer or dispute* your negative self-talk with positive, rational, self-supportive statements. Answer each negative statement you've written by *writing down* an opposing, positive statement. These counterstatements should be worded so that they avoid negatives, are in the present tense, and in the first person. They should also be *believable* and *feel good* to you (in other words you should feel comfortable with them).

In many cases you'll find it helpful to question and refute your negative statements with the Socratic questions enumerated earlier in this chapter.

In other instances, you may imagine a positive counterstatement immediately, without going through a process of rational questioning. This is fine, so long as you have some degree of belief in your counterstatement.

Exercise: The Daily Record of Dysfunctional Thoughts

On page 203 you'll find the *Daily Record of Dysfunctional Thoughts* designed by Aaron Beck, one of the pioneers in investigating self-talk. This form has been specifically designed to assist you in identifying and countering your negative thinking. The *Daily Record* is *particularly* appropriate to use at times when you're feeling anxious, depressed, self-critical, or otherwise upset. The columns should be filled in from left to right as follows:

1. *Situation:*   Describe in a few words the specific situation that led you to feel anxious or upset. If it was exclusively a matter of internal thoughts, anticipations, or memories that led you to feel upset, describe these instead.

2. *Emotion(s):*   What emotions (for example, anxiety, depression, shame) did you experience while you were upset? On a scale of 0-100, how intense were your emotions?

3. *Automatic Thought(s):*   Here is where you write down the negative self-talk which caused you to be anxious, depressed, or upset. Think back over what you were telling yourself when your strong emotions arose, and be careful to separate the actual thoughts that went through your mind from the resulting feelings. Ask yourself what thoughts led you to feel the way you did. If you're still feeling upset or tense at the time of doing this exercise, give yourself time to relax before attempting to identify self-talk. After you've determined what you were saying to yourself, rate your degree of belief in it: How valid does it seem to you on a scale from 0-100?

4. *Rational Response:*   In this column write positive statements to counter your negative self-talk. Think about how you could take a more constructive, self-supportive outlook and write statements that reverse your negative thoughts. Use Socratic questions to challenge negative self-talk if necessary. Be sure that you actually have some belief in your positive counterstatements. Also specify your degree of belief in these statements on a scale from 0-100.

5. *Outcome:*   First, rerate your degree of belief in your negative self-talk (as a result of having written positive counterstatements). Then rerate the initial feelings you experienced before doing the exercise. What is the intensity of your feelings now on a scale from 0-100?

Note: Before filling in the *Daily Record*, you will want to photocopy at least 50 copies for your future use.

If you are serious about overcoming your habits of negative self-talk, I recommend that you use the *Daily Record of Dysfunctional Thoughts* on a *daily* basis for at least two

Daily Record of Dysfunctional Thoughts

Date	Situation	Emotion(s)	Automatic Thought(s)	Rational Response	Outcome
	Describe: 1. Actual event leading to unpleasant emotion, or 2. Stream of thoughts, daydream, or recollection leading to unpleasant emotion	1. Specify sad anxious/ angry, etc. 2. Rate degree of emotion, 1–100	1. Write automatic thought(s) that preceded emotion(s). 2. Rate belief in automatic thought(s), 0–100	1. Write rational response to automatic thought(s) 2. Rate belief in rational response, 0–100	1. Rerate belief in automatic thought(s), 0–100 2. Specify and rate subsequent emotions, 0–100

Instructions: When you experience an unpleasant emotion, note the situation that seemed to stimulate the emotion. (If the emotion occurred while you were thinking, daydreaming, etc., please note this.) Then note the automatic thought associated with the emotion. Record the degree to which you believe this thought: 0=not at all; 100= completely. In rating degree of emotion. 1=a trace; 100=the most intense possible.

weeks. After that, use it every time you find yourself anxious, depressed, self-critical, angry, or otherwise upset during the next two months. It will take some time and effort to write down your negative self-talk along with positive counterstatements—however, this will be time and effort well spent. The practice of writing down counterstatements repeatedly will help you to internalize a new habit of reversing your negative thinking whenever you notice it beginning to start. After a month or two of writing everything out, you'll find that you begin to counter negative self-talk automatically and effortlessly as it comes up. *Cultivating the habit of countering is one of the most significant steps you can take in dealing with all kinds of anxiety as well as panic attacks.*

Disrupting Negative Self-Talk: Short Form

Using the *Daily Record of Dysfunctional Thoughts* will go a long way to help you overcome long-established mental habits that produce anxiety, depression, and low self-esteem. In many situations, however, you may neither have the time nor opportunity to write down negative self-talk and positive counterstatements. Follow the three steps below whenever you wish to disrupt a negative train of thought "on the spot."

1. *Notice* that you are engaging in negative self-talk. The best time to catch yourself involved in negative inner dialogue is when you are feeling anxious, depressed, self-critical, or upset in general.

2. *Stop*—Ask yourself any or all of the following questions:
   "What am I telling myself that is making me feel this way?"
   "Do I really want to do this to myself?"
   "Do I really want to stay upset?"

3. *Relax or Distract*—In order to break a train of negative self-talk, you need to "switch gears." This can be accomplished by slowing yourself down with deep, abdominal breathing *or* by finding some form of distraction to divert your mind from negative thoughts. Often doing something *physical* (such as exercise, dancing, or household chores) will have the greatest power to distract because it moves you out of your head and into your body. Other ready forms of distraction include engaging in conversation, reading, hobbies and games, relaxation tapes, and music.

   As an alternative to deep breathing or distraction, use a thought-stopping technique such as shouting "Stop!" or "Get Out!" or stomping your foot or snapping a rubber band against your wrist to divert your mind.

   See Appendix 6 for a more detailed list of methods for distracting yourself from anxious thinking and worrying.

The purpose of this section is to suggest convenient methods for disrupting negative self-talk "on the spot." It is *not* intended as a substitute for writing out counterstatements or using the *Daily Record of Dysfunctional Thoughts*. Only by using the latter, and practicing over a period of weeks, can you begin to effectively change your lifelong habits of negative thinking that arise from the subpersonalities and cognitive distortions described in this chapter.

Summary of Things to Do

1. Reread the section "Some Basic Points About Self-Talk" to reinforce your understanding of the automatic nature of self-talk and its role in maintaining both phobias and panic attacks.

2. Familiarize yourself with the four subpersonalities that contribute to much of your negative self-talk: the Worrier, the Critic, the Victim, and the Perfectionist. Determine their role in your daily life by completing the worksheets in the section "What Are Your Subpersonalities Telling You?" Then counter the negative self-talk of each subpersonality with positive statements. Read over your positive statements every day for a week or put them on a tape so that you can listen to them in the car or while going to sleep at night.

3. Make a list of all your phobias and other specific fears, then rank them from the most to least bothersome. Complete the Worry Worksheet for each of your most difficult phobias or fears. For each one, write down overestimating and catastrophic thoughts that keep the fear going. Then refute these negative thoughts with more reasonable and positive counterstatements. Finally, write down ways in which you would cope if what you feared were actually to come about.

4. Identify and challenge other types of cognitive distortions that may aggravate worry and anxiety. Use the *Cognitive Distortion Worksheet* to identify examples of overgeneralizing, filtering, emotional reasoning, and should statements that come up at times when you feel anxious, depressed, self-critical, or otherwise upset. Then use the Socratic questions to challenge distorted self-statements and write down corresponding positive counterstatements.

5. Become familiar with the six steps for identifying and countering negative self-talk: 1) *Notice*, 2) *Stop*, 3) *Relax* and slow down, 4) *Write down* negative self-statements, 5) *Identify* the relevant subpersonality or cognitive distortion, 6) *Counter* each negative self-statement with a rational, positive alternative. After you've completed the exercises for the subpersonalities, the *Worry Worksheet*, and the other cognitive distortions (which should take a few weeks), spend at least two more weeks filling out the *Daily Record of Dysfunctional Thoughts* every day. Make about 50 copies of the *Daily Record* for this purpose and for future use. A thorough effort on your part here will pay off.

6. Use the "short form" of disrupting negative self-talk when you want to divert yourself from a train of negative thinking "at a moment's notice." Remember, this is not a substitute for doing the exercises in 2, 3, and 4 above.

Further Reading

Barlow, David, and Craske, Michelle. *Mastery of Your Anxiety and Panic.* Albany, New York: Graywind Publications, 1989. (See especially Chapters 7, 8, and 9.)

Beck, Aaron T. *Cognitive Therapy and the Emotional Disorders.* New York: Meridian, 1979.

Beck, Aaron T., and Emery, Gary. *Anxiety Disorders and Phobias: A Cognitive Perspective.* New York: Basic Books, 1981. (This book is primarily intended for helping professionals.)

Burns, David. *Feeling Good.* New York: Signet, 1981. (The classic popular book on cognitive distortions.)

Ellis, A., and Harper, R. *A Guide to Rational Living.* North Hollywood, California: Wilshire Books, 1961.

Helmstetter, Shad. *What To Say When You Talk To Yourself.* New York: Pocket Books, 1982.

Helmstetter, Shad. *The Self-Talk Solution.* New York: Pocket Books, 1987. (Both of Helmstetter's books are timely and easy to read.)

McKay, Matthew; Davis, Martha; and Fanning, Patrick. *Thoughts and Feelings: The Art of Cognitive Stress Intervention.* Oakland, California: New Harbinger Publications, 1981. (See especially Chapters 2 and 3.)

McKay, Matthew, and Fanning, Patrick. *Self-Esteem.* Oakland, California: New Harbinger Publications, 1987.

Woolfolk, Robert L., and Richardson, Frank C. *Stress, Sanity and Survival.* New York: Signet, 1978. (See Chapter 7.)

10

Mistaken Beliefs

By now you may have asked "Where does negative self-talk come from?" In most cases it's possible to trace negative thinking back to deeper-lying beliefs or assumptions about ourselves, others, and life in general. These basic assumptions have been variously called "scripts," "core beliefs," "life decisions," "fallacious beliefs," or "mistaken beliefs." While growing up we learned them from our parents, teachers, and peers as well as from the larger society around us. These beliefs are typically so basic to our thinking that we do not recognize them as *beliefs* at all—we just take them for granted and assume them to reflect reality. Examples of mistaken beliefs that you might hold are "I'm powerless," "Life is a struggle," or "I should always look good and act nice no matter how I feel." There is nothing new about the idea of mistaken beliefs—they are a part of what people have in mind when they refer to your "attitude" or "outlook."

Mistaken beliefs are at the root of much of the anxiety you experience. As discussed in the preceding chapter, you talk yourself into much of your anxiety by anticipating the worst (what-if thinking), putting yourself down (self-critical thinking), and pushing yourself to meet unreasonable demands and expectations (perfectionist thinking). Underlying these destructive patterns of self-talk are some basic false assumptions about yourself and "the way life is."

You could save yourself quite a bit of worrying, for example, if you let go of the basic assumption, "I must worry about a problem before there's any chance it will go away." Similarly, you would feel more confident and secure if you discarded the mistaken beliefs, "I'm nothing unless I succeed" or "I'm nothing unless others love and approve of me." Once again, life would be less stressful and tense if you would let go of the belief, "I must do it perfectly or it's not worth bothering to try." You can go a long way toward creating a less anxious way of life by working on changing the basic assumptions that tend to perpetuate anxiety.

Mistaken beliefs often keep you from achieving your most important goals in life. You might ask yourself right now, "What is it that I really want out of life? What would I attempt to do if I knew I could not fail?" Take a few minutes to seriously reflect on this and write your answer in the space below. (Use a separate sheet of paper if you need more room.)

Now, if you don't yet have what you want, ask yourself the simple question, "Why not?" List what reasons you can come up with in the space below or write them on another sheet of paper.

In the process of doing the above exercise, you may have discovered certain beliefs or assumptions that have been holding you back. Are these assumptions truly valid? Examples of assumptions that people hold themselves back with might include, "I can't afford to have what I want," "I don't have the time to go back to school and study the subject that interests me," or "I don't have the talent to succeed." At a more unconscious level, you might even feel, "I don't deserve to have what I truly want." None of these ideas necessarily reflects the true nature of reality—they all involve assumptions that might well turn out to be false if actually tested. Often you don't realize how such assumptions are affecting your behavior until someone else points them out to you.

Mistaken beliefs often set limits on your self-esteem and self-worth. Many such beliefs involve the idea that your self-worth depends on something outside yourself, such as social status, wealth, material possessions, the love of another person, or social approval in general. If you don't have these things, somehow you believe that you are not worth much. The belief that "Success is everything" or "My worth depends on what I accomplish" places the basis of your self-esteem outside of you. So does the belief, "I'm nothing unless I'm loved (or approved of)."

The truth that takes some people a long time to realize is that self-worth is *inherent*. You have an essential value, worth, and dignity just by virtue of the fact that you're a human being. You have many qualities and talents regardless of your outer accomplishments or the approval of others. Without thinking, we respect the inherent value of dogs and cats as animals. So, too, human beings have inherent value *just as they are*, apart from what they accomplish, possess, or whose approval they enjoy. As you grow in self-esteem, you can *learn* to respect and believe in yourself apart from what you have accomplished and without relying on another for your good feeling (or making another reliant on you).

Examples of Mistaken Beliefs

There are innumerable mistaken beliefs. You have your own collection as a result of what you learned from your parents, teachers, and peers during childhood and adolescence. Sometimes you take on a false belief directly from your parents, such as when you are told "Big boys don't cry" or "Nice girls don't get angry." At other times you develop an attitude about yourself as a result of being frequently criticized (thus "I'm worthless"), ignored (thus "My needs don't matter"), or rejected (thus "I'm unlovable") over many years. The unfortunate thing is that you may "live out" these mistaken attitudes to the point where you act in ways—and get others to treat you in ways—that confirm them. Like computers, people can be "preprogrammed," and the mistaken beliefs of childhood can become self-fulfilling prophecies.

Below are some examples of fairly common mistaken beliefs that tend to influence many people. Following each are counterstatements which replace the negative belief with a positive one, much in the way negative self-talk was countered by positive self-statements in the preceding chapter. Positive statements that counter mistaken beliefs are known as *affirmations*.

1. I'm powerless. I'm a victim of outside circumstances.

   I'm responsible and in control of my life. Circumstances are what they are, but I can determine my attitude toward them.

2. Life is a struggle. Something must be wrong if life seems too easy, pleasurable, or fun.

   Life is full and pleasurable.
   It's O.K. for me to relax and have fun.
   Life is an adventure—and I'm learning to accept both the ups and downs.

3. If I take a risk, I'll fail. If I fail, others will reject me.

   It's O.K. for me to take risks.
   It's O.K. to fail—I can learn a lot from every mistake.
   It's O.K. for me to be a success.

4. I'm unimportant. My feelings and needs are unimportant.

   I am a valuable and unique person.
   I deserve to have my feelings and needs taken care of as much as anyone else.

5. I always should look good and act nice no matter how I feel.

   It's O.K. simply to be myself.

6. If I worry enough, this problem should get better or go away.

   Worrying has no effect on solving problems; taking action does.

7. I can't cope with difficult or scary situations.

   I can learn to handle any scary situation if I approach it slowly, in small enough steps.

8. The outside world is dangerous. There is only safety in what is known and familiar.

   I can learn to become more comfortable with the world outside.
   I look forward to new opportunities for learning and growth that the outside world can offer.

Just *recognizing* your own particular mistaken beliefs is the first and most important step toward letting go of them. The second step is to develop a positive affirmation to counter each mistaken belief and continue to impress it on your mind until you are "deprogrammed."

What follows is a questionnaire that will help you to identify some of your own unconstructive beliefs. Rate each statement on a 1-4 scale according to how much you think it influences your feelings and behavior. Then go back and check off the beliefs you rated 3 or 4.

Mistaken Beliefs Questionnaire

How much does each of these unconstructive beliefs influence your feelings and behavior? Take your time to reflect about each belief.

1 = Not at All   **3 = Strongly/Frequently**
2 = Somewhat/Sometimes   **4 = Very Strongly**

Place the appropriate number after each statement:

1. I feel powerless or helpless.
2. Often I feel like a victim of outside circumstances.
3. I don't have the money to do what I really want.
4. There is seldom enough time to do what I want.
5. Life is very difficult—it's a struggle.
6. If things are going well, watch out!
7. I feel unworthy. I feel that I'm not good enough.
8. Often I feel that I don't deserve to be successful or happy.
9. Often I feel a sense of defeat and resignation: "Why bother!"
10. My condition seems hopeless.
11. There is something fundamentally wrong with me.
12. I feel ashamed of my condition.
13. If I take risks to get better, I'm afraid I'll fail.
14. If I take risks to get better, I'm afraid I'll succeed.
15. If I recovered fully, I might have to deal with realities I'd rather not face.
16. I feel like I'm nothing (or can't make it) unless I'm loved.
17. I can't stand being separated from others.
18. If a person I love doesn't love me in return, I feel like it's my fault.
19. It's very hard to be alone.
20. What others think of me is very important.
21. I feel personally threatened when criticized.
22. It's important to please others.
23. People won't like me if they see who I really am.
24. I need to keep up a front or others will see my weaknesses.

25. I have to achieve or produce something significant in order to feel O.K. about myself.

26. My accomplishments at work/school are extremely important.

27. Success is everything.

28. I have to be the best at what I do.

29. I have to be somebody—somebody outstanding.

30. To fail is terrible.

31. I can't rely on others for help.

32. I can't receive from others.

33. If I let someone get too close, I'm afraid of being controlled.

34. I can't tolerate being out of control.

35. I'm the only one who can solve my problems.

36. I should always be very generous and unselfish.

37. I should be the *perfect* ... (rate each)

    a. employee   e. lover
    b. professional   f. friend
    c. spouse   g. student
    d. parent   h. son/daughter

38. I should be able to endure any hardship.

39. I should be able to find a quick solution to every problem.

40. I should never be tired or fatigued.

41. I should always be efficient.

42. I should always be competent.

43. I should always be able to foresee everything.

44. I should never be angry or irritable. Or: I don't like (or am afraid of) anger.

45. I should always be pleasant or nice no matter how I feel.

46. I often feel ... (rate each)

    a. ugly   c. unintelligent
    b. inferior or defective   d. guilty or ashamed

47. I'm just the way I am—I can't really change.

48. The world outside is a dangerous place.

49. Unless you worry about a problem it just gets worse.

50. It's risky to trust people.

51. My problems will go away on their own with time.

52. I feel anxious about making mistakes.

53. I demand perfection of myself.

54. If I didn't have my safe person (or safe place), I'm afraid I couldn't cope.

55. If I stop worrying, I'm afraid something bad will happen.

56. I'm afraid to face the world out there on my own.

57. My self-worth isn't a given—it has to be earned.

You may have noticed that some of the beliefs on the questionnaire fall into specific groups, each of which reflects a very basic belief or attitude toward life.* Go back over your answers and see how you scored with respect to each of the groups of beliefs below.

Add up your scores for each subgroup of beliefs. If your total score on the items in a particular subgroup exceeds the criterion value, then this is likely to be a problem area for you. It's important that you give this group special attention when you begin to work with affirmations to start changing your mistaken beliefs.

If your total score for questions **1, 2, 7, 9, 10, 11** is over 15:	You likely believe that you are powerless, have little or no control over outside circumstances, or are unable to do much that could help your situation. In sum, "I'm powerless" or "I can't do much about my life."
If your total score for questions **16, 17, 18, 19, 54, 56** is over 15:	You likely believe that your self-worth is dependent on the love of someone else. You feel that you need another's (or others') love to feel O.K. about yourself and to cope. In sum, "My worth and security are dependent on being loved."
If your total score for questions **20, 21, 22, 23, 24, 45** is over 15:	You likely believe that your self-worth is dependent on others' approval. Being pleasing and getting acceptance from others is very important for your sense of security and your sense of who you are. In sum, "My worth and security depend on the approval of others."
If your total score for questions **25, 26, 27, 28, 29, 30, 41, 42** is over 20:	You likely believe that your self-worth is dependent on external achievements such as school or career performance, status, or wealth. In sum, "My worth is dependent on my performance or achievements."
If your total score for questions **31, 32, 33, 34, 35, 50** is over 15:	You likely believe that you can't trust, rely on, or receive help from others. You may have a tendency to keep a distance from people and avoid intimacy for fear of losing control. In sum, "If I trust or get too close, I'll lose control."

---

*The idea for defining subgroups of beliefs was adapted from David Burns, M.D., *Feeling Good*, Chapter 10. See his book for further details on how to counter and work with mistaken beliefs.

If your total score for questions **37, 38, 39, 40, 52, 53** is over 25:   You likely believe that you have to be perfect in some or many areas of life. You make excessive demands on yourself. There is no room for mistakes. In sum, "I have to be perfect" or "It's not O.K. to make mistakes."

Countering Mistaken Beliefs

Now that you have an idea of those mistaken beliefs which have the greatest impact on you, how do you go about changing them? The first step is to ask yourself *how strongly do you believe in them*. There are three possible ways to maintain a mistaken belief:

1. You don't really believe it. You view the belief as a bad mental habit that you are truly ready to give up. You are convinced of the uselessness of the belief *and* you realize that it has no strong emotional hold on you.

   If that is the case, you are ready to develop a positive affirmation to counter the belief. You can proceed directly to the next section, "Guidelines for Constructing Affirmations," and follow the suggested steps for developing affirmations to counter the particular belief. You may also want to see the section "Examples of Affirmations" at the end of the chapter to get ideas for specific alternatives to any of the beliefs on the *Mistaken Beliefs Questionnaire*.

2. You don't really subscribe to the belief on an intellectual level, but it still has an emotional grip on you and influences the way you act. You *don't want to believe* that "It's always important to be pleasing to others," for example, but you find that you continue to feel and act as if it were true. It's hard to "get the belief out of your system."

   If that is the case, it's important to subject the belief to questions 4 and 5 under "Five Questions for Challenging Mistaken Beliefs" listed below. Identify any belief you rated 3 or 4 that still affects you despite your intellectual doubts. Then use questions 4 and 5 below to examine whether the belief is beneficial to your well-being and whether it developed out of your own choice or from your family history.

3. You may really have faith in a particular belief. You're not convinced that it's inaccurate; you'll need some persuading before you'll consider giving it up. The idea of substituting a positive affirmation in place of an attitude you've long believed in seems superficial or naively optimistic.

   If that is the case, it's important to subject the belief to questions 1, 2, and 3 under "Five Questions for Challenging Mistaken Beliefs" listed below. These first three questions are taken from the Socratic questions described in Chapter 9, and are especially useful for challenging a mistaken belief on a strictly logical level. If you discredit your belief on purely rational grounds, then proceed to questions 4 and 5. These questions will enable you to see how the belief affects your personal well-being and to determine whether it's your own belief or was acquired from your parents.

Five Questions for Challenging Mistaken Beliefs

1. What is the evidence for this belief? Looking objectively at all of my life experience, what is the evidence that this is true?

2. Does this belief *invariably* or *always* hold true for me?

3. Does this belief look at the whole picture? Does it take into account both positive and negative ramifications?

4. Does this belief promote my well-being and/or peace of mind?

5. Did I choose this belief on my own or did it develop out of my experience of growing up in my family?

A few words need to be said about this last question. Many of your mistaken beliefs were likely acquired from your family while growing up. There are at least two ways this could happen. First, one or both of your parents may have held the belief and you simply learned it from them. For example, beliefs such as, "The world outside is a dangerous place" or "It's risky to trust people" might have been attitudes held by your parents that you adopted wholesale, because no alternative views were presented to you as a child.

The other way you might have acquired a mistaken belief is as a *reaction to what happened* and/or *the way you were treated* as a child. For example, if your father died and then your mother went to work when you were five years old, you may have felt abandoned and developed the belief, "Being alone means being abandoned and unloved." Or if your parents expected you to achieve and criticized your mistakes and performance at school, your reaction would likely involve developing such beliefs as "My accomplishments are extremely important" and "It's not O.K. to make mistakes."

It's often helpful in the process of evaluating mistaken beliefs to see how they arose from unfortunate or dysfunctional circumstances during childhood. While such beliefs may have helped you to survive as a child, *they have long lost their usefulness and only serve to create anxiety or stress for you now*. To investigate connections between your childhood and mistaken beliefs, refer to the section "Childhood Circumstances" in Chapter 2, and complete the *Family Background Questionnaire* if you haven't done so already. You may also find it helpful to look at the section "Some Causes of Low Self-Esteem" in Chapter 15 to get a clearer idea of the various types of dysfunctional childhood situations that can provide the basis for developing mistaken beliefs.

Examples

The following examples illustrate the application of the above questions in challenging mistaken beliefs.

Mistaken Belief: "I am powerless or helpless" (Note: In challenging beliefs from the *Mistaken Beliefs Questionnaire*, reword any belief beginning with the words "I feel ... " to "I am ... " This provides a more direct statement of the belief.)

Questioning:	1. "What is the evidence for this?" 2. "Is this *always* true for me?" 4. "Does this belief promote my well-being?"
Counterarguments:	1. "What is the evidence for this?" "Though I often *feel* powerless or helpless, that doesn't necessarily mean that I *am* powerless or helpless." (Recognize that this is an example of an attitude typically held by the Victim subpersonality described in Chapter 9. It is also an example of a cognitive distortion based on emotional reasoning.) "After all, I can work on mastering the strategies in this workbook and can consult a therapist specializing in anxiety disorders to help me overcome my condition. Also, I have the support of my family and friends who are backing me all the way. Thus there is no strong evidence that I'm either powerless or helpless." 2. "Is this *always* true for me?" "Some days I certainly *feel* powerless or helpless, but other days I feel more capable and optimistic. It's just not true that I *always* feel that way." 4. "Does this belief promote my well-being?" "Believing that I'm powerless and helpless is destructive to developing confidence in myself and hope for recovery. Such a belief definitely does not promote my well-being or peace of mind."
Affirmations:	*I believe in myself.* *I trust I have the capacity to overcome my problem with anxiety.*
Mistaken Belief:	"It's very important to please others."
Questioning:	2. "Is this *always* true for me?" 4. "Does this belief promote my well-being?" 5. "Did I choose this belief on my own or did it develop from my childhood?"
Counterarguments:	2. "Is this *always* true for me?" "Certainly there are some situations where it's helpful to come across in a pleasing manner. If I'm interviewing for a job, going out on a first date, comforting my spouse, or hosting a party, I generally *want* to be pleasing. On the other hand, if I'm feeling exhausted or upset and need support from my partner or friends, it serves me better to ask them to be there for me rather than to have to deny my needs and keep up a pleasing front. In short, it's sometimes *more* important to attend to my own feelings." 4. "Does this belief promote my well-being?" "In some situations, probably yes. I feel good about myself

if I can be pleasant in situations where to come across as such might be appropriate. However, it doesn't serve me to try to be pleasing when I'm actually feeling upset or ill. I'll be more honest and in tune with myself to let people know what I'm feeling and ask for their support."

5. "Did I choose this belief on my own or did it develop from my childhood?"

"My mother was ill and frequently complained during much of my childhood. I felt I always had to be on guard to protect her from my own problems. It seemed that I had to be pleasing to maintain her approval. No wonder I grew up to be such a people pleaser! I guess that I didn't freely choose this belief, but rather it was imposed on me by the circumstances of my childhood."

Affirmations:	*It's O.K. to not always be pleasing.*
	I can enjoy being pleasing at those times when I genuinely feel like it.
Mistaken Belief:	"My accomplishments at work/school are supremely important."
Questioning:	2. "Is this belief *always* true?"
	3. "Does this belief look at the whole picture?"
	4. "Does this belief promote my well-being?"
	5. "Did I choose this belief on my own or did it develop from my childhood?"
Counterarguments:	2. "Is this belief *always* true?"

"No, in as much as other areas of my life (health, relationships, leisure time, creative pursuits) are also important. Accomplishing things at school or work is certainly important, but it's not *always important 24 hours a day, 7 days a week.*"

3. "Does this belief look at the whole picture?"

"It's true that what I accomplish at school or work is important. I need to maintain a certain level of competence in school in order to earn the degree that will help me find a job." (Or "I need to maintain a certain level of performance at work to hold my job.") "But is it looking at the whole picture to regard my accomplishments as *supremely* important? If that were the case, they would be more important than my health, peace of mind, my family, and everything else I value. Such an attitude would lead to an imbalanced and ultimately unhealthy lifestyle—a lifestyle where nothing else mattered except my success and accomplishments. Thus it's unreasonable to believe that my accomplishments are supremely important."

4. "Does this belief promote my well-being?"

"For reasons already mentioned, I recognize that an *exclusive* focus on accomplishments is unhealthy."

5. "Did I choose this belief on my own, or did it develop from my childhood?"

"My parents were both professionals who were successful in their careers and expected me to follow their example. I always had to do well in school to receive their approval and was criticized for any grade below a B. My attitude that achievement is so important came from living with them—I didn't freely choose it."

Affirmations: *My accomplishments are important and so are other things in my life.*
I am learning how to balance work and play in my life.

The above examples can serve as guidelines for challenging your own mistaken beliefs. If there is little evidence for a particular belief, if it is not always true, or if it doesn't promote your personal well-being, then it is most likely to be mistaken. If the belief was acquired out of dysfunctional family circumstances rather than having been freely chosen by you as an adult, it is equally likely to be mistaken. It is important to go through such a process of questioning if you feel at all attached to any particular belief.

Once you've completed the process of challenging all of those mistaken beliefs you rated 3 or 4, you're ready to develop positive affirmations to counter each one of them. The guidelines in the next section explain how to construct affirmations. Although it's preferable to develop your own affirmations, you can refer to the examples at the end of the chapter if you need help creating an affirmation for a particular mistaken belief.

After you've developed your affirmations, go back to the *Mistaken Beliefs Questionnaire* and write each affirmation in capital letters next to or under the particular mistaken belief it is intended to counter. (Refer to the examples of mistaken beliefs and affirmations earlier in this chapter.)

The process of countering mistaken beliefs with affirmations is very similar to that of countering negative self-talk with positive self-statements, which was described in Chapter 9. The difference is that affirmations are very compact statements that you can easily rehearse (not unlike the coping statements for panic attacks listed in Chapter 6). Writing affirmations repetitively on paper or listening to them repetitively on tape can, with persistence, actually result in their supplanting unwanted mistaken beliefs in your mind. In the chapter on self-talk, the important process to master was "countering." By continually writing out counterstatements to negative self-talk, you eventually develop a *habit* of noticing and countering the anxiety-provoking things you tell yourself. In this chapter, the important process is working with affirmations. This will actually change the core beliefs that underlie your negative self-talk. See the section "Ways to Work with Affirmations" for specific suggestions on using affirmations.

Guidelines for Constructing Affirmations

1. An affirmation should be *short, simple*, and *direct*. "I believe in myself" is preferable to "There are a lot of good qualities I have that I believe in."

2. Keep affirmations in the *present tense* ("I am prosperous") or *present progressive tense* ("I am becoming prosperous"). Telling yourself that some change you desire will happen in the future always keeps it one step removed.

3. Try to *avoid negatives*. Instead of saying "I'm no longer afraid of public speaking," try "I'm free of fear about public speaking" or "I'm becoming fearless about public speaking." Similarly, instead of the negative statement "I'm not perfect," try "It's O.K. to be less than perfect" or "It's O.K. to make mistakes." Your unconscious mind is incapable of making the distinction between a positive and a negative statement. It will respond to a negative statement in the same way as a positive affirmation (for example, "I'm not perfect" becomes "I am perfect").

4. Start with a direct declaration of a positive change you want to make in your life ("I am making more time for myself every day"). If this feels a little too strong for you just yet, try changing it to "I am willing to make more time for myself." *Willingness* to change is the most important first step you need to take in order to actually make any substantial change in your life. A second alternative to a direct declaration is to affirm that you are *becoming* something or *learning* to do something. If you're not quite ready for a direct statement such as, "I'm strong, confident, and secure," you can affirm "I am becoming strong, confident, and secure." Again, if you're not ready for "I face my fears willingly," try "I'm learning to face my fears."

5. It's important that you have *some* belief in—or at least a willingness to believe in—your affirmations. It's by no means necessary, however, to believe in an affirmation 100 percent when you first start out. The whole point is to shift your beliefs and attitudes in favor of the affirmation.

Ways To Work With Affirmations

Once you have made a list of affirmations, decide on a few that you would like to work with. In general, it's a good idea to work on only two or three at a time, unless you choose to make a tape containing all of them. Some of the more helpful ways you can utilize affirmations are listed below.

1. Write an affirmation repetitively, about five or ten times every day, for a week or two. Each time you doubt your belief in the affirmation, write down your doubt on the reverse side of the paper. As you continue to write an affirmation over and over, giving yourself the opportunity to express any doubts, you'll find that your willingness to believe it increases.

Example:

I'm learning to be fine by myself.	Yes, for a few hours, but how will I ever manage for a whole day?
I'm learning to be fine by myself.	What if I panic and no one is around?
I'm learning to be fine by myself.	I'm not sure I'll be able to do this.
I'm learning to be fine by myself.	

Later, go back and counter your doubts one by one with positive statements. In the example above, the three doubts might be countered by the following three affirmations:

> "Gradually, I can learn to extend the time I'm O.K. being alone to an entire day."

> "If I panic while I'm alone, I can do deep breathing, go with the feeling, and call _____."

> "If I break this down into small enough steps, I know I can do it."

2. Write your affirmation in giant letters with a magic marker on a blank sheet of paper (the words should be visible from at least 20 feet away). Then attach the sheet to your bathroom mirror, your refrigerator, or some other conspicuous place in your home. Constantly seeing the affirmation day in and day out, whether or not you actively attend to it, will help to reinforce it in your mind.

3. Put a series of affirmations on tape. If you develop 20 or so affirmations to counter statements on the *Mistaken Beliefs Questionnaire,* you may wish to put all of them on tape. You can use either your own voice or have someone else do the recording. Make sure the affirmations are in the first person and that you allow 5-10 seconds between them so that each one has time to sink in.

   Listening to the tape once a day for 30 days will lead to a major shift in your thinking and the way you feel about yourself. It's O.K. to play the tape at any time, even while cleaning the house or driving in your car. However, you can expedite the process by giving the tape your full attention in a very relaxed state when you've slowed yourself down enough to deeply feel each affirmation.

4. Work with a partner. Have your partner say the affirmation to you in the *second* person while looking into your eyes. After she or he says it (for example, "You are learning to overcome your fears"), you respond "Yes, I know." Your partner keeps repeating the affirmation to you until she or he is convinced that you really mean it when you say "Yes, I know." After you've completed this, reverse roles. This time you repeat the affirmation in the *first* person while looking into your partner's eyes. After each time you say the affirmation (for example, "I'm learning to overcome my fears"), your partner responds with the statement "Yes it's true!" Again, you need to continue this until your partner is convinced that you really mean what you're saying.

5. Take a single affirmation with you into meditation. Repeating an affirmation slowly and with conviction while in a deep meditative state is a very powerful way of incorporating it into your consciousness. Meditation is a state in which you can experience yourself as a "whole being." Whatever you affirm or declare with your whole being will have the strongest tendency to come true.

Increasing the Power of an Affirmation

There are two fundamental ways of reinforcing an affirmation or any new habit of thinking—*repetition* and *feeling*.

Repetition	It took repetition to "program" mistaken beliefs in your mind originally. Being told numerous times by your parents to "shut up" or "behave yourself" reinforced the fallacious belief "I'm unworthy" or "I'm unimportant." By the same token, repeated exposure to a positive affirmation can help instill it in your mind until it replaces the original false belief.
Feeling	Saying affirmations with deep conviction and feeling is the *most* powerful method, in my opinion, for strengthening them. Getting a new belief *into your heart*—as well as into your head—will give it the greatest power and efficacy. A good way to do this is to attain a deep state of relaxation first (through progressive muscle relaxation or meditation) and then to say the affirmation slowly, with feeling and a sense of conviction. It has been said before that what you believe in with your whole heart becomes a part of you.

Active Integration

You can also increase your conviction about an affirmation by keeping track of confirmations of it in real life. Select an affirmation you wish to work on and write it down on a note card. As you go through the day, write down on the other side of the card any event or situation, no matter how minor, which supports the affirmation. Keep this up for two or more weeks and see if you can compile a list of confirmations. For example, if you're working with the affirmation, "I can recover by taking small risks at my own pace," then you might list all of your successes in reducing your anxiety and/or confronting phobic situations. Or if you're working with the statement, "I'm learning that there is more to life than success in my career (or school)," you can list all the occasions when you derived enjoyment from other activities to demonstrate the truth of your new belief.

Reinforcing an affirmation by noting real-life events that confirm it will go a long way toward strengthening your conviction of its truth.

Examples of Affirmations

Below are examples of affirmations you can use to counter statements from the *Mistaken Beliefs Questionnaire*. Use any that feel right to you or use them as guidelines for making up your own.

1. I'm responsible and in control of my life.

2. Circumstances are what they are, but I can choose my attitude toward them.

3. I am becoming prosperous. I am creating the financial resources I need.

4. I am setting priorities and making time for what is important.

5. Life has its challenges and its satisfactions—I enjoy the adventure of life. Every challenge that comes along is an opportunity to learn and grow.

6. I accept the natural ups and downs of life.

7. I love and accept myself the way I am.

8. I deserve the good things in life as much as anyone else.

9. I am open to discovering new meaning in my life.

10. It's never too late to change. I am improving one step at a time.

11. I am innately healthy, strong, and capable of fully recovering. I am getting better every day.

12. I am committed to overcoming my condition. I am working on recovering from my condition.

13. I can recover by taking small risks at my own pace.

14/15. I am looking forward to the new freedom and opportunities I'll have when I've fully recovered.

16. I am learning to love myself.

17. I am learning to be comfortable by myself.

18. If someone doesn't return my love, I let it go and move on.

19. I am learning to be at peace with myself when alone. I am learning how to enjoy myself when alone.

20. I respect and believe in myself apart from others' opinions.

21. I can accept and learn from constructive criticism.

22. I'm learning to be myself around others. It's important to take care of my own needs.

23/24. It's O.K. to be myself around others. I'm willing to be myself around others.

25. I appreciate my achievements, and I'm much more than all of them put together.

26. I am learning how to balance work and play in my life.

27. I am learning that there is more to life than success. The greatest success is living well.

28/29. I'm a unique and capable person just as I am. I am satisfied doing the best I can.

30. It's O.K. to make mistakes. I'm willing to accept my mistakes and learn from them.

31. I'm willing to allow others to help me. I acknowledge my need for other people.

32. I am open to receiving support from others.

33. I am willing to take the risk of getting close to someone.

34. I am learning to relax and let go. I'm learning to accept those things I can't control.

35. I am willing to let others assist me in solving my problems.

36. When I love and care for myself, I am best able to be generous to others.

37. I'm doing the best I can as a _____ (optional: and I'm open to learning ways to improve).

38. It's O.K. to be upset when things go wrong.

39. I'm O.K. if I don't always have a quick answer to every problem.

40. It's O.K. to make time to rest and relax.

41/42. I do the best I can, and I'm satisfied with that.

43. It's O.K. if I'm unable to always foresee everything.

44. It's O.K. to be angry sometimes. I am learning to accept and express my angry feelings appropriately.

45. I'm learning to be honest with others, even when I'm not feeling pleasant or nice.

46. I believe that I am an attractive, intelligent, and valuable person. I am learning to let go of guilt.

47. I believe that I can change. I am willing to change (or grow).

48. The world outside is a place to grow and have fun.

49. Worrying about a problem is the real problem. Doing something about it will make a difference for the better.

50. I am learning (or willing) to trust other people.

51. I'm making a commitment to myself to do what I can to overcome my problem with _____.

52. I'm learning that it's O.K. to make mistakes.

53. Nobody's perfect—and I'm learning (or willing) to go easier on myself.

54. I'm willing to become (or to learn to become) self-sufficient.

55. I'm learning to let go of worrying. I can replace worrying with constructive action.

56. I am learning, one step at a time, that I can deal with the outside world.

57. I'm inherently worthy as a person. I accept myself just the way I am.

The purpose of this chapter has been to increase your awareness about mistaken beliefs and help you identify some of your own. Countering negative self-talk and mistaken beliefs with positive thinking and affirmations can go a long way toward helping you lead a calmer, more balanced and anxiety-free life. While the earlier chapters on relaxation and exercise were designed to help you overcome the physiological bases of anxiety, the intent of the last two chapters has been to give you tools to deal with that part of anxiety that is in your mind—what you say to yourself and what you believe. Chapter 13 will examine the important relationship between anxiety and feelings.

Summary of Things To Do

1. Complete the *Mistaken Beliefs Questionnaire,* checking off those beliefs you rated 3 or 4. Note any subgroupings of beliefs where your total score exceeds the criterion value for that group. The theme for that subgroup deserves your special attention.

2. Reread the section "Countering Mistaken Beliefs" until you are thoroughly familiar with various ways of challenging them. Use the "Five Questions for Challenging Mistaken Beliefs" to call into question any belief that a) has an emotional hold on you or b) seems intellectually plausible.

3. After challenging your mistaken beliefs, develop affirmations to counter each one of them. Use the "Guidelines for Constructing Affirmations" to assist you, and refer to the section "Examples of Affirmations" at the end of the chapter for a list of examples. On the questionnaire, write each of your affirmations in capital letters underneath the particular mistaken belief you're countering.

4. Reread the section "Ways To Work With Affirmations" and decide which method of rehearsing affirmations you want to use— for example, writing them repetitively, listening to them on tape, working with a partner or taking your affirmations into meditation. Work with this method for two weeks to one month on a daily basis, and afterwards whenever you feel the need.

Further Reading

Bloch, Douglas. *Words That Heal: Affirmations and Meditations for Daily Living.* New York: Bantam, 1990. (The best single book on working with affirmations I've seen.)

Handly, Robert, and Neff, Pauline. *Anxiety and Panic Attacks: Their Cause and Cure.* New York: Rawson Associates, 1985. (Popular book for phobics on how to utilize affirmations and visualization.)

McKay, Matthew, and Fanning, Patrick. *Prisoners of Belief.* Oakland, California: New Harbinger Publications, 1991.

Woolfolk, Robert L., and Richardson, Frank C. *Stress, Sanity and Survival.* New York: Signet, 1978. (A classic book on the types of mistaken beliefs that perpetuate anxiety—see especially Chapters 4, 5, and 7.)

11

Four Traits That
Perpetuate Anxiety

People who are prone to anxiety disorders tend to share certain personality traits. Some of these traits are positive—such as creativity, intuitive ability, emotional sensitivity, empathy, and amiability. Such traits as these endear anxiety-prone people to their friends and relatives. Other common traits tend to aggravate anxiety and interfere with the self-confidence of people with anxiety disorders. This chapter focuses on four of these traits, all of which need to be addressed at some point in the process of recovery.

- Perfectionism

- Excessive need for approval

- Tendency to ignore physical and psychological signs of stress

- Excessive need for control

You may not possess all four of these traits. But if panic, phobias, or generalized anxiety have been part of your life for any length of time, you probably identify with at least two or three of them.

Origins of Anxiety-Provoking Traits

What's the origin of these traits that perpetuate anxiety? Such traits as creativity and emotional sensitivity may well be part of the hereditary component of anxiety disorders (see Chapter 2). On the other hand, perfectionism and excessive need for approval or control most likely have their origin in early childhood experiences. There are various ways in which you can acquire such traits. If your parents have these traits, you may learn them directly by following their example. If your mother and father are high achievers, and demand perfection of themselves, you may internalize their values and behave in a similar way. Alternatively, such traits may develop out of your *response* to the ways in which you were treated by one or both of your parents. If, for example, you were frequently criticized or reprimanded, you may have decided early on that nothing you could do was good enough. As a result, you strive to do everything perfectly. Or you might constantly seek reassurance and approval. In the process, you may have also learned to deny your feelings and ignore signs of stress.

If you would like to obtain more insight about how you developed any of the traits considered in this chapter, you can start by referring to the *Family Background Questionnaire* in Chapter 2. Reflecting on your answers to the questions will help you better understand your past.

Below you'll find guidelines to help you identify, work with, and change each of the four traits that perpetuate anxiety: perfectionism, excessive need for approval, the tendency to ignore physical and psychological signs of stress, and the excessive need for control.*

Perfectionism

Perfectionism has two aspects. First, you have a tendency to have expectations about yourself, others, and life that are unrealistically high. When anything falls short, you become disappointed and/or critical. Second, you tend to be overconcerned with small flaws and mistakes in yourself or your accomplishments. In focusing on what's wrong, you tend to discount and ignore what's right.

Perfectionism is a common cause of low self-esteem. It is critical of every effort and convinces you that nothing is ever good enough. It can also cause you to drive yourself to the point of chronic stress, exhaustion, and burnout. Every time perfectionism counsels you that you "should," "have to," or "must," you tend to push yourself forward out of anxiety, rather than from natural desire and inclination. The more perfectionistic you are, the more often you're likely to feel anxious.

Overcoming perfectionism requires a fundamental shift in your attitude toward yourself and how you approach life in general. The following seven guidelines are intended as a starting point for making such a shift.

1. Let Go of the Idea That Your Worth Is Determined by Your Achievements and Accomplishments

Outer accomplishment may be how society measures a person's "worth" or "social status." But are you going to allow society to have the last word on your value as a person? Work on reinforcing the idea that your worth is a given. People ascribe inherent worth to pets and plants just by virtue of their existence. You as a human being have the same inherent worth just because you're here. Be willing to recognize and affirm that you're lovable and acceptable as you are, apart from your outer accomplishments. When self-reflective people are near death, there are usually only two things that seem to have been important to them about their lives: learning how to love others, and growing in wisdom. If you need to measure yourself against any standard, try these rather than society's definitions of value.

2. Recognize and Overcome Perfectionistic Thinking Styles

Perfectionism is expressed in the way you talk to yourself. Three types of thinking characteristic of a perfectionistic attitude were described in the chapter on self-talk: "Should/Must Thinking," "All-or-Nothing Thinking," and "Overgeneralization." Below

---

* Outlines of the sections on perfectionism and the excessive need for approval in this chapter were adapted with permission from Chapters 6 and 8 of *Anxiety, Phobias and Panic: Taking Charge and Conquering Fear* by Reneau Z. Peurifoy, M.A., M.F.C.C. See this useful book for more detailed discussions of these issues.

are examples of self-statements associated with each thinking style and corresponding, more realistic counterstatements.

Thinking Style	Counterstatements
Should/Must Thinking	
"I should be able to do this right."	"I'll do the best I can."
"I must not make mistakes."	"It's okay to make mistakes."
All-or-Nothing Thinking	
"This is all wrong."	"This is not *all* wrong. There are some parts of it that are O.K. and some that need attention."
"I just can't do it at all."	"If I break this down into small enough steps, I can do it."
Overgeneralization	
"I'll *always* foul things up."	"It's simply untrue that I *always* foul things up. In this particular case, I'll go back and make the necessary corrections."
"I'll *never* be able to do this."	"If I take small steps and keep making an effort, over time I'll accomplish what I set out to do."

Spend one week noticing all the instances when you get involved in should/must thinking, all-or-nothing thinking, or overgeneralization. Keep a notebook with you so that you can write down thoughts as they occur to you. Examine what you're telling yourself at times when you feel particularly anxious or stressed. Pay special attention to your use of the words "should," "must," "have to," "always," "never," "all," or "none." After you've spent a week writing down your perfectionist self-statements, compose counterstatements for each one. In subsequent weeks, read over your list of counterstatements frequently to encourage yourself to develop a less perfectionist approach to life. See Chapter 9 for further information on how to develop and work with counterstatements.

3. Stop Magnifying the Importance of Small Errors

One of the most problematic aspects of perfectionism is its mandate to focus on small flaws or errors. Perfectionists are prone to come down very hard on themselves for a single, minute mistake that has few or no immediate consequences, let alone any long-term effects. When you really think about it, how important is a mistake you make today going to be one month from now? Or one year from now? In 99.9 percent of cases, the mistake will be forgotten within a short period of time. There is no real learning without mistakes or setbacks. No great success was ever attained without many failures and mistakes along the way.

4. Focus on Positives

In dwelling on small errors or mistakes, perfectionists tend to discount their positive accomplishments. They selectively ignore anything positive they've done. A way to counter this tendency is to take inventory near the end of each day of positive things you've accomplished. Think about what ways, small or large, you've been helpful or pleasant to people during the day. Think of any small steps you've taken toward achieving your goals. What other things got done? What insights did you have?

Pay attention to whether you disqualify something positive with a "but"—for example, "I had a good practice session, but I became anxious near the end." Learn to leave off the "but" in the assessments of your attitudes and behavior.

5. Work on Goals That Are Realistic

Are your goals realistically attainable, or have you set them too high? Would you expect of anyone else the goals you set for yourself? Sometimes it's difficult to recognize the overly lofty nature of certain goals. It can be helpful to do a "reality check" with a friend or counselor to determine whether any given goal is realistically attainable, or even reasonable to strive for. Are you expecting too much of yourself and the world? You may need to adjust some of your goals a bit in line with the limiting factors of time, energy, and resources. If your determination of self-worth truly comes from within, rather than from what you achieve, you will be able to do this. Acceptance of personal limitations is the ultimate act of self-love.

6. Cultivate More Pleasure and Recreation in Your Life

Perfectionism has a tendency to make people rigid and self-denying. Your own human needs get sacrificed in favor of the pursuit of external goals. Ultimately this tendency can lead to a stifling of vitality and creativity. Pleasure—finding the enjoyment in life—reverses this trend.

The Sioux Indians have a wise saying: "The first thing people say after their death is—'Why was I so serious?'" Are you taking yourself too seriously and not allowing yourself time for fun, recreation, play, and rest? How can you make more time for leisure, and pleasure? You can change by taking time every day to do at least one thing you enjoy.

7. Develop a Process Orientation

If you engage in sports, do you play to win or just to enjoy the activity of playing? In your life in general, are you "playing to win," channeling your energies into excelling at all costs, or are you enjoying the process of living day by day as you go along?

Most people find, especially as they get older, that to get the most enjoyment out of life, it works best to place value on the *process* of doing things—not just on the product or accomplishment. Popular clichés which express this idea include: "The journey is more important than the destination," and "Stop and smell the roses."

The Excessive Need for Approval

All human beings need approval. Yet for many people struggling with anxiety and phobias, the need for approval can be excessive. Being overly concerned with approval often arises from an inner sense of being flawed or unworthy. This leads to the mistaken belief that you are unacceptable just the way you are ("If people really saw who I am, they wouldn't accept me."). Individuals with an excessive need for approval are always looking for validation from other people. In trying to be generally pleasing, they may accommodate themselves so well to others' expectations that they often ignore their own needs and feelings. Frequently they have a difficult time setting boundaries or saying "no."

The long-term consequence of always accommodating and pleasing others at the expense of yourself is that you end up with a lot of withheld frustration and resentment over not having taken care of your own basic needs. Withheld frustration and resentment form the unconscious foundation for a lot of chronic anxiety and tension.

There are many ways in which to get over being excessively needy for approval. The following three guidelines can help you start.

1. Develop a Realistic View of Other People's Approval

When people don't express approval toward you—or even act rude or critical—how do you receive it? Do you tend to take it personally—to see it as further evidence of your own ineptness or lack of worth? Below are some common attitudes characteristic of people who place excessive emphasis on always being liked. These might be called "people-pleasing" attitudes. Following each is an alternative view which represents, in most cases, a more realistic outlook.

"If someone isn't friendly to me, it's because I did something wrong."
Alternative View: People may be unable to express warmth or acceptance toward me for reasons having nothing to do with me. For example, their own problems, frustrations, or fatigue may get in the way of their being friendly and accepting.

"Others' criticism only serves to underscore the fact that I really am unworthy."
Alternative View: People who find fault with me may be projecting their own faults, which they can't admit to having, onto me. It's a human tendency to project unconscious flaws onto others.

"I think I'm a nice person. Shouldn't everyone like me?"
Alternative View: There will always be some people who just won't like me—no matter what I do. The process by which people are attracted to or repelled by others is often irrational.

"Others' approval and acceptance of me is very important."
Alternative View: It's not necessary to receive the approval of everyone I meet in order to live a happy and meaningful life—especially if I believe in and respect myself.

The next time you feel put off or rejected, take a moment to calm down and think about whether the person acting negatively is reacting to something you did, or might simply be upset about something that has little or nothing to do with you. Ask yourself whether you might be taking the other person's inconsiderate remarks or behavior too personally.

2. Deal With Criticism in an Objective Fashion

An excessive need for approval is often accompanied by an inability to handle criticism. You can learn to change your attitude toward criticism, ignoring those critical remarks that are unfounded and accepting constructive criticism as a positive learning experience.

The following three guidelines may be helpful:

Evaluate the source of the criticism. If you find yourself criticized, it's important to ask *who* is making the criticism. Is this person qualified to criticize you? Does he or she know enough about you, your skills, or the subject involved to make a reasonable assessment? Does this person have a bias that would make it impossible for him or her to be objective? (The more emotionally charged the relationship, the more likely this is to be true.) Is this person speaking emotionally or rationally? You can often soothe the sting of criticism by exploring the answers to these questions.

Ask for details. This is especially important if you receive a "blanket" or "global" criticism such as, "That was a lousy job," or "I don't think you know what you're doing." Don't accept a global judgment. Ask the person offering the criticism to indicate specific behaviors or issues that seem to fall short. Ask that person's point of view about what actions you can take to improve your performance or correct the situation.

Decide whether the criticism has some validity. You've evaluated the source of criticism and also, in the case of a global criticism, asked for details. The next question to ask is whether the criticism has some merit. Usually when a criticism has some truth to it, it has a little more sting—you may feel somewhat pained or disturbed by it. If a criticism has no validity, you're likely to have little emotional reaction to it at all: you may dismiss it as irrelevant, absurd, or uninformed.

The best way to handle criticism that rings true is to view it as important feedback which can help you learn something about yourself. Also be sure to remind yourself that the criticism is—or should be—directed toward only one aspect of your behavior, not to you as a total person. Here are some good affirmations to help cultivate a positive response:

- "This criticism is a good opportunity to learn something."

- "This criticism concerns only a few of my actions, not my entire being."

- "Although this criticism feels uncomfortable, it doesn't mean that I'm totally rejected or disapproved of."

3. Recognize and Let Go of Co-Dependency

Check off any of the following statements that generally reflect your beliefs:

- ☐ "If someone important to me expects me to do something, I should do it."
- ☐ "I should not be irritable or unpleasant."
- ☐ "I shouldn't do anything to make others angry at me."
- ☐ "I should keep people I love happy."
- ☐ "It's usually my fault if someone I care about is upset with me."
- ☐ "My self-esteem comes from helping others solve their problems."
- ☐ "I tend to overextend myself in taking care of others."
- ☐ "If necessary, I'll put my own values or needs aside in order to preserve my relationship with my significant other."
- ☐ "Giving is the most important way I have to feel good about myself."
- ☐ "Fear of someone else's anger has a lot of influence on what I say or do."

If you checked three or more statements, co-dependency is likely to be one of the issues you need to deal with.

Co-dependency can be defined as the tendency to put others' needs before your own. You accommodate to others to such a degree that you tend to discount or ignore your own feelings, desires, and basic needs. Your self-esteem depends largely on how well you please, take care of, and/or solve problems for someone else (or many others).

The consequence of maintaining a co-dependent approach to life is a lot of resentment, frustration, and unmet personal needs. When these feelings and needs remain unconscious, they often resurface as anxiety—especially *chronic, generalized anxiety*. The long-term effects of co-dependency are enduring stress, fatigue, burnout, and eventually serious physical illness.

Recovering from co-dependency in essence involves learning to love and take care of yourself. It means giving at least equal time to your own needs alongside the needs of others. It means setting limits on how much you will do or tolerate, and learning to say "no" when appropriate. The following list of affirmations will encourage you to develop a more self-nurturing attitude that can move you beyond co-dependency: (See Chapter 10 for suggestions on how to work with affirmations.)

- "I'm learning to take better care of myself."

- "I recognize that my own needs are important."

- "It's good for me to take time for myself."

- "I'm finding a balance between my own needs and my concern for others."

- "If I take good care of myself, I'll have more to offer others."

- "It's O.K. to ask for what I want from others."

- "I'm learning to accept myself just the way I am."

- "It's O.K. to say no to others' demands when I need to."

- "I don't have to be perfect to be accepted and loved."

- "I can change myself, but I accept that I can't make another person change."

- "I'm letting go of taking responsibility for other people's problems."

- "I respect others enough to know that they can take responsibility for themselves."

- "I'm letting go of guilt when I can't fulfill others' expectations."

- "Compassion toward others is loving; feeling guilty about their feelings or reactions accomplishes nothing."

- "I am learning to love myself more every day."

In order to work with your own co-dependency issues, you may want to read some of the classic books on the subject, such as *Co-Dependent No More* by Melody Beattie, *Facing Co-Dependence* by Pia Melody, and *Women Who Love Too Much* by Robin Norwood. Also consider attending a local meeting of Co-Dependents Anonymous, which offers a 12-step approach to overcoming co-dependent attitudes.

The above three guidelines are only a start in the direction of learning to be less concerned with others' approval. The chapters on assertiveness and self-esteem in this book will also help you learn to empower yourself, rather than rely on others, in developing a sense of your inherent worth and acceptability.

Tendency To Ignore Physical and Psychological Signs of Stress

People with anxiety disorders are often out of touch with their bodies. If you are anxious or preoccupied with worrying, you may, as the expression goes, be "living in your head"—not feeling strongly connected with the rest of your body below the neck. Try checking in with yourself as you are reading right now. Do you feel as if most of your energy—your "center of gravity"—is situated from your neck up? Or do you feel solidly connected with the rest of your body, in touch with your chest, stomach, arms, and legs?

To the extent that you are out of touch with your body, you may ignore—often unconsciously—an entire range of physical symptoms which arise when you're under stress. Examples of physical symptoms that may signify stress include fatigue, headaches, nervous stomach, tight muscles, cold hands, or diarrhea, to mention a few. Unfortunately, when you're unaware that you're under stress, you're likely to keep pushing yourself without taking time out or slowing down. You may keep going without resting until you reach a state of exhaustion or illness.

Many individuals with anxiety disorders have a long history of pushing themselves very hard and continually overextending themselves—trying to fit too much into too little time. Driven by perfectionist standards, they keep striving to do more and be more for everyone. Often they may go for months at a time—even years—without noticing, or simply ignoring, that they are under high levels of stress.

One possible outcome of chronic, cumulative stress is that the neuroendocrine regulatory systems in the brain begin to malfunction, and you develop panic attacks, generalized anxiety, depression, mood swings, or some combination of these three (see Chapter 2). You might also develop ulcers, hypertension, headaches, or other psychosomatic illnesses under conditions of chronic stress. If it is your neurotransmitter systems that happen to be vulnerable, the effects of chronic stress are likely to show up in the form of an anxiety or mood disorder. Although these disorders cause significant distress in themselves, *they are in fact warning signs*. The body has built-in mechanisms for preventing its own self-destruction. Developing panic disorder or depression may be viewed as a way in which your body forces you to slow down and alter your lifestyle before you push yourself into catastrophic illness or death.

One of the themes of this workbook is that your recovery from anxiety disorders depends in great measure on your ability to manage and cope with stress. And this, in turn, requires that you learn to *recognize* your own symptoms of stress and then *do* something about them—to relieve your symptoms through deep relaxation, exercise, "down time," supportive social interaction, recreation, and so on—so that stress does not become cumulative.

Stress can manifest itself not only in the form of physical symptoms but as emotional and psychological symptoms as well. The psychological symptoms are a *direct* indication that your nervous system (and possibly endocrine system) is being overtaxed. As previously mentioned, being out of touch with your body may cause you to miss physical symptoms of stress. It is more difficult to be unconscious about psychological symptoms, however, because they are so much a part of your immediate experience. The problem is that if you are too busy, rushed, driven, or preoccupied, you may choose to ignore both types of symptoms.

The *Stress Symptom Checklist* on page 235 is designed to help you increase your awareness of both physical and psychological symptoms of stress. You may want to make a number of copies of the checklist and complete it periodically to get a reading of your own stress level.

The *Life Events Survey* in Chapter 2 measured your level of cumulative stress over a period of two years. The *Stress Symptom Checklist* will enable you to determine the stress load on your body and psyche over the past month. Take some time to complete the checklist now.

Handling stress involves two steps. The first is to *recognize and identify* your own symptoms of stress. The second is to *decide not to ignore* them. If you would truly like to find relief from anxiety disorders, you need to *do* something to reduce and better manage your stress. Some of the stress management strategies described in this workbook include: deep relaxation, regular exercise, down time and time management, cultivating constructive self-talk and attitudes, expressing feelings, learning assertiveness and self-nurturing skills, and good nutrition.

Many other strategies for coping with stress are available. You will find them described in books on stress management such as: *Life After Stress* by Martin Shaffer, *Guide to Stress Reduction* by John Mason, and *The Relaxation and Stress Reduction Workbook* by Martha Davis, Elizabeth Eshelman, and Matthew McKay. A list of 24 positive coping skills for dealing with stress is presented on page 234. Which of these skills do you possess? Which of them would you like to add to your life?

24 Positive Coping Strategies for Stress

Physical and Lifestyle Strategies
(see Chapters 4 and 5)

1. Abdominal breathing and relaxation

2. Low-stress diet

3. Regular exercise

4. "Down time" (including "mental health days")

5. Mini-breaks (5-10-minute periods to relax during the day)

6. Time management (appropriate pacing)

7. Sleep hygiene (see Appendix 7)

8. Choosing a nontoxic environment

9. Material security

Emotional Strategies
(see Chapters 13 and 15)

10. Social support and relatedness

11. Self-nurturing

12. Good communication

13. Assertiveness

14. Recreational activities ("playtime")

15. Emotional release

16. Sense of humor—ability to see things in perspective

Cognitive Strategies
(see Chapters 9 and 10)

17. Constructive thinking—ability to counter negative thinking

18. Distraction—ability to distract yourself from negative preoccupations (see Appendix 6)

19. Task-oriented (vs. reactive) approach to problems

20. Acceptance (ability to accept/cope with setbacks)

21. Tolerance for ambiguity—ability to see shades of gray

Philosophical/Spiritual Strategies
(see Chapter 19)

22. Consistent goals or purposes to work toward

23. Positive philosophy of life

24. Religious/spiritual life and commitment

Stress Symptom Checklist

Instructions: Check each item that describes a symptom you have experienced to any significant degree during the last month; then total the number of items checked.

Physical Symptoms

- ☐ Headaches (migraine or tension)
- ☐ Backaches
- ☐ Tight muscles
- ☐ Neck and shoulder pain
- ☐ Jaw tension
- ☐ Muscle cramps, spasms
- ☐ Nervous stomach
- ☐ Other pain
- ☐ Nausea
- ☐ Insomnia (sleeping poorly)
- ☐ Fatigue, lack of energy
- ☐ Cold hands and/or feet
- ☐ Tightness or pressure in the head
- ☐ High blood pressure
- ☐ Diarrhea
- ☐ Skin condition (e.g., rash)
- ☐ Allergies
- ☐ Teeth grinding
- ☐ Digestive upsets (cramps, bloating)
- ☐ Heart beats rapidly or pounds, even at rest
- ☐ Stomach pain or ulcer
- ☐ Constipation
- ☐ Hypoglycemia
- ☐ Appetite change
- ☐ Colds
- ☐ Profuse perspiration
- ☐ Overeating
- ☐ Weight change
- ☐ When nervous, use of alcohol, cigarettes, or recreational drugs

Psychological Symptoms

- ☐ Anxiety
- ☐ Depression
- ☐ Confusion or "spaciness"
- ☐ Irrational fears
- ☐ Compulsive behavior
- ☐ Forgetfulness
- ☐ Feeling "overloaded" or "overwhelmed"
- ☐ Hyperactivity—feeling you can't slow down
- ☐ Mood swings
- ☐ Loneliness
- ☐ Problems with relationships
- ☐ Dissatisfied/unhappy with work
- ☐ Difficulty concentrating
- ☐ Frequent irritability
- ☐ Restlessness
- ☐ Frequent boredom
- ☐ Frequent worrying or obsessing
- ☐ Frequent guilt
- ☐ Temper flare-up
- ☐ Crying spells
- ☐ Nightmares
- ☐ Apathy
- ☐ Sexual problems

Evaluate your stress level as follows:

Number of Items Checked	Stress Level
0-7	*Low*
8-14	*Moderate*
15-21	*High*
22+	*Very High*

Excessive Need for Control

The excessive need for control makes you want to have everything in life be predictable. It's a kind of vigilance that requires all the bases to be covered—the opposite of letting go and trusting in the process of life.

Often an excessive need for control has its origins in a traumatic personal history. After living through experiences in which you felt frightened, vulnerable, or violated and powerless, it's easy to grow up feeling defensive and vigilant. You may go through life this way, ready to put up your defenses in response to any situation that seems to challenge your sense of security (whether it actually does or not). Survivors of severe trauma often develop highly controlled and/or controlling personalities; or else they may have been so distressed that they decided to give up, feeling depressed and discouraged about maintaining any control of their lives (the latter outcome has been referred to as "learned helplessness").

Overcoming the excessive need for control takes time and persistence. Four strategies which have been helpful to many people are described in the sections below.

1. Acceptance

Acceptance entails learning to live a little more comfortably with the unpredictability of life—with the unexpected changes that occur daily on a small scale and, less often, on a large scale. It's inevitable that you'll encounter changes in your environment, in the way others choose to behave, and in your own physical health that you are simply unable to predict or control. You may have resources to cope with these changes, but you are not always going to be prepared for them. There will be times when your personal life situation may seem relatively chaotic, disordered, or out of control. Developing acceptance means acquiring a willingness to take life as it comes. Rather than fearing and struggling with those occasions where circumstances don't obey your expectations, you can learn to go with the change. Popular expressions for this are "go with the flow" and "take things in stride." In a word, acceptance implies *nonresistance.*

There are numerous ways in which to cultivate greater acceptance. Certainly letting go of perfectionism, as described earlier in this chapter, will provide a good start. A willingness to let go of unrealistic expectations can save you a lot of disappointment. Relaxation is also an important key. The more relaxed you remain, the less likely you are to be fearful and defensive when circumstances suddenly change and don't go your way. When you're relaxed, you slow down, and it's easier to go with rather than balk against the unexpected.

Finally, a sense of humor toward life can be very helpful. Humor enables you to step back from those times when everything appears to be in disarray and to get some perspective. If you can remain relaxed and laugh a little at situations that appear out of control, your response begins to change from "Oh my God!" to "Oh well—that's the way it goes." Acceptance ensures that you will be able to cope better and sooner. You are likely to say, "Now what do I need to do?" a lot sooner after "Oh well..." than after "Oh my God!"

Affirmations that can help you develop acceptance include:

- "I'm learning to take life as it comes."

- "It's O.K. to let go and trust that things will work out."

- "I can relax and tolerate a little disorder and ambiguity."

- "I'm learning not to take myself or life so seriously."

2. Cultivating Patience

People who have an overcontrolled approach to life's problems want to have them all figured out by tomorrow. Yet it's often true that difficult situations cannot be worked out immediately. All the pieces that contribute to a solution come together gradually over a period of time. Developing patience entails allowing yourself to tolerate temporary muddles and ambiguity while you wait for all the necessary steps of the solution to unfold. As you develop patience, you learn to let go and wait for a resolution or an answer to emerge.

3. Trusting That Most Problems Eventually Work Out

Developing trust goes along with cultivating patience. You may not see the solution to a particular difficulty easily or quickly. But if you always need to see in advance how something is going to work out, you can end up making yourself very anxious. There is an old saying, "Life is a river—you can't always see what's coming around the bend." Developing trust means believing that just about everything *eventually does work out.* Either you find a solution, or, if the problem can't be changed externally, you learn to alter your attitude toward it, so that coping becomes easier. When you look back over the problems you've encountered in your life, you'll find that in most, if not all cases, the problem eventually worked itself out.

4. Developing a Spiritual Approach to Life

Developing a spiritual approach to life can mean many things (for further discussion of this topic, see Chapter 19). In essence, it means believing in a Higher Power, Force, or Intelligence which transcends the world as you ordinarily perceive and know it. Very often it also implies having a personal relationship—in your inner experience—with that Power, Force, or Intelligence.

Developing your spirituality offers at least two ways in which to reduce an excessive need for control. First, it gives you the option to "turn over" or let go of any problem that seems insoluble, overwhelming, or just plain worrisome to the care of your Higher Power. This possibility is expressed in the third step of all 12-step programs as: "[We] made a decision to turn our will and our lives over to the care of a Higher Power as we understood that Power." This does *not* mean that you relinquish responsibility for handling the problems that come up in life. It does mean that there is a higher resource (higher in the sense of being beyond your own capabilities) which can be of support and assistance when you've reached the point where a problem appears insoluble despite your best efforts. Faith in such a resource enables you to let go of the idea that you have to fully control everything. Some of my clients find that they can approach a phobic situation more easily by "turning over" their worry and anxiety to a Higher Power.

The second way in which developing your spirituality can reduce your need for control is in nurturing your belief that *there is a larger purpose in life beyond the overt appearance of what happens from day to day.* If you believe that there is no spiritual foundation to reality, then the unpredictable and unforeseen events of life can seem both random and capricious. You can feel distressed because there is no explanation for why this bad event happened or that apparent unfair situation occurred. Most forms of spirituality offer the alternative view that the universe is not random. Events that may appear meaningless and brutal from a human perspective have some meaning or purpose in a broader scheme of things.

A popular phrase that expresses this idea is "Everything happens for some purpose." Often hindsight provides us with clearer vision. When you reflect deeply on some of the unforeseen mishaps in your life, you may see in retrospect how they served you—either in an obvious way or simply in promoting your growth and development as a human being.

The four traits described in this chapter—perfectionism, excessive need for approval, tendency to ignore physical and psychological signs of stress, and excessive need for control—are shared by many people who deal with anxiety on a day-to-day basis. I hope by this point you've become more aware of which of these traits might be a problem for you. Actually changing traits such as perfectionism or the excessive need for control will take time and commitment on your part. Part of the process involves changing particular mistaken beliefs you may hold, as was described in Chapter 10. Ultimately, though, you may need to reevaluate and shift certain basic values and priorities in your life.

Summary of Things To Do

1. What are you willing to do today—and each day—to relax your quest for perfection? Can you let go of some of the demands you put on yourself in order to make time for your anxiety recovery program—or simply for rest and relaxation? Each day, find something you would ordinarily do that doesn't *have to* get done (such as work or household chores) and defer it to another day.

2. If excessive need for approval is an important issue, be sure to spend extra time with the chapters on assertiveness and self-esteem in this book. It's important to work on developing: 1) greater self-respect, 2) an ability to nurture yourself, 3) knowledge of your basic rights, and 4) a willingness to ask for what you want. If you suspect that co-dependency is an issue for you, consult the references on that subject below, or attend a Co-Dependents Anonymous meeting in your area.

3. Complete the *Stress Symptom Checklist* to get an idea of your level of stress over the past month. If stress is a real problem, focus on the chapters on relaxation, exercise, and nutrition in this book to get started with a program of stress management. Working on mistaken beliefs (Chapter 10) and perfectionism is also important. Consult the references on the subject of stress reduction below.

4. Learning to let go of the excessive need for control can be a challenge for people who are prone to anxiety. Cultivating a sense of humor and an ability to laugh at life's limitations is one way to get started. You tend to loosen up as you learn how to laugh and have more fun with your life. Another way to proceed, if you feel so inclined, is to develop your spirituality and trust in a Higher Power (See Chapter 19).

Further Reading

Beattie, Melody. *Codependent No More.* San Francisco: Harper/Hazelden, 1987.

Davis, Martha; Eshelman, Elizabeth Robbins; and McKay, Matthew. *The Relaxation and Stress Reduction Workbook.* Fourth Edition. Oakland: New Harbinger Publications, 1995.

Mason, John. *Guide to Stress Reduction.* Berkeley, California: Celestial Arts, 1985.

Melody, Pia. *Facing Codependence.* San Francisco: Harper & Row, 1989.

Peurifoy, Reneau. *Anxiety, Phobias & Panic: Taking Charge and Conquering Fear.* New York, New York: Warner Books, 1995.

12

Visualization

Imagery is one of the most basic ways in which your mind stores and represents information: it has been called the "language of the unconscious mind." There is evidence that before you learned to speak, you were able to "think" in terms of images. Every night while disengaged from verbal thought, you continue to dream in images.

Visualization is a method of deliberately using imagery to modify your behavior, the way you feel, and even your internal physiological state. Because imagery is one of the basic media in which your unconscious mind operates (along with feelings and kinesthetic sensations), visualization can affect your behavior or state of being in profound ways apart from your deliberate, conscious will. The French pharmacist Emil Coue asserted, almost one hundred years ago, that the power of the imagination exceeds that of the conscious will. You may or may not be able to will your way to a particular goal, yet repeatedly visualizing the attainment of that goal has a good chance of bringing about exactly what you seek.

It is through practicing visualizations that many athletes achieve peak performance in their particular sports. The baseball player can increase his batting average through visualizing making perfect contact with the ball, as can professional tennis players and golfers in their respective sports. Even marathon runners can improve their performance by visualizing in advance every aspect of their course in detail. It has been demonstrated that any type of performance can be improved through repeatedly visualizing success. Trial lawyers, salespersons, and students facing a difficult exam have all used this to their advantage. Visualizing that you can successfully negotiate a phobic situation you've been avoiding will also help you to confront and master that situation. An exercise for doing this is offered at the end of this chapter.

Visualization (imagery) not only can help you to act in ways that are likely to lead to success, but can alter subtle internal physiological states as well. O. Carl Simonton, in his book *Getting Well Again*, demonstrated how the use of imagery can arrest and even reverse the progress of cancer through enhancing immune system functions. Many researchers have followed his example; imagery is currently used as part of the treatment program for a variety of diseases.

You can demonstrate the power of imagery for yourself through a simple experiment. First, find a small pendulum (you can construct one by tying a small object to the end of a string). Now, close your eyes and relax while letting the pendulum hang from your dominant hand. While relaxed, imagine that the pendulum is turning in a clockwise direction. After a minute of repeating this visualization, open your eyes and observe the pendulum. Most likely it will be turning in a clockwise direction. Your visualization operated apart from your conscious will to cause micromuscle movements in your fingers that corresponded with your image. (The same experiment can be repeated, visualizing the pendulum moving counterclockwise or back and forth.)

This chapter offers a number of guided visualizations. Any of them may help you reduce anxiety—or any state of "worry" you can't seem to break out of—in a matter of 20 minutes or so. First, a series of guided visualizations for reducing anxiety is presented. You may want to experiment with all of these to find out which ones work best for you. The key to using imagery successfully is to use it when you are deeply relaxed. When you are relaxed, you'll be able to experience the images more vividly, and so they are likely to have a more profound effect. The first two in the series of anxiety-reduction visualizations—passive muscle relaxation and the sunlight meditation—are especially useful for achieving a deep state of relaxation. You may want to use these visualizations first to get yourself relaxed and then go deeper with any of the other visualizations that follow. By the same token, active progressive muscle relaxation or meditation (see Chapter 4) can serve effectively as preliminary relaxation techniques prior to implementing any of the visualization exercises in this chapter.

At the end of this chapter you'll find a guided visualization for successfully confronting a phobic situation. Practicing this visualization can decrease the time it takes you to master a particular phobia. Please note that positive visualization is *not* a substitute for the process of imagery desensitization presented in Chapter 7. However, imagery desensitization, as conceived in this workbook, incorporates elements of "success imagery." The concluding visualization in this chapter elaborates on this type of imagery in detail.

So that you have the optimal chance to relax, it is useful to record guided visualizations on tape—either in your own voice or by asking someone else to make the recording (the voice should be, naturally, one that sounds pleasant to you). After you've gone through the visualization a number of times on tape, you may recall it so well that you can do it on your own. Or you may prefer to continue using the tape indefinitely.

Guidelines for Effective Visualization*

1. Prerecord the visualization so that you can follow it from start to finish without having to deliberately concentrate or call up details from memory. In making the recording, pause briefly wherever three dots (…) are indicated and for a few seconds between each sentence. Read through the script *slowly*.

2. Get into a comfortable position, free of encumbrances and with your head supported.

3. Be sure that your environment is quiet and free from distractions.

---

* More detailed guidelines for effective visualization can be found in Chapter 2 of Patrick Fanning's book, *Visualization for Change*.

4. Give yourself time to relax before undertaking a guided visualization. To this end you can use progressive muscle relaxation or meditation (from Chapter 4) or the passive muscle relaxation or sunlight visualizations in this chapter. Of course any way of getting initially relaxed will do. You may find the beach, forest, or other visualizations in the following section to be so inherently relaxing that you don't need a "preliminary" relaxation technique.

5. One indication of the depth of your relaxation is your ability to "see" the imagery contained in a particular visualization in vivid, sensory detail. If colors, shapes, and sizes of objects in the visualization are not distinct, continue to work on relaxation until you can picture these details clearly. Practicing visualizations repeatedly will help increase your ability to see things in vivid detail. With practice you'll get more and more adept at visualization.

6. If you like, you can accompany your visualization for reducing anxiety with affirmations such as, "I am letting go," "I am at peace," "All tension is flowing from my body." For many people, affirmations can enhance the relaxing effect of a visualization.

7. Use the visualizations for anxiety reduction whenever you feel "stuck" in an anxiety state or in some worrisome mental preoccupation. Alternatively, you may want to use a specific visualization as your personal "deep relaxation technique"— the relaxation technique that you use every day on a regular basis, as discussed in Chapter 4. Guided visualizations can work just as well as progressive muscle relaxation or meditation for the purpose of achieving a more relaxed state of mind over the long term. As a general relaxation technique, try to use visualization at the same time each day and preferably on an empty stomach. Excellent times might be when you first awaken in the morning, during your lunch break, or between the time you get home from work and eating dinner.

8. At the conclusion of your relaxing visualization, bring yourself back to an alert state of mind with the following statement (which you can record at the end of your visualization tape):

    Now, in a moment you can begin to come back to an alert, wakeful state of mind. Pay attention as I count from one up to five. When I get up to five, you can open your eyes and feel awake, alert, and refreshed. One—gradually beginning to come back up to an alert, wakeful state. Two—more and more awake. Three—perhaps you might move your hands and feet as you become even more alert. Four—almost back to a fully alert state. And five—opening your eyes now, finding yourself fully awake, alert, and refreshed.

    After finishing with your visualization, get up and walk around a bit until you feel fully alert and grounded. Allow at least ten minutes to pass before driving a car or engaging in any other activity that requires complex coordination.

9. To summarize, your visualization should contain the following three parts:

    - Preliminary relaxation (5-15 minutes)
    - The visualization itself
    - Instructions for returning to an alert state of mind

Visualizations for Reducing Anxiety

Passive Muscle Relaxation

Start out by taking two or three deep breaths ... and let yourself settle back into the chair, the bed, or wherever you happen to be right now ... making yourself fully comfortable. Let this be a time just for yourself, putting aside all worries and concerns of the day ... and making this a time just for you ... letting each part of your body begin to relax ... starting with your feet. Just imagine your feet letting go and relaxing right now ... letting go of any excess tension in your feet. Just imagine it draining away ... and as your feet are relaxing, imagine relaxation moving up into your calves. Let the muscles in your calves unwind and loosen up and let go ... allow any tension you're feeling in your calves to just drain away easily and quickly ... and as your calves are relaxing, allow relaxation to move up into your thighs ... Letting the muscles in your thighs unwind and smooth out and relax completely. You might begin to feel your legs from your waist down to your feet becoming more and more relaxed. You might notice your legs becoming heavy as they relax more and more. Continuing now to let the relaxation move into your hips ... feeling any excess tension in your hips dissolve and flow away. And soon you might allow relaxation to move into your stomach area ... just letting go of any strain or uncomfortableness in your stomach ... let it all go right now, imagining deep sensations of relaxation spreading all around your stomach ... and continuing to allow the relaxation to move up into your chest. All the muscles in your chest can unwind and loosen up and let go. Each time you exhale, you might imagine breathing away any remaining tension in your chest until your chest feels completely relaxed ... and you find it easy to enjoy the good feeling of relaxation as it deepens and develops throughout your chest, stomach area, and your legs. And shortly, you might allow relaxation to move into your shoulders ... just letting deep sensations of calmness and relaxation spread all through the muscles of your shoulders ... allowing your shoulders to drop ... allowing them to feel completely relaxed. And you might now allow the relaxation in your shoulders to move down into your arms, spreading into your upper arms, down into your elbows and forearms, and finally all the way down to your wrists and hands ... letting your arms relax ... enjoying the good feeling of relaxation in your arms ... putting aside any worries, any uncomfortable, unpleasant thoughts right now ... letting yourself be totally in the present moment as you let yourself relax more and more. You can feel relaxation moving into your neck now. All the muscles in your neck just unwind, smooth out, and relax completely. Just imagine the muscles in your neck loosening up just like a knotted cord being unraveled. And soon, the relaxation can move into your chin and jaws ... allowing your jaws to relax ... letting your jaws loosen up, and as they are relaxing, you can imagine relaxation moving into the area around your eyes. Any tension around your eyes can just dissipate and flow away as you allow your eyes to relax completely. Any eyestrain just dissolves now and your eyes can fully relax. And you let your forehead relax too ... letting the muscles in your forehead smooth out and relax completely ... noticing the weight of your head against whatever it's resting on as you allow your entire head to relax completely. Just enjoying the good feeling of relaxation all over now ... letting yourself drift deeper and deeper into quietness and peace ... getting more and more in touch with that place deep inside of perfect stillness and serenity.

Sunlight Meditation

Picture yourself in a safe, beautiful place outdoors. Now imagine that you feel a warm, gentle breeze blowing over your body. Overhead you can see a beautiful blue sky and some white clouds. Shining directly overhead is the sun.

Now imagine that you can feel the warmth and light from the sun directly above you. You can feel it shining down—in and through your entire body. You feel it beginning to relax and soothe every part of your body. In a moment, you might concentrate on this sunlight and move it over to your right arm. Focus it there. Just experience the warmth and light from the sun penetrating the fingertips of your right hand. You can feel it soothing and relaxing your right hand. And in a moment it begins to move from your right hand to your forearm … and then to your upper arm … and then to your shoulder. Just feel the sunlight warming and soothing your entire right arm. You can feel it filling and soothing every muscle, tendon, and nerve in your right arm. And you feel your right arm—from the tips of your fingers to your shoulders—becoming completely relaxed. And you find yourself just letting go more and more … becoming more and more at peace.

Now move the light from the sun to your left arm. Imagine it entering and soothing your left hand. And in a moment you can begin to feel it moving from your left hand up your left arm … soothing your forearm … and then your upper arm … moving all the way up to your shoulder. You're relaxing all the muscles, nerves, and tendons in your left arm … feeling the light penetrating and soothing your entire left arm. Just continue to let yourself drift deeper and deeper into quietness and peace … feeling very safe, secure, and relaxed.

And, gently now, take the light from the sun and move it over to your right leg. Allow it to move from the tips of your toes all the way up your right leg to the big hip joint. Feel the warmth as the sunlight moves up through your right leg, from your right foot to your right calf … and then to your right knee … and then to your right thigh … and finally to your right hip bone. Just feel the sunlight penetrating and soothing every muscle, tendon, and nerve in your right leg and hip. Your entire right leg is feeling completely relaxed.

And in a moment, feel the sunlight move to your left leg. Again, allow it to move from your left foot up through your entire left leg to your hip bone. Feel it soothing and relaxing your left ankle … then your calf … and then your knee … and then soothing all the muscles in your thigh … and finally moving up into your hip. You can feel the sunlight penetrating every muscle, tendon, and nerve in your entire left leg. And in a moment you find your left leg feeling completely relaxed.

And now move the light from the sun into your stomach area. Just feel it warming and soothing every organ in the lower part of your body. Just feel the pressures and tensions of the day draining away from you … as your stomach and lower abdomen relax completely. Feel your stomach and lower abdomen becoming very relaxed.

Now take the light from the sun and move it into your chest area. Let it soothe and comfort that area. Just feel it streaming into your chest. You're feeling relaxation … peace … and comfort throughout your entire chest … feeling your chest becoming very relaxed and your breathing becoming easy.

Now, in a moment, you might bring the light from the sun down through the top of your head. Imagine it soothing and comforting the top of your head … and then the area around your eyes … and then your jaws. And in a moment, feel the warm, soothing sensations of the sunlight moving down into your neck, relaxing and releasing every tight muscle in your neck. And in a while you can feel your neck completely relaxing. Your head and neck are becoming completely relaxed.

And now let the sunlight move down your spine, down through your spine all the way to your tailbone … let it move down through your spine all the way to your tailbone. And then imagine the light moving out from your spine into every nerve of your body. Feel the sunlight moving into every nerve of your body, healing and relaxing all of those nerves. And as all of your nerves relax, you can enter into a very deep state of peace.

Just allow yourself to drift deeper and deeper into quietness and peace … becoming more and more relaxed. In a moment you can feel the sunlight relaxing and soothing every single cell in your body. Every single cell in your body is becoming very relaxed. And you feel yourself becoming very deeply relaxed … very much at peace.

The Beach

You're walking down a long wooden stairway to a very beautiful, expansive beach. It looks almost deserted and stretches off into the distance as far as you can see. The sand is very fine and light … almost white in appearance. You step onto the sand in your bare feet and rub it between your toes. It feels so good to walk slowly along this beautiful beach. The roaring sound of the surf is so soothing that you can just let go of anything on your mind. You're watching the waves ebb and flow … they are slowly coming in … breaking over each other … and then slowly flowing back out again. The ocean itself is a very beautiful shade of blue … a shade of blue that is so relaxing just to look at. You look out over the surface of the ocean all the way to the horizon, and then follow the horizon as far as you can see, noticing how it bends slightly downward as it follows the curvature of the earth. As you scan the ocean you can see, many miles offshore, a tiny sailboat skimming along the surface of the water. And all these sights help you to just let go and relax even more. As you continue walking down the beach, you become aware of the fresh, salty smell of the sea air. You take in a deep breath … breathe out … and feel very refreshed and even more relaxed. Overhead you notice two seagulls flying out to sea … looking very graceful as they soar into the wind … and you imagine how you might feel yourself if you had the freedom to fly. You find yourself settling into a deep state of relaxation as you continue walking down the beach. You feel the sea breeze blowing gently against your cheek and the warmth of the sun overhead penetrating your neck and shoulders. The warm, liquid sensation of the sun just relaxes you even more … and you're beginning to feel perfectly content on this beautiful beach. It's such a lovely day. In a moment, up ahead, you see a comfortable-looking beach chair. Slowly, you begin to approach the beach chair … and when you finally reach it, you sit back and settle in. Lying back in this comfortable beach chair, you let go and relax even more, drifting even deeper into relaxation. In a little while you might close your eyes and just listen to the sound of the surf, the unending cycle of waves ebbing and flowing. And the rhythmic sound of the surf carries you even deeper … deeper still … into a wonderful state of quietness and peace.

The Forest

You're walking along a path deep in the forest. All around you there are tall trees … pine, fir, redwood, oak … try to see them. The rushing sound of the wind blowing through the treetops is so soothing, allowing you to let go. You can smell the rich dampness of the forest floor, the smell of earth and new seedlings and rotting leaves. Now you look up through the treetops until you can see a light blue sky. You notice how high the sun is in the sky. As the sun enters the canopy of the treetops, it breaks into rays which waft their way down through the trees to the forest floor. You're watching the intricate patterns of light and shadow created as the light filters down through the trees. The forest feels like a great primeval cathedral … filling you with a sense of peace and reverence for all living things.

Off in the distance, you can hear the sound of rushing water echoing through the forest. It gets louder as you approach, and before long you are at the edge of a mountain stream. You're looking at the stream, noticing how clear and sparkling the water is. Imagine sitting down and making yourself very comfortable. You might sit down on a flat rock up against a tree or you might even decide to lie down on a grassy slope. You can see the mountain stream creating rapids as it moves, rushing around a variety of large and small rocks. These rocks are many shades of brown, gray, and white and some are covered with moss. You can see the sparkling water rushing over some and around others, making whirlpools and eddies. The rushing sound of the water is so peaceful that you can just let yourself drift … relaxing more and more.

You take in a deep breath of fresh air and breathe out, finding the subtle smells of the forest very refreshing. As you let yourself sink into the soft bed of grass or dead leaves or fragrant pine needles beneath you, you can let go of any strains or concerns … allowing the sights, sounds, and smells of this beautiful wooded area to fill you with a deep sense of peace.

Gas/Liquid Release

Take a moment now to focus on any discomfort you may be feeling in your body. It may be anxiety, tension, or emotional distress. Now see if you can pinpoint precisely where in your body this discomfort is. Is it in your stomach? Your chest? Your neck and shoulders? Your head? Or is it throughout your entire body? You might also notice if this discomfort has a specific shape and size. How much space does it take up in your body? Is it large or small?

Now imagine this discomfort to be like a gas—or a liquid—inside your body. See this as clearly as you are able. Imagine that your discomfort or anxiety is nothing more than a gas [or liquid] … a gas [or liquid] that can, in a moment, begin to flow out of your body. Again notice the location, shape, and size of this gas [or liquid]. Also take notice of its color. Does it have a color? How light or dark is it? However you see it is just fine.

Imagine now that all of your tension has become this gas [or liquid]. You can see it more and more clearly … its shape, size, color, and location in your body. And in just a moment, as you continue watching it, imagine that it is beginning to move out of your body in some fashion. You might see it leaving through your mouth or nose with each exhalation of your breath. Or you might see the gas [or liquid] flowing out through the pores of your skin. On the other hand, you might picture the gas [or liquid] flowing out an imaginary opening, or even several openings, throughout your body. However you see it leaving is fine. Just continue watching that gas [or liquid]. See it beginning to move in your body. And then see it moving toward the opening[s] ... slowly moving toward the opening[s] ... and then flowing out. Moving in your body and then flowing out. Flowing out and away from your body. And as it flows out and away you're beginning to feel more and more at ease ... more and more relaxed. As it leaves your body you can relax. Just see it flowing out continually. Flowing out more and more. Flowing out and away from your body ... off into the distance. And as it leaves your body, you're feeling more and more calm and at ease.

And in a little while this gas [or liquid] is going to clear out of your body altogether ... from your feet ... from your legs ... from your hips ... from your stomach and abdomen ... from your chest ... and then from your shoulders ... from your arms and hands ... and then finally from your neck ... from your head ... and any other place in your body. The gas [or liquid] is leaving your body altogether. And as it does, your body is feeling more and more comfortable ... more and more relaxed. As the gas [or liquid] completely leaves your body, you're growing more and more deeply relaxed.

And when the gas [or liquid] is completely gone from wherever it might have been, your body is going to feel even more deeply relaxed than it does right now. And it will continue to relax, as you're breathing deeply and easily. Allowing every last trace of the gas [or liquid] to leave your body, so that you're feeling completely at peace and relaxed. And in a few moments it will be completely gone. Completely gone. And you'll find your body is relaxing even more.

Globe of Light*

Now that you're feeling very relaxed and at peace, imagine that you can see a violet globe of light—about the size of a grapefruit—suspended just above the top of your head. Imagine that this globe of violet light is luminous and semitransparent. Now see this globe of light begin to turn clockwise [or counterclockwise, whichever you prefer]. As it turns it picks up any tension in or near the top of your head. Just imagine that as this globe of light turns right above your head, it is picking up and absorbing any tension you feel in your head. It is also picking up any racing, extraneous thoughts, allowing your mind to slow down and become calm. Just keep imagining the violet globe turning, picking up tension from the region of your head for as long as you like, until that area feels completely relaxed. [Pause for 45 seconds or as much time as you need.]

Now imagine that there is a luminous sphere of light, pastel violet, blue, or any color you prefer, out an inch or two in front of your face. Imagine that this sphere is beginning to revolve, slowly, clockwise [or counterclockwise, whichever you prefer]. As it turns, it picks up tension and strain from around your eyes. Just continue to imagine seeing the globe of light turning in front of your face, and, as it does so, it is picking up and absorbing any tension from around your eyes and face. [Pause for 45 seconds or as much time as you need.]

---

*It's especially important to be already relaxed before attempting this visualization.

Now imagine moving the globe of light down to a spot an inch or so away from your neck. Let it be pastel violet, blue, green, pink or whatever color feels most right. Again, see it revolving, slowly, clockwise [or counterclockwise]. As it does, it is picking up tension and constriction in your neck. The longer it continues to turn, the more tension and constriction it can pull up out of your neck. [Pause for 45 seconds or as much time as you need.]

Now move the globe of light down to your chest an inch or so above your sternum, which is at the level of your heart. Again, allow the sphere to be pastel green, pink, or any other color you like. Imagine seeing it turn slowly. As it turns, it is picking up tension in your chest area. The longer it continues to revolve, the more tension it can pull out of your chest. [Pause for 45 seconds or as much time as you need.]

Now move the globe of light down to the area of your solar plexus—a point in the middle of your abdomen right below your sternum. This is the place in your body where you're most likely to experience feelings of fear or hurt. Make the globe of light very luminous and pick the color for it that feels best to you. Then allow the globe to revolve slowly, picking up as it turns any fear, hurt, or other stressful feelings from the area of your solar plexus. Just continue seeing the globe of light turning right above your solar plexus, allowing it to pick up any tension, stress, or emotional discomfort you happen to be feeling there. [Pause for 45 seconds or as much time as you need.]

Now let go of the globe of light and imagine your whole body being bathed by luminous, golden-white light. Imagine that this light enters your body at the top of your head and flows down into your neck … your shoulders … your arms … your hands … your chest … your abdomen … your hips … your thighs … your calves … and your feet. Allow this light to enter and fill every single cell of your entire body … and as it does, just relax more and more. You're experiencing this as a very soothing, comforting light. As it spreads through your entire body and enters every single cell, it brings a sensation of comfort, calm, and deep relaxation. It allows you to feel very much at peace … deeply calm and at peace.

Mastering a Phobia

You can use the following visualization to gain confidence about confronting and mastering a particular phobic situation you've been avoiding. The visualization involves seeing yourself fully in your phobic situation. It's best to work with it *after* having used imagery desensitization (see Chapter 7) to overcome any anxiety that can come up initially when you picture yourself dealing with your phobia. If this visualization causes you anxiety, go back and work up to it gradually using imagery desensitization.

Take a few moments to imagine what you'll be doing and how you'll feel when you have successfully reached the goal you've set for yourself. See yourself fully involved in what used to be your phobic situation … doing what you want to do … feeling calm, comfortable, and confident … (Allow about one minute to visualize yourself successfully handling a situation you've been avoiding.)

You know that there is no longer any need to avoid this situation. You can find yourself in this situation feeling calm, safe, and assured. As you enter this situation, your breathing is calm and regular and all of your muscles are fully relaxed. It's truly easy to enter this situation and it feels just fine. You experience a sensation of relaxation all over …

You've succeeded in reaching your goal, and you feel proud of yourself for having reached it. You're feeling confident that you can handle this situation every time you return to it. It feels great to have the freedom to enter this situation … to have fully achieved your goal … to have fully left the past behind … to be able to do what you want. Your life is enlarged by your success.

You can be calm and at ease whenever you're in this particular situation … in fact, it doesn't really matter a lot one way or the other. You find being in this situation to be just routine … nothing special … just a part of everyday life. Comfortable … easy … calm … just fine. And you're happy to know that you've succeeded … you've reached your goal … gained the mastery of yourself you've wanted all along. You can enjoy life fully now … knowing that you feel safe and confident whenever you enter this particular situation. You truly enjoy your success and the freedom of choice you've gained.

Now take a few minutes once again to imagine how you would *think*, *act*, and *feel*, having achieved your goal with this particular situation … See yourself handling the situation in just the way you would like….

Notice what you're doing … (15 seconds or more)

Notice how you appear … perhaps you see a smile of confidence on your face … How does your face express your success and your sense of accomplishment? (15 seconds or more)

Now notice the inner feeling of accomplishment you feel deep inside … Can you feel that wonderful feeling of satisfaction you've gained from your success? (15 seconds or more)

Perhaps you might also notice friends and family in the picture, and the good feelings they express about your success. Can you see them expressing their good feelings toward you now? (15 seconds or more)

Now that you know you've reached your goal, take a little time to imagine how you would enjoy the new freedom you've gained in your life. Are there any new opportunities available to you now that you have more freedom? You might see yourself enjoying these opportunities now. (Allow up to 1 minute.)

Summary of Things To Do

1. Review the "Guidelines for Effective Visualization" so that you can make the most out of your experience using visualization.

2. Experiment with several of the six visualizations for reducing anxiety by having a friend read them to you. Make a tape of the one or two scripts you prefer in your own voice or someone else's. You can use any one of them for your daily

deep-relaxation practice or on the spur of the moment when you feel anxious or worried.

3. Try the visualization for mastering a phobia to increase your confidence about handling any particular phobic situation. It's preferable to do this *after* having overcome some of your anxiety toward the phobia through imagery desensitization (see Chapter 7).

4. Specific visualizations for improving your confidence and positive outlook toward mastering the following eight phobias are available on the "I Can Do It" series of audiotapes by the author:

   • Shopping in a Supermarket

   • Driving Further From Home

   • Driving Freeways

   • Flying

   • Public Speaking

   • Speaking Up in Groups

   • Heights

   • Fear of Illness

   See the description of these tapes in the notice at the end of this book.

Further Reading

Fanning, Patrick. *Visualization for Change*. Oakland, California: New Harbinger Publications, 1988.

Gawain, Shakti. *Creative Visualization*. Mill Valley, California: Whatever Publishing, 1978.

Mason, L. John. *Guide to Stress Reduction*. Berkeley, California: Celestial Arts, 1985.

Samuels, Mike, and Samuels, Nancy. *Seeing with the Mind's Eye: The History, Techniques and Uses of Visualization*. New York: Random House, 1975.

Simonton, O.C.; Matthews-Simonton, S.; and Creighton, J.L. *Getting Well Again*. New York: Bantam Books, 1980.

13

Identifying and Expressing
Your Feelings

As you progress in your recovery, you may notice unaccustomed emotions and feelings beginning to surface. This is particularly true if you're at the point where you're beginning to confront your phobias. It's entirely normal to experience feelings more intensely when you begin to face situations you've been avoiding for a long time. If this is happening to you, you're on the right track.

Many people who are phobic and prone to anxiety tend to have difficulty with feelings. Some of you may have a problem just knowing *what* you're feeling. Or you may be able to identify your feelings but are unable to express them. When feelings begin to come up in the course of facing phobias or dealing with panic, there is often a tendency to withhold them, which only aggravates your stress and anxiety. The purposes of this chapter are 1) to help you to increase your awareness of feelings and 2) to give you some tools and strategies for identifying and expressing them more readily.

Some Facts About Feelings

1. Feelings, unlike thoughts, involve a *total body reaction.* They are mediated both by a part of your brain called the limbic system and the involuntary, autonomic nervous system in your body. When you're emotionally excited, you "feel it all over" and experience bodily reactions such as increased heart rate, respiration, perspiration, and even shaking or trembling (note the similarity to panic, which is another type of intense emotional state).

2. Feelings do not come "out of the blue" but are *influenced by your thoughts and perceptions.* They arise from the way you perceive or interpret outer events and/or the way you react to your own inner thought processes or "self-talk" (see Chapter 9), imagery, or memories. If you can't identify a stimulus for a particular emotional reaction (for example, a spontaneous panic attack), that stimulus may be unconscious. Feelings are also affected by stress. When you're under stress, your body is already in a state of physiological arousal similar to that which accompanies an emotion. Since you're already primed to have emotional reactions, it may not take much to set you off. The particular type of emotion you happen to experience will depend on your view of external events and what you tell yourself about them.

3. Feelings can be divided into two groups—*simple* and *complex*. There is much controversy and disagreement about how to do this—and even whether it can be done—but for our purposes here, a distinction will be made between *basic emotions* such as anger, grief, sadness, fear, love, excitement, or joy, and more *complex feelings* such as eagerness, relief, disappointment, or impatience. Complex feelings may involve a combination of more basic emotions and are also shaped by thoughts and imagery. Many of the feelings on *The Feeling List* presented later in this chapter are complex. Complex feelings can last a long time and are more tied to thought processes, while basic emotions tend to be short-lived, more reactive, and more tied to involuntary physical reactions mediated by the autonomic nervous system. Fear or panic is a basic emotion while free-floating anxiety (anxiety without an object) is an example of a more complex feeling.

4. Feelings are what give you *energy*. If you're in touch with your feelings and can express them, you'll feel more energetic. If you're out of touch with your feelings or unable to give them expression, you may feel lethargic, numb, tired, or depressed. As you'll see shortly, blocked or withheld feelings can lead to anxiety.

5. Feelings often come in *mixtures* rather than in pure form. Sometimes you may experience a simple, basic emotion such as fear, sadness, or rage. More often, though, you'll find that you feel two or more emotions at the same time. For example, it's common to feel anger and fear at the same time when you're threatened. Or you may feel anger, guilt, and love all at the same time in response to arguing with your partner, parent, or close friend. The common expression *sorting out* feelings reflects the fact that you can feel several things at once.

6. Feelings are often *contagious*. If you're close to someone who is crying, you may start to feel sad or even cry yourself. Or you may pick up on another's excitement or enthusiasm. Phobic and anxiety-prone individuals are often particularly susceptible to taking on the feelings of people around them. The more you learn to be in touch with and comfortable with your own feelings, the less prone you'll be to "catch" those of others.

7. Feelings are *not* "right" or "wrong." As reactions, feelings simply *exist*. Fear, joy, guilt, or anger are not in and of themselves valid or invalid—you just happen to have these feelings and usually will feel better if you can express them. The *perceptions* or *judgments* you made which *led* to your feelings, however, may be right or wrong, valid or invalid. Be careful not to make yourself or anyone else wrong for simply having a feeling, whatever that feeling may be.

8. Feelings are often subject to *suppression*. Sometimes you may actively control or "hold in" your feelings. For example, you're still upset from an argument with your spouse and then you have to talk to a colleague at work. You deliberately and consciously hold back your feelings, because you know that it would be inappropriate for them to carry over into your work situation. On other occasions, you may start to experience feelings that are unpleasant and decide that you don't want to deal with them. Instead of deliberately suppressing them, you just get busy and put your mind on something else—in essence you ignore them. This avoidance or evasion of feelings is a subtler form of suppression (which some

people speak of as "repression"*). Over time the practice of continually suppressing your feelings can lead to increased difficulty in expressing or even identifying them. When the process of suppression begins in childhood, you tend to grow up being out of touch with your feelings and going through life experiencing a certain numbness or "emptiness."

Why Phobic and Anxiety-Prone People Have a Tendency to Suppress Their Feelings

People with anxiety disorders tend to withhold their feelings. There are several reasons for this.

First, many such persons tend to have a very strong need for control and/or a fear of losing control. It's difficult to surrender to the partial loss of control involved in a full experience of your feelings. When feelings have been chronically denied for a long time, they can loom very large and overwhelming when they first begin to surface. You can even experience irrational fears of "going crazy" or "coming apart" when you give in to the full force of these long-withheld feelings. Note that these are the very same fears that occur during a panic attack. In fact, in some cases *panic itself may be a signal that suppressed feelings are trying to emerge.* Instead of dealing with feelings that seem overwhelming, you panic instead. It's important to learn that feelings only *seem* overwhelming or scary at the point when they first begin to surface. This scariness goes away as soon as you allow yourself to accept and *feel* them. It's simply not possible to "go crazy" by fully feeling your emotions. In fact, "craziness"—or severe emotional disturbance—is more likely to develop as an outcome of *not* experiencing your feelings.

A second reason why phobic people have difficulty expressing their feelings is because they often grew up in families where their parents were overly critical and set unrealistically high or perfectionist standards. In such a situation a child doesn't feel free to express her or his natural impulses and feelings. Parental approval is so essential to every one of us that we will always suppress our natural reactions and feelings if they are in conflict with parental expectations. As adults, many of us continue to make that choice. Anger is typically the most common feeling to be withheld because it was frequently not tolerated in childhood or its expression was punished. To the child, anger becomes truly dangerous if its expression threatens the continued approval and affection of the parents, on whom that child is completely dependent for survival. More will be said about anger later in this chapter.

Identifying, Expressing, and Communicating Feelings

Because phobic persons, by their very nature, tend to be emotionally reactive and have very strong feelings, it is especially important for them to learn to express rather than withhold what they feel. Actually a three-stage process is involved here.

---

* In this workbook the terms "repression" and "repressed feelings" are avoided because there is frequently confusion between the popular use of these terms (where what is meant is usually similar to the term "suppression"—to consciously withhold feelings) and the more technical, psychoanalytic use of the word repression to refer to an unconscious defense mechanism.

Perhaps you have so withheld your emotions that much of the time you don't even know *what* you're feeling. An important first step is to learn how to *identify* your feelings. Once this awareness and your ability to identify feelings has developed, the second step is learning to *express* them. This usually involves being willing to share your feelings with another person. Alternatively, you may choose to "write out" your feelings in a journal, or physically discharge them (for example, by crying or venting anger into a pillow).

Once you've given some expression to your feelings, you're ready for the third and final step: *communicating* them to whoever you perceive to have contributed to "triggering" these particular emotions. For the purposes of this chapter, "communicating" a feeling means to let someone know that your feeling involves something they said or did. While *expressing* anger means simply finding a way to discharge it, for example, telling a neutral friend that you feel angry about something, *communicating* anger means to let someone know that you're angry about something *they* said or did.

The good news is that identifying, expressing, and communicating your feelings is something that can be learned—and something that can be improved upon with practice. It does take some time and perseverance, however, if you've been accustomed to withholding or ignoring feelings for much of your life.

To sum up, your ability to gain awareness of and express your feelings is an *essential* part of the process of recovering from anxiety disorders. It is just as important as relaxation, desensitization, and the cognitive skills discussed in previous chapters.

Identifying Your Feelings

How can you identify what you're feeling? It will help to follow these three steps:

1. Recognize the symptoms of suppressed feelings.
2. "Tune in" to your body.
3. Discriminate the exact feeling.

Symptoms of Suppressed Feelings

Held-in feelings frequently make themselves known through several types of bodily and psychological symptoms:

"Free-floating" Anxiety. Anxiety arises from many sources. Sometimes it's simply fear in the face of uncertainty. Sometimes it's the result of anticipating a negative outcome ("what-if" thinking). If anxiety doesn't seem to relate to any specific situation—if it's only a vague, undefined uneasiness—this may be because it arises from strong but unexpressed feelings. Every feeling carries a charge of energy. When we hold that energy in and do not give it expression, it may create a state of tension or vague anxiety. The next time you hold in your anger toward someone, notice whether you feel anxious afterward. Holding in enthusiasm or excitement about something can also produce anxiety.

Depression. In his well-known book, *The Road Less Traveled*, M. Scott Peck defines depression as "stuck feelings." Often we feel depressed when we're holding in unexpressed grief or sadness over some loss. Letting out tears and crying often helps us to feel better—we effectively mourn the loss. Depression can also result from holding in anger. Gestalt psychologists were the first to point out that depression can mask anger turned in against the self. If you find yourself feeling depressed without any obvious recent loss, it may help to ask yourself what you're angry about. This is an especially good question if you find that you're attacking and criticizing yourself.

Psychosomatic Symptoms. Common psychosomatic symptoms such as headaches, ulcers, high blood pressure, and asthma are often the end result of chronically withheld feelings. While psychosomatic symptoms can arise from any type of chronic stress, the holding in of feelings over many years is a form of stress that is especially likely to take its toll on your body. Learning to identify and express strong feelings can lead to a reduction or even a remission of many types of psychosomatic symptoms.

Muscle Tension. Stiff, tight muscles are an especially common symptom of chronically withheld feelings. We tend to tighten certain groups of muscles when we suppress and hold in what we feel. Different feelings are held in by tightening different muscle groups. Anger or frustration is often suppressed by tightening the back of your neck and shoulders. (These are the areas, incidentally, where tension is most commonly experienced in our society.) Grief and sadness can be held in by tightening muscles in the chest and around the eyes. Fear can be held in through tightening up in the stomach-diaphragm area. Withheld sexual feelings may be indicated by a tightening up of muscle groups in the pelvic region.

These correlations between areas of the body and suppression of specific feelings should not be viewed as absolute. Anger, for example, can be held in by tightening many different muscle groups from the eyes to the pelvis. The point is that tight muscles and physical tension in any region may be a sign of chronically bottled-up feelings. This relationship between suppressed feelings and muscular tension has been explored in great depth by the school of therapy known as *Bioenergetics*. The books of Dr. Alexander Lowen provide a good introduction to this approach.

Any of the above four symptoms may indicate that you've been withholding strong feelings. Once you've recognized this, the next step is to "tune in" to exactly what it is you're feeling.

Tuning In to Your Body

Staying "in your head," preoccupied with daily worries and concerns, tends to keep you out of touch with your feelings. To switch gears and gain access to your feelings, it's necessary to shift your focus from your head to your body. As indicated above, feelings tend to be held in the body. Our use of language reflects this in expressions such as *heart-broken, pain in the neck*, and *gut-level feeling*. By making time to tune in to your body, you can learn to get in touch with and identify your feelings. Many people have found the following steps to be useful. (They are based on a process called "experiential focusing" developed by Eugene Gendlin—see the reference at the end of this chapter.)

a. **Physically relax.** It's difficult to know what you're feeling if your body is tense and your mind is racing. Spend 5-10 minutes doing progressive muscle relaxation, meditation, or some other relaxation technique to slow yourself down.

b. **Ask yourself, "what am I feeling right now?"** or alternatively, "what is my main problem or concern right now?"

c. **Tune in to that place in your body** where you feel emotional sensations such as anger, fear, or sadness. Often this will be in the area of your heart or your gut (stomach/diaphragm), although it may be other areas higher or lower in the body. This is your "inner place of feelings."

d. **Wait and listen** to whatever you can sense or pick up on in your place of feelings. *Don't try to analyze or judge* what's there. Be an observer and allow yourself to sense any feelings or moods that are waiting to surface. Simply *wait* until something emerges.

e. If you draw a blank on Steps c and d or are still stuck in your head (your thoughts are racing), go back to Step a and start over again. Most likely you need more time to relax. A few minutes of slow, deep breathing will often help to increase your awareness of your feelings.

f. Once you've obtained a general sense of what you're feeling, it may help you to make it seem more concrete by answering the following questions:

- Where in my body is this feeling?

- What is the shape of this feeling?

- What is the size of this feeling?

- If this feeling had a color, what would it be?

If, after taking the time to relax and tune in to what you're feeling, you still have only a vague sense of what's there, it may be useful to look at a list of "feeling words" to help you to identify the exact feeling you're experiencing.

Identify the Exact Feeling: The Feeling List

The list of feeling words which follows may help you to identify exactly what you're feeling. Use the list anytime you have a vague sense of some feeling but are unsure of exactly what it might be. Read down the list until a particular feeling word stands out and then check to see if it matches your inner experience.

The Feeling List

Positive Feelings		Negative Feelings	
Accepted	Loving	Afraid	Melancholy
Affectionate	Loyal	Angry	Miserable
Alive	Passionate	Anxious	Misunderstood
Amused	Peaceful	Apprehensive	Muddled
Beautiful	Playful	Ashamed	Needy
Brave	Pleased	Awkward	Old
Calm	Proud	Bitter	Outraged
Capable	Quiet	Bored	Overwhelmed
Caring	Relaxed	Confused	Panicky
Cheerful	Relieved	Contemptuous	Pessimistic
Cherished	Respected	Defeated	Phony
Comfortable	Safe	Dejected	Preoccupied
Competent	Satisfied	Dependent	Prejudiced
Concerned	Secure	Depressed	Pressured
Confident	Self-reliant	Despairing	Provoked
Content	Sexy	Desperate	Regretful
Courageous	Silly	Devastated	Rejected
Curious	Special	Disappointed	Remorseful
Delighted	Strong	Discouraged	Resentful
Desirable	Supportive	Disgusted	Sad
Eager	Sympathetic	Distrustful	Self-conscious
Excited	Tender	Embarrassed	Shy
Forgiving	Thankful	Exasperated	Sorry
Friendly	Thrilled	Fearful	Stubborn
Fulfilled	Trusted	Foolish	Stupid
Generous	Understanding	Frantic	Terrified
Glad	Understood	Frustrated	Threatened
Good	Unique	Furious	Tired
Grateful	Valuable	Guilty	Touchy
Great	Warm	Hateful	Trapped
Happy	Witty	Helpless	Troubled
Hopeful	Wonderful	Hopeless	Unappreciated
Humorous	Worthwhile	Horrified	Unattractive
Joyful	Youthful	Hostile	Uncertain
Lovable		Humiliated	Uncomfortable
Loved		Hurt	Uneasy
		Ignored	Unfulfilled
		Impatient	Used
		Inadequate	Useless
		Incompetent	Uptight
		Indecisive	Victimized
		Inferior	Violated
		Inhibited	Vulnerable
		Insecure	Weary
		Irritated	Wishy-washy
		Isolated	Worn-out
		Jealous	Worried
		Lonely	

Expressing Feelings

Once you're able to identify what you're feeling, it's very important to express it. *Expressing* feelings, here, is defined as "letting them out" by 1) sharing them with someone else, 2) writing them out, or 3) physically discharging them (such as by hitting a plastic bat against your bed or crying into a pillow). Expressing your feelings does *not* mean "dumping" or directing them toward someone you perceive to be responsible for how you feel. The skill of letting someone know how you feel about them (or better, their behavior) is discussed later in the section, "Communicating Your Feelings to Someone."

Feelings can be compared to charges of energy that need physical release or discharge from the body. When unexpressed, they tend to be stored in your body in the form of tension, anxiety, or other symptoms previously described. Your physical health as well as your sense of well-being depend on your willingness to acknowledge and express feelings at or close to the time they occur. Here are some useful ways of expressing your feelings.

1. Talk It Out

Probably the best way to express feelings is to share them with a supportive friend, mate, or counselor. Sharing means not just talking *about* your feelings but actually letting them out. It's important that you have a high level of trust toward the person you share with in order to open up and fully disclose your true feelings. And it's important that they *listen carefully*—in other words, they do not offer advice, opinions, or suggestions while you're sharing. Your ability to share will in part be determined by your partner's willingness to do nothing more than "just listen." (This type of listening may still be "active," where the listener occasionally summarizes what you've said in order to confirm that it's been correctly understood.)

2. Write It Out

If your feelings are running high and there's no one immediately available to talk to, take a pen and paper and write out what you feel. You may wish to keep a "feeling journal" in which you enter your strong feelings from time to time (see Exercise 2 at the end of this chapter). Weeks or months later it will be very instructive to go back and read through the journal to get an idea of broad patterns or themes running through your life. Whether you keep a journal or not, the act of writing out your feelings will often suffice as an outlet until you have the opportunity to talk them out.

3. Discharging Sadness

You might want to ask yourself the following questions:

• Do you ever cry?

- Under what circumstances do you cry?

- Do you cry because someone hurt you? Because you feel lonely? Because you're scared?

- Do you cry for no apparent reason?

- Do you only cry alone or do you permit someone else to see you crying?

Sometimes you may have a feeling of being on the verge of tears. You feel like you would like to cry but are having difficulty "getting it out." At this point you may find that a particular artistic prodding will help. Evocative pieces of music that have personal significance can often help to elicit tears. Watching an emotional movie or reading poetry or literature or even certain television commercials may also bring an initially vague sense of sadness to the surface.

4. Discharging Anger

Often you may feel angry or frustrated but are reluctant to express it for fear of hurting others. It's quite possible, and often healthy, however, to discharge your anger in ways that are not destructive—ways that do not involve "dumping" your anger on someone else. *Going through the physical motions associated with aggression* will usually bring anger to the surface. The target of these motions, however, always needs to be an inanimate object. All of the following have been helpful to many people in ventilating angry feelings:

- Hitting a large pillow with both fists

- Screaming into a pillow

- Hitting a punching bag

- Throwing eggs against a wall or into a bathtub

- Yelling within the confines of a car

- Chopping wood

- Hitting a life-size inflatable doll

- Hitting an old tennis racket or plastic bat against the bed

- Having a vigorous physical workout

I do not recommend that you engage in any of the above (with the exception of physical exercise) on a daily basis. There is evidence, reported by Carol Tavris in her book *Anger: The Misunderstood Emotion*, that excessive ventilation of anger only tends to produce more anger. The popular term "rageaholic" describes the type of person who has become addicted to anger through *excessive* expression. On the other hand, many phobic and anxiety-prone people have a tendency to withhold or deny angry feelings under any circumstances. Anger may be such a difficult emotion for some of you that some additional comments are warranted.

Dealing With Anger

Of all the different emotions that can give rise to anxiety, anger is the most common and pervasive one. Anger comprises a continuum of emotions ranging from rage at one extreme to impatience and irritation at the other. Frustration is perhaps the most common form of anger that most of us experience.

A proneness to phobias and obsessive-compulsive behavior is often associated with withheld anger. *Your preoccupation with phobias, obsessions, and compulsions increases during those times when you're feeling most frustrated, thwarted, and otherwise angry with your situation in life.* Frequently, however, you are entirely (or almost entirely) unaware of these angry or frustrated feelings.

Why should people suffering from phobias and other anxiety disorders be predisposed to deny or withhold anger? There are several reasons:

1. Individuals who are prone to phobias and anxiety tend to be "people pleasers." They want to think of themselves—and appear to others—as pleasant and nice. And that leaves very little room for experiencing, let alone expressing, anger.

2. Such people, especially if they suffer from agoraphobia, are often unusually dependent on relationships with significant others. Outward expressions of anger are taboo because they might threaten to alienate the very person on whom the agoraphobic feels dependent for survival.

3. People who are prone to anxiety have a high need for control. But anger, when full-blown, is probably the least rational and least controllable of our feelings. Giving in to anger, with the attendant loss of control, is very frightening if you are someone who always feels the need to "keep a grip" on yourself.

The consequences of withholding anger over time have been discussed in the previous section detailing the symptoms of suppressed feelings. Generalized anxiety can be a sign of suppressed anger. So can depression or psychosomatic symptoms such as ulcers, neck and upper back tension, or tension headaches. Some additional signs of withheld anger include

- An *increase* in phobic concerns or sensitization to new situations without any obvious reason.

- An *increase* in obsessive thoughts and/or compulsive behaviors.

- Self-defeating behaviors, such as excessive self-criticism, maximizing what's wrong with your life while discounting the good, complaining about problems without taking any action, passive-aggressive behavior such as procrastination or always being late, blaming others, and worrying about the future instead of enjoying the present.

Some Guidelines for Learning To Deal With Anger

Once you've become aware of the signs and symptoms of suppressed anger, what can you do to better deal with these feelings? The following guidelines may be helpful:

1. *Be willing to let go of the standard of always having to be nice or pleasing in all situations.* Expand your self-concept so that you can allow yourself to express irritation or anger in situations where to do so might be appropriate. Examples would include occasions where someone keeps responding to you with snide remarks or subtle putdowns—or a situation where someone breaks an important agreement they made with you. Remember that expressing your anger does *not* mean dumping it on someone else, but rather sharing with someone (preferably *not* the person you feel angry at) that you're feeling angry. You need to do this with feeling, rather than merely talking in a detached manner about your anger. Expressing your anger might alternatively mean to write out or physically "exercise out" your angry feelings. When you're ready to tell someone you're angry with them or their behavior, there are specific skills you can learn to communicate your feelings without hurting or belittling the other person. See the section below, "Communicating Your Feelings to Someone," and Chapter 14 for guidelines about communicating anger or other feelings.

2. *Work on overcoming what-ifs about what might happen if you let your anger out.* Usually these what-ifs are exaggerated and unreasonable, for example, "What if I go berserk or crazy?" or "What if I do something terrible?" Remember that anger withheld for a long time may *seem* ominous at first. Its intensity may startle you during the first few moments you give it vent, but it is *not* going to cause you to "fall apart," "go crazy," or "do something destructive." The intensity of your angry feelings will diminish quickly as soon as you allow yourself to experience them. This is especially so if you express your anger in a benign way. If your anger is intense, try discharging it onto inanimate objects or on paper in the ways previously described, instead of "dumping" it onto someone you'd like to blame for your feelings.

3. *Work on overcoming fears about alienating people you care about when you allow your anger to show.* Being able to appropriately communicate angry feelings to significant others is, in fact, an indication that you *do* care about them. If you didn't care, you would be more likely to withdraw from them and withhold your true feelings. While overexpression of anger can be destructive to others or yourself, not ever communicating angry feelings to someone you love may convey either indifference or a kind of phony, "holier-than-thou" equanimity.

4. *Learn to communicate angry feelings assertively rather than aggressively.* It is quite possible to convey your anger or frustration toward other people in a way that respects their dignity—in a way that doesn't blame or put them down. One way is to begin what you say with *I* rather than *you*—in other words "I feel angry when you break your agreements," instead of "You make me so mad when you break your agreements." I-statements maintain respect for the other person; you-statements put people on the defensive and assign them the blame for your feelings.

   Believe it or not, other people don't *make* you angry. You react angrily to your own interpretation of the significance of another person's behavior. Something they say or do goes against your standards of what is acceptable or just, and so you feel angry. You can learn to convey your angry feelings without hurting, judging, or blaming others by using the communication skills discussed in the next section.

5. *Learn to discriminate different modes of expressing anger, depending on the intensity of your feelings.* If your anger is *very* intense, you're probably not ready to talk to someone yet. Instead, you need a direct and physical mode of expression such as pounding pillows, screaming into a pillow, or engaging in a vigorous physical workout.

   After your anger has lessened as a result of direct physical expression—or if it was moderate in the first place—talk it out with someone. If possible, it is best to share it with a neutral friend first before directly confronting the person with whom you're angry. If no such neutral person is available, use the communication guidelines presented below as well as those outlined in Chapter 14. If, finally, your anger is only a mild irritation, you can use the tried-and-true method of deep breathing and counting to ten to dispel it—or communicate it directly if you wish.

A Caveat

This section on dealing with anger is intended for those of you who have difficulty being aware of, or expressing, angry feelings. If you tend to withhold your anger, even when you are being taken advantage of or abused, then learning to be more in touch with your angry feelings can be empowering. If you have difficulty standing up for yourself in the face of manipulation or when your boundaries are violated, then appropriate, *assertive* communication of your anger is something that you will certainly want to learn.

On the other hand, if you feel angry often and find that your angry feelings interfere with your relationships, then obviously you don't need instructions on how to identify and express your anger! If you're tired of the emotional and physical toll that frequent anger can take, you're looking for a different solution. *When any emotion is excessive or destructive, the solution lies not in expressing it more but in changing the self-talk and mistaken beliefs which aggravate that emotion.* In brief, while this chapter will be useful if you have difficulty acknowledging or expressing feelings, a more *cognitive* approach is needed for any feeling that is excessive or destructive to you (for example, anxiety itself). Thus it may be useful, if anger comes too easily and interferes with your relationships, to review Chapters 9 and 10.

Anger, like all other emotions, is determined by your perceptions and your internal monologue. Other people and situations don't, *in themselves*, "make" you angry: it is your interpretations of what others do and say and your internal commentary about them that stimulate anger. Often these interpretations and this self-talk contain an element of distortion. Any of the following cognitive distortions can trigger anger:

1. *Global Labeling*—When you describe someone to yourself as a "bum" or a "jerk," you write them off in a way which ignores the whole person.

2. *Black-or-White Thinking*—You see things in extreme terms, so that people or situations are either all good or all bad; there are no shades of gray. You thus often lose sight of the truth of a situation.

3. *Magnification*—When you blow something up out of proportion, you increase your sense of being wronged and victimized. This is a common way of fueling and maintaining anger.

4. *Entitlement*—When you believe that you should always get what you want, everything should come easily, or life should always be fair, your thinking rests on the mistaken belief that you are *naturally entitled* to complete gratification of your needs all the time. This kind of misconception can lead to a lot of self-defeating anger and blame.

The above examples are just four among several types of distorted thinking that can lead to excessive and destructive anger. A more complete discussion of the mistaken beliefs that can trigger anger may be found in the book *When Anger Hurts*, by Matthew McKay, Peter Rogers, and Judith McKay. If excess anger is interfering with your well-being and relationships, I highly recommend this book.

Communicating Your Feelings to Someone

Communicating your feelings, for the purposes of this chapter, means letting someone know that your feelings have something to do with what they said or did. This level of dealing with your feelings is usually riskier than simply expressing them to someone else or setting them down on paper. Yet when you let someone know how you feel toward them, you have the greatest likelihood of being able to work through or "complete" the feeling—in short, to be done with it. You can live in fear or anger toward someone for a long time without any change until you finally let them know how you feel. Once you've let them know, you no longer need to "hold" the feeling in secret or silence. Sometimes the person you have feelings toward is no longer available or alive, in which case you can still communicate your feelings by writing a letter (see Exercise 3 at the end of this chapter).

There are two important rules for communicating your feelings:

1. Be sure that the person you disclose your feelings to is willing to hear you out and listen.

2. Avoid blaming or belittling the person you're addressing.

The first rule is important because your feelings are an intimate part of you that deserves respect. If someone isn't truly ready or willing to hear you, you're likely to go away feeling discounted and misunderstood. Your sadness, fear, or anger toward the person may even increase. When you're ready to tell someone how you feel, ask him to make time to listen to you. You might tell him, "I have something important to say and I'd appreciate it if you would listen." If the other person interrupts you, you might say, "Would you please wait until I'm finished?" When another person truly listens to you, it means that he gives you his undivided attention, doesn't interrupt, and doesn't offer any advice, opinions, or judgments. He just listens—silently and attentively. If he has any comments, these can wait until after you're finished with your communication. The only appropriate interruption by the other person would be an occasional summary of what you've said, just to confirm that he's heard you accurately. This occasional summarizing by the listener is called "active listening" and is a skill which you can learn about in any basic book or course on communication. Good listening skills on the part of the person you're addressing will actually *enhance* your ability to disclose and communicate what you're feeling.

The second rule is important because the person you're speaking to can best listen if you respect him and refrain from blaming or making him responsible for your feelings. Three skills are needed to accomplish this: 1) using I-statements, 2) referring how you feel to the other's *behavior* rather than to him personally, and 3) avoiding judging the other person.

1. *I-statements. When you communicate how you feel to someone, begin what you say with the expression "I feel ..." or "I'm feeling ..."* In this way you take responsibility for your feelings rather than putting them off onto the other. The moment you tell someone "You make me feel ..." or "You caused me to feel ..." you relinquish your responsibility and put the other person on the defensive. Even if part of you wants to blame the other, you'll get across more easily and get a better hearing if you begin with "I feel ..."

2. *Refer to the other's behavior rather than making a personal attack.* What do you have feelings about? Although initially it may *seem* that you're angry at or scared of the person himself, this almost invariably turns out to be an overgeneralization. On further reflection you'll find that you're angered or frightened by something specific that was *said* or *done*. Before communicating your feelings, it's important to determine what this is. Then, when you actually speak, complete your I-statement with a reference to that specific behavior or statement.

    "I'm feeling angry because you didn't call when you said you would."

    (*Not*: "I had a panic attack because you didn't call—not that you'd care," or "You didn't call, you jerk, and it made me feel awful.")

    "I felt threatened when I saw you dancing with your secretary at the party."

    (*Not*: "How could you dance with her when you knew how humiliated I'd feel?" or "You're so completely insensitive to my feelings.")

    "I feel scared when you talk about leaving."

    (*Not*: "I'm scared," or "How can you talk to me like that when you know how vulnerable I am?")

Although "right" and "wrong" ways of stating your feelings can involve little more than a difference in wording, it is an important difference. Referring your feelings to the person rather than his behavior results in putting either him or yourself in a "one-down" position. In the first example, dumping anger on the other person is likely to make him feel guilty or angry. Calling him a jerk will certainly put him on the defensive. In the third example, telling someone you're afraid of him is likely to make *you* feel more defensive and to promote distance in the relationship. In brief, referring your feelings to a specific statement or behavior lets other people know that you're upset with *something they can change*—rather than with who they are personally.

3. *Avoid judgments*—This point speaks for itself and is an extension of the previous point. When telling people how you feel about what they said or did, avoid judging them. Your problem is with their behavior, not them. Refraining from judging others will greatly increase the likelihood of their hearing you out.

Looking for the Need Behind Your Feelings

Strong feelings are often a clue to unmet needs. Perhaps you're feeling anxious because you're afraid of what other people will think of you if you show signs of panic. The need for acceptance underlies your fear. You experience sadness or grief because you're alone after the departure of someone you felt close to. The need beneath your grief is for companionship and affection. Or you're feeling angry because your partner broke an important agreement you had. The need behind your anger is for respect and consideration. Or you may be feeling bored, empty, or depressed because your life seems too dull or routine. The need behind your boredom is for a greater sense of meaning and purpose in your life.

By looking for the need behind your feelings, you give your feelings a new and deeper perspective. You're not just feeling anger or sadness without reason: you know you have a particular need. Once you've gained more insight into your needs, you can begin to address how to go about meeting them. If you ignore or fail to address the needs behind a feeling, you'll find that the feeling will come up more and more, to the point where it feels as if it will never leave you. Once again, you can view your excessive feelings as a sign rather than a problem. When it gets to the point where you're asking yourself why you feel sad all the time—or angry all the time—that is a sure sign that you need to uncover some unmet need or needs. The subject of how to ask for what you need is dealt with in detail in the following chapter on assertiveness. More will be said about the nature of human needs and the importance of acknowledging and addressing them in the chapter on self-esteem. If anxiety plays too big a part in your life, take that as a sign that you're denying some of your basic needs.

Self-Evaluations

The following two self-evaluations are intended to help you gain more awareness about how you handle two important emotions—anger and sadness. Use them as a basis for identifying any attitudes or habits that stand in the way of your ability to express and communicate what you feel.

Self-Evaluation 1: Developing Awareness of Anger

1. What messages did you receive as a child about expressing anger?

2. What types of people, situations, and events tend to make you angry?

3. Is it O.K. for you to feel anger?

4. How do you feel about expressing angry feelings? To others? To inanimate objects?

5. If you do express anger, how do you go about it? Are you aggressive? Assertive? Stubborn/resistant? Complaining? Rebellious?

6. What are you willing to do to increase your ability to recognize angry feelings? Express anger? Communicate anger appropriately?

Self-Evaluation 2: Developing Awareness of Sad Feelings

1. What messages did you receive as a child about crying?

2. What types of situations might lead you to cry? Do you usually cry for a reason—or for no apparent reason?

3. Do you always cry alone or can you cry in the presence of another?

4. How do you feel about crying? Relieved? Depressed? Ashamed? Other?

5. What are you willing to do to improve your ability to recognize sad feelings? Express sad feelings? Communicate sad feelings appropriately?

Exercises

The following three exercises offer direct ways to express your feelings.

Exercise 1: Establish a Listening Partner

Make an arrangement with your spouse, partner, or a close friend to set aside an hour or more each week for listening to each other. Then do a trade-off. First, your partner gives you his or her undivided attention for a half an hour, while you express what you've been feeling during the week. Then you switch roles. As a speaker in this process, you need to focus on how you've actually been *feeling* about what's happening in your life, not just chat about or describe it. If you are the listener, you need to give the speaker your undivided attention without interruptions. For the duration of the period that you're listening, refrain altogether from offering your advice, opinions, or comments. You may ask the speaker for clarification if you're confused about what he or she is saying. It also helps occasionally to summarize what you hear the speaker say, beginning with, "Let's see if I'm following you. You said ..." Giving these summaries is called *active listening*. (For a more complete description of active listening, see the book *Messages: The Communication Skills Book*, by Matthew McKay, Martha Davis, and Patrick Fanning.)

Exercise 2: The Feeling Journal

Set aside a notebook whose sole purpose is to provide a place where you can express your feelings. Make entries whenever you feel the need to release frustration, anger, anxiety, fear, sadness, or grief, as well as positive feelings such as joy, love, and excitement. Begin each entry with the words "I feel" or "I felt" and refer to *The Feeling List* to help identify the specific feelings you are experiencing.

Exercise 3: Write a Letter Communicating Your Feelings

Write a letter communicating your feelings to someone who is not available in person. Good candidates for this would be an ex-spouse or lover or a deceased parent. Make time to express *all* of your feelings toward this person, both positive and negative. Persist with the process until you feel that you've said everything you need to say. It's not uncommon for such a letter to run on for several pages.

When you've completed the letter, read it to a close friend or counselor, which will help make it more real. It's alright, on the other hand, if you prefer to keep the letter private.

Option: You may want to write a letter to someone who is available but to whom, for various reasons, you've avoided communicating your feelings. I suggest that you consult with a close friend, or, even better, a counselor before deciding to *send* such a letter.

Summary of Things To Do

1. Reread the section "Symptoms of Withheld Feelings" until you're familiar with both psychological and bodily signs of suppressed feelings such as free-floating anxiety, depressed moods, psychosomatic symptoms such as headaches or ulcers, muscle tension, and so on.

2. If you have difficulty identifying your feelings, practice the focusing exercise in the section "Tuning In to Your Body." Use *The Feeling List* to help you discriminate exactly what you're feeling.

3. Practice expressing your feelings on a daily basis. Establish a "listening partner" with whom you can talk out your feelings regularly (Exercise 1) and/or keep a feeling journal (Exercise 2). Notice changes in your level of body tension and mood after expressing what you feel.

4. If anger is an especially difficult feeling to deal with, reread "Some Guidelines for Learning to Deal With Anger." Practice getting comfortable expressing your anger to a neutral person or journal before attempting to communicate anger to someone directly.

5. In communicating anger or any other feeling to people directly, remember to 1) make sure that they're willing to listen to you, 2) use I-statements, 3) refer your feeling to their behavior (or statements) rather than to them personally, and 4) avoid judging them.

6. Write a letter communicating your feelings to someone who was or is important in your life (Exercise 3).

Further Reading

Gendlin, Eugene. *Focusing*. New York: Bantam Books, 1978.

Lowen, Alexander. *Bioenergetics*. New York: Penguin Books, 1976.

McKay, Matthew, Rogers, Peter, and McKay, Judith. *When Anger Hurts*. Oakland, California: New Harbinger Publications, 1989.

Rubin, I.R. *The Angry Book*. New York: Collier Books, 1969.

Tavris, Carol. *Anger: The Misunderstood Emotion*. New York: Simon & Schuster, 1982.

14

Asserting Yourself

Assertiveness is an attitude and a way of acting in any situation where you need to

- Express your feelings

- Ask for what you want, or

- Say no to something you don't want

Becoming assertive involves self-awareness and knowing what you want. Behind this knowledge is the belief that you have the right to ask for what you want. When you are assertive, you are conscious of your basic rights as a human being. You give yourself and your particular needs the same respect and dignity you'd give anyone else's. Acting assertively is a way of developing self-respect and self-worth.

If you are phobic or anixety-prone, you may act assertively in some situations but have difficulty making requests or saying no to family members or close friends. Having perhaps grown up in a family where you felt the need to be perfect and please your parents, you've remained a "people pleaser" as an adult. With your spouse or others you often end up doing many things you don't really want to do. This creates resentment, which in turn produces tension and sometimes open conflict in your relationships. By learning to be assertive, you can begin to express your true feelings and needs more easily. You may be surprised when you begin to get more of what you want as a result of your assertiveness. You may also be surprised to learn that assertive behavior brings you increased respect from others.

Alternative Behavior Styles

Assertiveness is a way of acting that strikes a balance between two extremes: aggressiveness and submissiveness.

Nonassertive or *submissive* behavior involves yielding to someone else's preferences while discounting your own rights and needs. You don't express your feelings or let others know what you want. The result is that they remain ignorant of your feelings or wants (and thus can't be blamed for not responding to them). Submissive behavior also includes feeling guilty—or as if you are imposing—when you do attempt to ask for what you want. If you give others the message that you're *not sure* you have the right to express your needs, they will tend to discount them. Phobic and anxiety-prone people are often submissive because, as previously mentioned, they are overly invested in being "nice" or "pleasing" to everybody. Or they may be afraid that the open expression of their needs will alienate a spouse or partner on whom they feel dependent.

Aggressive behavior, on the other hand, may involve communicating in a demanding, abrasive, or even hostile way with others. Aggressive people typically are insensitive to others' rights and feelings and will attempt to obtain what they want through coercion or intimidation. Aggressiveness succeeds by sheer force, creating enemies and conflict along the way. It often puts others on the defensive, leading them to withdraw or fight back rather than cooperate. For example, an aggressive way of telling someone you want a particular assignment at work would be to say: "That assignment has my name written on it. If you so much as look at the boss when she brings it up during the staff meeting, you're going to regret it."

As an alternative to being openly aggressive, many people are *passive-aggressive*. If this is your style, instead of openly confronting an issue, you express angry, aggressive feelings in a covert fashion through passive resistance. You're angry at your boss, so you're perpetually late to work. You don't want to comply with your spouse's request, so you procrastinate or "forget" about the request altogether. Instead of asking for or doing something about what you really want, you perpetually complain or moan about what is lacking. Passive-aggressive people seldom get what they want because they never get it across. Their behavior tends to leave other people angry, confused, and resentful. A passive-aggressive way of asking for a particular assignment at work might be to point out how inappropriate someone *else* is for the job, or to say to a co-worker, "If I got more interesting assignments, I might be able to get somewhere in this organization."

A final nonassertive behavior style is being *manipulative*. Manipulative people attempt to get what they want by making others feel sorry for or guilty toward them. Instead of taking responsibility for meeting their own needs, they play the role of victim or martyr in an effort to get others to take care of them. When this doesn't work, they may become openly angry or feign indifference. Manipulation only works as long as those at whom it is targeted fail to recognize what is happening. The person being manipulated may feel confused or "crazy" up to this point; afterward they become angry and resentful toward the manipulator. A manipulative way of asking for a particular assignment at work would be to tell your boss, "Gee, if I get that assignment, I think my boyfriend will finally have some respect for me," or to tell a co-worker, "Don't breathe a word about this—but if I don't get that assignment, I'm going to finally use those sleeping pills I've been saving up."

Assertive behavior, in contrast to the above-described styles, involves asking for what you want (or saying no) in a simple, direct fashion that does not negate, attack, or manipulate anyone else. You communicate your feelings and needs honestly and directly while maintaining respect and consideration for others. You stand up for yourself and your rights without apologizing or feeling guilty. In essence, assertiveness involves taking responsibility for getting your own needs met in a way that preserves the dignity of other people. Others feel comfortable when you're assertive because they know where you stand. They respect you for your honesty and forthrightness. Instead of demanding or commanding, an assertive statement makes a simple, direct request, such as, "I would really like that assignment," or "I hope the boss decides to give that particular assignment to me."

Which of the above five descriptions fits you most closely? Perhaps more than one behavior style applies depending on the situation. The following exercise will assist you in identifying your preferred behavior mode when you want something.

What's Your Style?

Think about each of the following situations one at a time. How would you typically handle it? Would your approach be nonassertive (in other words, you wouldn't do anything about it), aggressive, passive-aggressive, manipulative—or would you respond assertively? Note the style you'd use after each situation. If you have fewer than 25 out of 30 "assertive" responses, it would be useful for you to work on your assertiveness.*

1. You're being kept on the phone by a salesperson who is trying to sell you something you don't want.

2. You would like to break off a relationship that is no longer working for you.

3. You're sitting in a movie and the people behind you are talking.

4. Your doctor keeps you waiting more than 20 minutes.

5. Your teenager has the stereo on too loud.

6. Your neighbor next door has the stereo on too loud.

7. You would like to return something to the store and get a refund.

8. You're standing in line and someone moves in front of you.

9. Your friend has owed you money for a long time—money you could use.

10. You receive a bill that seems unusually high for the service you received.

11. Your home repair person is demanding payment but has done unsatisfactory work.

12. You receive food at a restaurant that is over- or undercooked.

13. You would like to ask a major favor of your partner or spouse.

14. You would like to ask a major favor of your friend.

15. Your friend asks you a favor which you don't feel like doing.

16. Your son/daughter/spouse/roommate is not doing their fair share of the work around the house.

17. You would like to ask a question, but are concerned that someone else might think it's silly.

18. You're in a group and would like to speak up, but you don't know how your opinion will be received.

19. You would like to strike up a conversation at a gathering, but you don't know anyone.

---

* The idea for this questionnaire was adapted from Shirley J. Mangini, *Secrets of Self-Esteem*. Canoga Park, California: N.O.V.A. Corp., 1986.

20. You're sitting/standing next to someone smoking, and the smoke is beginning to bother you.

21. You find your partner/spouse's behavior unacceptable.

22. You find your friend's behavior unacceptable.

23. Your friend drops by unexpectedly just before you were about to leave to run some errands.

24. You're talking to someone about something important, but they don't seem to be listening.

25. Your friend stands you up for a lunch meeting.

26. You return an item you don't want to the department store and request a refund. The clerk diverts your request and offers to exchange the item for another.

27. You're speaking and someone interrupts you.

28. Your phone rings but you don't feel like getting it.

29. Your partner or spouse "talks down" to you as if you were a child.

30 You receive an unjust criticism from someone.

The Assertiveness Questionnaire

To further clarify those situations in which you could be more assertive, complete the following questionnaire, developed by Sharon and Gordon Bower in their book, *Asserting Yourself*. Check those items that apply in Column A, and then rate the comfort level of those situations for you in Column B.

1 = comfortable
2 = mildly uncomfortable
3 = moderately uncomfortable
4 = very uncomfortable
5 = unbearably threatening

(Note that the varying degrees of discomfort can be expressed whether your feelings are angry, fearful, or passive.)

A Check here if the item applies to you	B Rate from 1-5 for comfort level	
		When do you behave nonassertively?
_____	_____	Asking for help
_____	_____	Stating a difference of opinion
_____	_____	Hearing or expressing negative feelings
_____	_____	Hearing or expressing positive feelings

		Dealing with someone who refuses to cooperate
_____	_____	Dealing with someone who refuses to cooperate
_____	_____	Speaking up about something that annoys you
_____	_____	Talking when all eyes are on you
_____	_____	Protesting a "rip-off"
_____	_____	Saying no
_____	_____	Responding to undeserved criticism
_____	_____	Making requests of authority figures
_____	_____	Negotiating for something you want
_____	_____	Having to take charge
_____	_____	Asking for cooperation
_____	_____	Proposing an idea
_____	_____	Asking questions
_____	_____	Dealing with attempts to make you feel guilty
_____	_____	Asking for service
_____	_____	Asking for a date or appointment
_____	_____	Asking for favors
_____	_____	Other _____

Who are the people with whom you are nonassertive?

_____	_____	Parents
_____	_____	Fellow workers, classmates
_____	_____	Strangers
_____	_____	Old friends
_____	_____	Spouse or significant other
_____	_____	Employer
_____	_____	Relatives
_____	_____	Children
_____	_____	Acquaintances
_____	_____	Salespeople, clerks, hired help
_____	_____	More than two or three people in a group
_____	_____	Other _____

What do you want that you have been unable to achieve with nonassertive styles?

_____	_____	Approval for things you've done well
_____	_____	To get help with certain tasks
_____	_____	More attention from, or time with, your partner
_____	_____	To be listened to and understood
_____	_____	To make boring or frustrating situations more satisfying
_____	_____	To not have to be nice all the time
_____	_____	Confidence in speaking up when something is important to you
_____	_____	Greater comfort with strangers, store clerks, mechanics, and so on
_____	_____	Confidence in asking for contact with people you find attractive
_____	_____	To get a new job, ask for interviews, raises, and so on
_____	_____	Comfort with people who supervise you, or work under you
_____	_____	To not feel angry and bitter a lot of the time
_____	_____	To overcome a feeling of helplessness and the sense that nothing ever really changes
_____	_____	To initiate satisfying sexual experiences
_____	_____	To do something totally different and novel
_____	_____	To have time by yourself
_____	_____	To do things that are fun or relaxing for you
_____	_____	Other _____

Evaluating Your Responses. What do your answers tell you about areas in which you need to develop more assertiveness? How does nonassertive behavior contribute to the specific items you checked on the What list? In developing your own assertiveness program, you might initially want to focus on items you rated as falling in the 2-3 range. These situations are likely to be the easiest to change. Items you rated as very uncomfortable or threatening can be handled later.

Learning To Be Assertive

Learning to be assertive involves working on yourself in six distinct areas

1. Developing *nonverbal assertive behaviors*

2. Recognizing and being willing to exercise your basic rights as a human being

3. Becoming aware of your own unique feelings, needs, and wants

4. Practicing assertive responses—first through writing and role-playing and then in real life

5. Learning to say no

6. Learning to avoid manipulation

Each of these areas is considered in the remainder of this chapter.

Developing Nonverbal Assertive Behavior

Some of the nonverbal aspects of assertiveness include

- *Looking directly at* another person when addressing them. Looking down or away conveys the message that you're not quite sure about asking for what you want. The opposite extreme, staring, is also unhelpful because it may put the other person on the defensive.

- Maintaining an *open* rather than closed *posture.* If you're sitting, don't cross your legs or arms. If standing, stand erect and on both feet. Face the person you're addressing directly rather than standing off to the side.

- While communicating assertively, do not back off or move away from the other person. The expression "standing your ground" applies quite literally here.

- *Stay calm*—avoid getting overly emotional or excited. If you're feeling angry, discharge your angry feelings *somewhere else* before you attempt to be assertive. A calm but assertive request carries much more weight with most people than an angry outburst.

Try practicing the above nonverbal skills with a friend by using role-playing in situations that call for an assertive response. A list of such situations can be found at the end of the section "Assertiveness on the Spot."

Recognizing and Exercising Your Basic Rights

As adult human beings we all have certain basic rights. Often, though, we have either forgotten them or else as children we were never taught to believe in them. Developing assertiveness involves recognizing that you, just as much as anyone else, have a right to all of the things listed under the *Personal Bill of Rights* on the following page. Assertiveness also involves taking responsibility to *exercise* these rights in situations where they are threatened or infringed upon. Read through the *Personal Bill of Rights*, reflecting on your willingness to believe in and exercise each one.

Personal Bill of Rights

1. I have the right to ask for what I want.

2. I have the right to say no to requests or demands I can't meet.

3. I have the right to express all of my feelings, positive or negative.

4. I have the right to change my mind.

5. I have the right to make mistakes and not have to be perfect.

6. I have the right to follow my own values and standards.

7. I have the right to say no to anything when I feel I am not ready, it is unsafe, or it violates my values.

8. I have the right to determine my own priorities.

9. I have the right *not* to be responsible for others' behavior, actions, feelings, or problems.

10. I have the right to expect honesty from others.

11. I have the right to be angry at someone I love.

12. I have the right to be uniquely myself.

13. I have the right to feel scared and say "I'm afraid."

14. I have the right to say "I don't know."

15. I have the right not to give excuses or reasons for my behavior.

16. I have the right to make decisions based on my feelings.

17. I have the right to my own needs for personal space and time.

18. I have the right to be playful and frivolous.

19. I have the right to be healthier than those around me.

20. I have the right to be in a nonabusive environment.

21. I have the right to make friends and be comfortable around people.

22. I have the right to change and grow.

23. I have the right to have my needs and wants respected by others.

24. I have the right to be treated with dignity and respect.

25. I have the right to be happy.

Photocopy the above list and post it in a conspicuous place. By taking time to carefully read through the list every day, you will eventually learn to accept that you are entitled to each one of the rights enumerated.

Becoming Aware of Your Own Unique Feelings, Needs, and Wants

Developing an awareness and ability to express your feelings was discussed in Chapter 13. Being in touch with your feelings is an important prerequisite for becoming assertive. Learning to recognize and take care of your needs and wants will be considered in some detail in the following chapter on self-esteem.

It's difficult to act assertively unless you're clear about 1) what it is you're feeling and 2) what it is you want or don't want.

Assertiveness involves saying how you feel inside *and* saying directly what changes you would like—such as, "I'm feeling upset right now *and* I would like you to listen to me." If you're feeling confused or ambivalent about your wants or needs, take time to clarify them first by writing them out or talking them out with a supportive friend or counselor. You might also use role-playing with a friend to ask for what you want in advance. Be sure not to *assume* that other people already know what you want: you have to make your needs known. Other people aren't mind-readers.

Practicing Assertive Responses

In learning to be more assertive it is often very helpful to play out your responses first on paper. Write out a problem situation that calls for an assertive response on your part. Then formulate in detail how you'll handle it. A trial run in writing can allow you to feel more prepared and confident when you actually confront the situation in real life.

Describing Your Problem Situation

In their book *Asserting Yourself*, Sharon and Gordon Bower suggest that you first select a problem situation from the *Assertiveness Questionnaire*. Write out a description of that situation, including the person involved *(who)*, time and setting *(when)*, *what* bothers you about the situation, *how* you would normally tend to deal with it, what *fears* you have about consequences that would follow if you were to be assertive, and finally, your behavior *goal*.

It's most important to be specific in these descriptions. For instance, the following description of a problem situation is too vague:

> I have a lot of trouble persuading some of my friends to listen to *me* for a change. They never stop talking, and I never get a word in edgewise. It would be nice for me if I could participate more in the conversation. I feel that I'm just letting them run over me.

Notice that the description doesn't specify *who* the particular friend is, *when* this problem is most likely to occur, *how* the nonassertive person acts, what *fears* are involved in being assertive, and a specific *goal* for increased involvement in the conversation. A more well-defined problem situation might be as follows:

My friend Joan (*who*), when we meet for coffee after work (*when*), often goes on nonstop about her marriage problems (*what*). I just sit there and try to be interested (*how*). If I interrupt her, I'm afraid she'll think I just don't care (*fear*). I'd like to be able to change the subject and talk sometimes about my own life (*goal*).

Exercise: Specifiying Your Problem Situations

On a separate sheet of paper write up two or three of your own problem situations. Be sure to specify the "who," "when," "what," "how," the "fear," and the "goal," as described above. If possible, choose situations that are current for you right now. Begin with a situation that's not *very* uncomfortable or overwhelming.

Developing an Assertive Response

Now that you've defined your problem situations, the next step is to develop an assertive response for each one. For the purposes of learning assertiveness skills, such a response can be broken down into six steps (adapted from the Bowers' work):

1. Evaluate your rights within the situation at hand.

2. Designate a time for discussing what you want.

3. Addressing the main person involved, state the problem in terms of its consequences for you.

4. Express your feelings about the particular situation.

5. Make your request for changing the situation.

6. Tell this person the consequences of gaining (or not gaining) his or her cooperation.

Let's consider each of these points in greater detail:

1. **Evaluate your rights**. Refer back to the *Personal Bill of Rights*. What do you have a right to ask for in this situation?

2. **Designate a time.** Find a mutually convenient time to discuss the problem with the other person involved. This step, of course, would be omitted in situations where you need to be spontaneously assertive on the spot.

3. **State the problem situation in terms of its consequences for you.** Don't make the mistake of expecting other people to be mind-readers. Most people are wrapped up in their own thoughts and problems, and will have very little idea about what's going on with you unless you state your case explicitly. Clearly outline your point of view, even if what you're describing seems obvious to you. This will allow the other person to get a better idea of your position. Describe the problem as objectively as you can without using language that blames or judges.

Examples

"I'm having a problem with your stereo. I need to study for an exam tomorrow and the stereo is so loud I can't concentrate."

"I don't have any way to get to the grocery store today. My support person is sick and I'm out of milk, vegetables, and meat."

"It seems to me that you do most of the talking when we're together. I'd like to have the chance to tell you some of my thoughts and feelings, too."

4. **Express your feelings.** By telling other people about your feelings, you let them know how greatly their behavior affects you and your reactions. Even if the person you're addressing completely disagrees with your position, he or she can at least appreciate your strong feelings on an issue.

Each of us owns our personal feelings. Though it might at first seem hard to believe, nobody else *causes* you to have feelings of fear, anger, or sadness. Other people say and do all kinds of things but it is your *perception*—your interpretation—of their behavior that is ultimately responsible for what you feel. You don't necessarily choose how you react to people—yet your reaction is based on your perception of the meaning of what they say or do.

In expressing feelings, always be sure to own your reactions rather than blaming them on someone else. You can still point out what the other person did to stimulate your feelings, but be willing to take ultimate responsibility for them.

The best way to ensure this is by always remembering to begin statements about your feelings with *I* rather than *you*. I-statements acknowledge your responsibility for your feelings, while you-statements generally accuse or judge others, putting them on the defensive and obstructing communication.

Examples

Instead of saying, "You make me angry when you don't hear what I say," you can say, "I feel angry when you don't listen to me."

Instead of saying, "You show that you have no respect for me or this household when you leave things lying around," you can say, "I feel demeaned and devalued when you leave things lying around."

Instead of saying, "You don't care about me or my getting better—you don't ever help," you can say, "I feel very sad and unloved when you don't seem to be helping me in my attempt to get better."

5. **Make your request.** This is the *key* step to being assertive. You simply ask for what you want (or don't want) in a direct, straightforward manner. Observe the following guidelines for making assertive requests:

- *Use assertive nonverbal behavior.* Stand squarely, establish eye contact, maintain an open posture, and work on staying calm and self-possessed.

- *Keep your request simple.* One or two easy-to-understand sentences will usually suffice, "I would like you to take the dog out for a walk tonight," "I want us to go to a marriage counselor together."

- Avoid asking for more than one thing at a time.

- *Be specific.* Ask for exactly what you want—or the person you're addressing may misunderstand. Instead of saying, "I'd like you to help me with my practice sessions," specify what you want, "I'd like you to go with me when I practice driving on the freeway every Saturday morning." Or instead of, "I would like you to come home by a reasonable hour," specify "I would like you to come home by 12:00 midnight."

- *Use I-statements of the form:*
  "*I would like...*"
  "*I want to ...*"
  "*I would appreciate it if...*"
  It's very important to avoid using you-statements at the point of actually making a request. Statements that are threatening ("You'll do this or else") or coercive ("You have to...") will put the person you're addressing on the defensive and decrease the likelihood of your getting what you want.

- *Object to behaviors—not personalities.* When objecting to what someone is doing, object to their *specific behavior—not to an individual's personality.* Let them know you're having a problem with something they are doing (or not doing), not with who they are as a person.

  It's preferable to say: "I have a problem when you don't call to let me know you're going to be late," rather than "I think you're inconsiderate for not calling me to let me know you'll be late."

  Referring to the problem *behavior* preserves respect for the other person. Judging others personally usually puts people on the defensive. When objecting to someone's behavior (for example, a lack of trustworthiness), always *follow up your complaint with a positive request,* such as "I would like you to keep your agreements with me."

- *Don't apologize* for your request. When you want to ask for something, do so directly. Say, "I would like you to..." instead of, "I know this might seem like an imposition, but I would like you to..." When you want to decline a request, do so directly but politely. Don't apologize or make excuses. Simply say, "No, thank you," "No, I'm not interested," or "No, I'm not able to do that." If the other person's response is one of enticement, criticism, an appeal to guilt, or sarcasm, just repeat your statement firmly until you've made your point.

- *Make requests, not demands or commands.* Assertive behavior always respects the humanity and rights of the other person. Thus an assertive response is always a request rather than a demand. Demanding and commanding are aggressive modes of behavior based on the false assumption that you are always right, or always entitled to get everything your way.

6. **State the consequences of gaining (or not gaining) the other person's cooperation**. With close friends or intimate partners, stating positive consequences of their compliance with your request can be an honest offer of give-and-take rather than manipulation.

Examples

"If you take the dog out, I'll give you a back rub."

"If you give me the time to finish this project, then we'll have more time to do something special together."

In cases where you are dealing with someone with a history of being resistant and uncooperative, you may describe the *natural* consequences (usually negative) of a failure to cooperate. If at all possible, any negative consequences should naturally flow out of the objective reality of the situation rather than being something that you arbitrarily impose. The latter will likely be perceived as a threat and may increase the other person's resistance.

Examples

"If we can't leave on time, then I'll have to leave without you."

"If you keep talking to me like this, I'm going to leave. We'll talk again tomorrow."

Sample Scenarios

The six steps of an assertive response are illustrated below:

Jean would like a half hour of uninterrupted peace and quiet while she does her relaxation exercise. Her husband, Frank, has had the tendency to disrupt her quiet time with questions and other attention-getting maneuvers. Before confronting him she wrote out an assertive response as follows:

1. *Evaluate your rights.*
   I have a right to have some quiet time to myself.
   I have a right to take care of my need for relaxation.
   I have a right to have my husband respect my needs.

2. *Designate a time.*
   When Frank gets home from work tonight, I'll ask him if we can sit down and discuss this issue. If it's not convenient for him tonight, we'll schedule a time within the next couple of days.

3. *State the problem situation in terms of its consequences.*
   I've let you know several times that I need half an hour each day for relaxation and I've even shut the door, but you still come in and ask me questions. This disturbs my concentration and interferes with an important part of my program for managing my anxiety.

4. *Express your feelings.*
   I feel frustrated when my attention is disrupted. I'm angry when you don't respect my right to have some time for relaxation.

5. *Make your request.*
   I would like to be uninterrupted during the time my door is closed, other than in

cases of dire emergency. I'd like you to respect my right to have half an hour of quiet time each day.

6. *State consequences of gaining cooperation.*
   If you respect my need to have some quiet time, I'll be much better able to spend some time with you afterwards and to be a good companion.

Sharon would like her boyfriend, Jim, to assist her in regaining the ability to drive on the freeway. Specifically, she would like him to accompany her for a one-hour practice session every Saturday. She has been reluctant to ask him for several months because of heavy demands he has had from his job.

1. *Evaluate your rights.*
   I have a right to ask Jim to help me, even if he is very busy.

2. *Designate a time.*
   This Saturday morning I'll ask him whether he has time to discuss my need for getting his help. If that's not a good time, we'll arrange another time that's convenient for both of us.

3. *State the problem situation in terms of its consequences.*
   My progress in overcoming my fear of driving freeways has been slow. I've had difficulty finding someone who will go with me on Saturdays, which is the time I can most easily practice. In order to make progress at this stage, I need someone to accompany me, although later I'll be able to practice alone.

4. *Express your feelings.*
   I've been feeling very frustrated that I haven't had many opportunities to practice driving freeways. I feel very disappointed about my rate of progress.

5. *Make your request.*
   I'd like you to go with me to practice driving on freeways for one hour every Saturday. I would really appreciate it if you would help me out with this.

6. *State consequences of gaining cooperation.*
   If you help me with my practice sessions, I'm sure that I'll be able to get over my phobia of freeways sooner. It'll be great for us if I don't have to ask you anymore to take me to all those places that are only accessible by freeway.

Exercise: Developing an Assertive Response

Now it's your turn.

Select one of the problem situations you previously described and write up an assertive response, following the six steps outlined above. You may want to make copies of this page before writing on it. (If you need more room, use a separate sheet of paper.)

1. *Evaluate your rights.*

2. *Designate a time.*

3. *State the problem situation in terms of its consequences.*

4. *Express your feelings.*

5. *Make your request.*

6. *State the consequences of gaining (or not gaining) the other person's cooperation.*

Once you've written out in detail your assertive response to a problem situation, you'll find that you feel more prepared and confident when you confront that situation in real life. This process of methodically writing out a preview of your assertive response is especially helpful during the time when you're learning to be assertive. Later on, when you have a fair degree of mastery, you may not need to write out your response in advance every time. It's never a bad idea, though, to prepare your response, especially when a lot is at stake. Attorneys do so as a way of life because they typically assert the rights of their clients in "high-stake" situations.

Finally, an important *intermediate step* between writing out an assertive response and confronting a problem in real life is to *role-play* your response with a friend or counselor. This can be an invaluable tool for developing the nonverbal aspects of assertiveness described earlier in this chapter. It will further increase your confidence and sense of being well-prepared when you come to deal with the actual situation. Assertiveness training, whether done in the context of psychotherapy or in a classroom situation, relies primarily on role-playing as a teaching tool.

Assertiveness on the Spot

Many situations arise in the course of everyday life that challenge you to be assertive spontaneously. Someone smokes right next to you, making you uncomfortable. Someone blasts loud music while you're trying to go to sleep. Someone cuts in front of you in line. (Many of the situations listed in the *What's Your Style* questionnaire at the beginning of this chapter fall into this category.) What do you do?

1. **Evaluate your rights.** Often you'll go through this step automatically, without the need to pause for reflection. The violation of your rights is obvious and perhaps flagrant. At other times you may need to pause and think about which of your rights is at stake.

2. **Make your request.** This is the *key* step in on-the-spot assertiveness. In many cases your assertive response will consist *only* of this step. Someone interferes with your rights and you simply ask them, in a straightforward manner, for what you want or don't want. As discussed previously, your statement can begin with such words as

   "I would like…"
   "I want…"
   "I would appreciate…"
   "Would you please…"

   Your statement needs to be

   - Firm
   - Simple and to the point
   - Without apology
   - Nonjudgmental, nonblaming
   - Always a request, not a demand

   If the person doesn't immediately cooperate or pretends not to notice, simply *repeat* your statement. Repeating your request in a monotonous fashion will work better in getting what you want than becoming angry or aggressive if the person you're dealing with is a stranger (see the "broken record technique," in the next section). Avoid monotonous repetition if you're dealing with family or close friends (with the exception of small children).

3. **State the problem in terms of its consequences.** This step is optional but can be helpful in on-the-spot assertiveness. If you feel that the person you're addressing might be puzzled by your request, you might want to explain why his or her behavior has an adverse effect on you. The other person may gain empathy for your position in this way, leading to a greater chance of cooperation.

   For example

   "Everyone here, including myself, has been waiting in line" (as a prelude to, "Would you go to the back of the line, please?").

   "I am allergic to cigarette smoke" (as a prelude to, "Would you please smoke somewhere else?").

4. **Express your feelings.** If you're dealing with a stranger with whom you don't wish to have any further relationship, it's usually O.K. to omit this step. The only occasion for using it with a stranger is if the person involved doesn't cooperate

after you've made your assertive request (for example, "I've told you twice that I'm not interested in your product and you're still trying to sell it to me. I'm starting to feel really irritated"). On the other hand, it's often a good idea to express your feelings when you need to be assertive on the spot with your spouse, child, or close friend ("I'm really disappointed that you didn't call when you said you would," or "I'm feeling too tired to clean up the kitchen right now").

5. **State the consequences of gaining (or not gaining) cooperation.** In situations with strangers, this step usually won't be necessary. On rare occasions, with someone resistant, you may choose to state negative consequences, although it will be difficult to keep this from coming across as a threat (for example, "If you continue smoking, I may have an asthma attack"). With family and friends a statement of positive consequences may be used to strengthen your request ("If you get in bed by 8:30, I'll read you a story").

The gist of being assertive on the spot is simply to *make your request* in as simple, specific, and straightforward a manner as possible. Whether you choose to mention your feelings or the consequences of the other person's behavior will largely depend on the situation. Mention consequences when you want the other person to better appreciate your position. Express your feelings when you want the other person to understand how strongly you feel about what they're doing (or not doing).

On-the-Spot Assertiveness Exercises

The exercises below* are designed to give you practice in responding assertively on the spot. The situations presented are common ones which you may have encountered before in your life. The task is to fill in the blank with an assertive response. Alternatively, you may wish to role-play these situations with a friend. This will give you direct practice with both the verbal and nonverbal aspects of assertive communication. As you practice, remember to stay calm.

1. You take your car to the garage for an oil change and receive a bill for that plus wheel alignment and new spark plugs. You say, _____
   _____
   _____

2. You arrange to take turns driving to work with a friend. Each day you drive she has an errand to run on the way home. When she drives, there are no stops made. You say, _____
   _____
   _____

3. When you entertain your co-workers, the conversation always turns to shop-talk. You are planning a party and prefer to avoid the usual topics. You say, _____
   _____
   _____
   _____

* Reproduced from the *TGRRAP Program Manual* by permission of Dr. Arthur B. Hardy.

4. You're in the bank. The teller asks, "Who's next?" It's your turn. A woman who came in after you says, "I am." You say, _____
_____
_____

5. You're in a taxi and you suspect that the driver is taking you by a roundabout route. You say, _____
_____
_____

6. You're in an airplane in the "No Smoking" section. The person next to you lights up a cigarette. You say, _____
_____
_____

7. You've frequently had adverse reactions to medications in the past. Your doctor gives you a prescription without telling you what side-effects to expect. You say,
_____
_____
_____

8. You're buying some new clothes. The saleswoman is pressuring you into buying something that makes you look ten pounds heavier. You say, _____
_____
_____
_____

9. You're playing miniature golf with your spouse. You're not doing very well but are having a good time. Your spouse is continually telling you how to do it "right." You say, _____
_____
_____

10. You've settled in for a quiet Sunday at home, the first in a long time. Your parents call and invite you over for the day. You don't want to go. You say, _____
_____
_____

11. You receive a notice informing you that your child has been placed in the classroom of a teacher whom you know to be notoriously incompetent. You call the principal and you say, _____
_____
_____

12. Someone rings your doorbell, wanting to convert you to their religion. You're not interested. You say, _____
_____
_____

13. A friend asks you to baby-sit for her but you have other plans for the day. You say, _____

_____

_____

14. You're feeling lonely and "left out." Your spouse is in the living room, reading. You say, _____

_____

_____

15. You've been rushing about all day. It's very hot and you don't have air conditioning. You prepare a salad for dinner because you don't want to turn the oven on. Your husband comes home hungry and wants a hot meal. You say, _____

_____

_____

_____

16. Friends drop by without an invitation at 5:00 PM. It is now 7:00 and you want to serve dinner to your family. You don't have enough to include the guests. You say, _____

_____

_____

Learning To Say No

An important aspect of being assertive is your ability to say "no" to requests that you don't want to meet. Saying no means that you *set limits* on other people's demands for your time and energy when such demands conflict with your own needs and desires. It also means that you can do this without feeling guilty.

In some cases, especially if you're dealing with someone with whom you don't want to promote a relationship, just saying "No, thank you," or "No, I'm not interested" in a firm, polite manner should suffice. If the other person persists, just repeat your statement calmly without apologizing. If you need to make your statement stronger and more emphatic, you may want to: 1) look the person directly in the eyes, 2) raise the level of your voice slightly, and 3) assert your position: "I said no thank you."

In many other instances—with acquaintances, friends, and family—you may want to give the other person some explanation for turning down their request. Here it's often useful to follow a three-step procedure:

1. Acknowledge the other person's request by repeating it.

2. Explain your reason for declining.

3. Say no.

4. (Optional). If appropriate, suggest an alternative proposal where both your and the other person's needs will be met.

Use Step 4 only if you can easily see a way for both you and the other person to meet each other halfway.

Examples

"I understand that you'd really like to get together tonight *(acknowledgment)*. It turns out I've had a really long day and feel exhausted *(explanation)*, so I need to pass on tonight *(saying no)*. Would there be another night later this week when we could get together?" (alternative option)

"I hear that you need some help with moving *(acknowledgment)*. I'd like to help out but I promised my boyfriend we would go away for the weekend *(explanation)*, so I'm not going to be available *(saying no)*. I hope you can find someone else."

Note that in this example the speaker not only acknowledges her friend's need, but indicates that she would have liked to help out if the circumstances had been different. Sometimes you may wish to let someone know that under different conditions you would have willingly responded to their request.

"I realize you would like to go out with me again *(acknowledgment)*. I think you're a fine person, but it seems to me that we don't have enough in common to pursue a relationship *(explanation)*, so I have to say no *(saying no)*."

"I know that you'd like me to take care of Johnny for the day *(acknowledgment)*, but I have some important errands I have to attend to *(explanation)*. So I can't babysit today *(saying no)*."

Are there any particular types of situations where you repeatedly have troubles saying no? Make a list of these situations in the spaces below:

Now take a sheet of paper and write a hypothetical assertive response for each of these situations where you say no, following the three-step procedure outlined above.

The following suggestions may also be helpful in learning to say no (adapted from Matthew McKay, *When Anger Hurts*, Chapter 12):

1. *Take your time.* If you're the type of person who has difficulty saying no, give yourself some time to think and clarify what you want to say before responding to someone's request (for example, "I'll let you know by the end of the week," or "I'll call you back tomorrow morning after sleeping on it.").

2. *Don't over-apologize.* When you apologize to someone for saying no, you give them the message that you're "not sure" that your own needs are just as important as theirs. This opens the door for them to put more pressure on you to comply with what they want. In some cases they may even try to play upon your guilt to obtain other things or to get you to "make it up to them" for having said no in the first place.

3. *Be specific.* It's important to be very specific in stating what you will and won't do. For example: "I'm willing to help you move, but (because of my back) I can only carry lightweight items"; "I can take you to work, but only if you can meet me by 8:15."

4. *Use assertive body language.* Be sure to face the person you're talking to squarely and maintain good eye-contact. Work on speaking in a calm but firm tone of voice. Avoid becoming emotional.

5. *Watch out for guilt.* You may feel the impulse to do something *else* for someone after turning down their request. Take your time before offering to do so. Make sure that your offer comes out of genuine desire rather than guilt. You'll have fully mastered the skill of saying no to others when you reach the point where you can do so without feeling guilty.

Techniques for Avoiding Manipulation

Much of the time you'll find that people listen to you and cooperate when you act assertively. Sooner or later, however, you'll encounter occasions where someone puts off your request by any of several means, including:

- changing the subject
- responding with a strong display of emotion (including anger)
- joking or making fun of your request
- trying to make you feel guilty about your request
- criticizing or questioning the legitimacy of your request
- asking you why you want what you asked for

These are just a few of the more common ploys other people can use if they simply want to ignore or avoid dealing with your request. The *true* test of assertiveness is not to back down in the face of such resistance, but to persist. The following techniques are proven ways of overcoming attempts to avoid or discount what you're asking for.

The Broken Record Technique

The broken record technique consists of stating repeatedly what you want in a calm, direct manner with the persistence of a broken record. You can use this technique in situations where you are unwilling to do what the other person suggests, but find yourself somewhat captive to the other person's persistence. Using the technique, you stay focused on what you want and don't give in to the other person's will. You simply state what you want as many times as you need to, without change or embellishment. Start with "I want..." or "I would like..."

Example: You wish to return a dress to the store and receive a refund.

Saleslady:	May I help you?
You:	Yes, thank you. I would like to return this dress and I would like my money back.
Saleslady:	We don't usually refund money. Why are you returning the dress?
You:	I would like to return this dress and I would like my money back.
Saleslady:	Didn't you try the dress on in the store?
You:	I would like to return this dress and I would like my money back.
Saleslady:	Well, if you're sure you don't want the dress, I'll give you a credit.
You:	I don't want a credit, thank you. I want my money back.
Saleslady:	Perhaps you would like to exchange the dress for another one. Let me show you some of the other dresses that would look nice on you.
You:	No, thank you. I would like to return this dress and I would like my money back.
Saleslady:	I've never done that before. I might get into trouble.
You:	I understand that this is a problem for you. However, I would like to return this dress and I would like my money back.
Saleslady:	I'll have to get some authorization from the manager.
You:	OK.
Manager:	May I help you?
You:	Yes, thank you. I would like to return this dress and I would like my money back.

Manager:	Is there something wrong with the dress?
You:	No. I would just like to return it and I would like my money back.
Manager:	I'm sorry that you don't like the dress. Here is your refund, and I do hope you will find something else you like in the store.
You:	Thank you very much.

Please note that the broken record technique is *not* designed to foster a relationship developing but rather to obtain what you want with a minimum of communication. It is generally *not* an appropriate technique in relationships with your spouse, partner, or close friends, although, on occasion, it can be useful with children.

Fogging

Fogging is best used with someone who is being critical of you. It involves agreeing in part with the criticism. You honestly agree with some part of the criticism even when you don't believe all of it. You need to do this in a calm, quiet tone of voice without being defensive or sarcastic. If you don't agree with the specific criticism, you can agree with the general principle behind the criticism and simply say "You may be right." When you agree with someone, they have little tendency to come back and criticize or argue with you further. When you respond defensively or argumentively to someone else's critical remarks, it gives them something to spar with. Fogging effectively stops communication before the other person can escalate a disagreement.

Example: Your mother criticizes the way you look.

Mother:	Your skirt is awfully short. Don't you think you should wear them longer? The style is longer skirts now.
You:	You're probably right—the style is longer skirts now.
Mother:	I think that if you cut your hair short, it might be easier for you.
You:	You could be right—shorter hair is easier.
Mother:	You'd look much more feminine if you put on some makeup.
You:	You could be right—I hadn't thought about it. I might look more feminine with makeup.
Mother:	You really should set a good example for your daughter. She copies you.
You:	Yes, she does copy me.
Mother:	Let's go out to lunch.
You:	I'm ready, let's go.

Like the broken record, fogging is useful in situations where you want to minimize communication—in other words, you don't want to listen to criticism and you don't want to argue. It's generally not a good idea to use fogging in situations with partners or friends where you wish to keep lines of communication open and give the other an opportunity to be heard or get their feelings out. In such instances, it is best to quietly listen to other people until they've spoken their mind. Then you can interject your own comments.

Content-to-Process Shift

The content-to-process shift changes the focus of your discussion with someone from the content to a description of what's going on between you. If someone responds to your asssertive request in almost any way *other* than hearing you and replying (for example, they get angry, laugh it off, or bring up something irrelevant) you can: 1) point out what they're doing (content-to-process shift) and 2) bring the focus back to your request.

Example:

You:	I'd like you to call me when you know you'll be getting home late.
Your Husband:	Yes, Sarge.
You:	Humor is fine, but it's getting us off the point.
Your Husband:	What's the point?
You:	I'd really appreciate it if you'd let me know when you'll be getting home late.
Your Husband:	You know, I just thought of something. Those nights I get home late, why don't you just not worry about saving dinner for me—I'll pick up something on the way home.
You:	You're getting off the point—and I'm beginning to feel very frustrated that you're not really listening. (Note: Here the content-to-process shift is amplified by an expression of feelings.)
Your Husband:	So, you want me to call you if I'm going to be late.
You:	Yes—you've got it.

Defusing

Defusing is a delaying tactic best used when someone responds to your assertive request with intense anger or any other extreme display of emotion. In close relationships, it's important to allow other people to express their strong feelings. Yet at such times they are unlikely to be open to hearing your assertive request. It's better to say "I can see that you're very upset— let's discuss this later."

Example:

You:	I'd like to have mother come down for the holidays.
Your Spouse:	What!? Not again! You're going to do this to me again! I absolutely won't have it!
You:	I can see that you're upset and I can even understand. Let's talk about it another time.

Assertive Inquiry

When someone attacks you for making an assertive request, you can often defuse their attack by asking them why they are having such a problem with your request.

Example:

You:	Could you drive with me to the store now?
Your Spouse:	Why don't you get off my case!
You:	Why is it such a problem for you to take me to the store now?
Your Spouse:	I'm tired of having to take you so many places.

This last example illustrates that being assertive can sometimes bring up basic issues in a relationship. In this case, the husband of an agoraphobic is having a genuine problem with his wife's need for him to drive her places. This one instance is of course just the tip of the iceberg. It may be appropriate for the husband and wife at this point to have a frank discussion about the larger issues of the wife's need and the husband's compliance. Or, if getting to the store quickly has higher priority, the wife may need to acknowledge the larger issues, but reach an agreement with her husband to discuss them another time. Obviously, being assertive can require other important communication skills, such as your ability to listen well and negotiate a compromise with the person to whom you make your request.

Learning to be assertive doesn't mean that you'll always get what you ask for one hundred percent of the time. Assertiveness can only be guaranteed to improve your chances of getting what you want. You should also work on developing skills of listening, negotiation, and compromise to complement your assertiveness skills and increase your odds of having your needs met by other people.

A disccussion of listening and negotiation skills is beyond the scope of this chapter. For further ideas, I suggest that you refer to the books listed under "Communication Skills" at the end of this chapter. You may also want to find a good classs or group situation that focuses on communication skills.

Ways in Which Someone Might Evade Your Request

It's helpful to prepare yourself against a number of typical blocking gambits that can be used to attack and derail your assertive requests. Some of the more common evasions (adapted from *The Relaxation and Stress Reduction Workbook*) include:

Laughing It Off. Your assertive request is responded to with a joke: "So what if my project is three weeks late? Healthy babies can be born a month late!" Use the content-to-process shift: "Humor is getting us off the point," and the broken record technique: "Yes, but your project is three weeks late."

Accusing Gambit. The other person blames you for the problem: "You're always so late cooking dinner that I'm too tired to do the dishes." Use the fogging technique: "That may be so, but you're still not honoring our agreement," or simply disagree: "Eight o'clock is not too late for the dishes."

The Beat-up. Your assertive request is responded to with a personal attack: "Who are you to protest being interrupted when you're the biggest loudmouth around here?" A good strategy is to respond with an ironic "Thank you" in conjunction with the broken record technique or defusing: "I can see that you're angry right now—let's talk about it after the meeting."

Delaying Gambit. Your assertive request is met with, "Not now, I'm too tired," or "Another time, maybe." Use the broken record technique, or insist on setting a specific time when the problem can be discussed.

Why Gambit. Your assertive request is blocked with a series of "why" questions ("Why do you feel that way?" "I still don't know why you don't want to go," "Why did you change your mind?"). The best response is to use the content-to-process shift: "Why isn't the point. The issue is that I'm not willing to go tonight," or the broken record technique.

Self-Pity Gambit. Your request is met with tears and an attempt to make you feel guilty. The best strategy is to acknowledge the other person is upset and then proceed with your request: "I know this is causing you pain, but I need to get this issue resolved." If the other person is really very upset, postpone the discussion until another time.

Quibbling. The other person wants to debate with you about the legitimacy of what you feel, the magnitude of the problem, or some such other distinction. Use the content-to-process shift: "We're quibbling now, and have strayed from the subject," along with an assertion of your right to feel the way you do.

Threats. You are threatened with such statements as, "If you keep harping at me like this, you're going to need another boyfriend." Use assertive inquiry: "What is it about my requests that bothers you?" as well as the content-to-process shift: "That sounds like a threat," or defusing.

Denial. You're told, "I didn't do that" or "You've really misinterpreted me." Assert what you've observed and experienced, and use fogging: "It may seem that way to you, but I've observed...."

Summary of Things To Do

Learning to be assertive will enable you to obtain more of what you want, and will help minimize frustration and resentment in your relationships with partners, family, and friends. It will also help you to take more risks and to ask more of life, adding to your sense of autonomy and self-confidence.

Becoming assertive does, however, take *practice*. When you first attempt to act assertively with family and friends, be prepared to feel awkward. Also be prepared for them not to understand what you're doing and possibly even to take offense. If you explain as best you can and give them time to adjust to your new behavior, you may be pleasantly surprised that they come to respect you for your new-found directness and honesty.

To get the most out of this chapter, I suggest you do the following:

1. Determine your dominant behavior style (submissive, aggressive, passive-aggressive, manipulative, or assertive) by asking yourself how you'd respond to each of the 30 situations listed in the *What's Your Style?* questionairre.

2. Clarify those situations and people with whom you'd like to be more assertive by completing *The Assertiveness Questionnaire*.

3. Make a copy of the *Personal Bill of Rights* and post it in a conspicuous place. Read it over a number of times until you feel thoroughly familiar with all of the rights listed.

4. Identify two or three problem situations in which you would like to be more assertive. Write them up under the exercise, *Specifying Your Problem Situations*. Make your description of each situation specific, by indicating *who* it involves, *when* it occurs, *what* bothers you, *how* you'd normally deal with it, your *fears* about being assertive, and, finally, your particular *goal*.

5. Write out an assertive response to each of your problem situations. Your narrative for each assertive response should contain the six steps listed in the exercise *Developing an Assertive Response*.

6. Become thoroughly familiar with the guidelines for making an assertive request: using assertive nonverbal behaviors, keeping your request simple, being specific, using I-statements, objecting to behaviors (not personalities), not apologizing for being assertive, and making requests instead of demands.

7. Review the guidelines for being assertive on the spot, and complete the *On-the-Spot Assertiveness Exercises*.

8. Role-play with a friend or counselor your assertive responses to your problem situations and/or the on-the-spot assertiveness exercises.

9. Review the section "Learning To Say No" and role-play saying no to unreasonable requests with a friend or counselor.

10. Review the section "Techniques for Avoiding Manipulation" and try practicing several of them with a friend or counselor.

11. Consult the books listed below under "Assertiveness Skills" for more thorough coverage of the topic. If you feel the need to seek extra help beyond this workbook, you'll find that most adult education programs through local colleges or high schools offer workshops and classes in asssertiveness training.

12. Consult the books listed below under "Communications Skills" or take a class in communication to back up your assertiveness training with other important interpersonal skills such as listening, self-disclosure, negotiating, and so on.

Further Reading

Assertiveness Skills

Alberti, Robert E., and Emmons, Michael. *Your Perfect Right*. Revised edition. San Luis Obispo, California: Impact Press, 1974.

Bower, Sharon, and Bower, Gordon. *Asserting Yourself*. Reading, Massachusetts: Addison-Wesley, 1976.

Davis, Martha; Eshelman, Elizabeth; and McKay, Matthew. *The Relaxation and Stress Reduction Workbook*. Third edition. Oakland, California: New Harbinger Publications, 1988. (See Chapter 12.)

Fensterheim, Herbert and Baer. *Don't Say Yes When You Want to Say No*. New York: David McKay, 1975.

McKay, Matthew; Rogers, Peter; and McKay, Judith. *When Anger Hurts*. Oakland, California: New Harbinger Publications, 1989. (See especially Chapter 12.)

Smith, Manuel J. *When I Say No, I Feel Guilty*. New York: The Dial Press, 1975.

Communication Skills

Bach, George R., and Wyden, Peter. *The Intimate Enemy*. New York: William Morrow, 1969.

Barker, Larry L. *Listening Behavior*. Englewood Cliffs, New Jersey: Prentice-Hall, 1971.

Fisher, Roger, and Ury, William. *Getting to Yes: Negotiating Agreement Without Giving In*. Boston: Houghton Mifflin, 1981.

Hopper, Robert, and Whitehead, Jack L. *Communication Concepts and Skills*. New York: Harper and Row, 1979.

Jourard, Sidney M. *The Transparent Self*. Revised edition. New York: Van Nostrand Reinhold, 1971.

Lieberman, Mendel, and Hardie, Marion. *Resolving Family and Other Conflicts: Everybody Wins*. Santa Cruz, California: Unity Press, 1981.

McKay, Matthew; Davis, Martha; and Fanning, Patrick. *Messages: The Communication Book*. Oakland, California: New Harbinger Publications, 1983.

Nierenberg, G.I., and Calero, H.H. *How to Read a Person Like a Book*. New York: Pocket Books, 1973.

15

Self-Esteem

Self-esteem is a way of thinking, feeling, and acting that implies that you accept, respect, trust, and believe in yourself. When you *accept* yourself, you can live comfortably with both your personal strengths and weaknesses without undue self-criticism. When you *respect* yourself, you acknowledge your own dignity and value as a unique human being. You treat yourself well in much the same way you would treat someone else you respect. *Self-trust* means that your behaviors and feelings are consistent enough to give you an inner sense of continuity and coherence despite changes and challenges in your external circumstances. To *believe* in yourself means that you feel you deserve to have the good things in life. It also means that you have confidence that you can fulfill your deepest personal needs, aspirations, and goals.

To get a sense about your own level of self-esteem, think of someone (or imagine what it would be like to know someone) whom you *fully* accept, respect, trust, and believe in. Now ask yourself to what extent you hold these attitudes toward yourself. Where would you place yourself on the following scale:

```
Very Low                                                              Very High
Self-Esteem _____ Self-Esteem
               0   1   2   3   4   5   6   7   8   9   10
```

A fundamental truth about self-esteem is that it needs to come from *within*. When self-esteem is low, the deficiency creates a feeling of emptiness which you may try to fill by latching on—often compulsively—to something external that provides a temporary sense of satisfaction and fulfillment. When the quest to fill your inner emptiness by appropriating something from outside becomes desperate, repetitive, or automatic, you have what is called an *addiction*. Broadly defined, addiction is an attachment to something or someone outside yourself that you feel you need to provide a sense of inner satisfaction or relief. Frequently this attachment substitutes preoccupation with a substance or activity for healthy human relationships. It may also substitute a temporary feeling of control or power for a more lasting sense of inner confidence and strength.

A healthy alternative to addiction is to work on building your self-esteem. Growing in self-esteem means developing confidence and strength from within. While still enjoying life fully, you no longer need to appropriate or identify with something or someone outside yourself to feel O.K. The basis for your self-worth is internal. As such, it is much more lasting and stable.

Ways To Build Self-Esteem

There are many pathways to self-esteem. It is not something that develops overnight or as a result of any single insight, decision, or modification in your behavior. Self-esteem is *built gradually* through a willingness to work on a number of areas in your life.

This chapter considers—in three parts—a variety of ways to build self-esteem:

- Taking Care of Yourself

- Developing Support and Intimacy

- Other Pathways to Self-Esteem

Most fundamental to your self-esteem is your willingness and ability to take care of yourself. This means first that you can *recognize* your basic needs as a human being and then *do* something about meeting them. Taking care of yourself also involves cultivating a relationship with that part of yourself known as the "inner child." Your inner child is a place deep inside that is the origin of your needs. It is the playful, spontaneous, and creative side of you—yet it also carries any emotional pain, fear, or sense of vulnerability you acquired from your childhood. By becoming a good parent to your own inner child now, you can overcome the limitations and deficiencies of your upbringing years ago. A popular saying these days aptly states "It's never too late to have a happy childhood."

Part I of this chapter focuses on this theme of taking care of yourself. It begins by enumerating a variety of dysfunctional family situations that can cause low self-esteem. Following this is a discussion of basic human needs to help you identify those needs which are most important to address in your life right now. Finally, a variety of methods for cultivating a relationship with your inner child are offered. Learning to meet your needs—to care for and nurture yourself—is *the most fundamental and important thing you can do to build your self-esteem.*

Part II of this chapter is an extension of Part I. Finding support and intimacy in your life is obviously a major part of taking care of yourself. Other people can't give you self-esteem, but their support, acceptance, validation, and love can go a long way toward reinforcing and strengthening your own self-affirmation. This part is divided into four sections. The first addressess the importance of developing a support system. The second presents ten conditions that I feel are critical to genuine intimacy. The third section offers a discussion of interpersonal boundaries. Having boundaries in your relationships is essential both to intimacy and to self-esteem. A final section underscores the relevance of assertiveness to self-esteem.

Part III presents four additional aspects of self-esteem:

- Personal wellness and body image

- Emotional self-expression

- Self-talk and affirmations for self-esteem

- Personal goals and a sense of accomplishment

Although these pathways to self-esteem are diverse among themselves, they can all be viewed as an extension of the basic idea of taking care of yourself.

Part I: Taking Care of Yourself

Taking care of yourself is the foundation on which all other pathways to self-esteem rest. Without a basic *willingness* and *ability* to care for, love, and nurture yourself, it is difficult to achieve a deep or lasting experience of self-worth.

Perhaps you had the good fortune to receive the love, acceptance, and nurturing from your parents that could provide you with a solid foundation for self-esteem as an adult. Presently you are free of any deep-seated feelings of insecurity and your path to self-esteem is likely to be simple and short, involving certain changes in attitude, habits, and beliefs. For those who have carried a life-long sense of insecurity, though, the way to self-worth involves developing the ability to give yourself what your parents could not. *It's possible to overcome deficits from your past only by becoming a good parent to yourself.*

Some Causes of Low Self-Esteem

What are some of the childhood circumstances that can lead you to grow up with feelings of insecurity or inadequacy?

1. **Overly Critical Parents**

   Parents who were constantly critical or set impossibly high standards of behavior may have left you feeling guilty; that somehow you could "never be good enough." As an adult, you will continue to strive for perfection to overcome a long-standing sense of inferiority. You may also have a strong tendency toward self-criticism.

2. **Significant Childhood Loss**

   If you were separated from a parent as a result of death or divorce, you may have been left feeling abandoned. You may have grown up with a sense of emptiness and insecurity inside that can be restimulated very intensely by losses of significant people in your adult life. As an adult, you may seek to overcome old feelings of abandonment by overdependency on a particular person or other addictions to food, drugs, work, or whatever works to cover the pain.

3. **Parental Abuse**

   Physical and sexual abuse are extreme forms of deprivation. They may leave you with a complex mix of feelings, including inadequacy, insecurity, lack of trust, guilt, and/or rage. Adults who were physically abused as children may become perpetual victims or may themselves develop a hostile posture toward life, victimizing others. Adults—especially men—who were sexually abused as children sometimes express their rage by turning to rape and abuse as adults. Or they may turn that rage inward in deep feelings of self-loathing and inadequacy. Survivors of abusive childhoods often, and understandably, have difficulty with intimate relationships in their adult lives. While less flagrant, constant verbal abuse can have equally damaging effects.

4. **Parental Alcoholism or Drug Abuse**

   Much has been written in recent years on the effects of parental alcoholism on children. Chronic drinking or substance abuse creates a chaotic, unreliable family atmosphere in which it is difficult for a child to develop a basic sense of trust or security. The attendant denial of the problem, often by both parents, teaches the child to deny his or her own feelings and pain connected to the family situation. Many such children grow up with poor self-esteem or a poor sense of personal identity. Fortunately, support groups are presently available to help adult children of alcoholics heal the adverse effects of their past. If one or both of your parents were alcoholic, you may wish to read the following books: *It Will Never Happen to Me*, by Claudia Black; *Adult Children of Alcoholics*, by Janet Woititz; and *Recovery: A Guide for Adult Children of Alcoholics*, by Herbert Gravitz and Julie Bowden. You may also want to join a support group or therapy group for adult children of alcoholics in your area.

5. Parental Neglect

Some parents, because they are preoccupied with themselves, their work, or other concerns, simply fail to give their children adequate attention and nurturing. Children left to their own devices often grow up feeling insecure, worthless, and lonely. As adults, they may have a tendency to discount or neglect their own needs.

6. Parental Rejection

Even without physical, sexual, or verbal abuse, some parents impart a feeling to their children that they are unwanted. This profoundly damaging attitude teaches a child to grow up doubting his or her very right to exist. Such a person has a tendency toward self-rejection or self-sabotage. It remains possible for adults with such a past to overcome what their parents didn't give them through learning to love and care for themselves.

7. Parental Overprotectiveness

The child who is overprotected may never learn to trust the world outside of the immediate family and risk independence. As an adult, such a person may feel very insecure and afraid to venture far from a safe person or place. Through learning to acknowledge and care for their own needs, overprotected individuals can gain the confidence to make a life of their own and discover that the world is not such a dangerous place.

8. Parental Overindulgence

The "spoiled" child of overindulgent parents is given insufficient exposure to "deferred gratification" or appropriate limits. As adults, such people tend to be bored, lack persistence, or have difficulty initiating and sustaining individual effort. They tend to expect the world to come to them rather than taking responsibility for creating their own lives. Until they are willing to take personal responsibility, such people feel cheated and very insecure because life does not continue to provide what they learned to expect during childhood.

Do any of the above categories seem to fit you? Does more than one? You may initially find it difficult to acknowledge problems in your past. Our memory of childhood is often hazy and indistinct—especially when we do not *want* to recall what actually happened. The point of remembering and acknowledging what happened to you as a child is not so that you can blame your parents. Most likely, your parents did the best they could with their available personal resources, which may have been severely limited as a result of deprivations they experienced with *their* parents. The purpose of remembering your past is to *release* it and *rebuild your present*. Old "tapes" or patterns based on fear, guilt, or anger will tend to interfere with your present life and relationships until you can identify and release them. Once you acknowledge and ultimately forgive your parents for what they were unable to give you, you can truly begin the journey of learning to care for yourself. In essence, this means becoming a good parent to yourself.

The balance of this section will consider three important ways in which you can learn to take better care of yourself:

1. Acknowledging and meeting your basic needs

2. Discovering and cultivating a relationship with your *inner child*

3. Making time for small acts of self-nurturing on a daily basis

Your Basic Needs

Basic human needs conjures an association with shelter, clothing, food, water, sleep, oxygen, and so on—in other words, what human beings require for their physical survival. It was not until the last few decades that higher-order *psychological needs* were identified. While not necessary for survival, meeting these needs is essential to your emotional well-being and a satisfying adjustment to life. The psychologist Abraham Maslow proposed five levels of human needs, with three levels beyond primary concerns for survival and security. He arranged these levels into a hierarchy, as follows:

Self-Actualization Needs (fulfillment of your potential in life, wholeness)

↑

Esteem Needs (self-respect, mastery, a sense of accomplishment)

↑

Belongingness and Love Needs (support and affection from others, intimacy, a sense of belonging)

↑

Safety Needs (shelter, stable environment)

↑

Physiological Needs (food, water, sleep, oxygen)

In Maslow's scheme, taking care of higher-level needs is dependent on having satisfied lower-level needs. It's difficult to satisfy belongingness and esteem needs if you're starving. On a subtler level, it's difficult to fulfill your full potential if you're feeling isolated and alienated for lack of having met needs for love and belongingness. Writing in the sixties, Maslow estimated that the average American satisfied perhaps 90 percent of physiological needs, 70 percent of safety needs, 50 percent of love needs, 40 percent of esteem needs, and 10 percent of the need for self-actualization.

Although Maslow defined esteem narrowly in terms of a sense of accomplishment and mastery, I believe that self-esteem is dependent on *recognizing and taking care of all of your needs.*

How do you recognize what your needs are? How many of the following important human needs are you aware of?

1. Physical safety and security

2. Financial security

3. Friendship

4. The attention of others

5. Being listened to

6. Guidance

7. Respect

8. Validation

9. Expressing and sharing your feelings

10. Sense of belonging

11. Nurturing

12. Physically touching and being touched

13. Intimacy

14. Sexual expression

15. Loyalty and trust

16. A sense of accomplishment

17. A sense of progress toward goals

18. Feeling competent or masterful in some area

19. Making a contribution

20. Fun and play

21. Sense of freedom, independence

22. Creativity

23. Spiritual awareness—connection with a "Higher Power"

24. Unconditional love

Now go back over the list carefully and ask yourself how many of these needs you are actually getting fulfilled at this time. In what areas do you come up short? What concrete steps can you take in the next few weeks and months to better satisfy those needs that are going unmet? Working up your exposure hierarchies to overcome your phobias will help you meet needs 17 and 18. Going dancing or to a movie tonight will help in a small way with your need for fun and play. The point is that learning to take care of yourself involves being able to 1) *recognize* and 2) *meet* your basic needs as a human being. The above list may give you ideas on areas of your life that need more attention. Use the chart on the following page to plan what you will actually do in the next month about five (or more) of your needs that could be better met.

Need	What I'm willing to do in the next month to better meet this need

Cultivating a Relationship With Your Inner Child

The concept of the *inner child*—the childlike part of yourself—has been around for many decades. The psychologist Carl Jung referred to it as the "divine child," while the religious thinker Emmet Fox called it the "wonder child." But what is it? How would you recognize your own child within? Some characteristics of the inner child include

- That part of you which feels like a little girl or boy.

- That part of you which feels and expresses your deepest emotional needs for security, trust, nurturing, affection, touching, and so on.

- That part of you which is alive, energetic, creative, and playful (much as real children are when left free to play and be themselves).

- Finally, that part of you that still carries the pain and emotional trauma of your childhood. Strong feelings of insecurity, loneliness, fear, anger, shame, or guilt— even if triggered by present circumstances—belong to the inner child. Actually there are very few new feelings. Especially when they are strong, most of our feelings reflect ways we reacted or failed to react a long time ago as a child.

How do you feel about the little child within you? If you are willing to allow the little girl or boy inside some freedom of expression, you'll find it easier to be more playful, fun-loving, spontaneous, and creative. You'll find it natural to give and receive affection, to be vulnerable, and to trust. You'll be in touch with your feelings and free to grow. On the other hand, to the extent that you suppress and deny your inner child, you will likely find it difficult to be playful or have fun. You may tend to be conventional and conforming and act out painful patterns repeatedly. You may feel constricted and inhibited, unable to let go and expand. It will be hard to be vulnerable or trusting, hard to give and receive affection. Finally, you will likely be out of touch with your feelings, inclined to be overly logical or overly in need of keeping everything under tight control.

How can you bring out and cultivate a healthy relationship with your inner child? In my experience there are four steps to this process:

1. Overcoming attitudes of criticism, rejection, and/or denial of your child within

2. "Bringing out" your inner child

3. Reevaluating negative feeling states in terms of positive needs of your inner child

4. Nurturing your inner child on a daily basis

1. Overcoming Negative Attitudes Toward Your Inner Child

A basic truth is that you tend to treat your own inner child in much the same way that your parents treated you as a child. For better or worse, you internalize your parents' attitudes and behaviors. If they were overly critical toward you, you likely grew up overly self-critical, especially of your "childish" or less rational, impulsive side. If they neglected you, you likely grew up tending to ignore or neglect the needs of your own inner child. If they were too busy for you as a child, you're likely to be too busy for your inner child as an adult. If they abused you, you may have become self-destructive as an adult or else may be abusive of others. If your parents placed a taboo on acknowledging and expressing your feelings and impulses, you may have grown up denying your feelings. The list goes on. To cultivate a healing, caring relationship with your own inner child—to become a good parent to yourself—you need to overcome any internalized parental attitudes that cause you to criticize, abuse, neglect, or deny the needs and feelings of your child within.

2. Bringing Out Your Inner Child

While learning to overcome negative patterns internalized from your parents, you may wish to begin bringing out your inner child. It's useful to begin this even *before* you work through all of the limitations you've imposed on your child within. There are a number of good ways to go about doing this, including 1) visualizations, 2) writing a letter to your inner child, 3) using photos as a reminder, and 4) real-life activities which give your inner child expression. You may be surprised to find that caring for your own inner child is a lot less time- and energy-consuming than bringing up a real one!

Visualization

Below is a detailed visualization to help you foster a closer relationship with your own inner child. Put this visualization on tape, pausing for a few moments between each sentence and for 10-20 seconds when the instructions say "Pause." You can do this yourself, or find a friend whose voice you like to prerecord the script for you. Make sure that you give yourself 10-15 minutes to deeply relax before beginning the visualization, since your capacity to remember and see yourself as a child will be greatly enhanced by deep relaxation. (You can use progressive muscle relaxation, meditation, or any deep-relaxation technique you wish.)

Healing Your Inner Child*

Imagine sitting down in a rocking chair and getting very comfortable. Feel yourself rocking easily back and forth. As you continue rocking, you might find yourself starting to drift ... drifting more and more. Rocking back and forth you might find yourself gently drifting back into time. Rocking gently and drifting ... slowly drifting back into time. Year by year you might imagine yourself getting younger and younger. The years are going by ... back through the 1980s ... back through the 1970s ... Gently drifting back ... feeling younger and younger. Back into time long ago. Drifting back to a time where you were perhaps very young. You're imagining now that you can see the little child you were a long time ago. Very soon you can imagine seeing yourself as a little child. Perhaps you can see her [him] there now. What does she look like? What is she wearing? About how old is she? Can you see where she is? Indoors or outdoors? Can you see what she's doing? Perhaps you can see her face, and, if you look carefully, you can see the expression in her eyes. Can you tell how this little child is feeling right now? (Pause) As you look at this little girl, can you recall anything that was missing in her life? Is there anything that kept her from being fully happy? (Pause) If there was anyone or anything that got in the way of this little girl being completely happy and carefree,

---

* I am indebted to David Quigley for some of the ideas in this visualization.

perhaps you can imagine seeing that person or situation. (Pause) If no one is there yet, perhaps you can imagine your dad or your mom or whoever you would like standing in front of you right now. (Pause) What does your little girl feel toward dad, mom, or whoever is standing in front of you right now? ... Is there anything that your child would like to say to that person right now? If so, it's O.K. to go ahead and say it right now ... you can go ahead and say it. (Pause) If your little child is feeling scared or confused about saying anything, imagine that your present-day, adult self enters the scene right now and goes up and stands next to your little child. (Pause) Now when you're ready, imagine your adult self, standing next to your little child, speaking up to whoever is there on your little child's behalf. Your adult self can say whatever she wants. Tell your parent—or whoever is there—whatever you need to say ... whatever it was that never got expressed. (Pause 30 seconds or longer) If you wish, you might complete the sentence "How do you think it makes me feel that ... " (Pause 20 seconds or longer) Or you might complete the sentence "I wish you had ... " (Pause 20 seconds or longer) Tell your parent or whoever is there anything you wish they had done, but they didn't. When you speak up, speak loud and clear so you can be sure that whoever is there really hears you. (Pause 20 seconds or longer) Does the person you're facing have any response? Listen to see if they have a response. (Pause 20 seconds or longer) If so, you can respond to what they say. If not, you can just finish what you need to say. (Pause) When you're finished speaking, you can ask whoever is there to either go away and leave you alone ... or to go away for a while until you're ready to talk again ... or else to stay ... and you're going to accept them as they are and give them a hug. (Pause)

Now go back and see your present-day, adult self standing next to your little child. (Pause) If you're willing, pick that little girl up in your arms this very second and love her. Wrap your arms around her and tell her that it's O.K. Tell her that you know how she feels. Tell her that you understand. You're here and you're going to help her and you love her very much. (Pause) If you could give a color to the love you feel, what color comes to mind? (Pause) Surround your little child with a light of that color and let her feel the peace of being in your arms. (Pause) Tell her that you think she's a great little girl ... that you love the way she talks, walks, laughs ... and does everything. Tell her that you care and that she's precious ... (Pause 30 seconds or longer)

Optional: *Now sit your child on your lap and talk to her. She's got a good mind, and if someone would only explain things, she would understand. Tell her that because of the problems mom and dad had in their own childhood, they couldn't care for her and love her in the way she deserved to be loved. It wasn't that they didn't want to love her ... it was because of their own difficulties that they couldn't love her the way she wanted. This little child simply needs someone to explain to her ... nobody ever explained to her about the problems her parents had when they were growing up. (Pause) Can your little child understand that because of their problems, mom and dad weren't able to love or take care of her in the way she truly deserved? Is your little child ready to forgive mom and dad for what happened? (Pause) If she's not ready right now, perhaps she'll be ready later. If she is ready now, go ahead and picture mom and dad standing in front of you. (Pause) Now tell them, in whatever way you wish, that you forgive them. You're willing to forgive them for their shortcomings because you know that their own problems interfered with their being the best parents they could. Go ahead and forgive them now ... (Pause 30 seconds or longer).*

(Give yourself instructions to wake up. See the section "Guidelines for Effective Visualization" in Chapter 12.)

Write a Letter to Your Inner Child

After having done the preceding visualization or as a result of looking at photos of yourself as a child, you may wish to write a letter to your inner child. You can tell your child about 1) how you feel about her or him 2) how you feel about what happened to her or him as a child, 3) how you would like to get to know her or him better, and 4) what you would like to learn from her or him. When you've completed this letter, open your mind and see if you can take the role of the little child. Then write a child's letter back to your adult self, saying how you feel about your adult self and what you would like from her or him. You might even try using child's handwriting for this letter to help get more in touch with how your little child feels. You will be surprised at how well this works in opening up communication between your adult and inner child "selves." Here is an example of such a letter from an adult to her inner child.

Dear Little Child,

I have long wanted to reach back in time to tell you how much I love you and how much I want to protect you from all the pain and suffering you've been going through. You're much too small and vulnerable to be facing such pain by yourself. I want you to know that you'll have me beside you from now on, and whenever you're frightened you can run to me. I'll be there to hold you and comfort you and protect you.

I know that seeing your daddy lose his temper is very, very frightening. He makes as much noise as he can, and sometimes he hits your mommy or your brother. He doesn't hit you and in a way this just makes you feel guilty. It makes it seem as if you're on his side, and that every time he hits one of them, it's your fault too.

I wish you could tell me more about how you feel, about yourself, your daddy, your mommy, and your brother. I think that a lot of things have happened to you that you just can't remember—either because they didn't make sense at the time or they were just too horrible to remember. It's hard to remember things that don't have any pictures, words, or even concepts attached to them—it's like trying to remember dreams.

As you remember more, I'll be able to understand more about who I am and how I act and what I feel. I know that it's painful trying to remember, and I want you to know how grateful I am to you for trying. Remember that from now on we'll always be there for each other.

Love,
(sign your name)

Photographs

Carry a photo of yourself as a child in your purse or wallet and take it out periodically as a reminder of your child within. Reflect on what was going on and how you felt in your life around the time the photo was taken. After a week or so with one photo, pick another from another age and repeat the process.

Real-Life Activities

A number of real-life activities can foster increased awareness of and closeness to your inner child. Spending 10 minutes daily doing any of the following may help:

- Hugging a teddybear or stuffed animal

- Going to a children's playground and using the swings or other playground equipment

- Playing with your own child as if you were a peer rather than an adult

- Having an ice-cream cone

- Going to the zoo

- Climbing a tree

- Engaging in any other activity you enjoyed as a child

Try to get into the spirit of being a child as you do any of the above. Your feelings in doing so will tell you a lot about your attitude toward your own inner child.

3. Reevaluate Negative Feelings as Positive Needs of Your Inner Child

If you were to encounter a small child who appeared scared, confused, or abandoned, you would likely do everything in your power to nurture and comfort her. Yet how do you treat yourself when you feel insecure, scared, lonely, abandoned, or otherwise needy? Too often we simply deny these feelings; or else we become critical or rejecting toward ourselves for having them. One of the most profound transformations you can make along the road to greater self-esteem is to *re-perceive feelings of insecurity and inadequacy as pleas for attention from your inner child rather than as signs of weakness to be gotten rid of.* You will heal yourself faster by acknowledging and nurturing the needy child behind your negative feeling states instead of trying to push away your inner child's needs.

The next time you feel frightened, insecure, inadequate, vulnerable, or angry, frustrated, and fed up, try asking yourself "What is the need behind this feeling? What is it that my inner child needs right now?" Then take the time to give your child within the attention, caring, or nurturing she or he needs, and you'll be surprised how much better you feel.

Learning to re-perceive negative feelings as pleas for attention from your inner child will transform your life and contribute greatly to your self-esteem. This is what "becoming a good parent to yourself" is all about.

Examples of Disguised Pleas for Help From Your Inner Child

You've just come home from a hard day at work. You see yourself in the bathroom mirror and you can't stand the way you look. Your makeup looks too heavy and it's smeared besides. You look and feel like an old floozy. You begin to think, "What's the use." You could choose to sink into a depression, but instead you ask your inner child what she wants at that very moment. Instead of fixing your make-up, you decide to fill the bathtub with warm bubbly water. You feel a little silly doing it, but you put some bath-toys in the tub with you—a little rubber ducky and a child's teapot. You had similar tub-toys when you were a child. You soak in the warm water and play with the toys, pouring pretend cups of tea and making the duck talk, just as you did when you were little. You stay in the tub as long as you feel like it, letting your fingertips and toes get wrinkled like prunes. When you look in the mirror again, you look pink and warm. You feel more forgiving of the way you look—after all, you've had a hard day!

You've spent two hours preparing a special meal for your sister, who was coming over to spend the evening with you. But at the last minute she calls and says she can't come because she's not feeling well. You suspect it's because she's been asked out on a date. Suddenly you feel a mixture of sadness and anger. You could indulge in these negative feelings, but instead you ask what your inner child needs. Instead of getting angry and throwing the food away, you decide to pretend that you're your own guest of honor, and you've just prepared this beautiful meal for yourself. You make yourself a paper tiara and sit at the head of the table between two candles. Several times during the meal, you raise your glass and make toasts to yourself. You eat slowly, enjoying every bite and noticing the texture, color, and taste—after all, you're in a good position to appreciate it. At the end of the meal, you thank yourself for providing such splendid company.

4. Nurturing Your Inner Child on a Daily Basis

How do you go about caring for and nurturing your child within? Earlier in this chapter I talked about recognizing and meeting 25 basic human needs. Meeting these needs would certainly be a good start. If you were to meet all of those needs you would go a long way toward developing a healthy relationship with your inner child. The exercises described above for bringing out the inner child will also foster a closer and more supportive relationship with this important part of yourself. Beyond this, there are hundreds of small acts of self-nurturing that can serve to cultivate a more caring relationship with yourself and ultimately a much improved sense of self-worth. Just as you would offer small gestures of caring and nurturing to deepen your relationship with your spouse, child, or a friend you love, you can do the same for yourself. The list below suggests 51 small ways in which you can nurture yourself on a daily basis.

Self-Nurturing Activities

The following list has been very helpful to many of my clients who suffer from anxiety disorders or depression. By performing at least one or two items from the list every day, or anything else you find pleasurable, you will grow in the important skill of becoming a good parent to yourself. You have nothing to lose but your sense of insecurity and inadequacy—nothing to gain except increased self-esteem.

1. Take a warm bath

2. Have breakfast in bed

3. Take a sauna

4. Get a massage

5. Buy yourself a rose

6. Take a bubble bath

7. Go to a pet store and play with the animals

8. Walk on a scenic path in a park

9. Visit a zoo

10. Have a manicure or pedicure

11. Stop and smell some flowers

12. Wake up early and watch the sunrise

13. Watch the sunset

14. Relax with a good book and/or soothing music

15. Go rent a funny video

16. Play your favorite music and dance to it by yourself

17. Go to bed early

18. Sleep outside under the stars

19. Take a "mental health day off" from work

20. Fix a special dinner just for yourself and eat by candlelight

21. Go for a walk

22. Call a good friend—or several good friends

23. Go out to a fine restaurant just with yourself

24. Go to the beach

25. Take a scenic drive

26. Meditate

27. Buy new clothes

28. Browse in a book or record store for as long as you want

29. Buy yourself a cuddly stuffed animal and play with it

30. Write yourself a love letter and mail it

31. Ask a special person to nurture you (feed, cuddle, and/or read to you)

32. Buy yourself something special that you can afford

33. Go see a good film or show

34. Go to the park and feed the ducks, swing on the swings, and so on

35. Visit a museum or another interesting place

36. Give yourself more time than you need to accomplish whatever you're doing (let yourself dawdle)

37. Work on your favorite puzzle or puzzlebook

38. Go into a hot tub or jacuzzi

39. Record an affirmation tape

40. Write out an ideal scenario concerning a goal, then visualize it

41. Read an inspirational book

42. Write a letter to an old friend

43. Bake or cook something special

44. Go window shopping

45. Buy a meditation tape

46. Listen to a positive, motivational tape

47. Write in a special diary about your accomplishments

48. Apply fragrant lotion all over your body

49. Masturbate

50. Exercise

51. Sit and hold your favorite stuffed animal

Part II: Developing Support and Intimacy

While self-esteem is something we build within ourselves, much of our feeling of self-worth is determined by our significant personal relationships. Others cannot give you a feeling of adequacy and confidence, but their acceptance, respect, and validation of you can reaffirm and strengthen your own positive attitude and feelings about yourself. Self-love becomes narcissistic in isolation from others.

Let's consider four pathways to self-esteem that involve relationships with others:

1. Close friends and support

2. Intimacy

3. Boundaries

4. Assertiveness

Close Friends and Support

When surveys of human values have been done, many people rank close friends near the top, along with career, a happy family life, and health. Each of us needs a support system of at least two or three close friends in addition to our immediate family. A close friend is someone you can deeply trust and confide in. It is someone who comfortably accepts you as you are in all your moods, behaviors, and roles. And it is someone who will stand by you no matter what is happening in your life. A close friend allows you the opportunity to share your feelings and perceptions about your life outside your immediate family. Such a person can help bring out aspects of your personality that might not be expressed with your spouse, children, or parents. At least two or three close friends of this sort, whom you can confide in on a regular basis, are an essential part of an adequate support system. Such friends can help provide continuity in your life through times of great transition such as moving away from home, divorce, death of a family member, and so on.

How many close friends of the type just described do you have? If you don't have at least two, what could you do to cultivate such friendships?

Intimacy

While some people seem content to go through life with a few close friends, most of us seek a special relationship with one particular person. It is in intimate relationships that we open ourselves most deeply and have the chance to discover the most about ourselves. Such relationships help overcome a certain loneliness that most of us would eventually feel—no matter how self-sufficient and strong we may be—without intimacy. The sense of belonging that we gain from intimate relationships contributes substantially to our feelings of self-worth. I want to reemphasize, however, that self-worth cannot be derived entirely from someone else. A healthy intimate relationship simply reinforces your own self-acceptance, and belief in yourself.

Much has been written on the topic of intimacy and on what ingredients contribute to lasting intimate relationships. Some of the most important of these are listed below (not in any rank order):

1. Common interests, especially leisure-time and recreational interests. (A few differences in interests, though, can add some novelty and excitement.)

2. A sense of romance or "magic" between you and your partner. This is an intangible quality of attraction that goes well beyond the physical level. It's usually very strong and steady in the first three to six months of a relationship. The relationship then requires the ability to renew, refresh, or rediscover this magic as it matures.

3. You and your partner need to be well matched in your relative needs for togetherness versus independence. Conflict may arise if one of you has a much greater need for freedom and "space" than the other, or if one of you has a need for protection and coziness that the other doesn't want to provide. Some partners may hold a double standard—in other words, they're unwilling to allow you what they require for themselves (such as trust and freedom).

4. Mutual acceptance and support of each other's personal growth and change. It is well known that when only one person is growing in a relationship, or feels invalidated in their growth by the other, the relationship often ends.

5. Mutual acceptance of each other's faults and weaknesses. After the initial romantic months of a relationship are over, each partner must find enough good in the other to tolerate and accept the other's faults and weaknesses.

6. Regular expressions of affection and touching. An intimate relationship cannot be healthy without both partners being willing to overtly express affection. Nonsexual

expressions such as hugging and cuddling are just as important as a sound sexual relationship.

7. Sharing of feelings. Genuine closeness between two people requires emotional vulnerability and a willingness to open up and share your deepest feelings.

8. Good communication. Entire books and courses are devoted to this subject. While there are many different aspects to good communication, the two most important criteria are that

   - The partners are genuinely willing to listen to each other, and

   - Both are able to express their feelings and ask for what they want directly (as opposed to complaining, threatening, demanding, and otherwise attempting to manipulate the other to meet their needs).

9. A strong sense of mutual trust. Each person needs to feel that they can rely on the other. Each also trusts the other with their deepest feelings. A sense of trust does not come automatically; it needs to be built over time and maintained.

10. Common values and a larger sense of purpose. An intimate relationship has the best opportunity to be lasting when two people have common values in important areas of life such as friendships, education, religion, finances, sex, health, family life, and so on. The strongest relationships are usually bound by a common purpose that transcends the personal needs of each individual—for example, raising children, running a business, or commitment to a spiritual ideal.

How many of the above 10 characteristics are present in your intimate relationship? Are there any, in particular, that you would like to work on?

Boundaries

Just as important as intimacy is the need for each of us to maintain appropriate boundaries within both intimate and other relationships.

Boundaries simply mean that you know where you end and the other person begins. You don't define your identity in terms of the other person. And above all, you don't derive your sense of self-worth and self-authority by attempting to take care of, rescue, change, or control the other person. In the past few years the terms "women who love too much" and "co-dependency" have been used to define those people who, because they lack a solid, internal basis of self-worth, attempt to validate themselves through taking care of, rescuing, or simply pleasing another person. The classic case of this is the person who attempts to organize his or her life around "rescuing" an alcoholic or otherwise addicted spouse or close relative. But loss of boundaries can occur in any relationship where you attempt to gain self-worth and security by overextending yourself to take care of, control, rescue, or change someone else. Your own needs and feelings are set aside and discounted in the process. A good indication of loss of boundaries is spending more time talking or thinking about another's needs or problems than your own.

Two excellent books are recommended if you want to further explore boundary issues in your own relationships. In her best-selling book, *Women Who Love Too Much*, Robin

Norwood advocates the following steps in overcoming co-dependency in a close relationship:

1. Going for help—giving up the idea you can handle it alone

2. Making recovery from co-dependency your highest priority

3. Finding a support group of peers who understand the problem

4. Developing a personal spiritual life where you can let go of self-will and rely on a "Higher Power"

5. Learning to stop managing, controlling, or "running the life" of another or others you love

6. Learning to let go of playing the game of "rescuer" and/or "victim" with the other person

7. Facing and exploring your own personal problems and pain in depth

8. Cultivating yourself: developing a life of your own and pursuing your own interests

9. Becoming "selfish," not in the unhealthy sense of egoism but instead putting your well-being, your desires, your work, play, plans, and activities first instead of last

10. Sharing what you have learned with others

Another excellent book which carefully defines co-dependency and provides a series of steps for overcoming the problem is *Co-Dependent No More,* by Melody Beattie. Some of her recommendations include

1. Practicing "detachment"—letting go of obsessively worrying about someone else

2. Letting go of the need to control someone else—respecting that person enough to know that he or she can take responsibility for his or her own life

3. Taking care of yourself, which includes finishing up "unfinished business" from your own past and learning to nurture and cherish the needy, vulnerable child within

4. Improving communication—learning to state what you want and to say no

5. Dealing with anger—giving yourself permission to feel and express anger at loved ones when you need to

6. Discovering spirituality—finding and connecting with a Higher Power.

Is co-dependency an issue for you? Have you considered joining a support group which focuses on co-dependency issues, such as Al Anon or Co-Dependents Anonymous?

Assertiveness

Cultivating assertiveness is critical to self-esteem. If you're unable to clearly get across to others what you want or do not want, you will end up feeling frustrated, helpless, and powerless. If you do nothing else, the practice of assertive behavior in and of itself can increase your feeling of *self-respect*. Honoring your own needs with other people in an assertive manner also increases *their* respect for you, and quickly overcomes any tendency on their part to take advantage of you.

The concept of assertiveness, along with exercises for developing an assertive style of communication, are presented in Chapter 14 of this workbook.

Part III: Other Pathways to Self-Esteem

The first two parts of this chapter focused on taking care of your needs through honoring your inner child and developing support and intimacy in your relationships. In this final part, I want to emphasize four other pathways to self-esteem which involve different levels of your whole being (as described in Chapter 3):

Body: physical well-being and body-image

Feelings: emotional self-expression

Mind: positive self-talk and affirmations for self-esteem

Whole Self: personal goals and a sense of accomplishment

Although these areas have been considered elsewhere in this workbook, they are discussed briefly here for their relevance to self-esteem.

1. Physical Well-Being and Body Image

Physical health and a sense of personal wellness, vitality, and robustness comprise one of the most important foundations of self-esteem. It's often difficult to feel good about yourself when you're feeling physically weak, tired, or ill. Current evidence points to the role of physiological imbalances—often caused by stress—in the genesis of panic attacks, agoraphobia, generalized anxiety, and obsessive-compulsive disorder. Upgrading your physical well-being will have a direct impact on your particular problem with anxiety, as well as contribute substantially to your self-esteem. The chapters on relaxation, exercise, and nutrition relate directly to physical well-being. Reading them and putting into practice the suggestions and guidelines offered will go a long way toward upgrading your personal wellness. The questionnaire below is intended to give you an overview of how you are doing in this area.

Personal Wellness Questionnaire

1. Am I exercising for at least one-half hour three to five times per week?

2. Do I enjoy the exercise I do?

3. Do I give myself the opportunity to deeply relax each day through progressive muscle relaxation, visualization, meditation, or some other relaxation method?

4. Do I give myself at least one hour of "down time" or leisure time each day?

5. Do I manage my time so that I am not perpetually rushed?

6. Do I handle stress or do I feel that it has control of me?

7. Do I give myself solitary time for personal reflection?

8. Do I get at least seven hours of sleep every night?

9. Am I satisfied with the quality and quantity of my sleep?

10. Am I eating three solid meals each day, including a good-sized breakfast?

11. Am I minimizing my consumption of stress-producing foods (those containing caffeine, sugar, salt, or processed "junk" foods)?

12. Do I take vitamin supplements on a regular basis to augment my diet—such as a multiple vitamin tablet and extra vitamin B-complex and vitamin C when I'm under physical or emotional stress?

13. Do I like my living environment? Is the place where I live comfortable and relaxing?

14. Does smoking tobacco interfere with my physical well-being?

15. Does excessive use of alcohol or recreational drugs compromise my well-being?

16. Am I comfortable with my present weight? If not, what can I do about it?

17. Do I value my personal appearance through good hygiene, grooming, and dressing in a way that feels comfortable and attractive?

18. Do I like my body and the way I appear?

2. Emotional Self-Expression

When you're out of touch with your feelings, it's hard to know who you are. You tend to feel internally detached from yourself and often fearful. By identifying and expressing the full range of your feelings, you can become better acquainted with your unique needs, desires, and yearnings. Literally you begin to *feel* yourself—your whole self—rather than walking around in a cloud of worried thoughts, fantasies, and anticipations. Learning to own and express your feelings takes time, courage, and a willingness to be vulnerable in the presence of others whom you trust. If you haven't already, read Chapter 13 for suggestions on how to increase your awareness and ability to express your feelings. This is a very important pathway to self-esteem.

3. Self-Talk and Affirmations for Self-Esteem

What you tell yourself, and your beliefs about yourself, contribute in an obvious and literal way to your self-esteem. If you are feeling inadequate and powerless, it's very likely because you *believe* that you are. By the same token, you can raise your self-esteem *simply* by working on changing your self-talk and basic beliefs about yourself.

Exercises for identifying and altering your negative self-talk and mistaken beliefs have been presented in Chapters 9 and 10. At this point, I'll simply highlight certain parts of those chapters that are relevant to self-esteem. First, I want you to consider two types of self-talk which are most damaging to your self-worth. Second, we will look at the use of affirmations to overcome negative beliefs and assumptions about yourself.

Of the four types of self-talk described in Chapter 9—the Worrier, the Critic, the Victim, and the Perfectionist—the Critic and the Victim are the most potentially destructive to your self-esteem. Indeed, it has been my experience that people with low self-esteem invariably have a strong Critic, a strong Victim consciousness, or both. It's the Critic's specific function to talk you down into feeling inadequate, inferior, and incompetent. Then Victim self-talk may add insult to injury by telling you that you're hopeless and powerless.

First, go back to Chapter 9 and review the sections on "Types of Negative Self-Talk" and "What Are Your Subpersonalities Telling You?" with particular attention to the Critic and Victim. Complete the worksheets for countering the destructive self-talk of each of these subpersonalities, if you haven't already. Then use the *Daily Record of Dysfunctional Thoughts* (make several copies) to track the occurrence of negative self-statements from your Critic and Victim as they occur spontaneously during a two-week time period.

When you catch yourself engaging in self-critical or self-victimizing inner dialogues, follow these three steps:

1. *Disrupt* the chain of negative thoughts with some method that diverts your attention away from your mind and helps you to be more in touch with your feelings and body. Any of the following may work:

   - Physical activity—for example, household chores or exercise

   - Taking a walk outside

   - Abdominal breathing

   - Five minutes of progressive muscle relaxation

   - Shouting "Stop!" aloud or silently

   - Snapping a rubber band against your wrist

   The point is to do *something* that slows you down and gives you a bit of distance from your negative thoughts. It's difficult to counter negative self-talk when you're tense and your mind is racing.

2. *Challenge* your negative self-talk with appropriate questioning, if necessary. Good questions to raise with your Critic or Victim might be, "What's the evidence for this?" "Is this *always* true?" or "Am I looking at both (or all) sides of this issue?" Review the list of Socratic questions in Chapter 9 for other examples of questions.

3. *Counter* your negative inner dialogue with positive, self-supportive statements. You may want to design your own positive statements specifically tailored to refute your Critic's or Victim's statements one by one. Alternatively, you can draw positive counterstatements from the following list of affirmations.

Affirmations for Self-Esteem

What I Am

I am lovable and capable.

I fully accept and believe in myself just the way I am.

I am a unique and special person. There is no one else quite like me in the entire world.

I accept all the different parts of myself.

I'm already worthy as a person. I don't have to prove myself.

My feelings and needs are important.

It's O.K. to think about what I need.

It's good for me to take time for myself.

I have many good qualities.

I believe in my capabilities and value the unique talents I can offer the world.

I am a person of high integrity and sincere purpose.

I trust in my ability to succeed at my goals.

I am a valuable and important person, worthy of the respect of others.

Others perceive me as a good and likable person.

When other people really get to know me, they like me.

Other people like to be around me. They like to hear what I have to say and know what I think.

Others recognize that I have a lot to offer.

I deserve to be supported by those people who care for me.

I deserve the respect of others.

I trust and respect myself and am worthy of the respect of others.

I now receive assistance and cooperation from others.

I'm optimistic about life. I look forward to and enjoy new challenges.

I know what my values are and am confident of the decisions I make.

I easily accept compliments and praise from others.

I take pride in what I've accomplished and look forward to what I intend to achieve.

I believe in my ability to succeed.

I love myself just the way I am.

I don't have to be perfect to be loved.

The more I love myself, the more I am able to love others.

What I Am Learning

I am learning to love myself more every day.

I am learning to believe in my unique worth and capabilities.

I am learning to trust myself (and others).

I am learning to recognize and take care of my needs.

I am learning that my feelings and needs are just as important as anyone else's.

I am learning to ask others for what I need.

I am learning that it's O.K. to say no to others when I need to.

I am learning to take life one day at a time.

I am learning to approach my goals one day at a time.

I am learning to take better care of myself.

I am learning how to take more time for myself each day.

I am learning to let go of doubts and fear.

I am learning to let go of worry.

I am learning to let go of guilt (or shame).

I am learning that others respect and like me.

I am learning how to be more comfortable around others.

I am learning to feel more confident in _____.

(name situation)

I am learning that I have a right to _____.

(specify)

I am learning that it's O.K. to make mistakes.

I am learning that I don't have to be perfect to be loved.

I am learning to accept myself just the way I am.

There are several ways you might want to work with the above list. The chapter on mistaken beliefs contains a number of suggestions for working with affirmations. The following two methods have been especially popular with my clients:

1. Select your favorite affirmations from the list and write them down individually on 3x5 cards. Then read through the stack slowly and with feeling once or twice a day. Doing this while alternately looking at yourself in a mirror is an excellent idea. You may also want to reword each affirmation in the second person: "You are lovable and capable" (rather than "I am lovable and capable") when repeating the phrases to your mirror image.

2. Alternatively, you can put the affirmations on tape. Repeat each affirmation twice and leave about 5-10 seconds between different statements. Listen to the tape once a day when you feel relaxed and receptive. You are most likely to internalize affirmations when you focus your attention on them fully while in a relaxed state. (Note that you may wish to construct your own list of self-esteem affirmations, drawing on those which are most meaningful to you from the above list; or make up new ones of your own.)

4. A Sense of Accomplishment

Accomplishment of personal goals always adds to your self-esteem. If you look back over your life to the times when you felt most confident, you'll find that they often followed the accomplishment of important personal goals. Although external achievements can never be the *sole* basis of a sense of self-worth, they certainly contribute to how you feel about yourself.

If you are dealing with phobias or panic attacks, a most significant accomplishment is the ability to enter into and handle situations that you previously avoided. An even more unassailable sense of achievement is reached when, in addition to confronting phobic situations, you become confident that you can handle any panic reaction that might arise. The mastery of phobias and panic reactions is a main theme of this book and is dealt with in detail in Chapters 6, 7, and 8. Those of you who have fully recovered from agoraphobia, social phobias, or panic disorder through conscientiously facing the very things you feared most know how much self-confidence and inner strength there is to be gained. Facing your phobias (including the phobia of panic itself) through a process of gradual exposure will, *in and of itself*, add considerably to your self-esteem.

Beyond the important goal of overcoming phobias and panic, however, are all the other goals you might have in your life. Your sense of self-esteem depends on the feeling that you're making progress toward *all* of your goals. If you feel "stuck" and unable to move toward something important that you want, you may begin to doubt yourself and feel somewhat diminished.

Beyond the issue of recovery from phobias and panic, then, you might ask yourself two questions:

1. What are the most important things I want out of life—now and in the future?

2. What am I doing about these goals right now?

Let's consider each of these. To answer the first question you need to define what your goals are. If this is presently unclear, thinking about what you want in each of the areas below might help you to be more specific:

Physical Health	Friends
Psychological Well-Being	Career
Finances and Money	Education
Intimate Relationships	Personal Growth
Family	Recreation and Leisure
Living Environment	Spiritual Life

Give yourself some time—up to several days if necessary—to clarify what your most important goals are in these areas over the following time intervals: the next month, the next six months, the next year, and the next three years. You may find the *Life Purpose Questionnaire* in Chapter 19 to be helpful in making an exploration of your lifelong goals—the focus of the present section is on your more immediate goals.

Write down your most important goals for each time period, using the chart below. You may wish to talk with a close friend or perhaps a counselor to assist you with the process of clarifying your specific personal goals.

The second question involves honestly evaluating what steps you're currently taking—or not taking—toward attaining your immediate and longer-range goals. Are you genuinely working toward what you want? Or are you making excuses and setting up obstacles to the attainment of what you want? The popular phrase "taking responsibility for your life" simply means that you take full responsibility for working toward your own goals. Avoiding self-responsibility is to not do anything about what you want and/or to expect someone else to do it for you. Avoiding self-responsibility will guarantee that you'll have feelings of powerlessness, inadequacy, and even hopelessness. A sense of personal self-worth is dependent on taking responsibility for yourself.

My Most Important Personal Goals

For the next month:

For the next six months:

For the next year:

For the next three years:

What are some of the obstacles you might be putting in the way of going after what you want? *Fear* is the greatest impediment to doing something about your goals, just as it is in the case of overcoming phobias. If you don't see yourself moving toward what you want, ask whether you're letting any of the following fears get in your way:

- Fear of losing present security

- Fear of failure

- Fear of personal rejection or the disapproval of others

- Fear of succeeding (*then* what would I have to deal with!)

- Fear of your goal involving too much work

- Fear of your goal involving too much time

- Fear of your goal involving too much energy

- Fear that your goal is too unrealistic—for example, that others will discourage you

- Fear of change itself

The solution to any of these fears about taking action on your life goals is exactly the same as the solution to dealing with a phobia: *face the fear and go forward in small steps*. There is no way to eliminate some risk and discomfort, but breaking a goal down into sufficiently small steps (much like an exposure hierarchy) will enable you to go forward.

While fear is the biggest obstacle to moving forward on goals, guilt can also be an impediment. You may wish to consider whether any of the following beliefs are keeping you from seeking what you want:

"I'm not good enough to have _____."

"I don't deserve to have _____."

"No one in my family has ever done something like that before."

"Others won't approve if I go after _____."

"No one will accept this idea if I try to put it into practice."

The latter two beliefs really could have been listed under fears, but they also involve guilt. To overcome the feeling of not deserving to achieve your goal, I suggest that you work intensively with the simple affirmation "I deserve _____" or "I deserve to have _____." Don't be sparing in the use of repetition with this particular affirmation. Continue to work with it until you develop an emotional conviction that it is true. Developing the belief that you deserve what you truly want will add significantly to your self-esteem.

After you've worked through your specific obstacles to taking action on your goals, it's time to develop a plan of action. Just as you would with a desensitization hierarchy, break down your goal into a series of small steps. Remember that this is a long-range plan. As an option, you may wish to specify a timeframe for accomplishing each step. Be sure that you reward yourself after the accomplishment of each step, just as you would with a phobia hierarchy. You might ask family or friends for their support in your undertaking, much as you would rely on a support person in tackling a phobia.

For example, you might be feeling increasingly dissatisfied with your present line of work and would like to be doing something else. Yet you're not quite sure about what you want to do, let alone how to go about training for it. The broad goal of "getting into another line of work" might seem a bit overwhelming, taken as a whole. But if you break it down into component parts, it becomes more manageable:

1. Find a career counselor you respect (or take a course in exploring career options at a local college).

2. Explore different options by

   • Working with the counselor or taking an appropriate course
   • Reading about different vocations in books such as *What Color Is Your Parachute?* and the *Occupational Outlook Handbook*
   • Talking to people who hold positions in vocations you feel drawn to

3. Narrow down vocational options to one particular type of work (obtain whatever help you need to do this)—focus is extremely important in achieving goals.

4. Obtain education or training for the line of work you've chosen.

- Find out where training is available in your area (your local library is a good resource for doing your research)
- Apply to appropriate schools or training programs
- Apply for an educational grant or loan if your education or training will require a full-time commitment

5. Complete your education or training (if possible while maintaining your current job).

6. Search for an entry-level position in your new career.

- Obtain resources that tell you where jobs are available (professional or trade newsletters, journals, alumni organizations, newspapers, and job hot-lines are all good resources)
- Prepare a professional-looking resume
- Apply for jobs
- Go for interviews

7. Begin your new career.

Provided it's physically possible, you can make any major goal manageable by breaking it down into sufficiently small steps. Use the worksheet below to list specific steps you might take to progress toward an important personal goal. Make photocopies of the sheet if there is more than one goal you want to pursue. You may find that you can clarify specific steps more easily by talking about them with a friend or counselor.

The advantage of developing a plan of action is that you then have a "map" to follow in going after what you want; you can always refer to it as you monitor your progress or if you get stuck at any time along the way. If you have trouble with any particular step, you may need to investigate once again any fears or sense of guilt that you're putting in your way.

Taking personal responsibility for achieving the things you want most out of life—and making tangible progress toward obtaining them—will add greatly to your sense of self-esteem. An excellent book for getting started that I've often recommended to my clients is Susan Jeffers' *Feel the Fear and Do It Anyway*.

Plan of Action: Steps Toward My Goal

1. My goal (be as specific as possible): _____
_____
_____

2. What small step can I take right now to make some progress toward achieving this goal? _____
_____
_____

3. What other steps will I need to take to achieve this goal? (Estimate the time required to complete each step.)_____

_____
_____
_____
_____
_____
_____
_____
_____

Remembering Previous Accomplishments

In identifying goals for the future, it's important not to lose sight of what you've already accomplished in your life. It's common to forget about past attainments at those times when you're feeling dissatisfied with yourself. You can raise your self-esteem in a few minutes by thinking about your life and giving yourself credit for those goals you've already achieved.

The following exercise is designed to help you do this. Think about your entire life as you review each area and make a list of your accomplishments. Keep in mind that while it's gratifying to have external, "socially recognized" achievements, the most important attainments are more intangible and internal. What you've given to others (for example, love, assistance, or guidance) and the life lessons you've gained on the road to maturity and wisdom are ultimately your most important accomplishments.

List of Personal Accomplishments

For each of the following areas, list any accomplishments you've had up to the present. Use a separate sheet of paper if you need.

School

Work and Career

Home and Family (for example, raising a child or taking care of a sick in-law)

Athletics

Arts and Hobbies

Leadership

Prizes or Awards

Personal Growth and Self-Improvement

Charitable Activities

Intangibles Given to Others

Important Life Lessons Learned

Other

Summary of Things To Do

So many different strategies for raising your self-esteem have been presented in this chapter that it would be impractical to summarize each one of them here. The following worksheet is intended to help you organize what you've learned from this chapter and decide which particular strategies for building self-esteem you want to try out in the immediate future.

Strategies for Building Self-Esteem

Go back through the chapter and decide which of the following strategies you want to implement in raising your self-esteem over the next month. I recommend that you stick with no more than three or four strategies and devote at least one week to each. In the spaces provided below, or on a separate sheet of paper, write out specifically what actions you'll take with respect to each intervention. When you're finished, design your own "four-week self-esteem program" by writing down which strategy you'll work with over each of the next four weeks.

1. Identify no more than three or four needs from the list of needs mentioned earlier in this chapter that you'd like to give special attention to. Then take action to do

something about meeting those needs you've singled out. What specifically will you do?

2. Work on bringing out your inner child.

   a. Record and listen to the inner child visualization.

   b. Write a letter to your inner child.

   c. Carry around a photo of yourself as a child.

   d. Engage in playful activities that give expression to your inner child. What activities will you practice?

3. Work on redescribing negative feeling states as pleas for attention from your inner child. Describe examples of when you do this over a period of at least one week.

4. Do one or more things from the list of self-nurturing activities. What will you do for each day of a given week?

5. Work on building your support system. How will you specifically do this?

6. Work on cultivating or enhancing an intimate relationship (for example, spending quality time with your partner, taking a course in communication skills, attending a marriage encounter weekend). How will you do this?

7. Work on improving your understanding and ability to maintain appropriate boundaries (for example, read the suggested books by Robin Norwood and Melody Beattie, attend Al Anon or Co-dependents Anonymous meetings, attend a workshop on co-dependency). How will you specifically do this?

8. Learn and practice assertiveness skills (see Chapter 14). What specifically will you do?

9. Work on upgrading your personal wellness and body image (for example, implement relaxation, exercise, and nutritional improvements in your life—see Chapters 4, 5, and 16). What are you willing to do in the next month?

10. Work on identifying and expressing your feelings (see Chapter 13). What specifically will you do?

11. Counter negative self-talk of your Critic or Victim subpersonalities (use *The Daily Record of Dysfunctional Thoughts*, in Chapter 9).

12. Work with self-esteem affirmations by

    a. Writing one or two of them out several times each day, or

    b. Reading them daily from a list, or

    c. Putting them on a tape which you listen to daily.

    Which one will you do?

13. Define your important personal goals over the next month, six months, year, and three years using the goals worksheet in this chapter. Then take action on one or more goals. What specifically will you do?

14. List personal accomplishments you've achieved to date, using the worksheet in the previous section.

Four-Week Self-Esteem Program

Which of the above interventions will you implement over the next four weeks?

Week 1:

Week 2:

Week 3:

Week 4:

Further Reading

Beattie, Melody. *Co-dependent No More.* San Francisco: Harper/Hazelden, 1987.

Black, Claudia. *It Will Never Happen to Me.* New York: Ballantine, 1981.

Bradshaw, John. *Homecoming: Reclaiming and Championing Your Inner Child.* New York: Bantam, 1990.

Brandon, Nathaniel. *The Psychology of Self-Esteem.* New York: Nash, 1969.

Gravitz, Herbert L. and Bowden, Julie D. *Recovery: A Guide for Adult Children of Alcoholics.* New York: Simon & Schuster (Fireside), 1985.

Jeffers, Susan. *Feel the Fear and Do It Anyway.* San Diego: Harcourt, Brace, Jovanovich, 1987.

Mangini, Shirley. *Secrets of Self-Esteem.* Canoga Park, California: N.O.V.A. Corp., 1985.

Maslow, Abraham. *Toward a Psychology of Being.* Second edition. New York: Van Nostrand Reinhold, 1968.

McKay, Matthew, and Fanning, Patrick. *Self-Esteem.* Oakland, California: New Harbinger Publications, 1987.

Missildine, Hugh. *Your Inner Child of the Past.* New York: Simon & Schuster, 1963.

Norwood, Robin. *Women Who Love Too Much.* New York: Pocket Books, 1985.

Whitfield, Charles. *Healing the Child Within.* Pompano Beach, Florida: Health Communications, 1987.

Woititz, Janet. *Adult Children of Alcoholics.* Hollywood, Florida: Health Communications, 1983.

16

Nutrition

To date, relatively little has been written on the subject of nutrition and anxiety disorders. Yet if it is assumed that there is at least some biological basis for panic attacks and anxiety, the subject of nutrition becomes important. What you eat has a very direct and significant impact on your body's internal physiology and biochemistry.

In the last 15 years the relationship between diet, stress, and mood has been well documented. It's known that certain foods and substances tend to create additional stress and anxiety, while others promote a calmer and steadier mood. Certain natural substances have a directly calming effect and others are known to have an antidepressant effect. Many of you may not yet recognize connections between how you feel and what you eat. You simply may not notice that the amount of coffee or cola beverages you drink aggravates your anxiety level. Or you may be unaware of any connection between your consumption of sugar and anxiety, depression, or PMS symptoms. This chapter may clarify some of these connections and help you to make positive changes in the way you feel.

The discussion of nutrition in this chapter is divided into three broad sections:

- Foods, Substances, and Conditions That Aggravate Anxiety

- Dietary Guidelines for Reducing Anxiety

- Supplements for Reducing Anxiety

The information in these sections is based on my personal experience and reading in the field of nutrition. It is intended to be suggestive only—not prescriptive. If you wish to make an in-depth assessment and reevaluation of your diet, I recommend that you consult a nutritionist, or a physician who is knowledgeable about nutrition.

Substances That Aggravate Anxiety

Stimulants: Caffeine

Of all the dietary factors that can aggravate anxiety and trigger panic attacks, caffeine is the most notorious. Several of my clients can trace their first panic attack to an excessive intake of caffeine. Many people find that they feel calmer and sleep better after they've reduced their caffeine consumption. Caffeine has a directly stimulating effect on several different systems in your body. It increases the level of the neurotransmitter norepinephrine in your brain, causing you to feel alert and awake. It also produces the very same physiological arousal response that is triggered when you are subjected to stress—increased sympathetic nervous system activity and a release of adrenalin.

In short, too much caffeine can keep you in a chronically tense, aroused condition, leaving you more vulnerable to generalized anxiety as well as panic attacks. Caffeine further contributes to stress by causing a depletion of vitamin B$_1$ (Thiamine), which is one of the so-called anti-stress vitamins.

Caffeine is contained not only in coffee but in many types of tea, cola beverages, chocolate candy, cocoa, and over-the-counter drugs. Use the chart on the next page to determine your total daily caffeine consumption in milligrams.

If you are prone either to generalized anxiety or panic attacks, I suggest that you reduce your total caffeine consumption to *less than 100 mg/day*. For example, one cup of percolated coffee or two diet cola beverages a day would be a maximum. For coffee lovers this may seem like a major sacrifice, but you may be surprised to find how much better you feel if you can wean yourself down to a single cup in the morning. The sacrifice may well be worth having fewer panic attacks. For those people who are very sensitive to caffeine, less than 50 mg/day would be advisable.

Please note that there are tremendous individual differences in sensitivity to caffeine. As with any addictive drug, chronic caffeine consumption leads to increased tolerance and a potential for withdrawal symptoms. If you have been drinking five cups of coffee a day and abruptly cut down to one a day, you may have withdrawal reactions including fatigue, depression, and headaches. It's better to taper off gradually over a period of several months—for example, from five cups to four cups per day for a month, then two or three cups per day for the next month, and so on. Some people like to substitute decaffeinated coffee, which has about 3 mg of caffeine per cup, while others substitute herbal teas. At the opposite extreme of the sensitivity continuum are people who are made jittery by a single cola or cup of tea. Some of my clients have found that even small amounts of caffeine predispose them to panic or a sleepless night. So it's important that you experiment to find out what *your own optimal* daily caffeine intake might be. For most people prone to anxiety or panic, this turns out to be less than 100 mg/day.

Nicotine

Nicotine is as strong a stimulant as caffeine. It stimulates increased physiological arousal, vasoconstriction, and makes your heart work harder. Smokers often object to this notion and claim that having a cigarette tends to "calm their nerves." Research has proven, however, that smokers tend to be more anxious than nonsmokers, even when there are no differences in their intake of other stimulants, such as coffee and over-the-counter drugs. They also tend to sleep less well than nonsmokers. I have found that smokers, after quitting, not only feel healthier and more vital but are less prone to anxiety states and panic. In short, if you presently smoke, here is one more reason for stopping.

Caffeine Chart

Coffee	_____cups	@_____mg =	_____mg
Tea	_____cups	@_____mg =	_____mg
Cola drinks	_____cups	@_____mg =	_____mg
Over-the-counter drugs	_____tablets	@_____mg =	_____mg
Other sources			

(chocolate 25 mg per bar, cocoa 13 mg per cup) _____

Daily Total   _____mg

Caffeine content of coffee, tea, and cocoa (milligrams per cup)
Coffee, instant . . . . .66 mg
Coffee, percolated . . . . .110 mg
Coffee, drip . . . . .146 mg
Teabag—5 minute brew . . . . .46 mg
Teabag—1 minute brew . . . . .28 mg
Loose tea—5 minute brew . . . . .40 mg
Cocoa . . . . .13 mg
Decaffeinated Coffee . . . . .4 mg

Caffeine content of cola beverages (milligrams per 12-ounce can)
Coca-Cola . . . . .65 mg
Dr. Pepper . . . . .61 mg
Mountain Dew . . . . .55 mg
Diet Dr. Pepper . . . . .54 mg
TAB . . . . .49 mg
Pepsi-Cola . . . . .43 mg

Caffeine content of over-the-counter drugs (per tablet)
Anacin . . . . .32 mg
Caffedrine . . . . .200 mg
Empirin . . . . .32 mg
Excedrin . . . . .65 mg
No-Doz . . . . .100 mg
Pre-mens Forte . . . . .100 mg
Vanquish . . . . .33 mg
Vivarin . . . . .200 mg

Stimulant Drugs

Over-the-counter drugs containing caffeine have already been mentioned. In addition to these medicines, you should be aware of prescription drugs that contain amphetamines, including Benzedrine, Dexedrine, Methedrine, and Ritalin. While these drugs used to be widely prescribed as appetite suppressants as well as antidepressants, they are rarely used today. Being strong stimulants, they are risky to use if you have a history of anxiety or panic attacks. The same is especially true for cocaine, whose recreational use has reached epidemic proportions in recent times. Cocaine use has been the initial cause of recurring panic attacks in countless people, including four whom I've treated personally. If you are at all concerned about panic, this is definitely a drug to avoid.

Substances That Stress the Body: Salt

Excessive salt (sodium chloride) stresses the body in two ways: 1) it can deplete your body of potassium, a mineral that's important to the proper functioning of the nervous system and 2) it raises blood pressure, putting extra strain on your heart and arteries and hastening arteriosclerosis. You can reduce the amount of salt you consume by avoiding the use of table salt, using a natural salt substitute (such as tamari) both in cooking and on the table, and limiting salty meats, salty snack foods, and other processed foods containing salt as much as possible. As a rule of thumb, it's good to limit your salt intake to one gram or teaspoon per day. If you must buy processed foods, choose those which are labeled "low sodium" or "salt free."

Preservatives

There are presently about 5,000 chemical additives used in commercial food processing. Common artificial preservatives include nitrites, nitrates, potassium bisulfite, monosodium glutamate (MSG), BHT, BHA, and artificial colorings and flavorings. Our bodies are simply not equipped to handle these artificial substances and, in most cases, very little is known about their long-term biological effects. To date, some that have been thoroughly tested have been found to be carcinogenic and thus have been removed from the market. Others currently in use, especially monosodium glutamate, nitrites, and nitrates, produce allergic reactions in many people. It is known that traditional societies which eat strictly whole foods without additives have a very low incidence of degenerative diseases such as cancer. You should try to eat whole, unprocessed foods as much as possible—the foods your body was designed to handle. Try to purchase vegetables and fruits that haven't been treated with pesticides (organically grown) if these are available in your area.

Hormones in Meat

Red meat, pork, and most commercially available forms of chicken are derived from animals that have been fed hormones to promote fast weight gain and growth. There is evidence that such hormones stress these animals (steers and hogs sometimes die of heart attacks on the loading platform). While there is at present no conclusive evidence, many people believe that these hormones might also have harmful effects for the human consumers of meat and meat products. One particular hormone, diethylstilbestrol (DES), has come to the public's attention because it has been implicated in the development of breast cancer and fibroid tumors.

Try to reduce your consumption of red meat, pork, and commercially available poultry, replacing it with organically raised beef, poultry, and fish such as cod, halibut, salmon, snapper, sole, trout, or turbot.

Stressful Eating Habits

Stress and anxiety can be aggravated not only by what you eat but by the *way* you eat. In our modern, fast-paced society, many of us simply do not give ourselves enough time for eating. Any of the following habits can aggravate your daily level of stress:

- Eating too fast or on the run

- Not chewing food at least 15-20 times per mouthful (food must be partially predigested in your mouth to be adequately digested later)

- Eating too much, to the point of feeling "stuffed" or bloated

- Drinking too much fluid with a meal, which can dilute stomach acid and digestive enzymes: one cup of fluid with a meal is sufficient

All of the above put a strain on your stomach and intestines in their attempt to properly digest and assimilate food. This adds to your stress level in two ways:

- Directly, through indigestion, bloating, and cramping

- Indirectly, through *malabsorption* of essential nutrients

If food is not properly digested in your mouth and stomach, much of it will pass undigested through your intestines and will subsequently putrify and ferment—causing bloating, cramps, and gas. The result is that you will get only a limited portion of the nutrition potentially available in your food, leading to a subtle form of undernourishment that you're not likely to be aware of.

So—in addition to reconsidering what you eat, you can decrease stress and a probable malabsorption problem by giving yourself adequate time to eat, chewing your food thoroughly, and not overtaxing your body by eating excessive amounts.

Sugar, Hypoglycemia, and Anxiety

Among nutritionally conscious people these days, sugar has become somewhat of a dirty word. The fact is, however, that your body and brain need glucose—or naturally occurring sugar—in order to operate. Glucose is the "fuel" your body burns; it provides the energy which sustains life. Much of this glucose is derived from carbohydrate foods in your diet such as bread, cereal, potatoes, vegetables, fruits, pasta, and so on. The starches in these foods are broken down *gradually* into glucose.

Simple sugars, on the other hand, such as refined white sugar, brown sugar, and honey, break down very quickly into glucose. These simple sugars can cause problems because they tend to overload your system with too much sugar too quickly. Our bodies are simply not equipped to process large amounts of sugar rapidly, and, in fact, it was not until the twentieth century that most of us (other than the very wealthy) consumed large amounts of refined sugar. Today, the standard American diet includes white sugar in most beverages (coffee, tea, cola), sugar in cereal, sugar in salad dressings, sugar in processed meat, along with one or two desserts per day and perhaps a donut or a cookie on coffee breaks. In fact, the average American consumes about *120 pounds* of sugar per year! The result of continually bombarding the body with this much sugar is the creation of a chronic disregulation in sugar metabolism. For some people this disregulation can lead to excessively high levels of blood sugar, or diabetes (whose prevalence has increased dramatically in this century). For an even larger number of individuals, the problem is just the opposite—periodic drops in blood sugar level *below* normal, a condition that is popularly termed *hypoglycemia*.

The symptoms of hypoglycemia tend to appear when your blood sugar drops below 50-60 milligrams per milliliter—or when it drops very rapidly from a higher to a lower level. Typically this occurs about two to three hours after eating a meal. It can also occur *simply in response to stress,* since your body burns up sugar very rapidly under stress. The most common subjective symptoms of hypoglycemia are

- Light-headedness

- Anxiety

- Trembling

- Feelings of unsteadiness or weakness

- Irritability

- Palpitations

Do the symptoms look familiar? All of them are symptoms that can accompany a panic attack! In fact, for *some* people panic reactions may actually be caused by hypoglycemia. Generally such people recover from panic simply by having something to eat. Their blood sugar rises and they feel better. (In fact, an informal, nonclinical way to diagnose hypoglycemia is to determine whether you have any of the above symptoms three or four hours after a meal, and whether they then go away as soon as you have something to eat.)

The majority of people with panic disorder or agoraphobia find that their panic reactions do *not* necessarily correlate with bouts of low blood sugar. Yet hypoglycemia can aggravate both generalized anxiety and panic attacks which have been caused for other reasons.

What causes blood sugar to fall below normal is an excessive release of insulin by the pancreas. Insulin is a hormone that causes sugar in the bloodstream to be taken up by the cells. (Insulin is used in the treatment of diabetes to lower excessive blood sugar levels.) In hypoglycemia the pancreas tends to overshoot in its production of insulin. This can happen if you ingest too much sugar, with the result that you feel a temporary "sugar high" followed half an hour later by a crash. This can also happen in response to sudden or chronic stress. Stress can cause a rapid depletion of blood sugar. You then experience confusion, anxiety, spaciness, and tremulousness because 1) your brain is not getting enough sugar *and* 2) a secondary stress response occurs. When blood sugar falls too low, your adrenal glands kick in and release adrenalin and cortisol, which causes you to feel more anxious and aroused and also has the specific purpose of causing your liver to release stored sugar in order to bring your blood sugar level back to normal. So the subjective symptoms of hypoglycemia arise *both* from a deficit of blood sugar *and* a secondary stress response mediated by the adrenal glands.

Hypoglycemia can be formally diagnosed through a clinical test called the 6-hour glucose tolerance test. After a 12-hour fast you drink a highly concentrated sugar solution. Your blood sugar is then measured at half-hour intervals over a 6-hour period. You will likely get a positive result on this test if you have a moderate to severe problem with hypoglycemia. Unfortunately, many *milder* cases of hypoglycemia are missed by the test. It's quite possible to have subjective symptoms of low blood sugar and test negative on a glucose tolerance test. Any of the following subjective symptoms are suggestive of hypoglycemia:

- You feel anxious, light-headed, weak, or irritable several hours after a meal (or in the middle of the night); these symptoms disappear within a few minutes of eating.

- You get a "high" feeling from consuming sugar and this changes to a depressed, irritable, or "spacey" feeling 20-30 minutes later.

- You experience anxiety, restlessness, or even palpitations and panic in the early morning hours, between 4:00 and 7:00 a.m. (Your blood sugar is lowest in the early morning because you have fasted all night.)

How do you deal with hypoglycemia? Fortunately, it's quite possible to overcome problems with low blood sugar by 1) making several significant dietary changes and 2) taking certain supplements. If you suspect that you have hypoglycemia or have had it formally diagnosed, you may want to implement the following guidelines. Doing so may result in a calmer disposition—less generalized anxiety, less emotional volatility, and less vulnerability to panic. You may also notice that you are less prone to depression and mood swings.

Dietary Modifications for Hypoglycemia

1. Eliminate as much as possible all types of simple sugar from your diet. This includes foods that obviously contain white sugar, such as candy, ice cream, desserts, Coke or Pepsi. It also includes subtler forms of sugar, such as honey, corn syrup, corn sweeteners, molasses, and "high fructose." Be sure to read labels on any and all processed foods to detect these various forms of sugar.

2. Substitute fruits (other than dried fruits, which are too concentrated in sugar) for sweets. Avoid fruit juices or dilute them 1:1 with water.

3. Reduce or eliminate simple starches such as pasta, refined cereals, potato chips, and white bread. Substitute instead "complex" carbohydrates such as whole grain breads and cereals, vegetables, and brown rice or other whole grains.

4. Have a complex carbohydrate or protein snack (nuts, whole grain toast and cheese, for example) halfway between meals—around 10:30–11:00 in the morning and especially around 4:00–5:00 in the afternoon. If you awaken early in the morning at 4:00 or 5:00, you may also find that a small snack will help you to get back to sleep for a couple of hours. As an alternative to snacks between meals, you can try having four or five small meals per day no more than two to three hours apart. The point of either of these alternatives is to maintain a steadier blood sugar level.

Supplements

1. Vitamin B-complex: 50-100 mg of all 11 B vitamins once per day with meals.

2. Vitamin C: 1,000 mg once or twice per day with meals.

3. Organic Trivalent Chromium (often called *glucose tolerance factor*): 200 mcg per day. This is available at your local health-food store.

4. A combination of "glycogenic" amino acids (including L-Glycine, L-Glutamic Acid, L-Tyrosine, L-Leucine, L-Alanine, L-Methionine, L-Lysine). These combinations are available at many health-food stores under the name of *hypoglycemia balancer* or *glycemic factors*. Take it as recommended either on the bottle or by a qualified nutritionist.

Vitamin B-complex and vitamin C help to increase your resiliency to stress, which can aggravate blood sugar swings. The B vitamins also help regulate the metabolic processes which convert carbohydrates to sugar in your body.

Trivalent chromium and the glycogenic amino acids have a direct, stabilizing effect on your blood sugar level.

If you're interested in exploring the subject of hypoglycemia in greater depth, you might want to read the following books:

Sugar Blues by William Dufty
Hypoglycemia: A Better Approach by Paavo Airola
Low Blood Sugar and You by Carlton Fredericks

Food Allergies and Anxiety

An allergic reaction occurs when the body attempts to resist the intrusion of a foreign substance. For some people, certain foods affect the body like a foreign substance, not only causing classic allergic symptoms such as runny nose, mucous, and sneezing but a host of psychological or psychosomatic symptoms, including any of the following:

- Anxiety or panic

- Depression or mood swings

- Dizziness

- Irritability

- Insomnia

- Headaches

- Confusion and disorientation

- Fatigue

Such reactions occur in many individuals only when they eat an excessive amount of a particular food, a combination of offending foods, or have excessively low resistance due to a cold or infection. Other people are so highly sensitive that only a small amount of the wrong food can cause debilitating symptoms. Often the subtler, psychological symptoms have a delayed onset, making it difficult to connect them with the offending foods.

In our culture the two most common foods causing allergic reactions are milk or dairy products and wheat. It is casein in milk and gluten in wheat that tend to cause problems. Other foods that can be a source of allergic response include alcohol, chocolate, citrus fruits, corn, eggs, garlic, peanuts, yeast, shellfish, soy products, or tomatoes. One of the most telling signs of food allergy is addiction. You tend to crave and are addicted to the very foods you are allergic to! While chocolate is the most flagrant example of this, you might also take pause if you find yourself tending to crave bread (wheat), dairy products, or another specific type of food. Many people go for years without recognizing that the very foods they crave the most have a subtle but toxic effect on their mood and well-being.

How can you find out whether food allergies are aggravating your problems with anxiety? As in the case of hypoglycemia, there are both formal tests you can obtain from a nutritionally oriented doctor as well as informal tests you can conduct on your own.

Among formal clinical tests for food allergies, the RAST test (Radio Allergo Sorbent Test) is probably the most reliable. This is a blood test which measures the presence of antibodies to a wide range of foods. Elevated levels of antibodies to specific foods in your blood suggest that you are allergic to those foods. Although expensive, the RAST test provides a detailed profile of all of the foods to which you're allergic, and can be a very helpful diagnostic tool.

A less formal and expensive way to assess food allergies is to conduct your own "elimination" tests. If you want to determine whether you are allergic to wheat, simply eliminate all products containing wheat from your diet for two weeks and notice whether you feel better. Then, at the end of the two weeks, suddenly eat a large amount of wheat and carefully monitor any symptoms which appear in the next few hours. After trying out wheat, you might want to try out milk and milk products. It's important to experiment with only one potentially allergic type of food at a time so that you don't confound your results.

It's also a good idea to keep a diary of symptoms comparing how you feel before, during, and following the elimination of a particular food type. Many people feel worse immediately after they eliminate a food for a few days, as though their body is going through withdrawal symptoms. This is a telltale sign of food allergy. In severe cases, such withdrawal symptoms may persist for several weeks, and the period for eliminating the food may need to be lengthened. If this happens, I suggest that you consult a nutritionist to assist you in conducting elimination tests.

An alternative way to test for food allergies is to take your pulse after eating a meal. If it is elevated more than 10 beats per minute above your normal rate, it's likely that you ate something you're allergic to.

The good news is that you do not have to permanently abstain from a food to which you are allergic. After a period of several months away from a food, it is possible to eat it again occasionally without adverse effects. For example, instead of having bread at almost every meal, you'll find that you feel better having it only two or three times per week.

Food allergies can definitely be a contributing factor to excessive anxiety and mood swings for certain people. If you suspect this to be a problem, try experimenting with the elimination method and/or consult a qualified nutritionist.

A more detailed discussion of the relationship between food allergies and anxiety is contained in Chapters 3 and 4 of the book *No More Fears* by Dr. Douglas Hunt. For more information on how to conduct your own elimination tests for food allergies, see the book *Dr. Mandell's Five-Day Allergy Relief System* by Marshall Mandell.

Note

Although the emphasis of this section has been on food allergies, some people have allergic symptoms to other environmental substances, both organic and inorganic, which can precipitate a host of psychological symptoms *including anxiety and panic.*

Offending substances can include food preservatives, natural gas, synthetic fabrics, household cleaners and detergents, hydrocarbons in smog, gasoline fumes, insect sprays, molds, newspaper print, kerosene, turpentine, tar or asphalt, asbestos, typewriter ribbons, cosmetics, lipstick, mascara, shampoos, perfumes, colognes, and hair sprays, to name a few. If you suspect that you might be chemically sensitive to any of these substances, you might want to consult an allergy specialist with a background in the relatively new field of clinical ecology.

Move Your Diet in the Direction of Vegetarianism

It has been frequently observed that people who eat vegetarian diets tend to be somewhat calmer and easier going than their meat-eating counterparts. It might be argued that low stress, "laid back" types of persons are more attracted to vegetarianism in the first place. However, impressions from clients and personal experience suggest otherwise. A dietary change toward vegetarianism can definitely promote a calmer, less anxiety-prone disposition.

If you're used to eating meat, dairy, cheese, and egg products, it is not necessary—or even advisable—to give up *all* sources of animal protein from your diet. Giving up red meat alone, for example—or restricting your consumption of cow's milk (and using soy or rice milk instead)—can have a noticeable and beneficial effect.

How can vegetarianism lead to a calmer disposition? Earlier in this chapter it was mentioned that steroid hormone residues in red meat can exert an effect not unlike the body's own steroid hormones, activating natural defenses against stress and suppressing immunity. Another reason, however, is that meat, poultry, dairy and cheese products, and eggs—along with sugar and refined flour products—are all *acid-forming* foods. These foods are not necessarily acid in composition, but they leave an acid residue in the body after they are metabolized, making the body itself more acid. This can create two kinds of problems:

When the body is more acid, the transit time of food through the digestive tract can increase to the point where vitamins and minerals are not adequately assimilated. This selective underabsorption of vitamins—especially B vitamins, vitamin C, and minerals—can subtly add to the body's stress load and eventually lead to low-grade malnutrition. Taking supplements will not necessarily correct this condition unless you are able to adequately digest and absorb *them.*

Acid-forming foods, especially meats, can create metabolic breakdown products which are congestive to the body. This is especially true if you are already under stress and unable to properly digest protein foods. The result is that you tend to end up feeling more sluggish, tired, and may have excess mucous or sinus problems. Although it's true that this congestion is not exactly the same thing as anxiety, it can certainly add stress to the body, which in turn aggravates tension and anxiety. The more free your body is from congestion due to acid-forming foods, the lighter and clearer-headed you'll be likely to feel. Be aware, also, that many medications have an acid reaction in the body and may lead to the same types of problems as acid-forming foods.

To maintain a proper acid-alkaline balance in the body, it helps to decrease consumption of acid-forming foods—most animal-based foods, sugar, and refined flour products—and increase the amount of alkaline-forming foods in your diet. Prominent among alkaline foods are all vegetables; most fruits, except plums and prunes; whole grains such as brown rice, millet, and buckwheat; and bean sprouts. Ideally, about 70 percent of the calories you consume should come from these foods—although in the winter it is okay to eat a slightly higher percentage of animal proteins. Try including more of the alkaline foods in your diet and see if it makes a difference in the way you feel.

Low Stress/Anxiety Dietary Guidelines

As with the rest of the information in this chapter, the following guidelines are intended to be suggestive rather than prescriptive. I've developed them out of my reading in the field of nutrition and after several years of personal experimentation with my own diet. These guidelines are not intended to take the place of a detailed dietary assessment, recommendations, and meal plan devised by a competent nutritionist, dietician, or nutritionally oriented physician. Although all of the guidelines below are important, they are listed in order of their direct relevance to anxiety reduction.

1. Eliminate as far as possible the stimulants and stress-inducing substances described in the first section of this chapter—caffeine, nicotine, other stimulants, salt (down to one gram or teaspoon per day), and preservatives. (Caffeine and nicotine are the most critical for reducing anxiety.)

2. Eliminate or reduce to a minimum your consumption of refined sugar, brown sugar, honey, sucrose, dextrose, and other sweeteners such as corn syrup, corn sweeteners, and high fructose. Replace desserts, sugary beverages, and sweet snacks with fresh fruit and sugar-free beverages. Moderate alcohol consumption, since your body converts alcohol to sugar.

3. Reduce or eliminate refined and processed foods from your diet as much as possible. Replace with whole and fresh foods (preferably organic).

4. Eliminate or reduce to a minimum any food that you establish as an allergen.

5. Reduce consumption of red meat as well as poultry containing steroid hormones and other chemicals. Replace these with organic poultry and/or seafood (fish such as halibut, salmon, snapper, sole, trout, and turbot are recommended).

6. Increase your intake of dietary fiber by eating foods such as whole grains, brans, and raw vegetables. (Note, though, that too much fiber can cause gas and bloating and interfere with the body's ability to absorb protein.)

7. Drink the equivalent of at least six 8-oz. glasses of bottled spring water or purified water per day.

8. Increase your intake of raw, fresh vegetables. A mixed-vegetable salad every day is an excellent idea.

9. Include one fresh (not frozen or canned) cooked vegetable in your diet each day.

10. Reduce animal fat and cholesterol-containing foods such as red meat, organ meats, gravy, cheeses, butter, eggs, whole milk, and shellfish to no more than 15 percent of the food you eat. Polyunsaturated vegetable-based fats contained in cooking and salad oils should also be taken in moderation. Monounsaturated oils such as unrefined olive oil are preferred.

11. To avoid excessive weight gain, consume only as much energy (calories) as you expend. Decrease caloric intake and increase exercise if you're already overweight.

12. Select foods from the four major food groups: 1) fruits and vegetables (four to five servings daily); 2) whole grains, including whole-grain rice, cereals, and whole-grain breads (three to four servings daily); 3) animal proteins, emphasizing organic poultry, seafoods, and eggs or legume equivalents if you are vegetarian (two to three servings daily), and 4) dairy products, emphasizing low-fat or nonfat dairy products (one or two servings daily). Your diet should emphasize the first two categories and only modest amounts of the latter two. In general, it's a good idea to move your diet in the direction of vegetarianism and away from excess consumption of animal-based foods. Protein should make up approximately 15-20 percent of what you eat, fat 15-20 percent (or less if your cholesterol is above 220), and complex carbohydrates about 60-70 percent.

Use the Food Diary on the next page to monitor what you eat for at least three days. In what ways might you improve your dietary habits? What would you actually be willing to change in the next month?

Supplements for Anxiety and Stress

B Vitamins* and Vitamin C

It is widely known that during times of stress your body tends to rapidly deplete stores of B vitamins and vitamin C. I recommend to all of my clients that they take a high-potency B-complex vitamin and a high dose of vitamin C every day. Many of them find that doing so makes a noticeable difference in their energy level and resiliency to stress. The B vitamins are necessary to help maintain the proper functioning of the nervous system. Deficiencies especially of vitamin B_1, B_2, B_6, and B_{12} can lead to anxiety,

---

* B vitamins include: thiamine (B1), riboflavin (B2), niacin or niacinamide (B3), pantothenic acid (B5), pyridoxine (B6), biotin, folic acid, choline, inositol, cyanocobalamin (B12), and PABA (para amino benzoic acid).

Food Diary

Instructions: Use the following chart to evaluate your eating habits for three days. The areas in which your average daily consumption varies the most from the ideal are the areas in which you can make the greatest improvement in what you eat. Make copies of this form so that you can track your diet for one or two weeks.

For three days, keep track of how many servings you have of each of these food categories. For each category, divide the total servings by three to get your daily average for the period. Compare your eating pattern to the ideal.					
Week of:_____ dates	Day one servings	Day two servings	Day three servings	Average servings per day	Ideal servings per day
Caffeine serving = 1 cup coffee or black tea, or caffeinated cola beverage					**0**
Fats and sweets serving = 1 candy bar, 2 tbs. salad dressing, 1 cup ice cream, 1 order french fries					**0**
Alcohol serving = 1 beer, 1 glass of wine, or cocktail					**0-1**
Vegetables and fruits serving = 1/2 cup, 1 apple, 1 orange, medium potato					**4-5**
Breads and cereal serving = 1 slice of bread, 3/4 cup cereal					**3-4**
Milk, cheese, yogurt serving = 1 cup milk, 1 medium slice cheese					**1-2**
Meat, poultry, fish, eggs, beans, and nuts serving = 3 oz. lean meat, two eggs, 1-1/4 cup cooked beans, 4 tbs. peanut butter, 3/4 cup nuts					**2-3**

irritability, restlessness, fatigue, and even emotional instability. It's best to take all 11 of the B vitamins together in a "B-complex" supplement, since they tend to work together synergistically. Vitamin C is well known for enhancing the immune system and promoting healing from infection, disease, and injury. Less well known is the fact that vitamin C helps to support the adrenal glands, whose proper functioning is necessary to your ability to cope with stress. Vitamin B5 (pantothenic acid) also supports the adrenal glands, and many people find that it is helpful in dealing with excess stress. (A high dose—such as 1,000 mg—of B5 actually has a calming effect for many individuals.)

Based on personal experience and work with clients, I would suggest that you try a B-complex and vitamin C in the following doses on a regular basis:

- B-complex: 50-100 mg of all 11 B vitamins once a day (twice a day under high stress).

- Vitamin C: 1,000 mg in a time-release form, twice a day (double this dose under high stress). Vitamin C in combination with bioflavonoids is preferred.

When under unusual stress, it is also a good idea to take extra B5 (pantothenic acid). Up to 1,000 mg in a time-release form may be needed to help mitigate the effects of pronounced anxiety and stress.

Please note that it is not possible to overdose on B vitamins, since they are water soluble. The one exception to this is vitamin B6. It is important not to exceed 100 mg/day if you're taking B6 on a long-term basis. (Higher doses of B6 may be taken on a short-term basis to relieve premenstrual symptoms, however.) High daily doses of Vitamin C are generally harmless and a good hedge against infections and colds. However, repeated daily doses in *excess of 8,000 mg/day* have been associated with stomach complaints and even kidney stones in some people.

It's important that you take B vitamins, vitamin C, and other vitamins *with meals.* Stomach acids and enzymes produced while digesting food are necessary to help break down and assimilate vitamins. Do *not* take vitamins on an empty stomach (with the exception of amino acids, as discussed in the following section). Capsule forms of vitamins are probably easier on the stomach than tablets.

Calcium

It is widely known that calcium can act as a tranquilizer, having a calming effect on the nervous system. Calcium, along with neurotransmitter substances, is involved in the process of transmitting nerve signals across the synapse between nerve cells. Depletion of calcium can result in nerve cell overactivity, which may be one of the underlying physiological bases of anxiety. It's important that you get at least 1,000 mg of calcium per day, either in calcium-rich foods such as dairy products, eggs, and leafy vegetables or by taking calcium supplements (chelates are preferred to calcium carbonate). If you take a calcium supplement, be sure to take it in combination with magnesium, as these two minerals balance each other and work in tandem. For some people, magnesium can have a relaxing effect equal to that of calcium. In your supplement, the ratio of calcium to magnesium should be either 2-to-1 or 1-to-1. You may also want to try taking liquid calcium-magnesium, available in most health-food stores, as a natural tranquilizer.

Note

You may want to have your nutritionist or doctor perform a hair analysis test if you are concerned about having a deficiency of calcium or other minerals. Utilizing a hair sample, the test detects deficiencies of a large number of different minerals. The presence of certain mineral deficiencies can be used to detect other conditions. For example, too little chromium suggests a problem in carbohydrate metabolism and possible hypoglycemia. Too little cobalt suggests a possible vitamin B_{12} deficiency. The test can also detect *excesses* of toxic metals such as aluminum, lead, or mercury in your body. High levels of mercury, in particular, have been associated with anxiety as well as xenophobia (an abnormal fear or dread of strangers).

Amino Acids

In the past few years, amino acids, which are the natural constituents of protein, have increasingly come into use in the treatment of both anxiety disorders and depression. Many people prefer them to prescription drugs because they have fewer side effects and are nonaddictive. You may wish to talk to a qualified nutritionist or the staff at your local health-food store to expand on the information presented below.

Tryptophan

Up until November 1989, many people found L-Tryptophan helpful as a natural relaxer, antidepressant, and sleep aid. Tryptophan has an effect similar to such antidepressant medications as Prozac, Zoloft, and Paxil: it increases levels of serotonin in the brain. Unlike the prescription antidepressant medications, however, tryptophan has few side effects. This is because it is converted directly into serotonin, while the antidepressant medications work by blocking the reuptake of serotonin at the synapses between neurons in the brain.

In November 1989, L-Tryptophan was removed from the market because it was linked to a rare but serious blood disease: eosinophilia myalgia. Over 3,000 cases of the disease occurred in the United States, with several hundred people suffering partial paralysis, and over 30 dying. Many people wondered how tryptophan, an amino acid, could cause such a serious and devastating problem, especially since it had been widely used for over 10 years prior to 1989. What was found was that all the tryptophan that caused the eosinophilia myalgia could be traced to a single manufacturer. Apparently an error occurred in this company's manufacturing process that caused a double tryptophan molecule (a molecular "diamer") to be formed. In susceptible individuals, this double molecule produced a severe allergic reaction, which caused the immune systems of these individuals to produce vast numbers of eosinophils, a type of white blood cell. When these eosinophils were deposited in the muscles of the people taking this tryptophan, the disease occurred.

L-Tryptophan has never been reintroduced in the United States. A different form of tryptophan—5-Hydroxy-Tryptophan—is available in the United States by prescription. It has been found useful in treating depression, but has a less sedative or tranquilizing effect than L-Tryptophan. After extensive testing and quality control, safe forms of L-Tryptophan are now available by prescription in Canada and several European countries, including Britain and Germany. As was the case before 1989, many people in these countries use it for anxiety, sleep, depression, and PMS symptoms. If you have any Tryptophan that was manufactured in 1989, please do *not* take it. If you are interested in using Tryptophan, be sure to consult with your doctor and obtain it from a safe source. (In the United States, 5-Hydroxy-Tryptophan may be obtained with a prescription by calling 1-800-888-9358.)

Gamma Amino Butyric Acid

As an alternative to tryptophan, you may want to consider trying gamma amino butyric acid (GABA for short), an amino acid which is available at most health-food stores. GABA has a mildly tranquilizing effect and many people have used it as an alternative to prescription tranquilizers such as Xanax and Ativan. Although it is not as potent as prescription drugs, GABA does have the advantage of having few side effects and being nonaddictive.

The usual dose of GABA recommended for its calming effect is 100-400 mg. It is fine to take it in this dose once or twice per day (do not exceed 800 mg in a 24-hour period). To my knowledge, three reliable vitamin companies presently offer this supplement in the form of tablets or capsules containing 100 mg GABA along with several other vitamins: Twin Lab (under the name "GABA Plus" or "AminoCalm"), Country Life (under the name "Relaxer"), and Source Naturals (under the name "GABACalm").

It's a good idea to take GABA either on an empty stomach or with a carbohydrate snack (such as a piece of toast, crackers, cereal, rice cakes, and so on). Carbohydrate foods actually enhance the calming or sedative effect. Avoid taking GABA with protein. There is nothing harmful in doing so, but the protein (which is made up of many different amino acids) will tend to compete with absorption of GABA.

DL-Phenylalanine and Tyrosine as Natural Antidepressants

Since depression frequently accompanies anxiety, it's important to consider two amino acids that have been used effectively in the past few years to treat depression. Both DL-phenylalanine and tyrosine increase the amount of a neurotransmitter substance in the brain known as *norepinephrine*, a substance whose deficiency has been implicated as a contributing cause of depression.

Many (though not all) of the depressed clients I've worked with have significantly benefited from taking one or the other of these amino acids. These supplements may allow you to feel better without resorting to prescription antidepressant drugs which, while effective, have numerous side effects.

DL-phenylalanine (DLPA) and tyrosine are available in 500-mg capsules or tablets in most health-food stores. If you are interested in experimenting with either of them, please observe the following guidelines:

1. Do not take either of them if you are pregnant, have PKU (a disease requiring a phenylalanine-free diet), or are taking an MAO-inhibitor medication (such as Nardil or Parnate). If you have high blood pressure, take them only under a doctor's supervision.

2. Take them with a carbohydrate snack or at least one-half hour before or after any meal containing protein. As with GABA, protein interferes with the absorption of DLPA and tyrosine.

3. Start with a dose of 500 mg/day and increase it to 1,500 mg/day over three or four days. If you experience no benefit, increase the dose to 2,000-3,000 mg/day after four days. Stay with one amino acid for at least two weeks (unless you experience an adverse reaction). If you experience no noticeable effect after two weeks, try the other one.

4. It's likely that you'll experience some benefit from either tyrosine or DL-phenylalanine after a few weeks if taken at the right dosage. Do not exceed 3,000 mg/day of either amino acid except under the supervision of a doctor who is familiar with the use of amino acid therapy for the treatment of depression. If you are severely depressed and/or have suicidal thoughts, do not rely on amino acids alone to deal with your problem. Please consult a professional.

An in-depth discussion of the use of amino acids in the treatment of depression can be found in Dr. Priscilla Slagle's book *The Way Up from Down*.

Relaxing Herbs

Several natural herbs can be used to help reduce anxiety. Though not as potent as prescription tranquilizers, they do have a definitely relaxing effect. Valerian root is probably the best known (its active ingredient was extracted and synthesized to form the basis for the tranquilizer Valium). Other herbs known for their relaxing effects include Passionflower, Skullcap, Hops, and Chamomile. Each of these relaxing herbs can be taken individually or in combination with the others. Most health-food stores offer these herbs in three forms: 1) the bulk herb, which can be boiled to make a tea, 2) liquid extract, in which the herb is distilled and preserved in alcohol or glycerine, usually in a small bottle with a medicine dropper, or 3) capsules. For most purposes, teas made from the bulk herb or a dropperful of the liquid extract (diluted in water) are likely to have a more deeply relaxing effect than the capsules. You might want to experiment with all three forms, though, to determine which you prefer.

Common Conditions Associated With Anxiety Disorders

In the past few years, I have seen an increasing number of cases in which an anxiety disorder coexists with, and is aggravated by, one or another physical syndrome which is not readily identifiable by standard medical tests. These syndromes, including PMS, adrenal exhaustion, yeast syndrome, and seasonal affective disorder, are disruptive and sometimes disabling to those who suffer from them. While they are caused by many complex factors, stress and poor nutrition often play a significant role. Four syndromes that can occur in conjunction with anxiety disorders are described below.

Premenstrual Syndrome (PMS)

Premenstrual syndrome (PMS) involves a constellation of disruptive physical and psychological symptoms that many women experience in the days or week prior to menstruation. Common physical symptoms include water retention, breast soreness, bloating, acne, headaches, and increased hunger and craving for sweets. Psychological symptoms can include depression, irritability, anxiety and tension, mood swings, distractibility and forgetfulness, fatigue, and even a feeling of "going crazy." Studies have found that 30-50 percent of all women experience a premenstrual increase in depression, anxiety, or irritability in addition to some of the above physical symptoms. Panic reactions can also be a symptom of PMS. The question to ask is whether your panic attacks typically occur—or increase in frequency and intensity—during the days before menstruation. *If so, treating your PMS may help to reduce or eliminate panic attacks.*

Most medical theories about PMS relate it to an imbalance in the amounts of estrogen and progesterone in a woman's body, particularly during the second half of the menstrual cycle. During this 14-day period, progesterone levels normally rise; estrogen levels also rise slightly. Insufficient levels of progesterone relative to the amount of estrogen tend to promote water retention. Water retention, in turn, is thought to lead to many of the problematic symptoms of PMS.

Other theories about PMS stress that menstruation allows the body to throw off excess toxins accumulated through improper diet, as well as from exposure to environmental contaminants and pollutants. Thus the symptoms experienced just prior to menstruation reflect the body's reaction to excess toxicity. The implication is that eating a healthy diet and reducing exposure to other toxins should help lessen PMS symptoms.

Both of these theories are probably valid. PMS symptoms can definitely be helped by eliminating foods that tend to aggravate them (described below). Symptoms can also be alleviated in many cases with the aid of vitamin and mineral supplements, herbs, and, in particular, by raising the body's level of progesterone.

The following recommendations describe strategies that have all been helpful in treating PMS. Before following any of them, you may first want to consult a physician, nutritionist, or practitioner of Chinese medicine who is well versed in treating the problem.

Dietary Guidelines
Avoid:
- Sugars and foods high in sugar content, as well as large amounts of simple carbohydrates (bread, chips, pasta, etc.). It's especially important to avoid the impulse to binge on sweets and carbohydrate foods. Observe the "Low Stress/ Anxiety Dietary Guidelines" described earlier in this chapter.

- Salty foods

- Foods high in fat

- Caffeinated drinks (coffee, tea, colas)

- Alcohol

- Chocolate

Vitamin and Mineral Supplements
When you have PMS symptoms, take 200 mg of vitamin B_6 once or twice daily (but, avoid taking this much vitamin B_6 for more than one week out of every month). During the entire month, take 25,000 IU per day of beta-carotene (pro-vitamin A). A high potency

B-complex in conjunction with calcium-magnesium (1,000 mg calcium to 500 mg magnesium) can also be useful if you are not already taking them regularly (see the previous section in this chapter on supplements).

Herbs

Angelica or dong quai is an herb that can help provide energy and stabilize your mood during PMS. It can be taken in capsule form (2-4/day) or as a tea. Ginger root and licorice root have also been found to be helpful (consult someone at your health-food store or a practitioner who is knowledgeable about herbs for further information).

Regular Physical Exercise

A program of regular physical exercise will liven up your metabolism and reduce stress levels. See the chapter on exercise.

Medical Treatments

Medical treatments prescribed by your doctor to alleviate PMS symptoms may include

- Diuretics to reduce water retention and breast swelling

- Natural progesterone (this is preferable to synthetic progesterone).

Adrenal Exhaustion

The well-known expert on stress, Hans Seyle, has described how prolonged stress on the adrenal glands results in a state of chronic underfunctioning or exhaustion. This condition develops over a series of stages. In the first stage of combatting stress, the adrenal glands tend to hyperfunction, producing high amounts of adrenalin and noradrenalin, as well as steroid hormones such as cortisol. As stress becomes prolonged, the glands begin to be overtaxed and go into a state of temporary underfunctioning. If you are relatively healthy, the glands will try to compensate, actually rebuilding themselves to the point of hypertrophy (growing larger). However, if high levels of stress continue, the glands will eventually exhaust themselves again and then remain in a chronic state of underfunctioning. At this stage they can oscillate between the overproduction of adrenalin, causing panic or mood swings, while underproducing adrenalin the rest of the time. With insufficient adrenal resources, you will tend to have a difficult time handling any stressful situation without overreacting or "going to pieces." In short, your stress tolerance is exhausted.

Symptoms of adrenal exhaustion include chronically low stress tolerance, frequent fatigue, depression, insomnia, light sensitivity, worsening allergies or asthma, and often a craving for substances that provide temporary stimulation and/or raise your blood sugar levels. Addiction to caffeine, sugar, tobacco, alcohol, and recreational drugs is frequently associated with adrenal exhaustion. Unfortunately, continued use of any of these substances will gradually worsen the condition. If you've had a long-standing addiction to caffeine, sugar, nicotine, or alcohol, your risk of adrenal insufficiency is high. Other factors which aggravate adrenal exhaustion are continuing stress, inadequate sleep, prolonged exposure to heat or cold, exposure to toxins, pollutants, and/or substances you're allergic to, and taking cortisone over a period of time. Sudden trauma or severe physical illness can also worsen the condition.

Recovery from chronic adrenal exhaustion requires consistent effort over time, but is possible. Try to follow these basic guidelines:

- Simplify your lifestyle to reduce stress as much as possible.

- Strive to obtain seven to eight hours of sleep at night and give yourself "down time" during the day (see Chapter 4).

- Eliminate caffeine, nicotine, alcohol, and recreational drugs altogether (substitute herb teas for caffeinated beverages—licorice tea is especially good if you're hypoglycemic).

- For three months, eliminate all forms of sugar, including white and brown sugar, honey, molasses, corn syrup, maple syrup, and dried fruit. After three months, you can reintroduce natural sugars such as honey in very small amounts.

- Eliminate processed foods and foods you're allergic to. Emphasize whole grains, fresh vegetables and fresh fruits in your diet. Protein in the form of beans and grains, organic poultry or fish is recommended.

- Supplements: Take B-complex and vitamin C as recommended in this chapter. You may also want to try raw adrenal extract, 50-200 mg per day, preferably under the supervision of a doctor or nutritionist experienced in using glandular extracts.

- Get plenty of fresh air and sunshine, but dress warmly if you're living in a cold climate (avoid getting chilled).

Yeast Syndrome

Candida or yeast syndrome refers to an overgrowth of a particular yeast—*candida albicans*—in the intestinal and/or genito-urinary tract. Although it affects a large number of people, especially women, it frequently goes undiagnosed due to a prevailing tendency by many physicians to ignore or dismiss the disorder. Symptoms can occur on two levels. Localized infections, particularly skin rashes and "yeast infections" (vaginitis) are common. More generalized, systemic symptoms include: 1) chronic fungus infections such as athlete's foot, ring worm, or "jock itch," 2) fatigue or feeling drained, 3) depression or mood swings, 4) chronic anxiety and tension, 5) poor memory, 6) headaches, 7) cramps or bloating, 8) severe PMS symptoms, 9) joint pains, and 10) cravings for sweets, bread, or alcohol. Factors that increase the risk for developing candida include: 1) having frequently used broad-spectrum antibiotics (such as ampicillin, amoxicillin, Ceclor, Bactrim, Septra), 2) having used birth control pills for more than a year, 3) living in a damp, moldy environment, and 4) consuming sweets in large quantities.

There are two ways of diagnosing candida. A common way is to use a diagnostic questionnaire, such as the one developed by Dr. Kenneth Crook in his classic book on the subject, *The Yeast Connection*. Alternatively, you can measure antibodies to candida (IgA, IgH, IgG) by blood test. Elevated antibody levels indicate that the candida organism has ventured beyond the intestine and become systemic.

Recovery from chronic candida takes time but can be achieved through a three-faceted program. First, it is necessary to eliminate foods from your diet which the candida organism feeds on. These include all kinds of sugar, dried fruits and fruit juices, alcohol, yeast, fermented foods, cheese, vinegar, and refined flour products, including bread. (All of these are eliminated for a month, then reintroduced in small quantities.) Second, it is often necessary to take an antifungal antibiotic such as Nystatin or Nizoral for a period of several months. Finally, you need to restore normal bacterial ecology in the intestine (candida tends to crowd out healthy intestinal bacteria) by implanting useful bacteria such as acidophilus and lactobacillus bifidus.

Persons who successfully recover from candida report that they have significantly increased energy and freedom from depression, lethargy, and a variety of physical complaints. If you suspect that candida could be affecting your overall health and well-being, I suggest that you read one of the well-known books on the subject such as *The Yeast Connection* by Kenneth Crook, M.D., or *The Candidiasis Syndrome* by Keith Sehnert.

Seasonal Affective Disorder

When the seasons change from spring/summer to fall/winter,

- ☐ Do you find that you have less energy than usual?

- ☐ Do you sleep more, but awaken still feeling tired?

- ☐ Do you experience mood changes? Do you generally feel more anxious, irritable, sad, or depressed?

- ☐ Do you feel less productive or creative?

- ☐ Do you feel that you have little control over your appetite or weight?

- ☐ Do you experience more memory and concentration problems?

- ☐ Do you find that you're less outgoing and social than usual?

- ☐ Do you find that you don't cope as well with stress?

- ☐ Do you feel less enthusiastic about the future and/or enjoy your life less?

If you checked two or more boxes, you may be one of the many people affected by Seasonal Affective Disorder (SAD), or a milder form of this disorder known as "subsyndromal SAD." Seasonal affective disorder is a cyclical depression that occurs during the winter months, typically during the period between November and March; it's brought on by an insufficient exposure to light. As the days get shorter and the angle of the sun changes during fall, the symptoms of SAD begin to appear. An estimated 20 percent of the American adult population, or 36,000,000 people are affected by SAD and subsyndromal SAD. The farther north you happen to live, the more susceptible you are.

It is this author's observation that many individuals dealing with anxiety disorders experience an aggravation of their condition during the late fall and winter. Panic attacks may occur more often, and generalized anxiety may increase along with depression. It's not surprising that this is so, because the same systems of the brain which contribute to the neurobiological basis of depression—the noradrenegic system and the serotonin system—are also implicated in anxiety disorders, particularly panic disorder, generalized anxiety disorder, and obsessive-compulsive disorder. Biochemical imbalances in these systems tipped one way may cause depression; tipped the other way they may aggravate anxiety disorders. And for many individuals, unfortunately, problems with anxiety and depression may co-exist, both becoming aggravated during the winter months.

Whether depression or anxiety, the symptoms of SAD are caused by decreased availability of light. SAD can be aggravated not only by reduced light outside during the winter months, but by spending too much time in indoor environments which have low levels of light, whether at home or work. SAD symptoms have been reported even in the summer among people who work in environments without windows. They can also occur in sensitive individuals at any time of the year after a long succession of cloudy days.

It used to be thought that SAD was caused by insufficient suppression of a hormone in the brain called melatonin. Melatonin is secreted by the pineal gland in the brain at night after several hours of darkness—it is one of the mechanisms by which your brain lets you know it is time to go to sleep. With light in the morning, melatonin secretion is suppressed and you know that it's time to wake up. Although popular for many years, the hypothesis that SAD is caused by insufficient melatonin suppression has not been borne out by systematic research. Results of studies have been mixed, and researchers have recently looked in other directions to find clues to the cause of SAD. The hypothesis that is currently receiving the most attention is that light insufficiency can cause a reduction in levels of serotonin in the brain. Norman Rosenthal, one of the leading researchers in this field, writes that when susceptible individuals are exposed to too little environmental light—such as during winter—they produce too little serotonin. Rosenthal and others believe that these low levels of serotonin are responsible for the symptoms of SAD.

Serotonin deficiencies are frequently associated with symptoms of depression and/or anxiety (see Chapter 2); that is why drugs that block the reuptake of serotonin in the brain—drugs such as Prozac, Zoloft, or Paxil—often alleviate depression and/or many of the anxiety disorders. But why should reduced light affect serotonin? And why only in certain individuals?

The answer to the first question is still being researched. In answer to the second question, some evidence exists that people who are susceptible to SAD may be less able to receive or process light at a neurological level relative to those who do not develop SAD. One hypothesis is that the visual receptive fields of individuals who develop SAD may tend to be smaller than the fields of those who do not. An experimental approach called neurosensory development training has shown some success in correcting this condition. The approach is discussed in a little more detail at the end of this section.

During the winter, people with SAD tend to crave sweets and carbohydrates. Eating high amounts of carbohydrates usually increases the amount of tryptophan (an essential amino acid derived naturally from protein foods) that gets into the brain. Once in the brain, tryptophan becomes serotonin, the neurotransmitter that is so critical to psychological well-being. Eating sweets and carbohydrates gives tryptophan a competitive edge over the body's other amino acids in terms of getting into the brain (for a detailed explanation, see the book by Judith Wurtman cited at the end of the chapter). So, if you tend to be drawn to sweets and starches in the wintertime, it may be your body's attempt to raise your levels of serotonin.

The treatment that most effectively reduces the symptoms of SAD is *light therapy*. In principle it would be possible to reduce SAD in the winter by spending prolonged periods of time outdoors every day. Unless you're a ski instructor or a snow plow operator, however, this is pretty impractical. Light therapy involves the use of one or more specific devices *indoors* to increase your exposure to bright light. Sometimes light-sensitive individuals can experience an improvement simply by increasing normal room light or installing brighter light bulbs. However, most SAD sufferers seem to require exposure to higher light levels—at least four times higher than normal household and office wattage.

"Light boxes" are commonly used to alleviate symptoms of SAD. A light box is typically a set of fluorescent bulbs in a box, with a diffusing plastic screen. Most of these devices deliver between 2,500 and 10,000 lux of light energy—considerably above the usual range of indoor lighting (approximately 200-1,000 lux). A typical light therapy session involves sitting within two to three feet of a light box for a period of half an hour to two hours in the morning. It's neither necessary nor advisable to look directly at the light; rather, you can use the time to read, write, eat, sew, or do whatever you need to do. The amount of time you spend in front of the light each day is something you need to work out on your own according to your individual needs.

Other devices used in light therapy are "dawn simulators" and "light visors." The dawn simulator creates an artificial dawn in your bedroom by having a light come on very dim at, say, 6:00 a.m. and gradually brighten until 7:00 a.m. The light visor is a lightweight source of light which you can wear on your head. It allows you to have more mobility than the light box.

Light therapy is very effective when administered properly. In experimental trials, it has been shown to help 75-80 percent of SAD sufferers within a week if used regularly. Before undertaking light therapy on your own, you should consult with a physician or another health professional who is knowledgeable about this therapy and its application. Although light therapy devices are available without a prescription, you can save yourself time—as well as such possible side effects as headache, eyestrain, irritability, or insomnia—by getting assistance on using them properly. Information on about a dozen companies which manufacture light therapy devices is available from the National Organization for Seasonal Affective Disorder (NOSAD), P.O. Box 40133, Washington, D.C. 20016. Another useful resource for learning about light therapy and SAD in general is a book by Norman Rosenthal, *Winter Blues: Seasonal Affective Disorder and How To Overcome It*.

NOSAD offers a number of resources, including basic information, a bibliography, and a support network of people across the country you can call. The organization also offers the following suggestions.

- Discuss your symptoms with your physician. You may be referred to a psychiatrist who may diagnose seasonal affective disorder or subsyndromal SAD and prescribe special light treatments to help relieve your symptoms. Some new antidepressants are also helpful in treating some people with seasonal depression.

- If you have a medical diagnosis of SAD or subsyndromal SAD, and your doctor prescribes light treatment, do not skip or shorten treatment because you're feeling better—you may relapse. Work with your doctor in adjusting the length of time, time of day, distance, and intensity of light for your own individualized treatment.

- Get as much light as possible and avoid dark environments during daylight hours in winter.

- Reduce mild winter depressive symptoms by exercising daily, preferably outdoors, to take advantage of natural light.

- If you are unable to exercise outdoors in the winter due to extreme cold, exercise inside. If possible, try sitting in front of sunlight from a south-facing window for short but frequent periods during the day.

- Rearrange work spaces at home, and work near a window; or set up bright lights in your work area.

- Stay on a *regular sleep/wake schedule.* People with SAD who get up every morning and go to sleep at preset hours report being more alert and less fatigued than when they vary their schedules.

- Be aware of cold outside temperatures and *dress to conserve energy and warmth.* Many affected by seasonal changes report sensitivity to *extreme temperatures.*

- Arrange family outings and social occasions for *day times and early evening in winter.* Avoid staying up late, which disrupts your sleep schedule and biological clock.

- Conserve energy by *managing time wisely and avoiding or minimizing unnecessary stress.*

- Try putting *lights on a timer in your bedroom* or use a dawn simulator set to switch on one-half hour or more before you get up. Some people with SAD report that this light technique has an antidepressant effect and helps them awaken more easily.

- When possible, postpone making major life changes until spring or summer.

- Share experiences regarding SAD as a way to get information, understanding, validation, and support.

- If you are able, arrange to vacation during the winter in a warm, sunny climate.

Finally, there exists a new approach to the treatment of SAD that is currently in an experimental stage. The approach, called "neurosensory development training," is based on the hypothesis that individuals susceptible to SAD have a reduced ability to process light—or to process nerve impulses associated with light perception—at the level of the brain. This inhibition of the ability to receive and process light is thought to be caused by cumulative stress or exposure to a severe stressor, and is potentially reversible. At present this technique is not yet widely available, although initial reports of its effectiveness are encouraging.

Summary of Things To Do

1. Evaluate the amount of caffeine in your diet, using the *Caffeine Chart* in this chapter, and attempt to gradually reduce your intake to less than 100 mg per day. If you are especially sensitive, you may want to eliminate caffeine altogether, substituting decaf coffee (or decaf teas) for regular coffee and decaf soft drinks for caffeinated ones.

2. Stop smoking. In addition to significantly reducing your risk for cardiovascular disease and cancer, you will lower your susceptibility to panic attacks and anxiety.

3. Reduce your consumption of substances which stress your body. Decrease your intake of salt to one gram per day. Replace processed foods containing preservatives with (preferably organic) vegetables and fruits and whole grains. If possible, substitute organic beef, poultry, and fish for commercially available meats. Avoid processed meats.

4. Allow eating to be a relaxing activity. Avoid eating on the run or eating excessively. Chew your food thoroughly and limit your fluid intake during a meal to eight ounces.

5. Evaluate whether you experience the subjective symptoms of hypoglycemia—light-headedness, anxiety, depression, weakness, or shakiness—three or four hours after a meal (or in the early morning hours) and whether they are quickly relieved by eating. You may want to follow this up with a formal six-hour glucose tolerance test. If you suspect that hypoglycemia is contributing to your problem with anxiety, strive to eliminate from your diet all forms of white sugar as well as brown sugar, honey, corn syrup, corn sweeteners, molasses, and high fructose. (Be careful also about aspartame or Nutrasweet. A recent study found a link between this substance and panic disorder for certain people.) Most fresh, whole fruits (not dried) are fine if you're hypoglycemic, although fruit juices should be diluted with water. Observe the *Dietary Modifications for Hypoglycemia* and consider taking the recommended supplements suggested in this chapter. You may want to consult a qualified nutritionist to assist you in setting up an appropriate dietary and supplement regime.

6. Evaluate your susceptibility to food allergies. Take note of any types of food that you crave (paying attention particularly to wheat and dairy products) and try eliminating that food from your diet for two weeks. Then reintroduce the food and notice if you have any symptoms. Consult the book by Marshall Mandell listed below, or a nutritionist, for further information.

7. Work toward complying with the "Low Stress/Anxiety Dietary Guidelines" described in this chapter. Use the *Food Diary* to monitor your intake of caffeine, fats, sweets, and alcohol, and try for a balanced number of servings of each major food group for several weeks. *Avoid pushing yourself to radically change your diet all at once,* or you may end up rebelling against the idea of making any changes. Introduce one small change each week—or perhaps even each month—so that you gradually modify your dietary habits.

8. Consider taking the supplements recommended for anxiety and stress, especially the B vitamins, vitamin C, and calcium-magnesium. You may want to consult with a nutritionist or physician who is supportive of the idea of high-potency vitamins (not everyone is) to assist you in this.

9. You may want to explore whether amino acids can be helpful, specifically, GABA for anxiety and 5-Hydroxy-Tryptophan, tyrosine, or DL-phenylalanine for depression. Consult the book by Priscilla Slagle (listed below) or a physician experienced in the use of amino acid therapy for further information.

10. If you are a woman, notice whether your anxiety or panic symptoms increase during the days or week preceding your period. If so, getting appropriate treatment for your PMS may help alleviate your anxiety.

11. If you suspect that you may have a problem with adrenal exhaustion, yeast syndrome, and/or seasonal affective disorder, give this issue your immediate attention. Dealing with such issues is an important part of your overall recovery program. Consult the references on yeast syndrome and SAD below as needed.

12. Among the many things your brain needs in order to function properly, the following three criteria are of particular importance to people who have panic attacks, phobias, and/or anxiety.

- **An adequate level of serotonin**
  This can be accomplished, if necessary, via the selective serotonin reuptake inhibitor medications, such as Prozac, Zoloft, or Paxil (see Chapter 17). Natural alternatives for increasing serotonin include: a) the use of the supplement 5-Hydroxy-Tryptophan (or L-Tryptophan if you live in Canada or Europe), b) eating tryptophan-rich foods such as turkey, tuna, eggs, or milk (if you're not allergic to dairy products), c) getting plenty of sunshine, and last, but not least, d) having that magic ingredient in your life known as "love and affection."

- **An adequate, stable level of blood sugar**
  Review the sections on hypoglycemia and dietary guidelines for hypoglycemia. Eliminate sweets from your diet other than fruits. Always have a nonsugar snack with you (in your car, at work, etc.) such as unsalted nuts or crackers and cheese should you start to experience hypoglycemic symptoms. Be sure to take supplemental B-complex and chromium. Consult the books on hypoglycemia in the reading list below.

- **Sufficient light**
  Review the section on seasonal affective disorder to determine whether light deficiency is an issue for you. If so, contact the National Organization for Seasonal Affective Disorder (NOSAD) and read the book by Norman Rosenthal cited below. In the meantime, increase your exposure to sunlight or bright light during fall and winter, if possible.

Further Reading

Airola, Paavo, *Hypoglycemia: A Better Approach.* Phoenix, Arizona: Health Plus Publishers, 1977.

Ballentine, Rudolph. *Diet and Nutrition: A Holistic Approach.* Honesdale, Pennsylvania: The Himalayan International Institute, 1982.

Bender, Stephanie. *PMS: Questions and Answers.* Los Angeles: Price Sloan, 1989.

Colbin, Annemarie. *Food and Healing.* New York, Ballantine Books, 1986. (Excellent introductory book on nutrition.)

Colimore, Benjamin, and Colimore, Sarah Stewart. *Nutrition and Your Body.* Los Angeles: Light Wave Press, 1974 (Excellent basic textbook on nutrition.)

Crook, William. *The Yeast Connection.* 3rd Edition. Jackson, Tennesee: Professional Books, 1989.

Dufty, William. *Sugar Blues.* New York: Warner Books, 1975. (Classic popular book on hypoglycemia.)

Fredericks, Carlton. *Low Blood Sugar and You.* New York: Grosset and Dunlap, 1969.

Fredericks, Carlton. *Psycho Nutrition.* New York: Grosset and Dunlap, 1976.

Haas, Elson M. *Staying Healthy With Nutrition.* Berkeley, California: Celestial Arts, 1992.

Hunt, Douglas. *No More Fears.* New York: Warner Books, 1988.

Lesser, Michael. *Nutrition and Vitamin Therapy.* New York: Grove Press, 1980. (Good basic introduction to vitamins and vitamin therapy.)

Mandell, Marshall. *Dr. Mandell's 5-Day Allergy Relief System.* New York: Pocket Books, 1980.

Mindell, Earl. *Vitamin Bible.* New York: Warner Books, 1979.

Robbins, John. *Diet for a New America.* Walpole, New Hampshire: Stillpoint Publishing, 1987.

Rosenthal, Norman. *Winter Blues: Seasonal Affective Disorder and How To Overcome It.* New York: Guilford Press, 1993.

Seyle, Hans. *The Stress of Life,* 2nd Edition. New York: McGraw Hill, 1976.

Slagle, Priscilla. *The Way Up from Down.* New York: Random House, 1987.

Tessler, Gordon. *The Lazy Person's Guide to Better Nutrition.* (Available from Better Health Publications, 90 Madison Ave., Ste. 507, Denver, Colorado 80206—a quick and easy-to-read primer on nutrition.)

Wurtman, Judith. *Managing Your Mind and Mood Through Food.* New York: Perennial Library, 1988.

17

Medications

As you will have gathered, this workbook offers a range of nonmedical strategies to help you overcome anxiety, panic, and phobias. My personal view is that natural methods should always be thoroughly explored before you develop a reliance on prescription drugs. All drugs induce unnatural changes in your body's physiology, with attendant short- and long-term side effects.

Many people find that they can avoid drugs—or eliminate those they have been taking—by implementing a comprehensive wellness program that includes

- Positive changes in nutrition

- A program of daily, vigorous exercise

- A daily practice of deep relaxation or meditation

- Changes in self-talk and basic beliefs which involve a less driven, more relaxed approach to life

- Human support—from family and/or friends

If you're not presently taking medications, I hope that you will give the methods in this book a fair trial before electing to use them.

If, on the other hand, you are currently taking a medication for anxiety or panic attacks, *don't* be in too much of a hurry to stop using it. You should first gain proficiency at using the various strategies for coping with anxiety, panic, and phobias presented in this workbook *before* curtailing your use of medication. Once you've acquired these skills, consult with your physician about setting up a program to gradually taper off your particular medication (this gradual approach is especially important if you're taking a tranquilizer).

When Are Medications Useful?

It would be misleading to state that prescription medications are never useful in the treatment of anxiety disorders. Indeed, they are sometimes quite necessary. Some further comments here are in order. There are two factors that influence whether medications should be used in the process of recovery. The first is severity. When panic attacks, obsessions and compulsions, or depressive symptoms are severe enough to prevent you from performing a large number of ordinary activities which you formerly accomplished with ease, you may need to rely on medications to expedite your recovery (in addition to the range of strategies presented in this workbook). When your symptoms have reached the point where just getting through each day is a struggle, you may find that *appropriate* medication may help give you sufficient control over yourself and inner stability to better utilize more natural approaches.

In my experience there are certain types of individuals, in certain types of situations, for whom medications are appropriate. What follows is a list of situations in which I would refer a client to a physician or psychiatrist for medication, along with the types of medications that might appropriately be used.

1. A person with panic attacks that are so frequent (for example, one or more per day) and severe that they interfere with his ability to work and earn a living, his primary personal relationships, and/or his sense of basic security and control over his life. Two types of medication are most frequently used to treat panic attacks. The first type are antidepressants. The most commonly used include Tofranil (imipramine), Pamelor (nortriptyline), Prozac (fluoxetine), and Paxil (paroxetine). The second type are the benzodiazepine tranquilizers. Among these, Xanax (alprazolam), Klonopin (clonazepam), and Ativan (lorazepam) are in frequent use these days, although older tranquillizers such as Valium are sometimes used. (Descriptions of the major types of drugs used to treat anxiety disorders follow this section.) Typically such drugs are prescribed for a period of three months to one year at a high enough dose to significantly reduce the frequency and severity of panic.

2. An agoraphobic who has a very difficult time undertaking real-life exposure to phobic situations (see Chapter 8). *Low* doses of a benzodiazepine tranquilizer such as Xanax (in the range of 0.25-1 mg/day) may enable such a person to negotiate graded exposure to her phobias. The benefits of exposure are likely to be retained even after the medication is discontinued, if the dose has been sufficiently low. This is less likely, however, for higher doses of Xanax (2-8 mg/day). It's necessary to experience some anxiety during exposure for the practice to be effective.

   Tricyclic antidepressants such as Pamelor (nortriptyline) and Tofranil (imipramine) are also helpful in enabling people to undertake and follow through with exposure. The newer SSRI antidepressants (see below), such as Paxil (paroxetine) and Zoloft (sertraline), often have the same benefits with fewer side effects.

3. A person with severe anticipatory anxiety related to phobias or severe generalized anxiety may need to rely on a benzodiazepine tranquilizer on a *short-term basis* to get him through a particularly stressful time (such as interviewing for a new job, exams, death of a close relative, a significant health crisis, and so on). Alternatively, a benzodiazepine sedative (Restoril or Dalmane) may be prescribed to help a person sleep during such a time.

4. A certain minority of individuals may have such severe and chronic generalized anxiety that they can only function by taking a low, "maintenance dose" of a tranquilizer on a long-term basis. Here a person's need for the medication must outweigh the likely risk of addiction, which commonly occurs in the long-term use of tranquilizers. Long-term use of tranquilizers, even at low dosages, carries

possible risks of impaired liver function (especially in older people), as well as depression and reduced vitality. I have witnessed a number of long-term users of tranquilizers (in other words, using tranquilizers for more than two years) who felt less depressed after they finally withdrew from the medication.

A recent possible alternative to long-term dependency on tranquilizers is a medication known as Buspar. Buspar is effective in diminishing chronic anxiety but is not physically addictive. However, it is not particularly effective in treating panic disorder.

5. People with chronic, severe depression accompanying panic disorder or agoraphobia will usually benefit from a prescription antidepressant medication, even if they've been unresponsive to amino acid therapy with tyrosine or DL-phenylalanine (see Chapter 16). Antidepressant medication will help relieve both depression and panic attacks.

6. Individuals who suffer from performance anxiety in public speaking or other performance situations—*especially* if the anxiety involves heart palpitations—may be helped by short-term doses of beta-blocking drugs such as Inderal (propranolol).

7. Severe social phobia or social anxiety may be helped by two classes of antidepressant medications: the MAO-Inhibitors (Nardil, Parnate, and Marplan) or the SSRIs (Prozac, Zoloft, and Paxil).

8. Sufferers of obsessive-compulsive disorder may respond to an antidepressant medication. At this time the medications Anafranil (clomipramine) and SSRIs such as Prozac (fluoxetine), Luvox (fluvoxamine), Zoloft (sertraline), and Paxil (paroxetine) look especially promising for the treatment of this disorder. In recent studies 50-60 percent of people with obsessive-compulsive disorder experienced an improvement in their symptoms while taking one of these drugs. All of these medications appear to be helpful in treating obsessive-compulsive disorder whether or not it is accompanied by depression. The former of those two, Anafranil, does have some undesirable side effects, however.

A second factor involved in the decision to rely on medication is your own personal values. Ultimately your values will play the largest role in determining whether or not you take prescription drugs. Many people with anxiety disorders are opposed altogether to the idea of taking medication. Either they fear medication or they have a philosophical commitment to the idea of recovering by natural means. This is an admirable choice. Anyone *can* recover by natural methods with sufficient motivation, persistence, and diligence. At the opposite extreme there are people who lack sufficient interest or motivation to put in the time and effort involved in practicing relaxation, exercise, desensitization, and cognitive skills on a daily basis. They seek immediate relief of symptoms through taking a drug. In many cases, this is also a viable choice. It is not for anyone to judge a person's decision to seek relief from anxiety disorders through medication. Medications certainly do provide a great deal of symptom relief for many people. Unfortunately, they don't do much more than relieve symptoms—and they have a cost in terms of side effects and/or a potential for addiction. As mentioned above, I believe that medications should remain a "second line of defense" to be used after natural methods have been given a fair trial. If, however, for reasons of severity or otherwise you choose to take medications, this should not lead you to judge yourself as being "weak" or unable to recover "on your own." Be easy with yourself.

Finally, the question is often raised, if medications really do help, should we assume that anxiety disorders are primarily caused by biological (as opposed to psychological) factors? Is anxiety a "disease," as one popular author has suggested? The answer to this (as discussed in Chapter 2) is that panic, phobias, anxiety, and obsessions are caused by a wide spectrum of factors ranging from the physical and behavioral to emotional, mental, and spiritual. Asking whether any one of these is the most basic or primary cause is like asking whether the chicken or egg came first. Factors at all of these levels work together in a mutually interdependent way. My own bias, however, is that the more *severe* and *chronic* a particular problem is, the larger the role biological factors are likely to play.

Types of Medications Used To Treat Anxiety Disorders

What follows is a description of the major types of prescription medications used in the treatment of anxiety disorders, with particular attention to their specific benefits and potential drawbacks.

Benzodiazepine Tranquilizers

The benzodiazepine tranquilizers (sometimes called "minor tranquilizers") include Xanax (alprazolam), Ativan (lorazepam), Klonopin (clonazepam), Librium (chlordiazepoxide), Valium (diazepam), Tranxene (chlorazepate), Serax (oxazepam), and Centrax (prazepam). Benzodiazepine sedatives used as "sleeping pills" include Dalmane (flurazepam), Restoril (temazepam), and Halcion (triazolam).

All benzodiazepine drugs tend to depress the activity of the central nervous system and thus directly and efficiently decrease anxiety. In higher doses the tranquilizers will induce sleep just like the sedatives. The main difference between various benzodiazepines is their "half-life" or the length of time their chemical metabolites tend to stay in your body (for example, Xanax and Halcion have short half-lives, while Dalmane and Valium have long ones). Although benzodiazepines produce rapid relief of anxiety, they all have the serious side effect of physical dependence and potentially difficult withdrawal, especially when taken over a long period of time.

At present the tranquilizer most commonly used to treat anxiety disorders is Xanax (alprazolam). (It's often said that Xanax was to the 1980s what Valium was to the 1970s.) Alprazolam differs from other benzodiazepines in that it has an additional antidepressant effect as well as the ability to relieve anxiety. It also has less of a sedative effect than most other tranquilizers. For nonspecific, generalized anxiety, Xanax is typically given in doses of 0.5–2 mg/day. It appears that relatively high doses, in the range of 2-9 mg/day, are needed to fully suppress panic attacks. Lower doses will significantly diminish the symptoms of panic, however. Xanax may be given on a temporary basis for acute anxiety as well as on a long-term basis, in lower doses, to treat panic disorder and agoraphobia.

The main problem with Xanax—a problem that it shares with all other benzodiazepines—is its potential for tolerance, physical dependence, and likely recurrence of panic and anxiety symptoms when it's withdrawn. Many people who have taken Xanax (or other benzodiazepines), even at low doses, for a few months report that it's very difficult getting off such medications. It's disheartening to hear stories confirming that withdrawal from long-term use of Xanax can be just as difficult as withdrawal from alcohol or heroin. (There is some recent evidence that withdrawal from Klonopin may be somewhat easier and less protracted than withdrawal from Xanax.) *Abrupt* withdrawal from these medications is *dangerous* and may produce panic attacks, severe anxiety, confusion, muscle tension, irritability, insomnia, and even seizures. A more gradual tapering of the dose, stretched out over many weeks or even months, is what makes withdrawal possible. People vary in the ease with which they can withdraw from Xanax, but as a general rule it's best to taper off very gradually over a period of one to four months under medical supervision. During this withdrawal period you may suffer a recurrence of panic attacks or other anxiety symptoms for which the drug was originally prescribed. Sometimes the symptoms can even be worse than what you experienced before taking the drug. Tapering off very gradually is the best way to minimize the risk of severe reactions. After you've fully withdrawn from Xanax or any other benzodiazepine, the likelihood of relapse—in other words, reexperiencing the original anxiety or panic for which the drug was recommended—approaches 100 percent. For many people, then, Xanax provides only a temporary respite from anxiety. The strategies described in this workbook provide a nonchemical alternative toward gaining more complete and enduring relief.

A final problem with Xanax and other benzodiazepines is that they tend to have a blunting effect not only on anxiety but on feelings in general. Many people report that their affective response is lower while they are taking these drugs (for example, they may have trouble crying or getting angry even at times when these reactions are appropriate). One of the chief components of recovery from anxiety disorders—the ability to identify, acknowledge, and express your feelings—thus becomes less feasible when you take tranquilizers, especially in higher doses. Insight-oriented psychotherapy, which involves working through suppressed emotions associated with present and past conflicts and traumas, is also made more difficult. To the extent that anxiety is related to suppressed and unresolved feelings, taking these drugs will only tend to alleviate symptoms rather than relieve the cause of the problem. (Some people have a paradoxical reaction to benzodiazepines where they actually become *more* emotional—but this tends to be the exception rather than the rule.)

In sum, Xanax and other minor tranquilizers are often used for treating short-term, acute anxiety or stress rather than long-lasting conditions such as agoraphobia. These tranquilizers may still be used for such conditions, however, when other types of drugs (to be described below) are ineffective or are poorly tolerated. Some people are able to take benzodiazepine tranquilizers, such as Xanax or Klonopin, long term at a low dose and in a responsible fashion. If they are over 50 and have been taking the medication for more than two years, they should periodically receive medical checkups, including an evaluation of liver function.

Antidepressant Medications

Antidepressant medications are most commonly used to treat panic attacks or agoraphobia with panic attacks. They may also be used to treat obsessive-compulsive disorder. These medications fall into four groups:

1. *Cyclic Antidepressants* such as Elavil (amitriptyline), Tofranil (imipramine), Pamelor (nortriptyline), Surmontil (trimipramine), Desyrel (trazodone), Sinequan (doxepin), Norpramin (desipramine), Vivactil (protriptyline), and Anafranil (clomipramine)

2. *MAO-Inhibitor Antidepressants* such as Nardil (phenelzine), Parnate (tranylcypromine), and Marplan (isocarboxazid)

3. *SSRI (Selective Serotonin Reuptake Inhibitor) Antidepressants* such as Prozac (fluoxetine), Zoloft (sertraline), and Paxil (paroxetine)

4. *Other Antidepressants* such as Wellbutrin (bupropion) and Effexor (venlafaxine)

The second of these catagories, the MAO-inhibitors, can be effective, but are not used much these days because they can cause serious or even fatal rises in blood pressure when combined with: 1) foods that contain the amino acid tyramine, such as wine and certain meats, or 2) certain over-the-counter medications, such as decongestants. MAO-inhibitor medications should *never* be combined with other classes of antidepressants. If you are taking an MAO-inhibitor, you should be under close supervision by your doctor.

Cyclic antidepressant medications (especially imipramine) are frequently used to treat panic attacks, whether such attacks occur by themselves or in conjunction with agoraphobia. For reasons that are unclear, these medications seem to reduce both the frequency and intensity of panic reactions for many people. They are also effective in reducing the depression that often accompanies panic disorder and agoraphobia. While it used to be believed that Tofranil was the most effective antidepressant for treating panic, current evidence indicates that any of the cyclic antidepressant medications can be helpful, depending on the individual. It is well known that different people respond differently to the various antidepressant medications, and sometimes several must be tried before the right one is found.

SSRI antidepressant medications have become increasingly popular over the past few years. They tend to be as effective as the older, cyclic antidepressants and, for many people, have fewer side effects (This is not universally true). Currently they are used most often to treat panic disorder, agoraphobia, and obsessive-compulsive disorder. The length of treatment for panic disorder and agoraphobia tends to be six to eighteen months (or longer), while obsessive-compulsive disorder often requires a long-term maintenance dose. In many instances, the SSRIs can be useful with generalized anxiety disorder as well, especially when generalized anxiety is accompanied by depression. People differ quite a bit in their response to the SSRIs. If you try one and experience no benefit, be willing to try another.

Other antidepressant medications such as Wellbutrin (bupropion) and Effexor (venlafaxine) tend to be prescribed when people have not shown beneficial response to either cyclic or SSRI antidepressants. Wellbutrin may be helpful for depression, but can be difficult for people with anxiety disorders to tolerate, since its side effects include anxiety and insomnia. Effexor combines a cyclic antidepressant with an SSRI in one pill. At the time of this writing there is insufficient information to evaluate its usefulness with anxiety disorders.

There are certain drawbacks associated with antidepressant drugs. All of them have side effects which are bothersome to some people during the first week or two of administration (afterwards, these effects usually diminish). Side effects tend to vary with the particular class of medication. Cyclic antidepressants may have anticholinergic side effects, such as dry mouth, dry skin, blurred vision, or constipation. They can also cause confusion, drowsiness, or agitation and anxiety, depending on the individual. The SSRIs are less likely to produce anticholinergic side effects, but can cause agitation, restlessness, anxiety, headaches or nausea, and gastrointestinal distress in certain individuals. *All of these side effects can be minimized by starting off with a very low dose of the medication and gradually increasing it over time to therapeutic levels*—for example, starting off with 5 mg/day of Pamelor or 10 mg/day of Zoloft, and gradually increasing the dose over two or three weeks to 100 mg/day for Pamelor or 50 mg/day for Zoloft. Still, in research on the effectiveness of antidepressant medications in treating panic, 25-30 percent of the participants stop taking these drugs because of initial side effects.

Another drawback of antidepressant medications is that they typically take 2-4 weeks to take effect. It is often easy to conclude that the medication isn't helpful while waiting this length of time for it to begin to relieve symptoms.

When use of an antidepressant medication is discontinued, quite a few individuals experience a relapse—that is, a return of the panic attacks for which the drug was originally prescribed. Relapse rates after taking antidepressant drugs are definitely lower than they are for Xanax, however. Research to date has found that approximately 50 percent of people experience an eventual return of panic after withdrawing from antidepressants, while 80-90 percent have a recurrence of panic symptoms after withdrawing from Xanax (this assumes they have received no other treatment for their problems besides medication).

Although the antidepressants have a major advantage over the benzodiazepines in that they are not physically addictive, some people become psychologically dependent on them and feel that they need to rely on them indefinitely. Occasionally, depressive symptoms also return after an antidepressant drug is withdrawn. In this instance some individuals choose to take a low, maintenance dose of an antidepressant medication for a period of several years.

Beta-Blockers

Although there are several different beta-adrenergic blocking drugs (popularly called *beta-blockers*), the two most commonly used with anxiety disorders are Inderal (propranolol) and Tenormin (atenolol). These medications can be helpful for anxiety conditions with marked bodily symptoms, especially heart palpitations (rapid or irregular heartbeat) and sweating. Beta-blockers are quite effective in blocking these peripheral manifestations of anxiety, but are less effective in reducing the internal experience of anxiety. Inderal or Tenormin may be used in conjunction with a benzodiazepine tranquilizer, such as Xanax, in treating panic disorder when heart palpitations are prominent. By themselves, beta-blockers are often given in a single dose to relieve severe physical symptoms of anxiety before a high-perfomance situation, such as public speaking, a job interview, final examinations, or a musical recital.

Although these medications are relatively safe, they can produce side effects, such as excessive lowering of blood pressure (causing dizziness or light-headedness), fatigue, and drowsiness. In some people they can also cause depression. Unlike tranquilizers, these medications do not tend to be physically addictive. Still, if you've been taking them for a while, it's preferable to taper your dose gradually to avoid rebound elevations of blood pressure.

Buspar

Researchers don't yet fully understand how Buspar (buspirone) works, but it is frequently used in the treatment of anxiety. To date it has been found useful in diminishing generalized anxiety, but is ineffective in reducing the frequency or intensity of panic attacks. Many practitioners prefer it over Xanax (and other benzodiazepines) for treating generalized anxiety because it does not cause sedation and is nonaddictive. There is relatively little risk of your becoming physically dependent on Buspar or requiring a protracted period of time to withdraw from it. More time is needed to fully evaluate the effectiveness and utility of this medication.

An ordinary starting dose for Buspar is 5 mg two to three times per day. It takes from two to three weeks before the full anti-anxiety effect of this medication is achieved. Some individuals with generalized anxiety respond well to Buspar, while others report side effects (lethargy, nausea, dizziness, or paradoxical anxiety).

Stopping Your Drug Use

If you've decided that you want to stop relying on prescription medications, observe the following guidelines:

1. *Be sure you've gained some level of mastery of the basic strategies for overcoming anxiety and panic presented in this workbook.* In particular, it would be a good idea to have established a daily practice of deep relaxation and exercise, along with skills in using abdominal breathing, muscle relaxation, and self-talk to counteract symptoms of panic. If you plan to withdraw from Xanax or a minor tranquilizer, these skills will serve you well in dealing with possible recurrences of anxiety and panic during the withdrawal period as well as over the long run. Be assured that any resurgence of high anxiety during withdrawal from a tranquilizer is *temporary* and should not persist after you've completed the withdrawal.

2. *Consult with your doctor to set up a program for gradually tapering off the dosage of your medication.* This is especially important if you've been taking a minor tranquilizer (the tapering-off period is dose-dependent, but may need to be as long as several months). A tapering-off period also needs to be observed if you're curtailing your use of an antidepressant medication such as Tofranil or a beta-blocker such as Inderal.

3. *Be prepared to increase your reliance on strategies described in this workbook during your tapering-off period*—especially relaxation, exercise, coping strategies for panic, self-talk, and identifying and expressing your feelings. Your withdrawal from medication is an opportunity to increase your skill at using these strategies. You'll gain increased self-confidence by learning to use self-activated strategies to master anxiety and panic without having to rely on medication.

4. *Don't be disappointed if you need to rely on medication during future periods of acute anxiety or stress.* Stopping regular use of a medication doesn't necessarily mean that you might not benefit from the *short-term* use of that medication in the future. For example, using a tranquilizer or sleeping medication for two weeks during a time of acute stress due to a traumatic experience is appropriate and unlikely to lead to dependence. If you're subject to seasonal affective disorder (pronounced depression during the winter months), you may stand to benefit from taking an antidepressant medication during that time of the year. Don't consider it a sign of weakness or a lack of self-control if you occasionally need to rely on prescription medications for a limited period of time. Given the stress and pressures of modern life, there are quite a few people who occasionally use prescription medications to help them cope. Such medications have their place if they are not used in a fashion that leads to physical or psychological dependence.

Working With Your Doctor

The purpose of this chapter has been to provide a balanced view of the role of medications in treating anxiety and phobias. There are certainly a variety of situations where the benefits of prescription drugs outweigh their associated risks and drawbacks. It's important, however, that before taking *any* medication you are fully aware of all of its potential side effects and limitations. It's your doctor's responsibility to 1) obtain a complete history of your symptoms, 2) inform you of the possible side effects and limitations of any particular drug, and 3) obtain your *informed consent* to try out a medication. As added insurance to being fully informed, you might look up the description of a medication you're considering in the *Physician's Desk Reference*, available at your doctor's office or your local library. It is your responsibility not to withhold information your doctor requests in taking your medical history, as well as to let him know, should he fail to ask, whether 1) you have allergic reactions to any drugs, 2) you are pregnant, or 3) you are taking any other prescription or over-the-counter medications.

Once this exchange of information has taken place between you and your physician, you will both be in a position to make a *fully informed and mutual decision* about whether taking a particular prescription medication is in your best interest. If your doctor is unwilling to take a collaborative rather than authoritarian stance or to allow for your informed consent, I strongly recommend that you find another doctor who will. Medications may enable you to "turn the corner" in recovering from your particular problem, but it is essential that they be used with the utmost care and responsibility.

Summary of Things To Do

1. Review this chapter to provide yourself with an overview of the various types of medications used to treat anxiety disorders. Be familiar with the benefits and limitations of those medications that may have relevance for your particular problems.

2. If you are not currently taking medication but wonder if you could benefit from doing so, contact a psychiatrist who is knowledgeable about anxiety disorders to discuss your options. The *National Treatment Directory for Phobias and Related Anxiety Disorders,* published by the Anxiety Disorders Association of America, lists psychiatrists specializing in anxiety disorders as well as other professionals who would know of such psychiatrists (see Appendix 1).

3. If you are currently taking a medication and would like to stop, consult your prescribing physician to discuss the appropriateness of doing so. If you and he jointly decide that you are ready to discontinue the medication, follow the guidelines in the section "Stopping Your Drug Use." Remember, it's preferable to discontinue medication only after you've gained some mastery of the skills discussed in Chapters 4-16 of this workbook.

Further Reading

Preston, John; O'Neal, John H.; and Talaga, Mary C. *Handbook of Clinical Psychopharmacology for Therapists.* Oakland, California: New Harbinger Publications, 1994.

Physician's Desk Reference, Oradell, New Jersey: Medical Economics Co., Inc., 1995.

Raynard, Richard C. *Guide to Panic and Anxiety Medications,* Braintree, Massachusetts: Healthguide Publishing, 1988. (This book may be obtained by calling 617-843-7689.)

18

Fears From the Past

Under most circumstances direct, real-life exposure to whatever situation you might fear is the most effective way to overcome that fear. Whether you're afraid of being home alone, driving far from home, speaking up in groups, or flying, simply facing the situation—in whatever small increments are necessary—offers the most likely resolution.

Sometimes, though, it's very difficult to begin exposure. No matter how small the initial step, your fear looms large. Or perhaps your experience with exposure is mostly successful, but some residual fear remains. While it becomes much easier to do what you previously avoided, it never becomes entirely comfortable or natural.

Having worked quite a few years with phobic clients has caused me to ponder the origins of these fears. In Chapter 2 of this book, you read that phobias are attributed to two causes: conditioning and trauma. Conditioning means learning a new association— for example, you're driving on the freeway, you suddenly start to panic, and then you subsequently form an automatic association between freeways and anxiety. The chapters on relaxation, imagery desensitization, and real-life desensitization provide detailed guidelines for overcoming fears that are due primarily to conditioning. What about fears that arise from past trauma? For example, you're in a car accident on the freeway and subsequently develop a fear of driving freeways. Certainly some of the fear is a result of conditioning. Yet the fear you felt at the moment the accident occurred was also likely to leave an emotional imprint. You don't have to approach the freeway to feel anxious— just thinking about the accident is enough.

The same implications also hold true for other types of trauma, such as natural disasters, violent assault, death of a loved one, and so on. Often such traumas can lead to an anxiety disorder that has only been briefly discussed in this book—Post-Traumatic Stress Disorder (PTSD). People with PTSD develop a constellation of symptoms either immediately or sometime after a traumatic incident. These symptoms include anxiety, recurrent distressing recollections of the event, distressing dreams of the event, avoidance of anything associated with the incident, emotional numbness, depression, feelings of estrangement and detachment, sleep disturbance, hypervigilance, and difficulty concentrating.

Although PTSD is usually associated with a discrete traumatic incident, the disorder seems to exist to some degree in anyone who has suffered an especially difficult or abusive childhood. Symptoms such as emotional numbness, a tendency to dissociate, and chronic anxiety can be the result of one particular incident in childhood, such as the death of a parent or abandonment by a parent through divorce. But more often such symptoms are the result of a series of traumatic incidents over a period of time, as is usually the case in instances of physical and sexual abuse, incest, parental alcoholism, or living with parents who by words or actions convey a sense of rejection.

Such incidents from the past can create a backdrop for the subsequent development of agoraphobia (in essence, a fear of being far from safety), social phobia (in essence, a fear of rejection or humiliation), and any number of other phobias. The more global fears associated with generalized anxiety disorder, such as fear of failure or fear of abandonment, often have roots in childhood. Even the fears evident in obsessive-compulsive disorder, such as fear of contamination or fear of loss of control, can often be traced back to early fears associated with being violated or losing control.

Core Fears

What has become apparent in my experience as a therapist is that most phobias seem to boil down to six underlying basic fears. These might be called "core fears"—they are the basic themes which underlie most of what we fear. The principal core fears are:

1. Fear of loss of control

2. Fear of death, injury, or pain

3. Fear of rejection, ridicule, or shame

4. Fear of confinement

5. Fear of abandonment, isolation, or loneliness

6. Fear of something strange or unknown

Almost any phobia you can imagine, when you trace it to its roots, involves one or more of these core fears. For example, fear of driving on freeways in most cases involves a fear of panicking while driving. But why would you be afraid of panicking on a freeway? The underlying fears here are likely to involve loss of control and/or fear of injury or death. In the same vein, fear of dentists can be traced back to a fear of confinement, fear of pain, or fear of loss of control.

Where do these core fears come from? Let's look at each one.

Fear of Loss of Control

Any traumatic experience that interferes with your sense of life being somewhat orderly and predictable can engender a fear of loss of control. Having a parent suddenly leave or die during childhood, for example, might leave you feeling not only vulnerable to loss and abandonment (see below), but fearful of anything that could upset your sense of having control over your life. Being in an accident, suffering a serious illness, or living through a natural disaster could also instill a fear of loss of control. Such experiences leave you with an increased sense of vulnerability about losing control again.

Fear of Death, Injury, or Pain

Traumatic experiences in which you have a close brush with death, or suffer injury or pain, can predispose you toward being fearful about any situation that could potentially lead to a similar experience. It also happens frequently that the death of someone close to you can lead to increased sensitivity and fearfulness about death, and perhaps any situation that can even remotely be associated with death. Two different clients of mine who experienced the death of a parent from chronic illness subsequently developed "illness phobia"—the fear that almost any minor ailment could be cancer or something terminal.

Fear of Rejection, Ridicule, or Shame

Growing up with parents who are overly critical or punitive can instill a sense of unworthiness or shame that a child may carry into adulthood. If you were frequently concerned about being accepted by your mother and father, you may still be walking around as an adult excessively concerned with getting approval, and fearful of criticism or rejection. This kind of background underlies many social phobias.

Fear of Confinement

Growing up in a dysfunctional family situation, in which your parents were physically or sexually abusive, or perhaps alcoholic, can instill a fear of being "unable to escape or get away." A child has no choice but to endure such mistreatment: it's easy to understand how a fear of being trapped might develop under such circumstances.

It's also evident that a fear of being trapped (in traffic, elevators, and so on) may point to a deeper sense of feeling trapped in a *current* life situation. Perhaps you feel trapped by your job, by your marriage, by loneliness, or possibly by a chronic illness. Because you haven't fully become aware of your deeper feeling of "existential entrapment," the fear is expressed in a specific phobia, such as fear of bridges, tunnels, elevators, or other enclosed places.

Fear of Abandonment, Isolation, or Loneliness

Frequently these fears are related to having experienced the loss of a parent or close relative during childhood. For some people, such losses can lead to a chronic fear of abandonment and difficulty being alone. Or perhaps there were occasions when your parents left you alone and you became quite frightened. Just as often, a fear of isolation and loneliness can refer back to having never felt close or bonded to either of your parents. Perhaps because they were neglectful, unavailable, or even abusive, you made the decision to withdraw into yourself and "go it alone" at an early age. Later on, you may have developed a fear of isolation and loneliness.

Fear of Something Strange or Unknown

A common manifestation of this fear is anxiety over unfamiliar or strange body sensations or symptoms. It can also arise in response to a new or unusual situation, especially when you are far from home. This particular core fear may have its origins in the "stranger anxiety" that many children display around the age of one in response to unfamiliar persons. Another possibility is that such fears arise from a "prewired" part of the brain, common not only to humans but also to other mammals, who often show fear when suddenly confronted with an unfamiliar person or other animal. (Such fear would have an evolutionary advantage in impelling flight from predators.)

Origins of Fear Before Childhood

In the past 15 years there has been considerable research into the possibility that some fears are imprinted even earlier than childhood. An emerging field of *perinatal psychology* is investigating the effect that traumatic birth has on subsequent personality development. It has been found, for example, that fears of confinement *may* have origins in a difficult birth during which the newborn was particularly slow to pass through the birth canal. Or a fear of death may derive from the experience of having come close to death at the time of birth—for example, when a newborn has to be revived from unconsciousness by artificial or mouth-to-mouth resuscitation. Evidence for fears from birth comes from the fact that some psychotherapy clients have been able to finally resolve some of their phobias when they were able to relive their original birth experience under hypnosis.

There is also evidence that even the fetus can be imprinted with fear prior to birth. Working in tandem with perinatal psychology, the field of *prenatal psychology* has proposed the hypothesis that the pregnant mother's predominant mood state—whether angry, sad, or fearful—can be adopted by the fetus. There is an emotional as well as physical symbiosis between mother and fetus to such a degree that an unborn child can actually take on the mother's predominant feeling. This even extends beyond feelings to attitudes: if the mother doesn't want the child, or is afraid of the responsibility the child might bring, the child somehow "knows" this and carries it into birth. The conclusions drawn by prenatal psychology are, as in the case of perinatal psychology, based on the experiences of clients in therapy. Under hypnosis these clients have actually returned to the intrauterine experience prior to their birth and "relived" the impact that their mother's feelings and attitudes had on them.

To the author's knowledge, there are no popular books exploring the realms of pre- and perinatal psychology. A comprehensive source book for professionals interested in this subject is *Regression Therapy: A Handbook for Professionals, Volume II*, edited by Winafred Lucas, Ph.D. (see the Further Reading section at the end of this chapter).

Recovery Approaches

How can you deal with your fears from the past? The first and most important approach to take is always *real-life exposure in the present*. Twenty-five years of research on psychotherapy has repeatedly demonstrated that desensitization and real-life exposure is the most effective treatment for phobias, always surpassing results of psychodynamic therapy approaches that explore childhood origins. *In the process of facing and overcoming what you fear in the present, you often reexperience and work through any possible unresolved emotions that might be left over from the past.* Going through all the feelings involved in facing what you fear—and developing an entirely new, more positive attitude toward what you previously avoided—can help you restructure the effects of a past trauma without necessarily remembering the trauma itself.

What is the purpose of this chapter then? In *some* cases it appears that exposure is not quite enough. Some residual anxiety remains even after successful exposure. Or you may have no particular phobias, but still be troubled by general fears of abandonment, rejection, loss of control, illness, death, and so on.

In such cases, it *may* be helpful to explore the possibility of a predisposing traumatic incident (or incidents). If you do recover memories of such an incident, it's important to reexperience any painful feelings you had at the time, and work through those feelings to the point where you are able to shift any negative decisions made, or beliefs held, as a result of the trauma. This process can be broken down into the following steps:

1. You recall and actually *reexperience*, to a significant degree, the circumstances of the early trauma which set up your fear.

2. You express and release the feelings—the fear, pain, sadness, shame, and anger—you had in response to traumatic circumstances.

3. You make a loving, caring response to your own inner child who had to endure these circumstances. You offer your inner child the caring, acceptance, and validation he or she was denied.

4. When you've completed the above steps, you can decide whether you are ready and willing to let go both of your old feelings and fearful attitudes about what happened, and to make room for new, constructive beliefs. You ask yourself: "What constructive belief would I like to hold instead of my old core fear?" For example, if you developed a fear of being trapped because a parent used to hold you down and hit you, you can reach the point where you formulate alternative, more positive beliefs: "The past is over. I'm free to feel safe in situations that are physically confining."

5. You reinforce your new belief—both with affirmations and by taking action in the world. That is, you keep affirming your new belief: "I'm free to feel safe in physically confining situations." Then you follow up your commitment with action, by continually exposing yourself to physically confining situations you used to avoid.

The above approach is particularly recommended for people who are survivors of physical or sexual childhood abuse.

Remembering and working through the effects of past trauma is a process that is best done in the context of psychotherapy. It's not something I would recommend attempting to do on your own. First, it's important to find a therapist with whom you feel safe and supported. Dealing with material from past trauma requires that you feel safe with and implicitly trust your therapist. Given this level of rapport, the process of recalling and exploring trauma from the past can take place in the context of insight-oriented talk therapy over a period of time. Usually this process takes a year or longer.

There are, at present, two methods that can accelerate this process considerably: 1) hypnosis and 2) eye-movement desensitization and reprocessing (EMDR). Each is described below.

Hypnosis

The word "hypnosis" may conjure up negative associations connected with sideshows and stage hypnotists. In fact, hypnosis is a *natural* phenomenon that all of us experience on a daily basis. Hypnotic trance, in its lighter form, is simply a state of focused attention or absorption. Every time you get involved in a TV program, or absorbed in driving on the freeway, you are essentially in a light trance state. The state of calm reverie induced by any relaxation technique is also a state of light hypnotic trance. Most of the therapeutic uses of hypnosis take place in a light to medium trance state. The deep trance states associated with magic shows and stage hypnotists are unnecessary for psychotherapeutic purposes and can only be reached by *highly* suggestible individuals—that is, by about 15-20 percent of the population.

Although there are many different types of hypnotic procedures, *age regression* is the technique most commonly used in retrieving unconscious memories and feelings associated with past traumatic incidents. One type of age regression technique involves giving clients explicit instructions to go back to their childhood and picture themselves as a small child. Further questioning enables clients to enter into specific scenes from the past and identify what they were doing, who was there, and how they felt about what happened. Another type of age regression technique involves having clients get in touch with a painful present day feeling such as fear, sadness, or shame and then to recall the earliest time they can remember when they felt that way in the past. Either of these techniques can help individuals to retrieve forgotten memories of past traumatic incidents. Often the recollection of trauma brings up very strong feelings. This happens because the person likely had very strong feelings of fear or terror at the time the trauma occurred, but was unable to experience such feelings because they were too overwhelming at the time. Instead, traumatized children repress or *dissociate* their feelings in connection with the trauma, subsequently developing symptoms of anxiety, emotional numbness, intrusive recollections, or even specific phobias. Not until the traumatic incident is recalled, and the original feelings are fully expressed, can such individuals entirely let go of what happened and be free to go on with their life. The purpose of hypnotic age regression is to help facilitate this retrieval, "reliving," and release of disturbing feelings associated with past trauma more fully and efficiently than might happen over the natural course of time.

It's better to undertake age regression with a skilled therapist than to attempt it on your own. There may be good reasons why you have been unable to recall a particular trauma in your past, and this may or may not be the right time to do so. Therapists using age regression always ask the client—addressing their unconscious rather than conscious mind—whether it's safe and appropriate to bring up repressed material from the past. The danger always exists that if too many repressed memories and feelings are brought up too fast, individuals can be flooded and consequently develop worse anxiety symptoms than they had in the first place. In the hands of a skillful therapist, however, age regression can be a very useful technique for helping you let go of fears from the past.

Eye-Movement Desensitization and Reprocessing (EMDR)

EMDR was developed from a phenomenon that was first observed by Dr. Francine Shapiro, a psychologist at the Mental Research Institute in Palo Alto, California. While walking through a park, preoccupied with disturbing thoughts, she noticed that by moving her eyes repetitively back and forth, the thoughts seemed to lose their intensity. Subsequently, she tested her observation on two groups of individuals suffering from PTSD, rape victims and Vietnam veterans. With both groups, the rapid-eye movement procedure reduced the intensity and frequency of disturbing symptoms related to the original trauma. When she followed up these groups a year later, they remained symptom-free.

Today, EMDR is a therapeutic procedure in which rapid-eye movements are induced while the individual focuses on a disturbing memory, feeling, image, or body sensation associated with a past traumatic event or a current disturbing issue. The process rapidly accesses repressed memories and feelings which the client often had not previously been able to recall or discuss. It is not uncommon to complete a process of remembering and working through a traumatic incident in four or five EMDR sessions, something that might have taken many months to accomplish with talk therapy. The process is referred to as "reprocessing" because clients not only access and work through traumatic memories, but also integrate new, more positive concepts—what they would *like* to believe about themselves, others, or life instead of the reactive, negative beliefs they likely took on automatically at the time of the trauma. For example, instead of concluding, "I'm vulnerable and unsafe," a rape victim might integrate a new, more constructive belief such as, "This is over, and I can go on with my life."

It appears that there is a biological basis for the efficacy of EMDR. Eye movements induced by the procedure are similar to those that occur naturally at night during rapid-eye-movement (REM) sleep. REM sleep corresponds to times at night when you are dreaming, and it is believed that one of the functions of dreaming is to integrate incomplete or unfinished experiences from the preceding day (or week, month)—that is, experiences you didn't fully think through and assimilate at the time they occurred. In the same manner, EMDR seems to enable the brain to access and reprocess "unfinished business" from past traumatic incidents. As long as traumatic material is unprocessed, it is likely to remain dissociated from consciousness and to produce disturbing symptoms such as anxiety, intrusive recollections, nightmares, emotional numbness and depression, and avoidance of anything associated with the trauma. There are, of course, other ways in which the brain may eventually be able to reprocess and integrate traumatic memories. EMDR, however, can speed up and help complete this process rather dramatically. The technique seems to be a way to remove excessive fear and emotional upset surrounding a past trauma so that you come to regard it as a memory with little or no emotional charge.

In the past few years, more than 4,000 therapists have been trained to use EMDR by Dr. Shapiro. To date, only licensed therapists have been trained. Utilizing the EMDR procedure properly is complex and best done in the context of working with a skilled therapist. It is not helpful or effective to try doing it on yourself.

The effectiveness of EMDR is currently being researched at several universities in the U.S. A study by Howard Lipke, Ph.D., of the North Chicago Veterans Administration

Medical Center, surveyed 1,200 EMDR-trained therapists about their opinion of the procedure. Approximately 75 percent felt that EMDR was more helpful than other techniques in relieving symptoms and difficulties associated with past trauma. Most of the remaining 25 percent of those surveyed found EMDR to be as helpful as other techniques they used.

The upshot of this section on recovery is that there are really two approaches to overcoming fears that have their origin in the past: 1) real-life exposure and 2) psychotherapy (possibly utilizing intensive approaches such as hypnosis and EMDR). The process of facing and working through a phobia in real life—*in vivo* exposure—may be sufficient to help you reprocess unfinished emotional business surrounding a past trauma. That is, the confidence you gain from successful exposure may itself help to undo long-standing fears. If exposure is not enough, though—or if you're dealing with core fears which persist after completing exposure to your phobias—then psychotherapy, exploring traumatic incidents in the past, may be useful. This is especially so if you are a survivor of childhood abuse.

Summary of Things To Do

1. Consider what core fears might underlie your more specific phobias and fears.

2. What circumstances in childhood might have contributed to any of your core fears? In reflecting on this question, it might be helpful to review the *Family Background Questionnaire* in Chapter 2.

3. If you decide that it's important for you to explore your fears from the past, be sure that you do this with a qualified psychotherapist with whom you feel a trusting, positive rapport.

Further Reading

Bass, Ellen and Davis, Laura. *The Courage to Heal.* New York: Harper & Row, 1988. (The most comprehensive source book for incest survivors.)

Farmer, Steven. *Adult Children of Abusive Parents.* Los Angeles: Lowell House, 1989.

Forward, Susan and Buck, Craig. *Toxic Parents.* New York: Bantam, 1989.

Lucas, Winafred B. (Ed.). *Regression Therapy: A Handbook for Professionals, Vols. I & II.* Crest Park, California: Deep Forest Press, 1993.

Matsakis, Aphrodite. *Post-Traumatic Stress Disorder: A Complete Treatment Guide.* Oakland: New Harbinger Publications, 1994.

Miller, Alice. *The Drama of the Gifted Child.* New York: Basic Books, 1983.

Missildine, Hugh. *Your Inner Child of the Past.* New York: Simon & Schuster, 1963.

Wickes, Frances. *The Inner World of Childhood.* Boston, Sigo Press, 1988.

19

Meaning, Purpose, and Spirituality

This chapter first considers how a sense of meaninglessness or lack of purpose in your life can contribute to anxiety. A second section examines the significance of developing your spirituality—one way to bring more meaning into your life. Raising questions about the meaning of life is important. Even if you have made the physical, behavioral, and attitude changes necessary to overcome panic attacks or phobias, a vague sense of anxiety may linger on if you feel that your life lacks meaning or a sense of purpose.

Existential psychologists such as Rollo May have used the term "existential anxiety" to refer to the type of anxiety that arises from having been unable to reach your full potential in life. This is a vague sense of tension, boredom, perhaps even "quiet desperation" that arises from feeling held back, for one reason or another, from being all that you can be. You live with a feeling of incompleteness—a sense that something vital is missing—although you may not consciously recognize what it is. If someone were to ask you, "Where is your life going?" or "What do you think your life is about?" you would tend to have trouble answering. Or you might think of things, which, on further reflection, don't seem "quite enough" to make your life as meaningful as you would like it to be.

For some people, a lack of purpose or meaningfulness in life can provide fertile ground for the development of panic attacks and phobias. Although panic may be caused by a number of factors, it sometimes reflects a sudden revelation (and desperation) that your life has no obvious direction. Similarly, the fear of being trapped or confined, or "unable to escape," that underlies so many phobias *may* reflect a deeper fear of being trapped by your current circumstances in life, whether involving a dead-end career, relationship, or any other situation that feels confining yet would require substantial risks to move out of. Phobic avoidance, in turn, *may* reflect a deeper avoidance of taking the very risks that are necessary to realize your full potential and life purpose. It has been my experience with a number of clients that their anxiety disorders (it doesn't seem to matter which particular type) did not fully resolve until they found something that could give their life a greater sense of meaning *and* they took the necessary risks to embrace it. In one case this involved a career change, in another it meant going back to school, and in still another it meant cultivating a creative talent with music.

Finding Your Unique Purpose

Each of us has one or more special purposes to fulfill that can give our life a sense of completeness. Those people who fully realize their special purpose often say, by the time they reach their senior years, that they feel satisfied with their life—that they did as much as they could to accomplish what they set out to do. Common examples of life purposes might include raising a family, succeeding in a fulfilling career, making a contribution to one's community, developing and expressing an artistic talent, completing an educational goal and using what you've learned to serve others, overcoming an addiction or the problems of a dysfunctional childhood, and conveying what you've learned to others. Life purposes appear to have a twofold function: 1) allowing you to feel more complete and whole, and 2) allowing you in some way to serve or contribute to the betterment of others. Realizing what truly gives your life meaning and purpose is likely to carry you beyond your own personal needs and to have a beneficial impact on someone else—whether that someone is a child, the people you work for, your community, or anyone to whom you convey what you've learned from your experience. In discovering your true purpose and potential, you move beyond immediate concerns for personal security and satisfaction toward making a meaningful contribution.

If you currently feel out of touch with your life purpose, how do you go about discovering what it is? The questionnaire which follows is designed to stimulate your thinking in ways that can help you to formulate your own unique goals. Your answers to the questions may give you some insights into what it is that is most important for you to do with your life. Give yourself at least *one full day* to reflect on these questions and write out your answers. You may even want to ponder these questions for a week or a month. After you've arrived at the answers for yourself, practice visualizing what your life would look like *if* you were truly fulfilling your special purpose. I also recommend that you share your answers to these questions with a close personal friend or counselor and get that person's input and feedback. If realizing your purpose involves making a career change, it might be helpful to work with a career counselor. If it involves going back to school, you'll want to talk to an academic guidance counselor at the school you're considering.

Life Purpose Questionnaire

1. Does the work I'm presently doing express what I truly want to be doing? If not, how can I begin to take steps toward discovering and doing work that would be more personally fulfilling?

2. Am I satisfied with the education I've obtained? Would I like to go back to school and increase my education and training? If so, how can I begin to move in that direction?

3. Do I have creative outlets? Are there any areas of my life where I feel I can be creative? If not, what creative activities could I develop?

4. Have I developed my spiritual life? Is doing so something I would like to explore further?

5. What would I like to do with my life if I could do what I truly wanted? (Assume, for the purpose of this question, that money and the responsibilities of your current job and family are *not* a limitation.)

6. What would I like to accomplish with my life? What would I like to have accomplished by the time I reach 70 in order to feel that my life has been productive and meaningful?

7. What are my most important values? What values give my life the greatest meaning? Some examples of values include:

Happy family life	Material success
Intimacy	Career achievement
Friendship	Creative expression
Good health	Personal growth
Peace of mind	Spiritual awareness
Serving others	Dedication to a social cause

8. Is there anything that I deeply value and yet feel I haven't fully experienced or realized in my life? What changes do I need to make—or what risks do I need to take—to more fully realize my most important values?

9. Do I have any special talents or skills that I haven't fully developed or expressed? What changes do I need to make—or what risks do I need to take—in order to develop and express my special talents and skills?

10. In the light of the above questions, I feel that my most important life purposes would include (list):

11. What obstacles exist to pursuing and realizing my life purposes?

12. What am I willing to *commit* to doing in the next month, year, and three years to eliminate the obstacles in Question 11 and move toward realizing my special purposes?

One month:

One year:

Three years:

Life Purpose Visualization

Write a scenario on a separate sheet of paper of what your life would look like if you were to fully realize your unique life purposes. You can design separate visualizations for each purpose or incorporate the realization of all of your life purposes into a single description. Be sure to make your scenario sufficiently detailed to include where you're living and working, who you are with, what activities make up your day, and what a typical day would look like. Once you've completed a detailed description, record it on tape, preferably in your own voice. You may want to record it after a few minutes of preliminary instructions to relax. Visualizing the fulfillment of your life purpose on a regular, consistent basis will go a long way toward accelerating the process of actually realizing your goal.

Spirituality

This section on spirituality is included because many clients of mine have achieved breakthroughs in their condition as the result of developing their spiritual life. If this section speaks to you, I hope that it may serve to motivate you to cultivate your spirituality. For those of you who already have a deep spiritual commitment, what follows may simply reinforce what you know, more than teach you anything new. For those to whom this section seems repellant or inapplicable, you need not feel compelled to read it or incorporate it into your recovery program. You can entirely overcome your particular problem with anxiety by relying on all of the strategies and guidelines presented in previous chapters of this workbook.

Spirituality involves the recognition and acceptance of a Higher Power beyond your own intelligence and will, with whom you can have a relationship. This Higher Power can provide you with an experience of inspiration, joy, security, peace of mind, and guidance that goes beyond what is possible in the absence of the conviction that such a power exists.

For our purposes here, spirituality can be seen as being distinct from religion. Different world religions have proposed various doctrines and belief systems about the nature of a Higher Power and humanity's relationship with it. Spirituality, on the other hand, refers to the *common experience* behind these various points of view—an experience involving an awareness of and relationship with something that transcends your personal self as well as the human order of things. This "something" has been given various names ("God" being the most popular in Western Society) and defined in ways that are too numerous to count. For purposes of this chapter, I will refer to it simply as the (or "your") *Higher Power*. You can choose to define what that means for yourself in whatever way feels most appropriate. Your own sense of a Higher Power can be as abstract as "cosmic consciousness" or as down-to-earth as the beauty of the ocean or mountains. Even if you regard yourself an agnostic or atheist, you may get a sense of inspiration from taking a walk in the forest or contemplating a beautiful sunset. Or a small child's smile may give you a special sense of joy. Whatever inspires you and takes you beyond yourself into a larger perspective points in the direction of what is referred to here as your Higher Power.

The purpose of this section is to emphasize that there is much healing and benefit to be obtained by cultivating your spiritual life (if that is something you feel drawn to or which feels right for you). Of all the methods and guidelines suggested in this workbook, a personal spiritual commitment is likely to reach the deepest in helping you to overcome the basic sense of fear or insecurity which underlies the various types of anxiety disorders. Whereas other methods described in previous chapters work at different levels—body, feelings, mind, or behavior—spiritual awareness and growth can effect a transformation in your whole being. It can help you to develop a basic trust and faith which is unshakable. Of course, the other methods described in previous chapters are still important and necessary. Please keep in mind that the ideas and exercises presented in this chapter are not a substitute for working with all of the other strategies and skills in this book.

A number of my clients have experienced major turnarounds in their condition as a result of cultivating their spirituality. Developing a relationship with their Higher Power did not necessarily cure a specific phobia or obsession, but it provided the moral support, courage, hope, and faith for them to follow through with their personal recovery program. It provided them with a sense that they are not alone in the universe, and that there is a source of guidance and support that is available at times of confusion and discouragement.

What are some of the specific benefits to be gained by developing your spirituality? Before enumerating several of these, it is important to understand that no one pursues spiritual growth in order to "get" such benefits. You will develop yourself spiritually only because you feel a deep, inner prompting to do so. The benefits are simply a consequence that follows from choosing to cultivate a relationship with your Higher Power. If you have already developed your spiritual life, you will already understand the "benefits" listed below.

Security and Safety

A sense of inner security and safety is especially important if you frequently deal with anxiety, worries, panic attacks, or phobias. Through developing a connection with your Higher Power, you gain security through the conviction that you are not all alone in the universe, even at those times when you feel temporarily separated from other people. You feel increasingly safe as you come to believe that there is a source you can always turn to in times of difficulty. There is much security to be gained through the understanding that there is no problem or difficulty, however great, that cannot be resolved through the help of your Higher Power.

Peace of Mind

Peace of mind is the *result* of feeling a deep, abiding sense of security and safety. The more reliance and trust you develop in your Higher Power, the easier it becomes to deal without fear or worry with the inevitable challenges life brings. It is not that you give up your self or your will to such a power; rather you simply learn that you can "let go" and turn to your Higher Power when you feel stuck with a problem in living and don't know how to proceed. Learning how to let go when solutions to problems aren't immediately apparent can go a long way toward reducing worry and anxiety in your life. Peace of mind is what develops in the absence of such anxiety.

Self-Confidence

As you develop a relationship with your Higher Power, you come to remember that you did not create yourself. You are reminded that you are a part of the universe of creation as much as the birds, stars, and trees. If this is a benign and supportive universe we live in—and developing a relationship with your Higher Power will help you to believe that it is—then in essence you're good, lovable, and worthy of respect just by virtue of the fact that you're here. However you behave—whatever choices you make— you are still inherently good and worthwhile. Your own judgments of yourself, however negative, do not ultimately count if you are a creation of the universe as much as everything else. As one person humorously put it: "God doesn't make junk." (It is, of course, a mistake to assume that this type of reasoning can be used to justify ignorant or unethical behavior. It's important to keep in mind the distinction between how a person behaves and what they are in essence.)

The Capacity To Give and Receive Unconditional Love

The most fundamental characteristic of your Higher Power is that it offers you an experience of unconditional love. This is a kind of love which differs from romantic love or even ordinary friendship. It entails an absolute caring for the welfare of another without any conditions. That is, no matter how another person appears or acts, you have compassion and care for them without judgment. As you develop a deeper connection with your Higher Power, you come to experience greater degrees of unconditional love in your life. You feel your heart opening more easily to people and their concerns. You feel freer of judgment toward them or of making comparisons among them. Unconditional love shows up both in your increased capacity to give love to others and to experience more of it coming into your life. You begin to experience less fear and more joy in your life and help to inspire others to experience their own capacity for unconditional love. This kind of love also manifests itself through the experience of having everything you need in your life to get on with what you want to do. This is spoken of in the Bible by the saying, "Seek ye first the Kingdom, and all will be added unto you."

Guidance

Developing a relationship with your Higher Power will provide you with guidance for making decisions and solving problems. Your Higher Power has a universal wisdom that goes beyond what you can accomplish through your own intellect. In traditional religions this has been referred to as the "all-knowingness of God" or "divine intelligence." Through connecting with your Higher Power, you can draw upon this greater wisdom to help you resolve all kinds of difficulties. You have probably already experienced this aspect of your Higher Power at moments when you've felt a deep conviction about something or have had an intuitive flash that turns out to be quite accurate. By learning to ask your Higher Power for guidance, you'll be surprised to find that every sincere request sooner or later is answered. And the quality of that answer generally exceeds what you could have figured out through your own conscious intellect or will.

These are some—by no means all—of the characteristics which define a close relationship with your Higher Power. All of them can contribute in a significant way to your personal recovery process. Keep in mind that there are many different paths you can take in coming into a greater awareness of your Higher Power. The particular path you choose, whether traditional or nontraditional, is up to you. The extent and sincerity of your commitment to your chosen path will determine the degree of personal healing you experience.

Changes in Beliefs Associated With Spirituality

Developing spiritually not only leads to new experiences and changes in the way you feel, it also can lead to a shift in your basic beliefs and assumptions about life and the world. As you develop spiritually, many of your beliefs about the meaning of life in general, and what your life is about specifically, can shift dramatically. And as these basic beliefs change, so too does your view of your condition—your personal struggle with anxiety—begin to change.

These shifts in beliefs can lead to having more compassion and tolerance toward yourself, as well as to finding a deeper meaning in the challenges you face, instead of viewing them as arbitrary and meaningless. You may feel less like a victim who has a particular problem with anxiety. Instead, you may come to regard your condition as an *opportunity* to grow and expand who you are.

What follows is a list of ten assumptions that are frequently associated with spirituality. They are not taken from any one source, tradition, or creed, but are based on the author's personal experience. Although they represent my own personal point of view, these ideas have been useful points of departure for discussion with a number of my clients. As you read through the ideas, give consideration to those that fit or make sense to you, and feel free to discard those that do not. Each of us has a basic philosophy about life which we have to formulate on our own.

Some of these ideas may stimulate questions which you may want to discuss with a significant other, a trusted friend, or even a minister, priest, or rabbi. All of the ideas can lead to a more optimistic and tolerant view of life. As you adopt any of these ideas that fit for you, you may find your attitude about your condition—as well as life in general—becoming a little more positive and a little less burdensome.

1. Life is a school. The primary meaning and purpose of life is that it is a "classroom" for growth in consciousness.

Most people tend to define their life's meaning in terms of those people, activities, self-images, or objects to which they attach the greatest value. Whatever you value most in life—whether family, another individual, work, a particular role or self-image, your health, or material possessions—these things are probably what define your life's meaning. If you lost what you valued the most, your life might seem to lose its meaning. Think for a moment about what you value most highly in your life and what gives you the greatest satisfaction and comfort. Then imagine what your life would be like if these things were all suddenly taken away.

The truth, of course, is that everything you value most *will* eventually pass away. Nothing that you cherish lasts forever. Yet if everything you value must someday cease to be, what is the *ultimate* meaning of life? And as long as you assume that there is nothing more to existence than your present life—what there is right now—then there doesn't seem to be *any* ultimate meaning. You end up saying (along with Jean Paul Sartre and other existentialists) that the only meaning life has is what you make of it in the present moment. Apart from this, life appears to have no meaning in and of itself. Since everything, including life itself, eventually passes away, how can there be any ultimate point to any of it?

Most forms of spirituality, traditional and modern, move beyond this existential predicament. Most of them make some kind of assumption that human life is *not* all there is. Something of us persists beyond human life, and so life comes to be seen as a temporary sojourn—not the final destination. Life comes to be understood as a preparation or training ground for something else that cannot be fully understood or revealed while you are alive.

It is this particular interpretation of life's "ultimate" meaning that the author has found to be most valid and helpful. If the final meaning of life is that it is a classroom or school for growth in consciousness—for the development of wisdom and the capacity to love—then the fact that everything passes away takes on an entirely new meaning. The tasks and challenges that come up in life, and your response to them, do not have eternal repercussions. Nor do they have no meaning at all. They are more like lessons in a school, lessons to which you apply yourself, and which you try to master as best you can. Each lesson is repeated until it is mastered. As you master old lessons, new ones are put before you. This "earth school" is thus a place where you learn and grow; it is not your final dwelling place. Eventually it is time to leave this classroom and move on.

2. Adversity and difficult situations are lessons designed for your growth—they are not random, capricious acts of fate. In the larger scheme of things, everything happens for a purpose.

If you accept the idea that life is a classroom, then the adversity and difficulties that come into your life may be viewed as part of the curriculum—as lessons for growth. This is a very different point of view from one that sees life's misfortunes as random quirks of fate. The latter perspective leads to a sense of victimization. You can end up feeling powerless in a capricious world which appears to be completely inequitable in its treatment of people, some of whom have such good luck, while others have misfortune heaped upon them.

The view proposed here is that the difficulties of life are lessons to promote growth in wisdom, compassion, love, and other positive qualities (some religious traditions refer to "tests," although I prefer the notion of "lessons"). The greater the difficulty, the greater the potential for learning and growth. If you accept this idea, then the next question you may ask is who establishes the curriculum or "assigns" your life lessons? Many of us may ask this question in one form or another when a given life challenge seems particularly difficult. We tend to protest and even rail against some of the misfortunes and limitations we're faced with. The question arises: "How could a loving God permit this?"

There is no easy answer to this question. None of us can fully understand how our life lessons are administered and assigned, though different spiritual traditions have different views on this matter (Eastern traditions speak of "karma," while Judeo-Christian traditions speak of "tests" and "temptations"). Each of us has to struggle with the challenges life brings without fully understanding why. What does seem apparent is that growth could not occur if the lessons were *always* easy. If the purpose of life is for us to grow in wisdom, consciousness, and compassion, then at least some of the lessons need to be difficult. This may not be an altogether consoling view, but it at least makes some sense out of the difficult situations that occur in life.

Given this view, you can stop asking, "Why did this happen to me?" and instead ask the more constructive questions: "What is this meant to teach me? How can I learn from this?" You might take whatever worry or concern is bothering you the most in your life at this time and try asking the latter two questions instead of the first.

3. Your personal limitations and flaws are the "grist" you have to work with for your inner growth. Sometimes you can heal and overcome them with modest effort. In other cases, they may stay with you for a long time in order to push you to evolve and develop to your fullest potential. You are not "wrong" or in any way to blame because of your limitations.

Think for a moment about some of your own personal limitations—the ones you find most difficult to live with. If you are dealing with an anxiety disorder, think about your condition. You may ask why anyone should have to deal with a difficult condition such as panic disorder, agoraphobia, social phobia, or an obsessive-compulsive disorder even for a few months, let alone a longer time. Hopefully you have utilized all of the best treatments—including medication, if necessary—and have experienced a significant and genuine recovery. In many cases, a full recovery from an anxiety disorder is certainly possible. Suppose, however, that you have received all the best treatments, worked very hard for one or two years, and have experienced *some* improvement—yet you are still dealing with your condition to a degree. Is that a reason for you to think of yourself as a failure? A reason to think that you are somehow less skillful or persistent than those people who overcame their condition quickly?

If you've worked hard on overcoming your condition, but are still troubled by it, perhaps there is some significant growth experience to find in the process of having to work with your difficulty for a long time. It all depends upon the lesson you happen to be learning. Having a difficult condition that is easily dispensed with in a short time would certainly help develop your confidence in your own self-mastery—an important lesson in itself. Yet it wouldn't necessarily develop qualities of compassion or patience. It often seems that only through having to struggle with our own infirmities for a time can we learn fully how to feel compassion or have patience with others' difficulties.

As a second example, suppose that your lesson is to learn how to let go of the excessive need for control—even more, to learn how to let go and allow your Higher Power or God to have an impact on your life. One way (not the only way) this might be learned is to have to deal with a difficult situation in which all your efforts to control just don't work. The ability to let go of control is often fostered by those very difficulties in life that are most challenging. Some conditions and situations are so challenging that they *compel* us to let go. There is no other alternative. To struggle or fight against the condition only creates more distress and suffering. It is often at the exact moment when you fully let go of your worry or stop struggling that you may experience some kind of response or relief from your Higher Power. To let go and trust in your Higher Power should not be thought of as relinquishing responsibility for your life. Rather, it involves doing all you can to help yourself first, and then, turning things over to another source of assistance.

In sum, it is a mistake to fault yourself for having any intractable condition, no matter how disabling or how long you've had it. It is there to foster and deepen certain qualities of your inner self. *How you respond to it and what you learn from it is what's important—not the condition itself.*

4. Your life has a creative purpose and mission. There is something creative which is yours to develop and offer.

Your life is not a random sequence of accidental events but follows a plan. This plan is *created* from a level that none of us can fully understand. Part of this plan consists of the lessons for growth in consciousness that were described in the preceding three sections.

Another very important aspect of the plan is your creative endowments, talents, or "gifts." Each of us has at least one personal form of creativity which can give our life meaning and purpose. The development and full expression of your creative talents and gifts is your "life purpose" or "life mission" spoken of earlier in this chapter.

Your life purpose is something that you feel you *need* to do in order to feel whole, complete, and fulfilled in your life. It's uniquely your own—something that can't be duplicated. Only you can do it. It comes from within, and has nothing to do with what your parents, partner, or friends might want you to do. Generally it moves you beyond yourself and has an impact on something or someone else.

Your purpose or mission can be a vocation or avocation—its scope can extend to the entire world or to just one other person. Examples would include: raising a family, mastering a musical instrument, volunteering your services to help youth or the elderly, writing poems, speaking eloquently before groups, or tending the garden in your backyard.

Until you develop and express your creative gifts, your life will seem incomplete. You will feel more anxiety because you are not making time to do what you truly want to do, what you were in fact born to do. The first part of this chapter was designed to help you get in touch with your creative purpose and mission. If you are not quite sure yet what it is, you may want to discuss your answers to the *Life Purpose Questionnaire* at the beginning of this chapter with a trusted friend or counselor. You may also find the book *Finding Your Life Mission* by Naomi Stephan to be useful.

5. A Higher Source of support and guidance is always available.

This idea is the basis of this entire section on spirituality. Much fear and anxiety is based on the perception that you are separate and alone—or else on the anticipation of rejection or loss that might eventually result in being separate and alone. The truth is that you are not alone. Even at those times when you might find it difficult to turn to other human beings for support, there remains another source of support that can always be called on. Your Higher Power is not merely an abstract entity that created and sustains the universe. It is a force, power, or presence with which you can enter into a personal relationship. This relationship is as personal as any you could have with another human being.

In this personal relationship, you can experience both *support* and *guidance.* Support often appears in the form of inspiration or enthusiasm that can help lift and sustain you at times of low motivation and discouragement. Guidance can come in the form of clear insights and intuitions that provide discrimination and direction about what you need to do. Frequently this type of inspired insight or realization is wiser than anything you might have figured out with your rational mind.

You may experience a dilemma about this. If you think of inspiration and intuition originating in your own subconscious mind, how do they come then from a Higher Power—from something seemingly separate from you? Certainly from the perspective of the conscious mind, everything does seem separate—you perceive yourself as separate from others, the world, and most likely from a Higher Power. There is another level, though, which the conscious mind can't comprehend, where all things are joined. Eastern philosophy refers to this as "the One in which all things reside." The modern physicist David Bohm speaks of the "implicate order" in which everything is connected. In the

Bible (New Testament) this idea is expressed in the statement: "The Kingdom of Heaven is within you."

To receive support and guidance from your Higher Power, you simply need to ask. Nothing more is necessary. While this might seem easy enough, it may not be in practice if you believe that you're supposed to figure out and handle everything entirely on your own. Or it may not be easy if you feel that it's irrational, weak, or in some other way beneath your dignity to rely on an invisible power for support. To trust and rely on your Higher Power, it takes a certain willingness to let go of control as well as a certain humility (it's often humbling to come to the realization that you can't handle something completely on your own). The ability to let go and trust *is* something that can be learned. Often the life lessons that are the hardest—the ones that push you to your absolute limit—tend to be the ones that have the most to teach about letting go.

As you increasingly learn to allow your Higher Power (Spirit) to assist in your life, you can grow in trusting that it is sometimes appropriate to relinquish control.

6. Contact with your Higher Power is directly available within your personal experience.

You can discover a personal relationship with your Higher Power within your own immediate experience. It is as personal a relationship as any you might have with another human being. It is a two-way relationship. You can receive support, guidance, inspiration, peace of mind, inner strength, hope, and many other gifts from your Higher Power; you can also communicate your needs to Spirit through prayer, and directly communicate feelings of gratitude and reverence. Such a relationship can deepen and grow to the extent that you choose to give it attention and time.

There are numerous ways in which your Higher Power can manifest in your personal experience. Some fairly common examples follow:

- Feeling supported by a loving presence.

- An inner knowing or intuitive recognition. Some deep insight comes to you and you have a clear, unequivocal sense that it is true.

- After a period of stress or struggle, you suddenly feel an influx of calmness or peace. Because it comes to you without any effort on your part, there is a sense that it comes from a place beyond your personal ego.

- Feelings of awe and wonder when beholding the beauty of nature.

- Visionary experiences—actually having a visual impression within or outside of your mind of a spiritual being or presence.

- Synchronicities—something in the outside world coincidentally matches what is going on in your mind. It feels like more than just a coincidence. For example, you're obsessively worrying about something while driving and a car pulls in front of you with a personalized license plate that says, "Let Go."

- Miracles—for example, spontaneous healings that defy medical explanation.

As you read this, think about some of the ways in which you have experienced the presence of a Higher Power within your own experience. There are many forms other than those listed above.

7. Questions sincerely asked of your Higher Power are answered.

This idea is really an extension of the previous point about your Higher Power being a source of support and guidance. The reason for making this point separately is to underscore the fact that your Higher Power's support and guidance is not only bestowed on you—you can deliberately ask for it. The famous quote of Jesus, "Ask and you shall receive," is true regardless of the particular spiritual tradition or orientation you follow.

It is the assumption of all religious approaches that incorporate prayer that prayer will be answered. Perhaps some of you reading this right now have had experiences of your prayers being answered. It often seems that the degree of earnestness of your request has something to do with how readily the prayer receives a response. A common example is when you feel overwhelmed with some situation and you almost literally cry out for help to your Higher Power. In many, if not most, cases something about the situation improves or shifts, often within a short time.

There is actually scientific research that confirms the efficacy of prayer. Several well-controlled empirical studies of prayer are reported in the book *Recovering The Soul: A Scientific and Spiritual Search* by Larry Dossey, M.D.

In sum, there is both anecdotal and research support for the idea that prayer is effective. This doesn't mean that whatever you pray for will come true. There are some qualifications, which, in this author's experience, need to be kept in mind: 1) the request or plea needs to be made with genuine earnestness and sincerity, 2) the "answer" or response to prayer may not come immediately—it may take days, weeks, or months, 3) the answer may not come all at once—instead, only a step in the direction of the answer may come (for example, if you're praying for healing from chronic pain, the answer may come in the form of a strong intuition to visit a particular doctor or healing practitioner). Prayer can be answered in many ways, and sometimes the answer may not be what you expected. It is not possible to know in advance how a particular prayer will be answered (that is when faith comes in). What can be trusted is that there will be an answer, and that that answer will serve your highest good.

8. What you truly ask for or intend from the deepest level of yourself—from your heart—will tend to come to you.

One of the most powerful things that can foster positive change and healing is a sincerely held intention. With clients, and in my own experience, I have observed how the power of intention can promote miraculous consequences. What you believe in and commit to with your whole heart tends to come true. When the intention is for your own highest good—and when it doesn't conflict with anyone else's highest good—it is most likely to become manifest.

A deeply held intention shifts and focuses your own consciousness. It also appears to have ramifications on events in the world apart from you. Events in the outer world will tend to align with your most deeply held intention. Goethe summed this up in his famous remark:

> Concerning all acts of initiative or creation,
> there is one elementary truth;
>
> The ignorance of which kills countless ideas and splendid plans:
> the moment one definitely commits oneself,
> then Providence moves too.

All sorts of things occur to help one
that would never otherwise have occurred.

A whole stream of events issue from the decision,
raising in one's favor
all manner of unforseen incidents and assistance,
which no person could have dreamt
would have come their way.

9. Love is stronger than fear. Pure, unconditional love emanates from your Higher Power (God) and is at the very center of your being and all beings. All fears can be understood as different forms of separation: separation from others, ourselves, and God—separation from the love that unites all things.

Love is stronger than fear because it goes deeper. On a conscious level love is the experience of feeling your heart go out toward unity with someone or something other than yourself. On a deeper level, love is the "ground state" or essential foundation of the entire universe. This is a view that is common both to Eastern and Western religions. Love is not something we either possess or do not possess, because it literally *defines* what we are at our core and in essence. Fear may go deep, but never as deep as love, because fear only arises when we feel separate from the ground state that unifies us with everything else.

The popular phrase, "We are all one," expresses the truth about love and is, on a level beyond what our conscious mind can fully comprehend, literally true.

Most of the anxiety you experience may be related to specific fears of abandonment, rejection and humiliation, loss of control, confinement, injury, or death. Fear can take on any of these forms, based on your conditioning and past experience. Yet none of these fears could ever arise if you did not experience separation. The existence of fear always points to a degree of separation—separation of your conscious mind from your innermost being, separation from others, and/or separation from God. If it is true that in essence all of us are united as one, then every fear we feel—no matter how much we believe it—is, in fact, just an illusion. If we could perceive things the way they truly are, there would be no reason to have any more fear.

Love and fear constitute perhaps the most profound duality in human existence. Yet the former can always overcome the latter.

10. Death is not an end but a transition. Our essential nature or soul survives physical death. (To fear death as "the end" is simply an illusion.)

This basic idea is shared by all of the world's religions. They all assume that an individual's soul continues to exist after physical death, although they differ somewhat in their conceptions about the nature of the afterlife.

Actual evidence for this view has emerged in the past 15 years from the widespread research on "near-death experiences." As you most likely already know, near-death experiences are based on reports of what people experienced between the time when their vital signs indicated imminent or actual death and when they were subsequently revived. These reports all share several things, such as passing through a tunnel, meeting a being of light that radiates love and understanding, witnessing a scene-by-scene review of one's entire life, and sometimes meeting relatives who have already died. A smaller number of these reports describe other-worldly scenes and locales associated with the events that are experienced. Though the thousands of such reports that have been collected worldwide don't "prove" that consciousness survives death, they certainly make a strong case in that direction. Further evidence that near-death survivors get a peek into an afterlife comes from the fact that many of them lose their fear of death and become more deeply spiritual following their experience. If what they went through was simply a dream, why would it have such a deep and lasting impact?

Does fear of death come up for you or underlie other fears you might have about illness or injury? If so, I would suggest that you read the literature on near-death experiences and come to your own conclusions about life after death. The books *Life After Life* and *Reflections On Life After Life* by Raymond Moody are a good start, but I would especially recommend the book *Heading Toward Omega* by Kenneth Ring.

Exercise 1: Spirituality and Your View of Your Condition

Go back over the ten assumptions above. Decide which ones fit for you, which ones you would want to question or discuss, and which, if any, don't fit or make sense to you.

If some of these ideas strike you as true, how would believing them change your view of your anxiety condition? Your view of life in general? On a separate sheet of paper, write down your answers to these two questions.

Exercise 2: Connecting With Your Higher Power

The following exercise is intended to help you get in touch with your Higher Power and obtain assistance to deal with any issue causing you worry or anxiety. Use the exercise only if it feels appropriate to you. (You may have your own methods of prayer and meditation which you find preferable.) Give yourself time to get relaxed and centered first before working with the affirmations and visualization.

1. Get comfortable in a seated position (or lie down if you prefer). Spend at least five minutes using any technique you wish to get relaxed. You can do abdominal breathing, progressive muscle relaxation, visualize going to your peaceful place, or meditate (see Chapter 4 for instructions for specific relaxation techniques).

2. If you're not already aware of it, bring to mind the situation, person, or whatever about which you are worried or anxious. Focus on this for several moments until you have it clearly in mind. If feelings of anxiety come up, allow yourself to feel them.

3. Affirm over and over, with as much conviction as you can,

   "I turn this over to my Higher Power (or God)."

   "I release this problem to my Higher Power (or God)."

   Simply repeat these statements slowly, calmly and with feeling as many times as you wish until you begin to feel better. While doing this, it is good to bring to mind the following ideas about your Higher Power:

- It is "all knowing"—in other words, it has wisdom and intelligence that go beyond your conscious capacity to perceive solutions to problems.

- In its greater wisdom, your Higher Power has a solution to whatever you're worried about.

- Even though you can't see the solution to your worry right now, you *can* affirm faith that there is no problem that can't be resolved through the help of your Higher Power.

4. If you are visually inclined, imagine that you're going to meet your Higher Power. You might see yourself in a garden or a beautiful setting of your choice, and then imagine that you see a figure—your Higher Power—approaching you. It may be indistinct at first and grow gradually clearer. You may notice that this figure exudes love and wisdom. It might be a wise old man or woman, a being of light, Jesus, the supreme being in your particular religion, or any other presence that adequately represents your Higher Power.

5. While in the presence of your Higher Power—whether you visualize it or not— simply find a way to ask for help. For example, you might say, "I ask for your help and guidance with_____." Keep repeating your request until you feel better.

   You may want to listen to see if your Higher Power has an immediate answer on an insight to offer you about your request. It is quite all right, though, simply to make your request and ask for help without getting an answer. The purpose of this process is to develop trust and belief in your Higher Power (what has traditionally been called "faith in God").

   The key to this part of the process is an attitude of genuine humility. By asking for help from your Higher Power, you relinquish some of your conscious control of the situation, and exercise a willingness to trust.

6. *Optional:* If it feels appropriate, visualize a beam of white light going to that place in your body that feels anxious or worried. Often this will be the solar plexus region (in the middle of your trunk right below the center of your rib cage) or the "pit" of your stomach. Let that area be filled with the light until the anxiety dissolves or fades away. Keep directing white light to that region until it completely settles down and is free of anxiety.

Give this entire process time. It may be necessary to persist with it for as long as half an hour to 45 minutes in order to feel a genuine connection with your Higher Power and a deeply felt trust that the problem you're worried about can truly be resolved. If, after completing this process, your worry comes back the next day, simply repeat the exercise every day until you've mastered your worry. To many readers, the above process will appear to be a variation on traditional prayer.

Options for Developing Your Spiritual Life

You can deepen your commitment to spirituality through any of the following means:

1. Regular participation in church or your preferred spiritually based organization.

2. Regular reading of inspirational literature of your preference. It's good to do this at least once per day, either upon awakening, during your lunch break, or before retiring.

3. Regular practice of meditation (see the section on meditation and relevant references in Chapter 4).

4. Regular practice of prayer or spiritual affirmations (see the books by Louise Hay and Shakti Gawain below for how to work with spiritual affirmations).

5. Involvement in a 12-step program that is relevant to your needs. The 12-step programs offer many people a well-conceived and effective approach for healing addictions. Although they began with Alcoholics Anonymous 50 years ago, they now include a wide range of programs such as Emotions Anonymous, Co-Dependents Anonymous, Overeaters Anonymous, Sex and Love Addictions Anonymous, Workaholics Anonymous, and so on. Consult your local chapter of the National Council on Alcoholism for a list of 12-step groups in your area.

A Final Caveat

Reading the previous sections may have made spirituality sound as if it were a "cure-all." You might even be left with the idea that developing a relationship with your Higher Power is *all* that is necessary for you to overcome your problem with panic, phobias, or anxiety. This is very unlikely to be true. You're still going to need to draw on all of the strategies presented in this workbook to deal with your particular problem with anxiety. Relaxation, exercise, coping strategies for panic, imagery and real-life desensitization, changing self-talk and mistaken beliefs, expressing feelings, developing assertiveness, and working on self-esteem will all be necessary.

What developing your spirituality can do is to give you the inspiration and hope to persist in following through with your recovery program. And it can also provide you with a powerful means for breaking through to your next step forward at those times when you're feeling stuck, discouraged, or confused.

Summary of Things To Do

1. Do you feel aware of your own unique life purpose or purposes? Use the *Life Purpose Questionnaire* to assist you in clarifying what you would most like to do with your life.

2. Reflect on the ten ideas presented in the section "Changes in Beliefs Associated With Spirituality" and complete Exercise 1.

3. Practice the meditation "Connecting With Your Higher Power" when you feel up against a personal issue that you've been unable to resolve through your own conscious efforts.

4. Among the list of options for developing your spiritual life, decide which one(s) you'd be willing to commit more time to during the next month.

Further Reading

For those readers who are already on a traditional religious path, written sources of inspiration and guidance are well-marked. The Bible has a tremendous amount of insight and wisdom to offer those of you who follow the Christian or Jewish faith. Islamic, Buddhist, Hindu, and other traditional cultures all possess a rich literature of spiritual wisdom.

Other readers exploring alternative spiritual points of view may feel drawn to what has been popularly called "new age spirituality." Much has been written in this area, although little of it is entirely new. New age spirituality, in fact, involves the rediscovery and reemergence of ancient spiritual wisdom that has been around for thousands of years. Recommended books in this vein include:

Dass, Ram, and Gorman, Paul. *How Can I Help?* New York: Alfred A. Knopf, 1986.

Dossey, Larry. *Recovering the Soul: A Scientific and Spiritual Search.* New York: Bantam, 1989.

Gawain, Shakti. *Creative Visualization.* Mill Valley, California: Whatever Publishing, 1978.

Gawain, Shakti, with King, Laurel. *Living in the Light.* Mill Valley, California: Whatever Publishing, 1986.

Hay, Louise. *You Can Heal Your Life.* Santa Monica, California: Hay House, 1984. (Many helpful tools and affirmations for developing self-worth.)

Jampolsky, Gerald. *Love Is Letting Go of Fear.* Millbrae, California: Celestial Arts, 1979.

Jampolsky, Gerald. *Good-Bye To Guilt.* New York: Bantam Books, 1985.

Miller, Carolyn. *Creating Miracles.* Tiburon, California: HJ Kramer, 1995.

Moody, Raymond. *Life After Life.* New York: Bantam, 1976.

Norwood, Robin. *Why Me. Why This. Why Now.* New York: Carol Southern Books, 1994.

Peck, M. Scott. *Further Along The Road Less Traveled.* New York: Simon & Schuster, 1993.

Ring, Kenneth. *Heading Toward Omega.* New York: William Morrow, 1985. (A comprehensive and compelling study of near-death experiences.)

Rodegast, Pat. *Emmanuel's Book.* New York: Bantam, 1985.

Roman, Sanaya. *Spiritual Growth.* Tiburon, California: H. J. Kramer Inc., 1989.

Stephan, Naomi. *Finding Your Life Mission.* Walpole, New Hampshire: Stillpoint Publishing, 1989.

Williamson, Marrianne. *A Return To Love.* New York: HarperCollins, 1992.

Williamson, Marianne. *Illuminata.* New York: Random House, 1994. (An outstanding collection of thoughts and prayers for modern times.)

Zukav, Gary. *The Seat of the Soul.* New York: Fireside Books, 1990.

Appendix

1

Resources

The Anxiety Disorders Association of America

The Anxiety Disorders Association of America (ADAA) is a nonprofit, charitable organization founded in 1980 by leaders in the field of treatment for phobias, agoraphobia, and panic/anxiety disorders. Its purpose is to promote public awareness about anxiety disorders, stimulate research and development of effective treatments, and offer assistance to sufferers and their families in gaining access to available specialists and treatment programs.

The Association publishes a quarterly newsletter and a *National Treatment Directory*, now in its sixth edition, which lists professionals and programs throughout the United States and Canada specializing in the treatment of anxiety disorders. It also publishes several relevant books and pamphlets.

For further information about the Anxiety Disorders Association of America, its services, publications, and conferences, as well as how to join, please contact

> The Anxiety Disorders Association of America
> 11900 Parklawn Drive, suite 100
> Rockville, Maryland 20852-2624
> (301) 231-9350

Other Resources

> Agoraphobic Foundation of Canada
> P.O. Box 132
> Chomedey, Laval, Quebec
> H7W 4K2, Canada

> Agoraphobics In Action, Inc.
> P.O. Box 1662
> Antioch, TN 37011-1662
> (615) 831-2383

Agoraphobics in Motion-A.I.M.
605 West 11 Mile Road
Royal Oak, MI 48067
(313) 547-0400

CHAANGE
128 Country Club Drive
Chula Vista, CA 91911
(619) 425-3992

ENcourage Newsletter
13610 North Scottsdale Road, Suite 10-126
Scottsdale, AZ 85254

Free From Fear Foundation
1137 Gloucester Square
Pickering, Ontario, Canada, L1V 3R1

National Institute of Mental Health—Information Service
Call 1-800-64-PANIC for free information on the nature and treatment of
panic disorders.

National Panic/Anxiety Disorder Newsletter
1718 Burgundy Place, Suite B
Santa Rosa, CA 95403
(707) 527-5738

New Beginnings Foundation for Agoraphobia
P.O. Box 9327
Glendale, CA 91226
(818) 549-9966

Obsessive Compulsive Foundation, Inc.
P.O. Box 9573
New Haven, CT 06535

The Open Door
608 Russell Avenue South
Minneapolis, MN 55405

PASS-Group, Inc.
P.O. Box 1614
Williamsville, NY 14221
(716) 689-4399

Phobics Anonymous
P.O. Box 1180
Palm Springs, CA 92263
(619) 322-COPE

Terrap
932 Evelyn Street
Menlo Park, CA 94025
(800) 274-6242

Appendix

2

Imagery Desensitization with a Helper
(Instructions for the Helper)*

1. Administer 10-15 minutes of relaxation instructions. Use the instructions for progressive muscle relaxation in Chapter 4 or one of the visualizations described in Chapter 11.

2. When your partner is fully relaxed, present the first scene from the hierarchy as follows: "Imagine that you are _____. Picture this fully in your mind. See all the details—the colors, shapes, and sizes of everything in the scene. Notice anything you can hear or smell. Notice how you're feeling as you enter the scene." (Pause 15 seconds.)

3. If your partner experiences any anxiety, she should signal you by raising her right index finger. When you introduce or reintroduce a given scene, you can give her the instruction "If you're feeling any anxiety, let me know by raising your right index finger." (After a while it may not be necessary to keep repeating this, as your partner will understand that she is supposed to signal her anxiety.)

4. If your partner signals anxiety, have her *stay* in the scene another minute but give her instructions as follows: "Now imagine you're still in the scene but you can begin to relax by taking a deep breath and then breathing any anxiety you're feeling away. Just breathe away any tension you're feeling. Imagine any anxiety you feel just flowing out of your body as you become more and more relaxed. Just let go of all the anxiety completely ..." (Allow one minute to pass.)

5. After the minute in Step 4 has elapsed, ask your partner to "switch off" the scene, and then give her further relaxation instructions. These can consist of muscle relaxation techniques or a suggestion to visualize a peaceful scene at the beach, in the woods, or wherever she likes. For example: "Now switch off the scene and let yourself completely relax.... Go to your peaceful scene." Have your partner stay in her peaceful scene for one minute.

---

* For the sake of clarity and brevity, I've used feminine pronouns in this section. Obviously, these instructions can be used when either male or female partners are involved.

6. After the minute in Step 5 has elapsed, ask your partner to signal with her right index finger if she is experiencing any anxiety.

   a. If so, continue giving her suggestions to relax or to stay in her peaceful scene for another minute. Then ask her again to signal whether she is experiencing any anxiety. Do not proceed until she *doesn't* signal any anxiety.

   b. If she doesn't signal anxiety, proceed to Step 7.

7. Reintroduce the same scene as in Step 2 and repeat the entire desensitization process (Steps 2-6) a second time: "Now I want you to imagine you are _____ _____ again." (etc.)

8. Continue repeating the entire desensitization sequence until you can give your partner the phobic scene without her signaling anxiety at all (in other words, she never raises her finger). When you get to this point, go on and administer the next scene up in the hierarchy. Typically a given scene must be presented and your partner desensitized two to four times before you can proceed up to the next scene.

Note: If your partner experiences intense anxiety or the early symptoms of panic during imagery desensitization (above Level 4 on the Anxiety Scale—see Chapter 6), she should signal this to you by lifting *two* fingers of her right hand. If this happens, instruct her to let go of the "problem scene" in the hierarchy and return to her peaceful scene or "safe place" immediately. Have her stay there until she's fully relaxed. After one minute or so, ask her to signal if she still feels any anxiety (by raising her right index finger). If so, let her continue relaxing. If not, have her return to *one scene below* the problem scene in the hierarchy. After presenting and desensitizing to this lower-intensity scene twice, have her return to the more difficult scene. If this scene still causes strong anxiety, you need to introduce an intermediate scene "between" the earlier scene and the one that is causing difficulty.

Appendix

3

Additional Hierarchies*

Use the following hierarchies as guidelines for attaining your own goals. You may want to add steps or develop your own hierarchies. Space is left between the steps of each hierarchy for adding in additional steps. There are also blank pages at the end of this appendix for developing hierarchies to meet your own unique needs.

Remember to repeat each step in the hierarchy until you become comfortable with it. *Do not advance to the next step until you are comfortable with all of the preceding steps.*

---

* These additional hierarchies are reproduced from the *TERRAP Program Manual*, Menlo Park: TSC Publications, 1986, with the permission of Dr. Arthur B. Hardy.

Being in a Supermarket

1. With your partner, sit in the parking lot and look at the store.

2. With your partner, walk to the door and remain there for one to five minutes.

3. Without your partner, walk in and out of the door. (In Steps 3-8, have your partner wait outside the store.)

4. Walk to the checkout area alone.

5. Walk to the first aisle alone.

6. Walk one-quarter of the way to the back of the store alone.

7. Walk halfway to the back of the store alone.

8. Walk all the way to the back of the store alone.

9. With your partner, remain in the back of the store for one to five minutes.

10. Remain in the store, browsing in different areas, alone, five to ten minutes.

Shopping in a Supermarket

Work through the steps first with your partner waiting outside the store. Then repeat on your own.

1. Spend five minutes in the store alone, browsing.

2. Purchase one item through the express line (with no more than one person ahead of you).

3. Purchase two to five items through the express line (with no more than one person ahead of you).

4. Purchase six to ten items through the express line (with one to three people ahead of you).

5. Purchase two or three items through the regular checkout line (with one or two people ahead of you).

6. Purchase five to ten items through the regular checkout line (with two to four people ahead of you).

7. Purchase ten or more items through the regular checkout line.

8. Select ten or more items and change checkout lines while waiting to purchase them.

9. Purchase ten or more items through the regular checkout line and ask the clerk to take back one item you've decided you don't want.

10. At a different supermarket, purchase ten or more items through the regular checkout line (with two to four people ahead and behind).

Riding as a Passenger in a Car

1. Sit in a car for one to five minutes with your partner in the driver's seat.

2. Ride, with your partner driving, for one block.

3. Ride with your partner in a residential area for ten to fifteen minutes.

4. Ride with your partner on a minor arterial for five to ten minutes.

5. Ride with your partner on a major arterial for ten to fifteen minutes.

6. Ride with your partner on the freeway for ten to fifteen minutes.

7. Ride with your partner on the freeway in heavy traffic.

8. Ride with your partner on a curving, mountainous road.

9. Ride on the freeway with a less familiar person driving.

10. Extend the distance that you ride away from home.

Driving With a Partner as Passenger

1. Sit in a car for one to five minutes with your partner in the passenger seat.

2. Drive one block making smooth stops and starts.

3. Drive in a residential area making right turns.

4. Drive in a residential area making left turns.

5. Drive in the right lane of a minor arterial.

6. Drive on a minor arterial making left turns at a stop sign or traffic light.

7. Drive on a major arterial in the right lane.

8. Drive on a major arterial, changing lanes, and making left and U-turns.

9. Drive on the freeway in the right lane for one to two exits.

10. Drive on the freeway, changing lanes and passing cars for two to five exits.

Driving Alone

When you practice driving alone, first have your partner follow you in another car as you go through the steps. When you feel comfortable, have your partner drive ahead of you in another car. When you're comfortable with this, then practice by yourself.

1. Sit in the car for one to five minutes alone.

2. Drive one block making smooth stops and starts.

3. Drive in a residential area making right turns.

4. Drive in a residential area making left turns.

5. Drive in the right lane of a minor arterial.

6. Drive on a minor arterial making left turns at a stop sign or traffic light.

7. Drive on a major arterial in the right lane.

8. Drive on a major arterial, changing lanes and making left and U-turns.

9. Drive on the freeway in the right lane for one or two exits.

10. Drive on the freeway, changing lanes and passing cars for two to five exits.

People

1. Go to a street or mall where there are stores and look around.

2. In the same area, look at the people walking around.

3. In the same area, pick out one person and look at what that person is doing.

4. In the same area, pick out one person and look at what that person is wearing.

5. In the same area, pick out one person and make eye contact.

6. In the same area, pick out one person and smile, making eye contact.

7. In the same area, go into a store and make eye contact with the clerk and smile.

8. In the same area, go into a store and talk to a clerk, making eye contact and smiling.

9. In the same area, pick out a person, go over, smile, make eye contact, and ask the person a question.

10. In a different area, pick out a person, go over, smile, make eye contact, and ask the person a question.

Crowds

1. With your partner, approach a small store with a few people inside.

2. With your partner nearby, remain in the small store for two to five minutes.

3. Approach and enter a small store alone for five to ten minutes.

4. With your partner, approach a busier store (such as a department store) and remain for one to five minutes.

5. Approach a crowded store alone (or with your partner waiting in the car), and remain nearby for five to ten minutes.

6. With your partner, approach a large shopping center and browse for five to fifteen minutes.

7. Approach and enter a store in a large shopping center and browse for five to fifteen minutes. Do this with your partner, then alone.

8. Approach and enter a large department store in a shopping mall and browse for five to fifteen minutes. Do this with your partner, then alone.

9. Attend a small sporting event, party, or concert with your partner.

10. Attend a larger sporting event, party, or concert with your partner and then try Steps 9 and 10 alone.

Groups

1. With your partner, join a small group of acquaintances and remain five to ten minutes, participating only minimally.

2. Without your partner, join a small group of acquaintances and remain ten to thirty minutes, participating only minimally.

3. With your partner, enter into conversation with one or two friends for five minutes.

4. With your partner, talk with two to four people for five to ten minutes.

5. Talk with one to three friends alone.

6. With your partner, talk with a less familiar person or a total stranger for one to five minutes.

7. Talk with some less familiar people alone for five to ten minutes (such as people you see every day around your place of work, but aren't acquainted with personally).

8. Enter a larger group of people with your partner and talk with them for five to fifteen minutes.

9. Enter a larger group of people without your partner and talk with them for fifteen to thirty minutes. (You'll probably have to search around for an opportunity like this. A church social, a group meeting such as Alanon, or a community college seminar would all be possibilities.)

10. Enter a larger group of people without your partner and give a short presentation on some topic on which you have some expertise.

Restaurants

1. With your partner, drive around the outside of a restaurant.

2. With your partner, sit in the restaurant parking lot for one to five minutes.

3. With your partner, enter the restaurant, stand inside for thirty to sixty seconds, then leave.

4. Enter the restaurant alone, stand inside for one to two minutes, then leave.

5. Enter the restaurant alone, select a table near the door, and order a beverage.

6. Enter the restaurant alone, select a table near the door, and order one item of food.

7. After ordering food, wait for it to arrive and eat it.

8. Enter the restaurant alone, select a table away from the door, and order a beverage.

9. Enter the restaurant alone, select a table away from the door, and order a small meal; wait for it and eat it.

10. Enter a larger restaurant, select a table away from the door, order a small meal, wait for it, and eat it.

Heights

1. Look out the window of a one-story building for ten to sixty seconds.

2. With your partner, look out from the top window of a two-story building for thirty to sixty seconds.

3. With your partner, look out from the top window of a two-story building for two to five minutes; look straight ahead and then down.

4. Look out the window of a two-story building alone for thirty to sixty seconds; look straight ahead and then down.

5. With your partner, look out from the top window of a three-story building for one to two minutes; look straight ahead and then down.

6. Look out the window of a three-story building alone for one to two minutes; look straight ahead and then down.

7. With your partner, look out the window of a four-story building for one to two minutes; look straight ahead and then down.

8. Look out from the top window of a four-story building alone for two to five minutes; look straight ahead and then down.

9. With your partner, look out from an open area of a five- to ten-story building, trying each floor from the fifth floor to the tenth; look straight ahead and then down at each level.

10. Without your partner, look out from an open area of a five- to ten-story building, trying each floor from the fifth to the tenth; look straight ahead and then down at each level.

Elevators

1. Approach an elevator with your partner; look at it, and then retreat.

2. Walk with your partner into an elevator with the door remaining open (have your partner make sure the door remains open).

3. Walk with your partner into an elevator and allow the door to close.

4. With your partner, ride up one floor.

5. With your partner, ride up two or more floors.

6. Ride up two or more floors with your partner waiting at the floor where you exit the elevator.

7. Ride up two or more floors with your partner waiting for you on the ground floor.

8. Ride the elevator while your partner is somewhere else in the building.

9. Ride the elevator alone for two or more floors without your partner being available.

10. Ride a less familiar elevator alone, without your partner being available.

Bridges

1. With your partner driving, approach a short bridge, stop, walk around, and look at the bridge.

2. With you driving, approach a short bridge, stop, and look at the bridge.

3. With your partner driving, drive across the same short bridge and return.

4. With you driving, drive across the same short bridge and return.

5. With your partner following in another car, drive across the same bridge and return.

6. With your partner waiting at each end, drive across the same bridge and return.

7. Without your partner around, drive across the same bridge and return.

8. Repeat the above procedure with a longer and/or higher bridge.

Buses and Trains

This hierarchy is described for buses but can be used in the same manner for trains.

1. With your partner, ride on a bus for one stop, sitting on the aisle near the door.

2. With your partner, ride the bus for two to five stops, sitting on the aisle near the door.

3. With your partner, ride the bus for five or more stops, sitting in the back of the bus.

4. With your partner following in a car, ride the bus one stop, sitting on the aisle near the door.

5. With your partner following in a car, ride the bus for two to five stops, sitting on the aisle near the door.

6. With your partner following in a car, ride the bus five or more stops, sitting in the back of the bus.

7. Alone, without your partner following, ride the bus one stop, sitting on the aisle near the door.

8. Alone, without your partner following, ride the bus two to five stops, sitting on the aisle near the door.

9. Alone, without your partner following, ride the bus two to five stops, sitting in the back of the bus.

10. Alone, without your partner following, ride the bus more than five stops, sitting in the back of the bus.

Dentists and Doctors

This hierarchy is designed for people with a fear of dentists but can be used in the same manner for doctor phobias.

1. With your partner, walk in and out of a dentist's office.

2. With your partner, sit in the waiting room for two to five minutes.

3. With your partner, sit in the waiting room for ten to fifteen minutes.

4. Make an appointment with the dentist just to talk to him for five to ten minutes. Tell him about your problem and explain that you are trying to desensitize yourself. Ask for his cooperation.

5. With your partner, sit in the dentist's chair five to ten minutes without the dentist being in attendance, then leave.

6. With your partner, sit in the dentist's chair ten to twenty minutes without the dentist being in attendance, then leave.

7. Make an appointment with your dentist to just look in your mouth, and not to do any work, with your partner staying with you.

8. Make an appointment with your dentist to clean your teeth only, with your partner staying with you.

9. Make an appointment for the dentist to do more work while your partner is with you.

10. Repeat Steps 7 through 9 without your partner.

Airports and Flying

1. Approach the airport with your partner and drive around it.

2. Park in the airport garage or lot; remain observing people for five minutes.

3. Park in the airport lot, enter the terminal with your partner, and remain one to five minutes.

4. Enter the terminal alone and remain five minutes, browsing and observing.

5. Arrange to visit a grounded plane; enter with your partner.

6. Enter a grounded plane alone and remain inside for five minutes.

7. Enter a grounded plane with your partner and get buckled into a seat. Remain five minutes.

8. Enter a grounded plane alone, browse, and then stay buckled into a seat for ten to fifteen minutes.

9. Schedule a short flight (ten to thirty minutes) and go with your partner.

10. Schedule a longer flight and go with your partner.

11. Repeat Steps 9 and 10 alone.

Extra Hierarchies

Extra Hierarchies

Appendix

4

Audiocassettes for Relaxation

Recommended Verbal Relaxation Tapes

You may wish to use any one of these as an alternative to progressive muscle relaxation or meditation for your daily deep-relaxation session.

Letting Go Of Stress by Emmett Miller, M.D.

    Available from: Source
                      P.O. Box W
                      Stanford, California 94305
                      1-800-52-TAPES
                      1-415-328-7171

Relaxation Training Program by Thomas Budzynski, Ph.D.
Read by Judith Proctor (three-tape set)

    Available from: Guilford Publications
                      72 Spring St.
                      New York, New York 10012
                      1-800-365-7006
                      1-212-431-9800

Recommended Instrumental Music for Relaxation

Though not an alternative to practicing deep relaxation, any of the following instrumental music tapes can help promote a state of inner peace and serenity.

Spencer Brower—*Emerald*
                  Portraits

Jim Chappell—*Living the Northern Summer*
                  Tender Ritual

Steve Halpern— *Ancient Echoes*
                  Spectrum Suite

Alex Jones and Doug Cutler—*Awake and Dreaming*
Kali's Dream

Michael Jones— *After the Rain*
Pianoscapes

David Lanz—*Christofori's Dream*
Nightfall

Jonathan Lee—*Piano Solos*, Vols. I-III

George Winston—*Autumn*
December

Appendix

5

Some Thoughts on Obsessive-Compulsive Disorder

The predominant focus of this workbook has been on panic attacks, phobias, and anxiety. Relatively little attention has been given to obsessive-compulsive disorder, and yet this is a problem that affects an estimated two to three percent of the population.

In the past few years it has been established that the behavioral methods of exposure and response prevention are probably the most effective treatments for the more common forms of obsessive-compulsive disorder, such as cleaning and checking (see the fourth example in Chapter 3, Mike, for further explanation of these techniques). It has also been discovered recently that antidepressant medications such as clomipramine (Anafranil) and fluoxetine (Prozac) have helped many people suffering from obsessive-compulsive disorder, although both of these medications have a number of side effects.

Despite what is known at present, obsessive-compulsive disorder remains a difficult problem to treat. This is especially true for the numerous clients who have obsessions (intrusive thoughts) only, for whom the technique of response prevention isn't pertinent. Moreover, many people suffering from obsessive-compulsive disorder opt not to take any prescription medications, which leaves them and their therapists with genuine questions about how they might best be helped.

In this appendix, I would like to share some observations I've made about people suffering from obsessive-compulsive disorder, along with some suggestions for remediation. These comments are especially directed to the numerous people who experience obsessions only.

It has been my repeated impression that obsessive-compulsive individuals are very wound up and tense. They appear to be almost continually in a state of high stress—hurried or "speeded up" to the point where they can't relax and slow down. Accompanying this state of high tension is a tendency to be very out of touch with their bodies and their feelings. Sufferers from this disorder are frequently very intelligent and tend to spend a lot of time ruminating in their heads, at the expense of being centered and relaxed in their bodies and able to experience their feelings. In short, such individuals often appear dissociated from their body—perhaps a little more so than people suffering from panic attacks or phobias.

Because of this, obsessive-compulsive sufferers do not experience sensitization to external situations, as does the phobic, but rather to *their own internal thoughts, sensations, or impulses.* While many people with obsessive-compulsive disorder may appear to be sensitized to external situations such as dirty clothes or stoves that are left unchecked, what they are actually sensitized to is the *idea* of dirt or the *idea* of something left unchecked. They then choose particular situations in their environment in which to play out these anxiety-laden ideas. In the case of a person with obsessions only—such as obsessions with death or illness or causing injury to someone else—there is even less dependence on an external situation to be avoided. Unpleasant internal thoughts or impulses alone become phobic. Unfortunately, there are relatively few ways to avoid something that causes you anxiety when it's strictly in your own head. Distraction and performing rituals are probably the most common recourses taken. Either can be helpful for a while—but intrusive thoughts have a tendency to come back.

I believe a more lasting solution to this problem may be found in dealing with the tension that I mentioned before; that is, trying to undo the condition of being "speeded up" and out of touch with your body and feelings. This is not something you can do quickly on the spur of the moment. It requires lifestyle changes and a fundamental change of attitude. If you're willing to incorporate some of the changes suggested below on an ongoing basis, you may be surprised to find that your problem with obsessions tends to diminish.

1. **Attempt to slow down and pace yourself.** Back off from always keeping busy and give yourself more time for rest, relaxation, and recreation. Recreation should consist of activities that you find genuinely enjoyable. Take more vacations and "mental health days" off if you need them. The point is to stop driving and pushing yourself—to take life more slowly and live more in the present. Often this will require fairly basic changes in your priorities and your attitudes.

2. **Engage in activities that help you to be more in touch with your physical body.** A regular exercise program, as described in Chapter 5, will be helpful. Other physical disciplines such as yoga, martial arts, dancing, or working in the garden, practiced on a regular basis, can be helpful too. Some of you may choose to experience body therapies such as bioenergetics, Reichian therapy, rebirthing, or various types of bodywork such as Rolfing, Trager, or other forms of massage. All of these activities will help you to feel more "grounded" and in your body. And this, in turn, will reduce your tendency to become sensitized to your inner thoughts and impulses.

3. **Be willing to experience your feelings.** The Freudian theory of obsessive-compulsive disorder explains obsessions and compulsions in terms of suppressed feelings (or impulses) that become so dissociated from your conscious mind that they take on a life of their own. When these feelings/impulses seek discharge without having been understood and integrated into your conscious awareness, what you experience is an intrusive, anxious thought or a compulsion that feels "out of control."

You can learn to be more aware of your feelings, first, by slowing down enough so that you can live more in the present moment instead of in your thoughts, as described in 1, above. Then you can begin to bring out your feelings by writing them down or sharing them on a regular basis with someone you trust. Simple *willingness* to be more available to experience your feelings is an important first step. Use the strategies and exercises in Chapter 12 to assist you in gaining more awareness of your feelings.

4. **Overcome isolation.** Social isolation tends to aggravate obsessions and compulsions, whereas connecting with, and feeling close to, other people will tend to reduce the problem because it brings you more into the present—more in contact with your whole self and your feelings. If you're dealing with obsessive-compulsive disorder and find you spend a lot of time alone, work on increasing your support system and make time to be with people. If you are already with someone a lot of the time, then work on upgrading your level of intimacy and communication with that person. You'll find, as a rule, that you will tend to let go of obsessions when you're having a good time being with someone.

Other Approaches To Help Obsessions

In the past few years, several new self-help books on OCD have appeared. Most of these books present a cognitive-behavioral approach to overcoming obsessions and compulsions, offering a variety of techniques which can be helpful. In particular, adopting an attitude of *accepting* obsessions when they occur, rather than trying to fight them head on, helps to make them less disruptive. Repeating affirmations such as "It's okay to have these obsessions," or "I don't have to pay attention to this. I'll go on about my business," or simply "This will pass," may be useful at times when obsessive thoughts start to intrude.

Other cognitive-behavioral techniques that have been helpful with obsessions include:

Postponing obsessing. You decide to delay obsessing for just 30 seconds or a minute at first, then gradually increase the length of time. You don't actually suppress obsessing, rather you gain an increasing sense of control by determining when you're going to do it. (Note: This technique may be quite useful for worry in general, not just obsessions.)

Creative distractions. Finding an interesting distraction to focus (or even obsess) on may divert your mind from negative obsessive thoughts. Good reading material, audio or video tapes, or conversation with a significant other or friend works well in this regard. Puzzles (crossword, jigsaw, mathematical, and so on) are particularly useful distractions because they provide an alternative, more positive way to obsess. See Appendix 6 for further suggestions.

Continuous loop tapes. If your obsessive thoughts have negative or frightening themes—such as fear of hurting someone or getting into an accident—it may help to write down the worst-case scenario and then record it on a 30- or 60-second continuous loop tape. Then, no matter how unpleasant it may seem, you listen to the loop tape over and over again for half an hour or longer every day. Eventually, after one or two weeks, you will *desensitize* to the content of the tape so that it no longer distresses you when you hear it out loud *or when it loops in your mind*. Remember that, in the case of OCD, you are primarily sensitized to internal thoughts or images in your mind. Your constant attempt to avoid these thoughts, whether or not you have rituals to dispel them, is what helps keep them going. Direct and continuous exposure to a worst-case example of these thoughts or images will help you desensitize to them.

For a more detailed discussion of the preceding three techniques and other cognitive-behavioral approaches to obsessions and compulsions, see especially the book *Stop Obsessing* by Edna Foa and Reid Wilson, cited below.

Further Reading

Foa, Edna, and Wilson, Reid. *Stop Obsessing: How To Overcome Your Obsessions and Compulsions*. New York: Bantam, 1991.

Rapoport, Judith L. *The Boy Who Couldn't Stop Washing: The Experience & Treatment of Obsessive-Compulsive Disorder*. New York: New American Library (Plume), 1990.

Schwartz, Jeffrey M. ***Brain Lock: Free Yourself from Obsessive-Compulsive Behavior.*** New York: Regan Books, 1996. (Self-help approach with demonstrated effectiveness. Highly recommended.)

Appendix

6

How To Stop Obsessive Worry

Obsessive worry is like a *negative spiral*. The longer you spend time with it, the deeper into it you can get. It may also be viewed as a form of trance. The more you induce it by repetition, the more entranced you get, and the more difficult it may be to "break the spell."

It takes a deliberate act of will to stop it. You need to make a deliberate effort to move away from circular mental activity and *get out of your head* by "shifting gears" to another modality of experience, such as bodily activity, expressing emotions, interpersonal communication, sensory distraction, or a specific ritual. (In some cases, an alternative obsession will do.)

The downward pull of an obsessive spiral can be very compelling. Following the path of least resistance is likely to keep you going round and round. Although deliberately choosing to break out of the obsessive thinking may be difficult at first (especially if you're highly anxious), with practice it will get easier.

Below are some examples of alternative activities and experiences that will help you shift out of your mind and away from obsessive thinking.

1. *Do physical exercise.* This can be your favorite outdoor or indoor exercise, dancing, or just household chores.

2. *Do progressive muscle relaxation alone or in combination with abdominal breathing.* See Chapter 4 for more detail. Keep this up for 5-10 minutes until you feel fully relaxed and free from obsessive thoughts.

3. *Use evocative music to release repressed feelings.* Such feelings—usually sadness or anger—may underlie and "drive" the obsessive thinking.

4. *Talk to someone.* Converse about something other than the worry, unless you want to express your feelings about it, as in point 3.

5. *Use visual distractions.* This can be TV, movies, video games, your computer, uplifting reading, or even a rock garden.

6. *Use sensory-motor distraction.* Try arts and crafts, repairing something, gardening.

7. *Find an alternative positive obsession.* For example, work out a crossword or jigsaw puzzle.

8. *Practice healthy rituals.* Combine abdominal breathing with a positive affirmation that has personal significance. Keep this up for 5-10 minutes, or until you're fully relaxed. (This is actually a positive trance induction to overcome the negative trance enforced by the obsessive worry.)

Examples of affirmations: (for the spiritually inclined)

- "Let it go."   • "Let go and let God."

- "These are just thoughts—   • "I abide in Spirit (God)."
  they're fading away."

- "I'm whole, relaxed, and   • "I release this negativity to God."
  free of worry."

Appendix

7

Guidelines for a Good Night's Sleep

The following guidelines are recommended to help you improve both the quality and amount of your sleep.

1. Exercise during the day, preferably in the late afternoon before dinner. Aerobic exercise (20 minutes or more) is better, but 45 minutes to an hour of brisk walking will suffice.

2. Go to bed and get up at regular times, even if you're tired in the morning. Don't vary your time of going to bed or getting up. Getting up half an hour earlier in the morning may help you get to sleep that night.

3. Don't try to make yourself sleep. If you're unable to fall asleep after 20-30 minutes in bed, leave your bed, engage in some relaxing activity (such as watching TV, sitting in a chair and listening to a relaxation tape, or having a cup of herb tea), and do not return to bed until you're sleepy.

4. Avoid heavy meals before bedtime, or going to bed hungry (a small snack before bedtime may be helpful).

5. Avoid heavy alcohol consumption before bedtime (for some people, a small glass of wine before bed may help).

6. Turn yourself down during the last hour or two of the day. Avoid vigorous physical or mental activity, emotional upsets, and so on.

7. Reduce caffeine and nicotine consumption as much as possible. If you must have coffee, have it only in the morning.

8. Instead of prescription drugs, try natural supplements that foster sleep. GABA, 200-500 mg before bedtime or in the middle of the night, may induce sleep for many persons. (GABA is available in many health-food stores under two names: "Relaxer" made by Country Life or "AminoCalm" made by Twinlab.) Safe forms of L-Tryptophan (taken off the market in the U.S. in 1989) are available by prescription in Canada. Recently, many people have been using the hormone melatonin to help them get to sleep. Herbal tinctures containing valerian, hops, passionflower, or skullcap may also be of help. Finally, you may find a Chinese

herbal preparation, "Anmien Pien," to be of assistance. Take four tablets at bedtime. As with any drugs or medicinal herbs, it's important to consult a knowledgeable practitioner to make sure that a given supplement or herb is safe and appropriate for you. This is especially important if you take other medications.

9. Develop a sleep ritual before bedtime. This is some activity you do every night before you get into bed. A hot shower or bath before bedtime may help you relax.

10. For relaxing tense muscles or a racing mind, use deep relaxation techniques such as progressive muscle relaxation or guided visualization on tape (see Chapters 4 and 12). Get an auto-reverse recorder that can play a tape in a continuous loop.

11. Eliminate nonsleep activities in bed (such as work or reading) to strengthen the association between bed and sleeping—unless these activities are part of your sleep ritual.

12. Avoid napping during the day.

13. Try varying the firmness of your mattress by buying a new one or adding a board underneath, a featherbed, or an "egg-crate" foam pad.

14. Reduce noise through the use of ear plugs or a noise-masking machine.

15. Keep your room temperature between 60 and 70 degrees. Too warm or cold a room tends to interfere with sleep. Use fans for a hot room if air conditioning is unavailable.

16. If your partner snores, kicks, or tosses and turns, have separate beds at whatever distance is mutually acceptable.

17. Don't let yourself be afraid of insomnia. Work on *accepting* those nights when you don't sleep as well. You can still function the next day, even if you had only a couple of hours of sleep. The less you fight, resist, or fear sleeplessness, the more it will tend to go away.

18. If pain is causing sleeplessness, analgesics are more appropriate than sleeping pills.

19. Sex (when physically and emotionally satisfying) helps sleep.

20. If you suspect that emotional problems are causing sleeplessness, consult a competent psychotherapist. Depression and anxiety disorders commonly produce insomnia. Getting more emotional support and expressing your feelings often will help you sleep.

ABOUT THE AUTHOR

Edmund J. Bourne received his Ph.D. in psychology from the University of Chicago and did postdoctoral research at Michael Reese Medical Center in Chicago. He has taught at several colleges and universities, authored numerous publications, and is the recipient of two national awards. Dr. Bourne specializes in the treatment of anxiety, phobias, and stress-related disorders. He was formerly director of the Anxiety Treatment Center in San Jose and Santa Rosa, California. Currently he resides and practices in Kona, Hawaii, and California.

Phone counseling for problems with panic attacks, phobias, and other anxiety difficulties is available with Dr. Bourne. For information, please call 1-808-334-1847. For resources in your local area, please see Appendix 1.

Anxiety & Phobia Audio Series

I CAN DO IT

Based on the popular *Anxiety & Phobia Workbook*, these new tapes provide step-by-step instructions for approaching frightening situations. Listeners are guided through exercises designed to gradually desensitize them to their phobia. Narrated by Edmund J. Bourne and Jerry Landis. Each program is one 120-minute cassette. **$11.95 each.**

HEIGHTS. Helps listeners visit high rise apartments, stay in tall hotels, work in skyscrapers, and drive mountain roads and high bridges. ISBN 1-879237-91-1 Item 51.

FLYING. Helps listeners reduce fear of flying to a level that allows them to take the vacation, family, and business trips that they currently dread. ISBN 1-879237-90-3 Item 52.

SHOPPING IN A SUPERMARKET. Helps reduce the fear of panic attacks or losing control so that shopping in a supermarket is no longer a dreaded ordeal. ISBN 1-879237-89-X Item 53.

DRIVING FREEWAYS. Helps reduce fear of driving freeways so that you can get where you need to go without plotting elaborate routes on surface streets. ISBN 1-879237-88-1 Item 54.

GIVING A TALK. Teaches phobic listeners how to give lengthy presentations to large audiences of strangers without overwhelming fear. ISBN 1-879237-86-5 Item 55.

SPEAKING UP IN PUBLIC. Builds confidence so that you can join in, contribute your ideas, and ask questions in meetings, workshops, discussions, and casual conversations. ISBN 1-879237-87-3 Item 56.

FEAR OF ILLNESS. Reduces fears arising from unexplained pain or symptoms and teaches you to relax while you contemplate your physical symptoms without panic and make realistic assessments of risk factors. ISBN 1-57224-015-6 Item 57.

DRIVING FAR FROM HOME. Reduces fears associated with leaving the safety of your home base and helps you challenge the catastrophic thoughts that can turn car travel into a nightmare. ISBN 1-57224-014-8 Item 58.

To order, please call 1-800-748-6273, toll-free.

Some Other New Harbinger Self-Help Titles

The Headache & Neck Pain Workbook, $14.95
Perimenopause, $13.95
The Self-Forgiveness Handbook, $12.95
A Woman's Guide to Overcoming Sexual Fear and Pain, $14.95
Mind Over Malignancy, $12.95
Treating Panic Disorder and Agoraphobia, $44.95
Scarred Soul, $13.95
The Angry Heart, $13.95
Don't Take It Personally, $12.95
Becoming a Wise Parent For Your Grown Child, $12.95
Clear Your Past, Change Your Future, $12.95
Preparing for Surgery, $17.95
Coming Out Everyday, $13.95
Ten Things Every Parent Needs to Know, $12.95
The Power of Two, $12.95
It's Not OK Anymore, $13.95
The Daily Relaxer, $12.95
The Body Image Workbook, $17.95
Living with ADD, $17.95
Taking the Anxiety Out of Taking Tests, $12.95
The Taking Charge of Menopause Workbook, $17.95
Living with Angina, $12.95
PMS: Women Tell Women How to Control Premenstrual Syndrome, $13.95
Five Weeks to Healing Stress: The Wellness Option, $17.95
Choosing to Live: How to Defeat Suicide Through Cognitive Therapy, $12.95
Why Children Misbehave and What to Do About It, $14.95
Illuminating the Heart, $13.95
When Anger Hurts Your Kids, $12.95
The Addiction Workbook, $17.95
The Mother's Survival Guide to Recovery, $12.95
The Chronic Pain Control Workbook, Second Edition, $17.95
Fibromyalgia & Chronic Myofascial Pain Syndrome, $19.95
Diagnosis and Treatment of Sociopaths, $44.95
Flying Without Fear, $12.95
Kid Cooperation: How to Stop Yelling, Nagging & Pleading and Get Kids to Cooperate, $12.95
The Stop Smoking Workbook: Your Guide to Healthy Quitting, $17.95
Conquering Carpal Tunnel Syndrome and Other Repetitive Strain Injuries, $17.95
The Tao of Conversation, $12.95
Wellness at Work: Building Resilience for Job Stress, $17.95
What Your Doctor Can't Tell You About Cosmetic Surgery, $13.95
An End to Panic: Breakthrough Techniques for Overcoming Panic Disorder, $17.95
Living Without Procrastination: How to Stop Postponing Your Life, $12.95
Goodbye Mother, Hello Woman: Reweaving the Daughter Mother Relationship, $14.95
Letting Go of Anger: The 10 Most Common Anger Styles and What to Do About Them, $12.95
Messages: The Communication Skills Workbook, Second Edition, $13.95
Coping With Chronic Fatigue Syndrome: Nine Things You Can Do, $12.95
The Anxiety & Phobia Workbook, Second Edition, $17.95
Thueson's Guide to Over-the-Counter Drugs, $13.95
Natural Women's Health: A Guide to Healthy Living for Women of Any Age, $13.95
I'd Rather Be Married: Finding Your Future Spouse, $13.95
The Relaxation & Stress Reduction Workbook, Fourth Edition, $17.95
Living Without Depression & Manic Depression: A Workbook for Maintaining Mood Stability, $17.95
Coping With Schizophrenia: A Guide For Families, $13.95
Visualization for Change, Second Edition, $13.95
Postpartum Survival Guide, $13.95
Angry All the Time: An Emergency Guide to Anger Control, $12.95
Couple Skills: Making Your Relationship Work, $13.95
Self-Esteem, Second Edition, $13.95
I Can't Get Over It, A Handbook for Trauma Survivors, Second Edition, $15.95
Dying of Embarrassment: Help for Social Anxiety and Social Phobia, $12.95
The Depression Workbook: Living With Depression and Manic Depression, $17.95
Men & Grief: A Guide for Men Surviving the Death of a Loved One, $13.95
When the Bough Breaks: A Helping Guide for Parents of Sexually Abused Children, $11.95
When Once Is Not Enough: Help for Obsessive Compulsives, $13.95
The Three Minute Meditator, Third Edition, $12.95
Beyond Grief: A Guide for Recovering from the Death of a Loved One, $13.95
The Divorce Book, $13.95
Hypnosis for Change: A Manual of Proven Techniques, Third Edition, $13.95
When Anger Hurts, $13.95

Prices subject to change without notice.